# Communication for Work



Carol Carysforth

Heinemann Educational Publishers
Halley Court, Jordan Hill, Oxford OX2 8EJ
a division of Reed Educational & Professional Publishing Ltd
Heinemann is a registered trademark of Reed Educational & Professional Publishing Limited

OXFORD MELBOURNE AUCKLAND
JOHANNESBURG BLANTYRE GABORONE
IBADAN PORTSMOUTH (NH) USA CHICAGO



First published 1998
00 01 02 03 11 10 9 8 7 6 5 4 3

A catalogue record of this book is available from the British Library on request.

ISBN 0 435 45542 7

Designed by Wendi Watson

Typeset by Tek-Art, Croydon, Surrey

Printed and bound in Great Britain by The Bath Press

# Contents

# INTRODUCTION

Between the ages of eighteen months and five years you accomplished one of the major achievements of your life. You learned the skill which sets the human race apart from animals – that is, you learned to speak a language. Most of you who are reading this book probably learned English as your first language. However, if you are one of those people who learned English as your second language then you have undertaken this feat at least twice in your life so far!

As a young child you never consciously 'learned' to speak but copied the sounds you heard. From a basic vocabulary of about fifty words between the ages of one and two, you increased the number of words you used to many thousands before starting school. You also practised sentence construction, starting with a base word such as 'mine', progressing to 'this mine' and finally 'this is mine' – which is a grammatically correct sentence. And all this happened long before you received any formal education in reading and writing!

Everyone learns additional words and phrases both consciously and unconsciously. We are taught new words and given information about the meanings of different words at school. Television, books, magazines, our friends, music and films are all additional sources. Some of the words and phrases we adopt and use, some we learn but rarely use and others we ignore or discard altogether. Usually, we retain words we find useful or those in vogue at the time and disregard the others – and the words *you* find useful will depend upon your own circumstances and situation. For instance, you will learn specialist terms when you study a particular subject, such as geography or science. You may use these whilst you take the exam – and forget them afterwards. You will speak a different version of your language when you are at school from the one you use at home – and a different version again with your friends, who will possess roughly the same vocabulary as yourself, but not exactly. We each have our own personal 'wordbank' representing our personal and linguistic experiences to date.

By now, I have no doubt that you have command of virtually all the words you need to live your life quite satisfactorily on a day to day basis. I am also sure that you are capable of speaking in perfectly acceptable sentences that are understood by everyone around you. You may therefore wonder why it is that, at this stage of your life, you are still being taught 'communication' and why so much emphasis is put on this subject. There are four main reasons.

**1** When you go to work, you are likely to find that your existing vocabulary does not include many words and specialist terms used by the people around you. It obviously helps if you know what people are talking about and are able to understand the documents you read or create and why they are used.

**2** At work, you will be expected to communicate with a variety of people both inside and outside the organisation. You may do this now if you have a part-time job and deal with customers. In this case, you should know already that there are several terms and phrases you use with your friends and family that you wouldn't repeat at work when talking to a customer or your boss! In fact, the whole 'tone' of your communication will be very different. This is why many new employees are hesitant about answering the telephone – even though they may talk on the phone for hours at home! When you have to write something – a letter, a message – you are likely to find that the wording is rather more formal than you are used to and you may be nervous about making spelling mistakes or grammatical errors which would make you look silly.

**3** Languages don't stand still – in fact you may often hear English described as a 'living language'. The expression is used to describe how the language changes and develops. This is why words and phrases used by writers such as Shakespeare can be virtually incomprehensible today, unless they are explained to you. New words and phrases are being added all the time – to explain technological developments (eg telethon, virtual reality, laser printer), to describe current issues (eg greenhouse effect, global warming, computer hacker) or to reflect our current lifestyles (eg fast food, couch potato, cash point). Each generation adds its own words and phrases, some of which are adopted for all time and some of which fall by the wayside as time moves on. The word 'teenager' was new to your great grandparents, the terms 'trendy' or 'commuter' to your grandparents, the phrases 'chill out' or 'he's sound' might have to be explained to your parents! The rules which govern the way we speak and write also change and are influenced by the media and general usage.

**4** Everyone communicates on a daily basis and the ability to send and receive information accurately and quickly is vital – particularly in business. Missing a zero out of a number in an important contract or writing down the wrong date for an appointment 50 miles away could cost a company thousands of pounds – as could annoying or upsetting an important customer by writing or saying the wrong thing. At work, you *are* the company when you deal with customers directly, whether face to face, over the phone or in writing, and you therefore have the power to influence their behaviour. You are paid to take responsibility – both for your own actions and the consequences – and the results of being a poor or inadequate communicator can range from minor difficulties to major disasters!

The aim of this book is to help you to speak more confidently and write more competently and appropriately in the working world. It does not assume that you know nothing about English, and it builds on the skills you already have – though in a rather different way. In this book, you won't just learn a topic and move on. Instead, you will return to topics you have met before and continually improve your knowledge and skills until you become proficient.

By now, you may feel you have read enough and want to move on. Please don't! The paragraphs below explain the way in which this book has been designed to help you. If you read them carefully then you will not only understand why it is different from many other communication books, you will also know which sections will help you to develop particular skills. Only you – and perhaps your tutor – know your individual strengths and weaknesses at this moment.

## Features to note

Each chapter has similar features.

- **In the spotlight** – introduces you to a new topic and checks your understanding of the words and phrases used.
- **Making headway** – returns to a topic you have met before and takes it to a more advanced level. This occurs throughout the book to enable you to develop your skills in an area progressively. Therefore you can not only write business communications from the first chapter but can also vary your activities as you progress through the book.
- **Tools of the trade** – concentrates on the practical skills you will have to use to communicate effectively at work.
- **Wordbank** – is designed to help you increase your vocabulary, particularly with 'work-related' words.
- **Spellchecker** – because despite modern technology you still need to be able to spell. A word of warning for people who think they can rely on an electronic spellchecker to do the work for them: it was reported recently that council officials in Cambridge had to apologise to tenants in the district after their spellchecker failed to notice that a recent letter had been addressed Dear Sir or Madman. You are asked to *learn* the spellings shown, unless you can confidently claim to have no problems with any of the words listed – and your tutor agrees!
- **Say it!** – helps you to pronounce some difficult words which you cannot guess from the spelling.
- **The good grammar guide** – helps you to conform to the rules of written English. The word 'grammar' is apt to trigger the reaction 'boring, boring' in most students but, although grammatical rules cannot easily be converted into fascinating titbits of information, there are many occasions when a knowledge of them is essential. At the very least, they stop you from making a fool of yourself, like the driver who submitted an insurance claim that read: 'I hit the tree because it was still moving.' It may be of some comfort to know that the rules of grammar are much more relaxed today than in the past. In each case, practical applications of the main points are shown and only the important rules are included – which you *must* learn and practise!
- **Polish your punctuation** – revises the main points to make certain that you know the usual conventions in business correspondence.
- **Double trouble** – gives pairs of words which are commonly confused.
- **Don't you dare** – identifies howlers commonly found in communication, and other 'don'ts' which you must avoid.

- **Communication in practice** – contains exercises to help you to practise and develop all the skills you have learned.
- **Word wizard** – provides some light relief to show you how words *can* be used very inventively and imaginatively by the experts.

Getting the most out of your course and this subject is entirely up to you. You improve only one related skill by studying this book – that of reading. You also need to *use* the words you meet for the first time and to practise your speaking and writing skills to improve – and no-one else can do this for you. It is rather like driving a car – you can only learn to do it properly by practising. If you do well, then you will find your new-found skills will prove very useful, not least in your personal life. Using words skilfully can even be fun! And, after all, if as a baby you could learn 10 new words every week and understand the basic rules of grammar well enough to be able to talk, why stop now?

Carol Carysforth-Neild

July 1998

# IN THE SPOTLIGHT – COMMUNICATION AT WORK

People at work constantly communicate. They talk on the telephone, write letters and reports, meet in the corridor to chat or exchange ideas and transmit information by computer. Today, information can be sent to Australia as easily and quickly as to the next town. Wherever you work, and whatever you do, you are likely to be surrounded by documents and messages and expected to communicate regularly with colleagues, customers and your counterparts in other organisations.

There are different ways of classifying the different types of communication in any organisation:

- by method
- by recipient
- by formality.

## BY METHOD

There are two main categories of communication – spoken (usually called **oral**) and **written**.

- **Oral communication** may be face to face (when we meet someone) or over the telephone. Today we can telephone someone and leave a message on an answering machine or use 'voice mail', which is a type of electronic answering service. People carry pagers or bleepers so that they can receive messages at a distance and security guards and engineers often use private radios to communicate with their base.
- **Written communications** can be sent through the post or transmitted electronically. They may contain illustrations or graphics as well as text. The most obvious example of a written communication is a letter, but other types include telephone messages, notices (on notice boards), newsletters and reports. Advertising materials are prepared as brochures or catalogues. Every purchase made by the organisation and every sale to a customer results in various documents being produced, all of which 'communicate' different types of information about the goods and the price.

The method of communicating we choose will often depend upon the speed and urgency of the situation. If we need information quickly we normally make a telephone call. However, if the content is complicated, will need to be used many times or retained as evidence, then a written method is better. The fastest methods of transmitting written information today are by fax or electronic mail (**e-mail**). An e-mail message is one which is sent from one person's computer to another.

### BY RECIPIENT

Some documents are meant to be seen only by people who work for the organisation, in which case they are known as **internal**. Others are prepared for people outside such as customers, suppliers or other organisations and are classed as **external**.

- Internal communications include staff meetings and newsletters, a telephone call to a colleague and a conversation with someone in the same organisation. A **memo** is the 'internal' equivalent of a letter. Today, many organisations also operate an internal e-mail system by linking all their computers in a network.
- External communications include business letters, advertisements, telephone calls, fax messages, invoices ('bills') and face to face meetings with customers who call and other visitors. Many organisations have their own Internet site which gives information about the company and its products. E-mails may also be sent externally over the Internet.

### BY FORMALITY

Some methods of communicating are **formal**, others are **informal**. A school report or a letter from a head teacher is a more formal method of communicating with a parent than a two-minute chat at the school gate. The reason for the communication and the nature of the recipient will determine whether it should be formal or informal.

- **Formal** methods are used for important or serious matters, when you do not know the recipient very well, or when you want to keep a record of something. If you apply for a job you may be asked to attend an **interview**, which is more formal than a discussion or chat. If you spend too much money and become overdrawn at the bank, you are likely to find a letter on your doormat telling you to make an appointment to see someone immediately. You are unlikely to receive a friendly telephone call!
- **Informal** methods of communication are used between people who contact each other frequently – both internally and externally. If you regularly liaise with people in another organisation, particularly those with a similar job to your own, you would probably make a telephone call or send a brief e-mail, unless the matter was very serious.

There are more 'rules' attached to formal, external communications than any others. Your organisation may ask that you set out a letter in a certain way (known as the 'house style') or obtain approval before you send a letter to a customer. This is because there is more danger of something going wrong if the communication is flawed in some way. There may be information your boss doesn't want sent outside the organisation. Equally, customers who receive a badly written or inaccurate document may take their business elsewhere or – even worse – have grounds for a legal claim against the organisation.

Today the trend is for fewer very formal communications. Most business letters are worded more informally than they used to be and many telephone calls to customers are relatively informal. However, this does not mean that you can use the same words and phrases as you do with your friends or colleagues!

## Your role as a communicator

Regardless of where you work or what you do, you will be expected to be able to communicate effectively with people *on your own*. This means being able to use the equipment (eg a telephone, fax machine and computer) and – even more importantly – being able to speak and write appropriately. Organisations are busy places. No-one will expect to pay you a salary and also spend several weeks showing you how to take a basic message, talk politely to a customer or answer the telephone. You will also be expected to communicate in writing precisely and accurately. Modern technology has *increased* the need for this skill, rather than reduced it. Whereas you may not be expected to write a formal business letter at the start of your career, if you have your own computer and are linked to an e-mail system, no-one will ever write your e-mails for you! In addition, your colleagues will expect you to give them accurate information when they need it – otherwise you prevent them from being able to do their own jobs properly.

You will also be expected to work harmoniously with your colleagues. This will be important to *you*, if you want to enjoy being at work. After all, nobody wants to spend a day with a group of people they don't like or don't get on with – let alone every day! At work, your colleagues are likely to be a rather more mixed bunch than they are at school or college. Some will be much older than you and senior to you in rank. Some will be easy to work with and naturally friendly, others may be less so. However, you will be paid to get on with them all! This means learning a few skills of tact and diplomacy so that you don't upset people unnecessarily or unintentionally. When you first start work you may find that it takes time before you are truly accepted as a member of your working group. In the early days, people may be guarded about what they say in front of you, in case you repeat their remarks to someone else outside the group. You will also be judged on how easy you are to work with – if you are helpful, courteous and pleasant then you are likely to be accepted much more quickly than if you grumble or complain a lot, are very noisy (or too reserved) or are thought to be lazy or inconsiderate to other people's needs. The aim is to be your own ideal co-worker!

## Check your aptitude as a communicator

Your ability to communicate now and to improve your skills over the next few months is likely to depend upon the following factors.

1 Your attitude to this subject. This will largely depend on whether you chose to do your course voluntarily, whether you were persuaded to do it by other people, or were given no choice but to do it.

2 Your attitude to learning. Whilst learning *can* be enjoyable – even fun on occasions – there are times when some hard slog is required. For instance, you will have to learn some spellings – and no-one can learn them for you!

3 Your ability to 'know yourself' – particularly your strengths and weaknesses. Only in this way can you build on your strengths and try to overcome your weaknesses.

## Self-assessment quiz

As a guide, do the following quiz and then score yourself from the key below. In each case, select one option from those given. Try to be as truthful as possible – even if this means you would rather not tell anyone else the result!

| | |
|---|---|
| **1** At school, English Language was | **a** my favourite subject.<br>**b** quite enjoyable, but not my favourite subject.<br>**c** just average, I had no strong feelings for or against it as a subject.<br>**d** the worst subject I had to do. |
| **2** What made you decide to study communication now? | **a** I like the subject and want to improve my skills.<br>**b** I think it's necessary if I want to get a job.<br>**c** It was part of my course – I didn't choose to do it as a subject.<br>**d** I had no choice. |
| **3** Which of the following best describes your current feelings towards studying communication? | **a** I'm really pleased I'm doing it and look forward to the lessons each week.<br>**b** Quite positive, I think it'll be useful to improve my skills.<br>**c** Open minded, if I enjoy the lessons then I'll work hard.<br>**d** Dire – I dread the lessons. |
| **4** If you are given homework, do you | **a** do it carefully at home and before the deadline?<br>**b** do it before the deadline – but sometimes in a rush the night before?<br>**c** do it on the bus or in a quick break before class?<br>**d** ignore it and hope you won't be asked for the answer in class? |
| **5** If a task is difficult or takes time to do properly, do you | **a** enjoy the challenge of getting it right?<br>**b** do your best, but accept that you may not always be perfect?<br>**c** struggle to concentrate for any length of time?<br>**d** give up quite quickly? |
| **6** How would you describe yourself? | **a** A hard conscientious worker at all times.<br>**b** An average human being who tries hard.<br>**c** An average human being who sometimes tries hard.<br>**d** Someone who prefers enjoying life to working. |

| | |
|---|---|
| **7** If someone criticises or corrects your work, do you | **a** get upset and then try your very best never to repeat the error?<br>**b** accept it, if it is justified, and then try to learn from it?<br>**c** note it at the time, but then often forget?<br>**d** take offence or ignore it? |
| **8** What is your attitude to reading (books or magazines)? | **a** I will read anything I get my hands on.<br>**b** I like reading books and articles in magazines if I find them interesting.<br>**c** I only read when I have to.<br>**d** I don't read at all – I just look at the pictures. |
| **9** How do you see yourself in five years' time? | **a** I hope to be in a really good job earning a reasonable salary.<br>**b** I would like to be in a job I enjoy and happy in my private life.<br>**c** I haven't really decided, but I certainly want to be working.<br>**d** With luck I'll have won the Lottery and won't have to think about work. |
| **10** On a scale of 1–5, where 1 is excellent and 5 is poor, how would you rate your ability to | **a** spell correctly?<br>**b** speak to a group of strangers?<br>**c** use a variety of words in the correct way?<br>**d** punctuate a sentence correctly?<br>**e** write a letter to your previous head teacher asking for a reference? |

## NOW SCORE YOURSELF

*Questions 1–9*

**Mostly As** If you have been truthful throughout then you are likely to be quite a perfectionist. You are unhappy with anything that seems second-rate in any way and work hard to do your best – all the time. Whilst this may seem ideal, it can be too much of a good thing if it means life is all work and no play. Try to relax more – you are keen enough to do well in the subject.

**Mostly Bs** You are a realistic person with a good sense of balance in your life, as well as being keen to do well when it matters. Work hard, and good luck!

**Mostly Cs** It's make-your-mind-up time! You have the ability to make headway if you can see a reason for it, but will have to discipline yourself more to make progress. Nobody can do this for you!

**Mostly Ds** Good luck with the Lottery – you're going to need it! In the meantime, a long straight talk with your tutor is essential. Perhaps a change of course may be advisable – there are lots of options these days and you really need to be looking for a job with little emphasis on communication skills, just in case you don't win the Lottery!

*Question 10*

Your scores for this question should highlight the particular areas on which you should focus your attention. It is better to think about each score separately rather than to add them together – as you will need all these skills at work. You should now concentrate on checking that your tutor's assessment of your ability matches your own. If it does, this enables your tutor to give you the best advice and help and means you will learn from it. If your tutor scores you lower than you score yourself, then you may need to review your own opinion of your current ability. However, if you are a perfectionist you may find you score yourself lower than your tutor does – in which case you need to review the way you think about yourself – perhaps you could be more positive and confident?

## TOOLS OF THE TRADE – using reference books

You need to be able to use two main reference books to develop your vocabulary. The first is a **dictionary**, the second is a **thesaurus**.

### DICTIONARIES

You should already know that a dictionary is a book which lists words in alphabetical order, together with their meanings, and that there are also pocket versions which are light enough to carry with you everywhere! But did you know that a good dictionary also gives you

- information on the part of speech of the word (eg whether it is a noun or verb). This is dealt with later in the book, but it is important you realise that this can result in a word having an entirely different meaning, eg

  | | |
  |---|---|
  | to desert | a desert |
  | to ring | a ring |
  | to wave | a wave |

- advice on spelling and the spelling variations that are allowed
- guidance on the usage of words
- hints on pronunciation.

You may also find there are reference pages relating to abbreviations and other useful facts.

The quick way to use a dictionary is to focus on the top right-hand corner of every page, which always gives the final word on that page. Use this to rapidly locate the initial letter of your word and a word near to yours in spelling. Then look at the tops of other columns, which again have the final word highlighted. This helps you to find the appropriate column as quickly as possible. You can then look down for the word you need.

Many people who do not know how to spell a word often complain that this makes it very hard – if not impossible – to find the word they want in a dictionary. A typical example is the word lieutenant (pronounced *lef-ten-ant*). A friend of mine once spent hours looking for the spelling of 'ceilidh', which is a Gaelic word for a party and is pronounced *kalee*. In these situations a dictionary may not be much help, but in the majority of cases if you are persistent and appreciate some of the differences between spelling and pronunciation in English, you can find the word you want. On other occasions, you may have to resort to a thesaurus to look up a substitute.

### A THESAURUS

A thesaurus is a dictionary of **synonyms**, or words similar in meaning. A thesaurus can also be useful for finding a difficult spelling. If you knew 'lieutenant' was an army rank, you could find the word this way, instead of trying to find it in a dictionary.

Using synonyms helps you to vary your writing. If you had written the word 'promptly' in a sentence and didn't want to repeat it, you could substitute 'quickly' or 'soon'. However, do be careful you don't alter the meaning. Substituting the word 'pain' instead of 'ache', for instance, would give a different impression. **Antonyms** are words which are opposite in meaning (eg quickly/slowly, forbid/allow). Finding out the antonyms of a new word can often help you understand its meaning more precisely. Many word processing packages incorporate a thesaurus which has both synonyms and antonyms.

## WORDBANK 1

The best way to increase your vocabulary is to keep a small notebook in which you can enter new words you come across. This will be your Wordbank book. Use a page for each letter of the alphabet and enter the word and its definition alongside. Start your book now by doing each of the following exercises.

**1** All the following words were used in the passage on Communication at Work. Use a dictionary to find out the meaning of each one and write a brief definition. Check, too, that you can spell each one correctly.

**a** counterpart **b** classifying
**c** recipient **d** graphics
**e** evidence **f** overdrawn
**g** liaise **h** flawed
**i** guarded **k** co-worker

**2** Use a thesaurus to suggest alternative words which could have been used instead of

**a** bunch **b** judged
**c** reserved **d** lazy

**3** What is meant by the phrase 'have grounds for a legal claim' at the top of page 7?

Enter all your new words in your Wordbank book. Now select at least 10 words from those you have researched above, which you don't normally use as part of your vocabulary, and try to practise using them over the next two weeks.

## THE GOOD GRAMMAR GUIDE
### Sentences

We are all ungrammatical when we are talking informally to our friends. After all, we aren't likely to stay friendly for long with someone who keeps correcting our sentences! However, using ungrammatical sentences when you are trying to create a good impression (such as at an interview) can be disastrous. If you answered 'I weren't with them long', in response to a question about how long you worked for a previous organisation, you would be unlikely to impress the interviewer. In writing, ungrammatical sentences make you look incompetent, and sometimes very silly. So let's start with basic sentences, which you know and use every day, and see how they are created. Then we can look at what can go wrong.

## WHEN IS A SENTENCE NOT A SENTENCE?

It is important to be able to recognise (and write) proper sentences. Sentences can be divided into two types – sometimes called 'major' and 'minor' sentences. We are mainly concerned with major sentences as these are the only ones used in formal conversation and business correspondence.

All major sentences:

- contain a connected group of words
- express a thought or an idea
- can stand alone – no further words are necessary to understand the thought or idea
- contain both a **subject** and a **finite verb**.

We usually write the subject first and then the verb.

| | (subject) | (finite verb) |
|---|---|---|
| Examples: | *Susie* | *swam.* |
| | *The child* | *laughed.* |
| | *People* | *stared.* |

A minor sentence is different, because this may contain only a verb, eg *Go!*

Consider each of the following:

*Run!*
*Bill ran.*
*Bill ran as fast as he could.*
*Bill ran twice round the track.*
*Bill ran faster than his brother and won the county championships last year.*

All of these, with one exception, are major sentences. Can you identify the minor sentence? In all but one 'Bill' is the subject and 'ran' is the finite verb.

The first sentence is the only one without a subject – and this is the minor sentence. You will often see this type of sentence on notices, posters and in advertisements: *Stop. Give Way. No smoking. Storm warning.* Apart from when you are drafting notices and posters yourself, you will only write major sentences at work – and you therefore need to make sure that all your sentences contain at least a subject and a finite verb.

■ What is a **subject**? The term 'subject' is used to describe the focus of the sentence – and this may be a place, a group of people or an inanimate object. To find the subject, look at the verb and ask yourself who, or what, is carrying out the action eg

| | |
|---|---|
| ***The team*** *played yesterday.* | (Who played? The team = subject) |
| ***The paper*** *fell on the floor.* | (What fell? The paper = subject) |

■ A **verb** is often known as a 'doing word'. It describes the action taking place. A **finite verb** is one that has a tense – which says when the action took place, either in the past, present or future. Therefore, 'looked', 'look' and 'will look' are all finite verbs, whereas 'looking' – the '-ing' form of a verb, is not.

You are unlikely to write the words 'We are looking' and think it is a sentence, but many people write 'Looking forward to hearing from you' and think they have written a sentence. They have not. Why? Firstly, because there is no subject (who is looking forward?) And secondly, because there is no finite verb. To be correct the sentence must be 'We look forward to hearing from you'.

Note that a group of words without a finite verb is called a phrase – and a phrase is not a sentence!

## Test your understanding

Identify the subject and the finite verb in each of the following sentences.

**1** The child slept.
**2** The dog barked.
**3** The car stalled at the traffic lights.
**4** The caretaker locked the doors.
**5** London has many attractions for tourists.
**6** After a while, Bill went home.
**7** The old man said, 'Tomorrow never comes.'
**8** The British film won three awards.
**9** I hope this answers your query.
**10** In this modern age, many people own a computer.

**DON'T YOU DARE!**

*...start a major sentence with the '-ing' form of a verb, eg looking, hoping or thanking.*

## MAKING HEADWAY – writing a short notice

Most organisations have a notice board – there will be several in your college. In addition there will be a fire notice in every classroom and other safety notices near doors, fire extinguishers and other relevant points. The aim of a notice is often to communicate information quickly – often at a glance. You will find the same technique used by advertisers on poster hoardings. Too many words cannot be read by drivers who are passing quickly, so the main aim is to attract attention. Sometimes a catchy slogan is used, which people then associate with the product or the organisation. Microsoft, for instance, use 'Where do you want to go today?', whilst Coca Cola's 'The real thing' is even shorter.

If you are writing a notice at work you will be expected to produce a short, yet courteous message which people can read quickly, especially if the notice is about a straightforward matter. You will often use a minor sentence as a heading to attract attention, eg FIRE DOORS. However, the text that follows usually comprises major sentences, eg 'Please keep doors closed at all times'. This is because too many minor sentences often sound abrupt or rude.

Other techniques used include:

- different sizes of print and the use of emboldening to emphasise the heading and other important words
- spacing out the information so there is plenty of 'white space' – this is much clearer than a cramped, crowded notice.
- the use of bullet points (as here) if there are several key items of information to include
- the use of coloured tape to section off areas of the noticeboard for a particular reason or to emphasise an important new notice.

It is also usual to put the name of the person issuing the notice on the bottom, together with a date. It may be your job to check the notice board regularly to remove out-of-date information and move the notices around. This is important, because people's attention is attracted by something new and different. If the notice board appears never to change, people will ignore it.

## Test your understanding

**1** Examine a noticeboard in your college and identify the notices which can be classed under the following headings:

**a** notices about safety or security
**b** notices announcing social events or activities
**c** notices on items of interest (eg a club or society, a trip abroad, etc)
**d** notices advertising something, eg jobs, car share required

What other notices are there and how would you categorise them?

**2** Critically evaluate the notices and select one or two that you think have particular impact and one or two that do not. What appeals to you about the first ones – and what puts you off about the others?

### SPELLCHECKER 1

First, a word about learning spellings. Chanting the letters of a word is *not* the way to learn to spell it. Instead, there are two far more productive ways.

- Write or type the word several times to get the 'feel' of it. It will then start to feel wrong if you spell it differently. This is why many people have to write down a word when you ask them how to spell it. Many skilled typists make the finger movements instead!
- While you are writing it, see it as a shape. Then a wrongly spelled version will look wrong. Some people can check a spelling by closing their eyes and visualising the word. People who are keen on reading are often better at spelling because they are more used to seeing the shape of words.

Second, a word about computer spellcheckers. If you use a word processing package you will no doubt be delighted to find that you can check your spelling automatically. However, no spellchecker that has yet been invented will be able to find all your errors! Why? Because if you typed 'form' instead of 'from' it will never know you made an error. Any error which results in another correctly spelt word cannot be identified by a spellchecker – so beware!

Third, it is very sensible to keep a Spellchecker book, similar to your Wordbank book, again with one letter of the alphabet for each page. Use this to enter any words which cause you difficulties – either those that you identify from the exercises in this book or those that your tutor points out to you. Regularly test yourself on spelling your entries by asking someone to read you a list from your pages.

Now start improving your spelling by reviewing the following common words that often cause difficulties in spelling. Check that you wouldn't make a mistake with any of them. *Learn* those that you think could pose a spelling trap for you.

| | |
|---|---|
| February | colleague |
| argument | awful |
| separate | definite |
| parallel (note: paralleled) | occurred (note: occurrence) |
| proceed (note: procedure) | leisure |

## POLISH YOUR PUNCTUATION

You already know that a sentence starts with a capital letter and ends with a full stop – or should do! However, at work many people hesitate over capitals and full stops in other places, because they are not sure where they should be used. To solve this problem, we will first revise the basics and then see how capitals and full stops are used in business correspondence today.

### *Capital letters*

Capital letters are used for three main reasons.

**1** They show where a new sentence starts.
**2** They denote proper names and proper nouns.
**3** They are used for some abbreviations.

Example: *I cannot see you on Tuesday. I am visiting some friends in Leeds.*

At work you may hear the terms 'upper case' for capitals and 'lower case' for non-capitals, as these are often used in relation to a typescript. Although you are unlikely to write or key in dialogue, unless you work in the media, you should know that a capital is used to begin sentences in quotation marks, such as

*The Prime Minister said, 'My aid adviser will be visiting Indonesia next month.'*

However, a capital is not required if the speech is interrupted, eg

*'Chris Kennedy is visiting Indonesia next month,' said the Prime Minister, 'to discuss this matter.'*

A modern trend is for a capital to appear in the middle of commercial names, products or processes. WordPerfect, for instance, is a word processing package and InterLink is a device used with medical injections.

A proper name is an individual name, such as your own, which you would always write with an initial capital, eg Bill Bloggs or Sally Smith. A proper noun refers to an item of which there is (usually) only one, eg Berwick Grammar School, Australia, Alice in Wonderland, Prime Minister.

Most people have little trouble with this rule for place names, titles of books or people, names of organisations and institutions and words such as the days of the week and the months of the year. Note, however, that the *seasons* of the year do *not* take an initial capital – hence 'spring', 'summer', etc.

Capitals are also used for some standard abbreviations such as BBC, USA, EU, IBM. Today full stops are not inserted between the letters. A standard abbreviation which makes a pronounceable word is known as an **acronym**, eg NATO (which stands for North Atlantic Treaty Organisation) and AIDS (Acquired Immune Deficiency Syndrome). Many of these words are not usually written completely in capitals, eg *Aids,* and may eventually drop the initial capital and become part of the language. The main example is 'laser' – which started as LASER (Light Amplification by Stimulated Emission of Radiation). Most people don't know what the letters stand for these days and the word has become an accepted part of our language, hence laser beam, laser printer, laser pen, etc.

The main problems with capitals occur in three areas:

- some words related to geography
- long headings on documents
- general words which are sometimes used specifically.

## PLACE NAMES

A specific place takes initial capitals, eg Northern Ireland or Western Australia. However, capitals are not used if you are indicating a direction, eg the *west coast of Scotland.* The word 'continent' can sometimes create problems. If you are referring to a continent generally, then don't use a capital. If you write 'the Continent' people will assume you are talking about Europe. Similarly, if you write 'the City' it is assumed you are referring to the City of London.

## LONG HEADINGS

If you had to type 'report on an investigation into security issues' as a heading where would you put the capital letters? The answer is to put the capitals on the important words only. The small words in between *don't* take an initial capital. Therefore you should type *Report on an Investigation into Security Issues.*

### GENERAL AND SPECIFIC WORDS

Confusion can be caused by words like 'manager', or names of departments in an organisation. For instance, many people always write 'Manager' with an initial capital – yet there are many managers in the world and even within one organisation! Remember that a capital is not normally used unless you are giving a specific title. Therefore words such as 'manager', 'department',' 'school', and 'university' do not take an initial capital, unlike Sales Manager, Personnel Department, Westcombe School and Manchester University, which do. The modern trend is to reduce the number of capitals, so that today in many books you may find even titles such as *personnel department* or *sales director* written without an initial capital – although this is still unusual in business communications.

## Full stops

You already know you should use a full stop at the end of a sentence. Today they are usually omitted in all abbreviations, including those written with small letters such as am, pm or etc, and they are also omitted in dates and addresses, as you will see in unit 2.

An extension of the use of full stops is the **ellipsis**. This is used to indicate that words are missing in a sentence. Three spaced dots are usually printed to show where words have been omitted in the middle of a sentence, with a fourth dot added as the full stop if the omission is at the end of a sentence.

*The report included many useful points of interest . . . and included a specific section on temporary work.*

*Bryant and Jones plc have contracts in Malaysia and Australia . . . . They have none in Europe.*

# Test your understanding

Insert capitals and full stops correctly in each of the following sentences.

**1** we are going to prague for our holidays as we have always wanted to visit eastern europe

**2** the board of directors usually meets on a tuesday

**3** he was appointed chair of the governors for westbury college last week

**4** the governor-general of the bbc has written a report for the government entitled public sector broadcasting in the digital age

**5** the chairman said although profits are down because of problems in south east asia, our decision to sell slimco products in the usa has resulted in high sales, particularly in california and florida

## COMMUNICATION IN PRACTICE

# Test your skills

**1** There is at least one mistake in each of the following sentences. It may be spelling, punctuation, grammar or the wrong use of a word. In each case find and correct the errors.

**a** In Summer, we often go with our colleeges to france.
**b** Asking you to understand on this ocassion.
**c** He said it was definate i would get a pay rise in febraury.
**d** I herd the rumour he was going to the U.S.A. as he has just seperated from his wife.
**e** the prime minister liased with the editor of the daily telegraph about this matter.
**f** Hoping to see you Wednesday.

**2** Use a dictionary or other reference book to find out the meaning of each of the following abbreviations.

PLC BA AA (2 meanings) COD FBI HRH HQ ITA MD MP (2 meanings) PS RSVP SOS UK UN

**3 a** The following abbreviations are often used in standard speech but would not be appropriate in a formal business communication. In each case, identify the full word and write it down, spelling it correctly.

**i** ad
**ii** pro
**iii** demo
**iv** mike
**v** flu
**vi** phone
**vii** prep
**viii** rep
**ix** vet
**x** exam

**b** People often use abbreviations when they write a note to someone. Can you say what each of the following mean?

**i** asap
**ii** pto
**iii** wef
**iv** aka

**4** Insert full stops and capital letters into the following passage at every point where they are needed.

bill tidied up his desk and sighed the report he was writing was causing problems phrasing some of the government regulations on safety so that everyone would understand them was not easy the report was required for the safety committee meeting on thursday when the managing director would be present john tomlinson was a busy man who would quickly show his impatience if he was not happy bill looked again at the title of the report he had decided on health and safety in the workplace but now had second thoughts then he glanced at the clock it was time he left he stuffed the draft document into his briefcase and headed for the car park

**5** Select one word from the list on the right which would make an appropriate substitute for the word on the left, in terms of meaning.

**a** alert — awake vigilant wary suspicious
**b** tired — exhausted ill sleepy annoyed
**c** stubborn — awkward wilful obstinate argumentative
**d** hurt — troubled injured maimed ill

**e** observe recognise differentiate see notice
**f** solemn serious sensible strict formal
**g** looked glimpsed stared watched glanced
**h** risk gamble endanger menace threat
**i** finished won achieved obtained concluded
**j** candid frank clear tactless brazen

## Apply your skills

Jane Mitchell was having a bad day. As senior receptionist at Riverside Small Animal Centre she liked to arrive early and had a set of keys to open up and disarm the burglar alarm. She collected the post from the wire basket behind the door. This morning she was wet through – the weather was awful. She took off her dripping mac and then looked around in annoyance. For the third night in succession whoever had locked up had left all the lights on in the back office. No wonder the electricity bill was so high! She moved over to the photocopier and switched it on, so that it would have time to warm up before she needed it. She then checked the reception area. As she was doing so, John Higgins, the senior vet, arrived looking very bedraggled.

'What a day!' he said. 'I could have done without an early morning call to Mrs Winter's house but her cat was struggling. Anyway, there are six healthy, black and white kittens to show for her troubles! Three males and three females. I've promised Mrs Winters we'll try to find homes for them all. Any chance of making me a coffee,' he asked, 'while I just go upstairs and check on our inmates?'

Jane heard him climb the stairs to the area reserved for the animals who were staying in the centre overnight. She suddenly heard a loud squawk, a muttered exclamation and a crash. 'Are you all right?' she shouted.

'Just about,' called John down the stairs. 'Someone forgot to lock the parrot cage last night. The beggar can get it open with his beak and he's had a wonderful night flying around. It looks like he's been in a scuffle with somebody – there are a few tail feathers near the window. It'll be great explaining *that* to his owners.'

Later that morning John Higgins caught up with Jane once again. 'There's a couple of interesting things in the post today,' he said. 'There's a report on Betty Holden's dog, Nipper, which I'd like Asif to see fairly quickly. I'd welcome his opinion. Can you photocopy it for me immediately? And there's confirmation from Petneeds that they can provide ID tags for us. They inscribe the name and address of the pet on one side and our name and phone number on the other. The tag fixes on to any collar and they cost £4 each – takes a week apparently. Can you do a brief notice for our clients? They can ask for details at reception but I'd warn them of the price.'

'Fine,' replied Jane. 'I've a few notices to do this morning.'

She went into the photocopying room and smothered an annoyed cry. Someone had switched it off. '*How* many times must I tell people it must be left on during the day and only switched off at night?' she muttered to herself. 'That must be five notices I've to do at least!'

**1** Identify the five notices Jane Mitchell has to prepare.

**2** Prepare each one, using a minor sentence for your heading to attract attention and then courteous major sentences for the main information. Don't be tempted to use more than two colours, fancy writing or elaborate borders on your notices. These spoil, rather than enhance, the overall look.

## *WORD WIZARD*

Whilst many word wizard sections in this book introduce you to word plays you can do yourself, in this chapter you can see how someone who is clever with words can use them for a purpose. Mark Twain was a writer and also a word wizard. The item below may strike a chord with you – particularly if you hate learning spellings. It is his progressive plan for improving spelling! The challenge for you is to be able to read it – right through to the end!

### A PLAN FOR THE IMPROVEMENT OF ENGLISH SPELLING
*(MARK TWAIN)*

For example, in Year 1 that useless letter 'c' would be dropped to be replased either by 'k' or 's', and likewise 'x' would no longer be part of the alphabet. The only kase in which 'c' would be retained would be the 'ch' formation, which will be dealt with later. Year 2 might reform 'w' spelling, so that 'which' and 'one' would take the same konsonant, wile Year 3 might well abolish 'y' replasing it with 'i' and Iear 4 might fiks the 'g/j' anomali wonse and for all.

Jenerally, then, the improvement would kontinue iear bai iear with Iear 5 doing awai with useless double konsonants, and Iears 6–12 or so modifaiing vowlz and the rimeining voist and unvoist konsonants. Bai Iear 15 or sou, it wud fainali bi posible tu meik ius ov thi ridandant letez 'c', 'y' and 'x' – bai now jast a memori in the maindz ov ould doderez – tu riplais 'ch', 'sh' and 'th' rispektivli.

Fainali, xen, aafte sam 20 iers ov orxogrefkl riform, wi wud hev a lojikl, kohirnt speling in ius xrewawt xe Ingliy-spiking werld.

# IN THE SPOTLIGHT – BUSINESS LETTERS

Some people think that because communications can now be sent electronically, there must be fewer letters sent by post these days. In fact, the reverse is true! The growth in computers and word processors has meant a huge increase in the amount of 'direct mail' sent to people's homes. This is personalised letters and leaflets advertising products and services and – when sent by charities – asking for donations. At present, the Royal Mail handles over 70 million items every day, and while not all of these are letters, the vast majority are business communications.

Throughout this book you will be introduced to a range of business letters, from straightforward replies to letters dealing with more complex or sensitive information. First of all, a brief word about the term 'business'. It may be that your final ambition is not to work for a 'business' – such as a manufacturer or an accountant – nor to work in an office all the time. You may want to work in leisure, travel, retail or the health service, for example. However, from the communication aspect *all* these different areas can be classed as businesses.

Therefore, when we refer to 'business' communication and 'business' letters, do think on a broader basis than a local factory or the solicitor down the road.

## Why send a letter?

Letters are sent for many reasons, but can basically be divided into the following categories.

1 **Confirmatory letters** that confirm an arrangement already agreed verbally, such as the details of an appointment or meeting or a hotel booking.

2 **Letters of acknowledgement** that confirm receipt of a letter, request or order that cannot be dealt with immediately.

3 **Reminder letters** that are sent to jog someone's memory, eg that an account is overdue for payment or that their annual check-up is due.

4 **Letters of enquiry** that ask for information, such as an enquiry about goods or a service or for details of a prospective customer.

5 **Letters of response** that provide information, eg a response to a letter of enquiry about goods or services.

6 **Sales letters** and **circular letters** sent to interest customers in a new product or service or to inform customers of a change to an existing product or service or a special promotional event which may interest them.

7 **Letters of complaint and adjustment** where the first is the letter that describes the problem and the second is the response to the complaint.

8 **Job application letters** including letters from candidates, letters asking for or supplying a reference, letters relating to interview arrangements and letters to the successful and unsuccessful candidates.

9 **Personal letters**, including letters that congratulate or thank someone, letters of condolence or sympathy sent if a close business associate or colleague suffers a bereavement, letters that ask a personal favour or give personal details.

## Letter-headed paper

Heinemann

Halley Court
Jordan Hill
Oxford OX2 8EJ UK

*Telephone* +44 (0)1865 311366
*Fax* +44 (0)1865 314140
*URL* http://www.heinemann.co.uk
*e-mail* reed.educational@bhein.rel.co.uk
*Direct Line*

Heinemann Educational
A Division of Reed Educational
& Professional Publishing Limited

*Registered Office*
Quadrant House, The Quadrant,
Sutton, Surrey, SM2 5AS

*Registered in England* 3099304

A member of the Reed Elsevier plc group

***Figure 2.1*** *Letter-headed paper*

All business letters are written on letter-headed paper – usually referred to simply as 'headed paper' (see Figure 2.1). This paper has the name of the organisation, its address, fax and phone number and other appropriate information printed on it. Today the e-mail and Internet addresses are often included, as well as the company logo. This is an illustration designed to represent the organisation (for instance, Lloyds Bank is represented by a black horse and the Princess of Wales Memorial Fund uses Diana's signature in purple). In many cases, if people see the logo they know the organisation to which it relates, therefore as well as being a trademark a logo is also a form of advertising. At the bottom of the paper you will often find the address of the 'registered office' and a registration number. This is a legal requirement for limited companies but does not apply to professions such as solicitors or doctors.

Organisations often spend a considerable amount of money on the design and printing of their letter heads because they want to give the impression that they provide a high quality, professional service to their customers and clients. This is ruined, of course, if the letter itself is not of the same standard!

Some organisations also produce special **continuation paper** for multi-page letters, which simply repeats the name and the logo at the top. However, many organisations simply use plain, good quality paper known as **bond paper** for second and subsequent pages, to save printing costs.

## The layout and components of a business letter

Many companies have a specific 'house style' for their letters which you must follow. This is to ensure that all the letters sent from the organisation look the same. The house style is likely to be similar to that shown below. Do check when you start work and follow the rules of your employer – never argue that they are wrong! Sometimes you may hear the word 'format' used instead of 'layout'. Both words have the same meaning.

Usually, the left hand margin for the text follows the design of the letter heading and the point at which the printer's left margin begins. The standard format is often called **fully blocked** because every line starts at the left margin. There is a particular place for each of the components (or parts) of the letter. These are listed below.

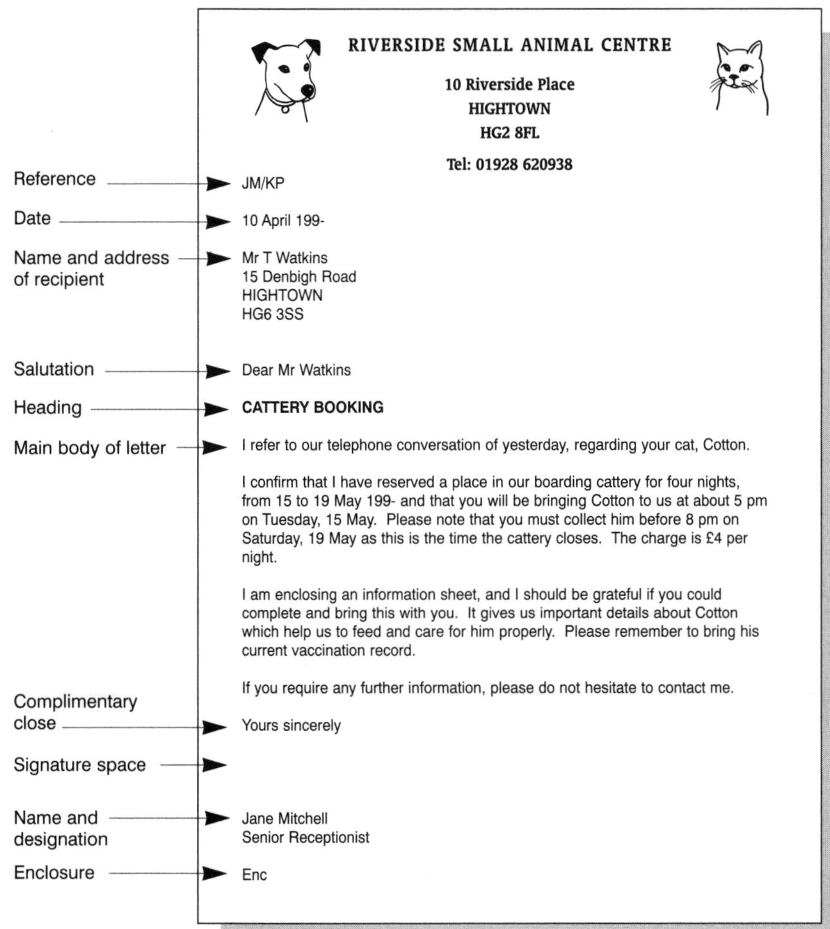

RIVERSIDE SMALL ANIMAL CENTRE

10 Riverside Place
HIGHTOWN
HG2 8FL

Tel: 01928 620938

JM/KP

10 April 199-

Mr T Watkins
15 Denbigh Road
HIGHTOWN
HG6 3SS

Dear Mr Watkins

**CATTERY BOOKING**

I refer to our telephone conversation of yesterday, regarding your cat, Cotton.

I confirm that I have reserved a place in our boarding cattery for four nights, from 15 to 19 May 199- and that you will be bringing Cotton to us at about 5 pm on Tuesday, 15 May. Please note that you must collect him before 8 pm on Saturday, 19 May as this is the time the cattery closes. The charge is £4 per night.

I am enclosing an information sheet, and I should be grateful if you could complete and bring this with you. It gives us important details about Cotton which help us to feed and care for him properly. Please remember to bring his current vaccination record.

If you require any further information, please do not hesitate to contact me.

Yours sincerely

Jane Mitchell
Senior Receptionist

Enc



***Figure 2.2*** *The layout and components of a business letter*

**The reference** is usually the initials of the writer and the person who typed the letter. The file number may also be added, eg KT/ML/3729.

**The date** is normally written as 14 February 1999 and not 14/2/99.

**The name and address of the recipient** (the person who will receive the letter) usually has no punctuation in the address and the town should be shown in CAPITALS. If possible, put the postcode on a separate line and *never* punctuate it.

Some organisations include the title of the person (Mr, Mrs, Miss, Dr). Many women prefer the title 'Ms', and you should certainly use this if a woman's marital status is unknown. Others simply write the name, eg John Smith or Fazana Patel.

**The salutation** is the part that says 'Dear Mr Smith' or 'Dear Miss Patel'. The title used here must match that used in the address line. A formal letter may start Dear Sir or Dear Madam, but this is becoming quite rare these days as organisations prefer to use a personal approach. *Never* write Dear John Smith! It's either Dear John or Dear Mr Smith but not both!

**A heading** is often included, particularly on long or complex letters, so that the recipient quickly sees what it is about. If you use capitals and/or bold type there is no need to underscore your heading.

**The main part of the letter** is known as the 'body' of the letter. A standard business letter has about three paragraphs but there are no rules on this – a very basic letter may have only one or two paragraphs, whereas a complex letter may have several more. Each paragraph normally deals with a different idea or sub-section of the overall theme. Remember always to leave a blank line between paragraphs.

**The complimentary close** used today is normally either 'Yours faithfully' or 'Yours sincerely'. Note the spelling of 'sincerely'! The complimentary close must match the salutation.

Dear Sir or Dear Madam = Yours faithfully

Dear Mr Smith = Yours sincerely.

A business letter starting Dear John may end with just the word Sincerely. This is the only time when a capital letter is used for the word. Normally neither 'faithfully' nor 'sincerely' have an initial capital. Few letters today end 'Yours truly' – but if you have to put this word, note there is no 'e' in it!

**The signature space** is for the writer to sign the letter – you must leave sufficient space. A standard gap is between 2 cm and 2.5 cm, and most people leave about five blank spaces.

**The name and designation of the person signing the letter** is shown below the signature. The designation is that person's official title in the organisation, eg Customer Services Co-ordinator, Promotions Assistant.

**An enclosure abbreviation** is added if any documents are being sent with the letter. This is usually typed as Enc (for one) and Encs (for more than one). This tells the recipient to look for something else in the envelope. It is also a useful reminder to you to include the enclosure!

## The conventions of a business letter

There are also several other conventions you need to know when writing business letters. The most important ones are given below.

- Contracted words are never used in a business letter, such as *can't, isn't* or *won't*. Instead write *cannot, is not* or *will not*.
- Abbreviated words, such as *rep, phone* and *photo* are not used – the full version is written. However, the word *fax* is used (rather than facsimile transmission) as this is now an accepted word in the English language.
- Slang phrases and expressions are *never* used. If you were confirming an appointment you would not say

  *Mr Blake wants you here dead on nine then we can get going on time.*

  Instead you should write:

  *We should be grateful if you could arrive promptly at nine o'clock so that the interviews can start on time.*

  This says the same thing – only in a much more courteous way!
- All the sentences you write must be *complete* sentences – with a subject and a finite verb. But you knew this already, didn't you?

## Writing a simple business letter

The first thing to remember is that all business letters (and most other business documents) are composed using the **KISS** principle. This stands for **K**eep **I**t **S**hort and **S**imple! People are too busy to read flowery phrases and to have to search through pages to find out why you are writing to them. So get to the point – but politely!

One of the most straightforward types of letter is a letter of confirmation. In this case you are referring to arrangements already made. All the details are usually included, to prevent any misunderstandings.

A letter of confirmation was shown in Figure 2.2 on page 23.

- The first paragraph sets the scene by referring to when the arrangements were first made. If the letter confirms a telephone call, an easy way to start the letter is as shown in the example – simply refer to the call and the topic discussed.
- The second and third paragraphs give the details. If there had been very few details to confirm, then only one paragraph would have been necessary. It is important to make sure that
  - all the facts you give are accurate
  - you clearly state both the day and date of any arrangements to prevent misunderstandings
  - you do not omit any essential information.
- A final sentence is included, out of courtesy, to round off the letter. Final sentences tell the recipient what to do next, or how to raise any problems.

**DON'T YOU DARE!**

*...start a letter with the phrase 'I am writing ...' It is quite obvious that you are writing, you don't need to tell them! The phrase 'Regarding our telephone conversation' should also be avoided, as this is apt to lead to an incomplete sentence with no finite verb.*

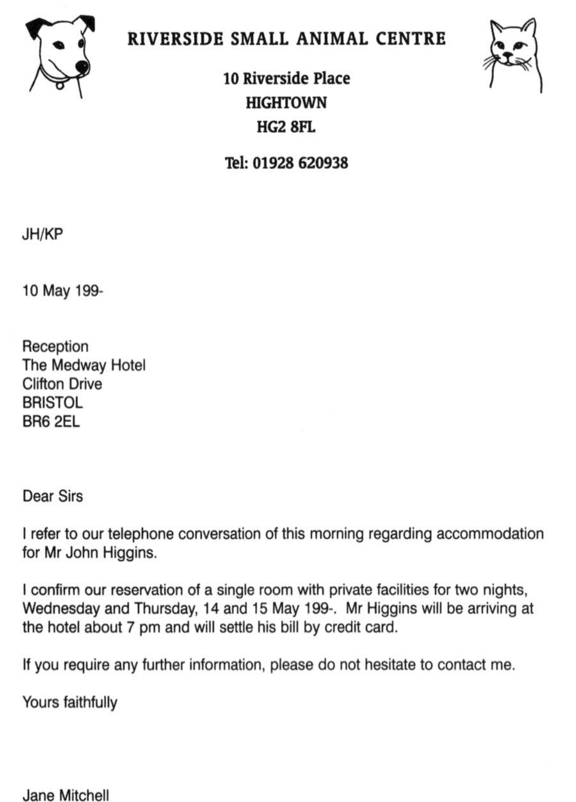

RIVERSIDE SMALL ANIMAL CENTRE

10 Riverside Place
HIGHTOWN
HG2 8FL

Tel: 01928 620938

JH/KP

10 May 199-

Reception
The Medway Hotel
Clifton Drive
BRISTOL
BR6 2EL

Dear Sirs

I refer to our telephone conversation of this morning regarding accommodation for Mr John Higgins.

I confirm our reservation of a single room with private facilities for two nights, Wednesday and Thursday, 14 and 15 May 199-. Mr Higgins will be arriving at the hotel about 7 pm and will settle his bill by credit card.

If you require any further information, please do not hesitate to contact me.

Yours faithfully

Jane Mitchell
Senior Receptionist

***Figure 2.3*** *A letter of confirmation from the files*

## Test your understanding

**1** The Riverside Small Animal Centre is owned by John Higgins, the senior veterinary surgeon in the practice. His Senior Receptionist, Jane Mitchell, asked you to help her this morning by making a telephone call to the Criterion Hotel in Liverpool (Portways Road, Liverpool L23 1SX) to book accommodation for John Higgins and then write a letter of confirmation. To help, she has given you a previous letter of confirmation from the files to use as your model (see Figure 2.3). The booking you made was for a single room for two nights for next Monday and Tuesday. John Higgins will arrive about 9 pm and Jane has stressed you must mention this, otherwise the hotel may re-let the room after 6 pm. As usual, he will pay by credit card. Write the letter in your name and use the title Clerical Assistant. Use today's date.

**2** At midday John Higgins receives a telephone call from Mr Peter Aspin from Fenlow and Associates, 16 Grange Road, Hightown HG3 3OS. This is the firm of architects responsible for planning the new extension to the practice. Mr Aspin has asked John Higgins if he can attend a meeting at Fenlows at 2 pm next Thursday to discuss the plans in more detail. John Higgins has agreed and has passed you the following notes for a letter of confirmation.

- Please start the letter Dear Peter and end it Yours sincerely
- I will sign the letter
- Use today's date and start by referring to our telephone conversation this morning
- Then confirm I will attend a meeting at their office next Thursday (please state time and date)

- Please say that I would be grateful if they would reserve me a parking space in their car park as parking is very difficult in the town centre.
- End by saying that I look forward to seeing him again.

Check your finished letters with your tutor.

## SPELLCHECKER 2

Several common words appear frequently in business letters. Learn these carefully so that you can write them automatically, without any errors. Enter any that give you problems into your Spellchecker book, for future reference.

| | | |
|---|---|---|
| acceptance | accommodation | appointment |
| efficient | faithfully | fulfil (note: fulfilled) |
| incur (note: incurred) | independent | immediately |
| negotiate | prefer (note: preference/preferred but preferable) | |
| receive | refer (note: reference/referred) | |
| regrettable | relevant | responsible |
| sincerely | truly | unnecessary |

## DOUBLE TROUBLE!

There are many pairs of words which can cause problems when you are writing a letter, and whilst you may be perfectly aware that 'dear' is an endearment or a salutation, whereas 'deer' is an animal, you may not be so aware of other commonly mistaken words. In the case of each word below, note the definition given and then write a sentence containing the word to show you understand the context in which it should be used.

- accept = to consent, agree or believe
  except = not including
- may be = might be
  maybe = perhaps or possibly
- descent = a movement downwards
  dissent = to protest against; a difference of opinion
- stationary = not moving
  stationery = paper, envelopes and related items
- personal = specific to a particular person
  personnel = the department that deals with staff
- principal = the chief or main one
  principle = a fundamental belief
- confident = feeling self-assured
  confidant = a person you confide in
- formerly = before or earlier
  formally = in a formal manner

- summary = a brief account
  summery = linked to summer, as in a type of dress
- proceed = to continue or go further
  precede = to be in front of

**DON'T YOU DARE!**

*...mix up the words 'loose' and 'lose' (which are pronounced differently as well as having different meanings)!*

*Loose = not tight*
*Lose = to mislay or be deprived of*

*The easy way to remember this is that 'lose' has lost an 'o'!*

## TOOLS OF THE TRADE – think first, communicate later

If you are unprepared when you are communicating then you will make mistakes, and sometimes this can cause problems. Lack of 'thinking time', preparation and planning can result in:

- wrong information being included (simply mistaking the day or date can cause havoc)
- forgetting important information that should have been given
- giving information that is confusing or ambiguous and makes no sense to the recipient
- saying (or writing) the 'wrong thing' – so that you upset or annoy someone
- the recipient not doing what you wanted them to do.

At best you are likely to look hesitant, at worst you will look foolish and create more problems than you solve. Therefore careful preparation, particularly for important or complex communications, is essential. How do you go about this?

- The first stage is to check that you have all the information that you need beforehand and that you *understand it*! If someone asks you to do something quickly and uses words that you don't understand you should ask them to repeat it in language you do understand, not guess!
- The second stage is to focus on the desired outcome. What are you trying to accomplish by sending the communication? How can this best be achieved?
- The third stage is to consider who will be receiving the communication. What do they know already and what do they not know? What words and phrases will they understand and what will they not understand? How formal should you be?

- The final stage is to check that you have included all the information required by the recipient. This should include everything the person cannot be expected to know already and the appropriate facts and reasons. Don't expect your recipients to possess second-sight!

## Jargon, gobbledegook and officialese

**Jargon** is the term used to describe words that are specific to a particular activity or occupation. If you go to a doctor – or to a vet – and he or she described a complaint in medical terms it is highly likely you wouldn't be very sure what was meant. This is the problem with jargon – only the people who use it regularly can understand it! Computer programmers talk about 'memory', 'code' 'bytes' and 'interfaces', solicitors talk about 'plaintiff', 'defendant', 'litigation' and 'executors', whilst even your local DJ may be into 'hip hop' and 'drum and bass' or 'apache loop' and 'Amen break'. Whilst this is fine for anyone 'in the know' such terms can create serious problems for anyone else. You might as well have used a foreign language.

You are bound to learn jargon when you work for any organisation, but do remember that its use is only appropriate in internal communications to other specialists.

**Gobbledegook** and **officialese** are two words used to describe language written in such a way that the recipient cannot possibly be expected to understand it. In the past, criticisms have been levelled at government offices, tax offices, insurance and pension companies and many others for sending out unintelligible instructions and information. As an example, read the following sentence, which is taken from the conditions of a life insurance policy:

*This policy shall be void if the Life Assured dies by his or her own hand within thirteen calendar months of the commencing date or the date of any reinstatement except to the extent of the interests of any third parties proved to the satisfaction of the Company to have been acquired for value.*

The basic message is that if the person holding the policy commits suicide the company is unlikely to pay out any money. Beyond that it is virtually incomprehensible! Today, however, many organisations have supported the Plain English Campaign so that booklets on savings accounts, benefit rules and tax regulations are written in such a way that everyone will understand them.

## Test your skills

Each of the following sentences would be unsuitable in a business letter. Your task is to say why! Rewrite the phrase so that it would be acceptable in any letter you wrote. To help you, words and phrases that could be written more simply are highlighted in bold.

**1** Looking forward to hearing from you.

**2** Can you pop in for a couple of minutes next week?

**3** We **endeavour** to **expedite** all orders by **despatching** them by first class post.

**4** Mr Higgins can see you on Monday at 4 pm but if you can't manage that, please give us a call.

5 **At this present moment in time** our spring brochure is still being produced, but I enclose a copy of our winter brochure which you can **peruse at your leisure**.

6 We **anticipate** that **employment** will **commence** on Monday, 25 May and your **remuneration** will be £10,000 **per annum**.

DON'T YOU DARE!

*...write the words 'thank you' as one word! There is no such word as thankyou in the English language!*

## MAKING HEADWAY – choosing your method of communication

In Unit 1 you learned that there are many different methods of communicating in business. Some are oral, others are written. External communications go outside the organisation whereas internal ones do not. In addition, some methods of communicating are more formal than others.

## Degrees of formality

In this chapter you have seen how business letters are written. They are external written communications. However, letters may be very formal or quite friendly and informal – even in business. The degree of formality will be influenced by:

- the reason for writing the letter
- how well the writer and the recipient know each other
- the status of the writer and recipient. If they are at the same level (eg both senior managers) *and* know each other well, the letter will be more informal than if one is senior in rank to the other.

Compare the following extracts from three letters. How would you rank them in formality?

**A** Dear Bill

I was pleased to hear that you will be able to attend the conference next week. It seems a long time since we last met. I think it would be interesting for both of us to ...

**B** Dear Mr Brown

I understand that you will be attending the conference in Brighton next week. You may remember that we met last year at the same event. I was wondering if you would be available to ...

**C** Dear Bill

It was great to hear that you will be at Brighton next week. It seems ages since we last met. Apart from anything else, I particularly wanted to talk to you about ...

You should have decided that B was the most formal and C the most informal with A somewhere in-between. The degree of formality affects the tone you will use in a letter. Tone is discussed in more detail in the next unit.

## Additional types of communications

Examples of different types of communication were given in Unit 1. A more complete list is shown in Figure 2.4 below.

- A **presentation** can be internal or external. It is normally a fairly brief session to introduce a new product, service, idea or staff procedure to a relatively small group of people. It is normal for a brief talk to be illustrated by using a video, a computer presentation package or overhead transparencies containing graphics or illustrations. This provides more information and helps to keep the attention of the audience. Further details may be given in a leaflet or pack of information.
- A **conference** is an occasion when a group of people meet – sometimes over several days – to attend talks and discussions on topics in which they are all interested. Conferences can be internal or external. An organisation may hold a sales conference for all its sales staff. Many professional groups hold conferences for all their members each year – and hundreds of people may be invited.
- You already know about **reports** from your schooldays! Basically, a report is an account of something. An example is an accident report – the details are often recorded on a special form. In some cases a person may be asked to investigate something and produce a written report. You will see how reports should be written in Unit 8.
- An **agenda** and **minutes** are both types of meetings documents. An agenda states the topics to be discussed at a meeting, in the order in

| **ORAL** | | **WRITTEN** | |
|---|---|---|---|
| **Internal** | **External** | **Internal** | **External** |
| Telephone<br>Voice mail<br>Pager or bleeper<br>Private radio<br>Face-to-face conversation with colleague<br>Meeting<br>Interview<br>Presentation<br>Conference | Telephone<br>Voice mail<br>Answering machine<br>Face-to-face conversation with caller or visitor<br>Meeting<br>Interview<br>Presentation<br>Conference | Memo<br>E-mail<br>Telephone message<br>Report<br>Summary<br>Staff newsletter or magazine<br>Notice<br>Agenda or minutes relating to a meeting<br>Business accounts (in a privately funded organisation) | Letter<br>E-mail<br>Fax<br>Form<br>Catalogue, brochure or prospectus<br>Advertisement<br>Invitation<br>Purchase and sales documents, eg order, invoice, statement<br>Business accounts and chairman's report (in a publicly funded organisation) |

***Figure 2.4*** *Types of communication*

which they will be dealt with. The **minutes** are the official record of the discussions that took place at a meeting and the decisions made. Note that the word 'minutes' is *always* used in the plural form.

- **Business accounts** are produced at the end of the year, giving information on the money earned and spent and the profit (or loss) made. They usually include the *profit and loss account* and the *balance sheet.* In a private organisation (such as a professional association or a limited company) the accounts are private and are not disclosed externally. A public limited company (plc), which obtains money from shareholders, must make its accounts public, so they are also external.
- **Purchase and sales documents** are many and various. They include orders, delivery notes, invoices, receipts and statements.

## The advantages and disadvantages of different methods of communications

You will often have to choose how to communicate with someone. You may, for instance, contact someone by telephone or write a letter – or you could send a fax. If the person is a colleague, you could write a note (or memo), go and speak face to face – or send an e-mail. What factors should influence your decision?

The first is obvious. You cannot fax or e-mail someone if either you, or they, do not have the equipment!

The second factor is the urgency of the situation. Some methods of communication – telephone, fax, e-mail, finding someone and speaking directly – are much quicker than writing a letter and posting it or putting a memo into the internal mail system.

The third factor is the *reason* for the communication, eg

- is it something complex, and better written down?
- is it something that could be disputed in future, so that a permanent record would be useful?
- is about a formal matter, which would be better in writing?
- or is it very personal, or a request, where you may wish to gauge the recipient's reactions – in which case you would be better speaking privately?

All these factors should influence your choice. Both verbal and written forms of communication have specific advantages and disadvantages, which are shown in Figure 2.5 opposite. Study this and then do the task below.

## Test your understanding

State whether you would choose a verbal or written method in each of the following situations. In each case give a reason for your decision.

**1** You want to ask your boss if you can finish early tonight because of a dental appointment.

**2** You have been asked to confirm your attendance at an interview in two weeks' time.

| | Verbal | Written |
|---|---|---|
| **Advantages** | Rapid<br>Relatively cheap<br>Voice can be used for emphasis or to show feelings<br>Immediate feedback possible<br>Can check listener(s) paying attention<br>Body language (gestures, facial expressions) emphasise meaning and attitude | Has formal authority<br>Provides a permanent record as evidence and for future reference<br>Can be studied at leisure<br>Can be copied for other people<br>Creates a 'distance' between sender and recipient – useful for difficult communications (eg bad news)<br>Can include visual information and colour to aid understanding/ emphasis |
| **Disadvantages** | Clear speech essential<br>Message must be clear and unambiguous<br>Listener must be able to hear the message without distortion<br>Long or complex messages are easily forgotten<br>External factors may distract speaker or listener<br>Can be difficult to handle open hostility or disagreement shown by listener | Takes time to produce – particularly if long or complex<br>Keyed-in documents need skill to be produced quickly and accurately<br>Will be spoiled by poor command of language, spelling or punctuation<br>Must be legible – may depend upon handwriting ability of writer<br>Delivery may take time<br>Permanency may prove a disadvantage if contents are inaccurate, out-of-date or writer later regrets sending message |

***Figure 2.5*** *Advantages and disadvantages of different methods of communication*

3 You need to make an urgent doctor's appointment.

4 Your great-aunt, who lives some distance away, has invited you to her diamond wedding celebration but you will be on holiday that day. You want to apologise very tactfully for not being able to attend.

5 You have agreed to work late in an emergency and need to contact a friend to cancel an arrangement for tonight.

6 You have received a council tax bill even though you are a student. The document says that you must give full details of your current situation if you wish to contest the charge.

7 You have been asked to give information to a group of visitors on the products you sell and the price of each.

## THE GOOD GRAMMAR GUIDE

### Building a sentence

Sentences can include other components besides a subject and a verb. Many also include an **object**. You may remember that the subject of a sentence is the person or thing carrying out the action. The object is the person or thing that is being acted upon, eg

*John* (subject) *met* (verb) *Paul* (object).

Sometimes there may be more than one object in a sentence, eg

*John met Paul* (1), *Frank* (2) and *Natalie* (3).

*John passed Paul* (1) *a pen* (2).

All of these sentences are **simple** sentences because they contain just one clause. A clause is a short statement that includes a verb. A **multiple** or **complex** sentence contains more than one clause, eg

*Simon is eating a biscuit* (1) *and writing a letter* (2).

Clauses can be joined together by means of a **conjunction** such as 'and', 'but', 'then', 'so', 'yet', eg

*She is staying at the Royal Hotel in Bradford, then travelling to Edinburgh for three days. She will be there for one week.*

The use of conjunctions helps you to lengthen some sentences. This is useful as varying the length of sentences in a piece of writing makes it more interesting as well as being easier to understand.

Not all sentences start with the subject. For instance you could say

*Tom stroked the cat* or *The cat was stroked by Tom.*

In the second case the object of the stroking comes before the subject. This is a **passive** sentence (see Unit 9, page 155)

However, do test that sentences beginning with an object make sense and aren't ambiguous. For instance,

*Mary was visiting Florida* can hardly be converted, sensibly, into *Florida was being visited by Mary!*

## Test your understanding

**1** Identify the subject, finite verb and object(s) in the following sentences.

- **a** Joanne has ordered a new desk and chair.
- **b** Most young people can use a computer these days.
- **c** A copy of the newsletter has been sent to Sahida.
- **d** Chinese restaurants offer a variety of dishes.
- **e** This answering machine uses a disk, not tapes.
- **f** For her birthday, Simon bought Paula some flowers and a CD.
- **g** The cost of the equipment is £1,500.
- **h** The new branch of the bank opened yesterday.
- **i** Personally, I do not think he should go.

**2** Write six sentences saying what you did last weekend. Try to vary the length of your sentences with at least two quite long and two short ones.

## WORDBANK 2

### GOOD NEWS: BAD NEWS?

Extend your vocabulary by reading each of the following sentences and deciding whether the statement gives good news or bad. The first time you can guess your answers. Then check the definition of each in a dictionary and see whether you were right. Add any new words to your wordbank book.

1 You discover your boss is very **parsimonious**.

2 You meet someone who is extremely **presentable**.

3 You find out a signed record by John Lennon is **authentic**.

4 You are given a **gratuity** by a customer.

5 Your new colleague is forever trying to **ingratiate** herself with the boss.

6 Your tutor tells you your work is **mediocre**.

7 You work for a **prestigious** company.

8 When you ask your boss if you can have a day off next week he **prevaricates**.

9 Your best friend says you are **obdurate**.

10 The new manager is very **charismatic**.

## POLISH YOUR PUNCTUATION

### The comma

The comma is the most frequently used punctuation mark in a sentence. It indicates a short break in the speaking or reading of a sentence. In some cases a comma is absolutely essential for the correct meaning to be obvious – otherwise a sentence is ambiguous (which means it could be understood in more than one way).

As an example, look at the following sentence.

*Mary is sick and tired of filing dozens of documents.*

Now look at this one.

*Mary is sick, and tired of filing dozens of documents.*

In the second case the sentence has an entirely different meaning.

Generally, the longer the sentence the more commas you should insert. If you are talking to someone then you automatically pause several times in a long sentence. Read the sentence below as if you were saying it out loud to a friend and note where you pause. Then check if this coincides with the commas inserted in the sentence (shown again on the next page).

*Jo goes on holiday to Ibiza each year not just because she likes the club scene but because she also likes to sunbathe providing she manages to get up whilst it is still daylight!*

When you are writing a sentence, commas are therefore essential to give the reader a breathing space, as well as to show the sense of a sentence.

The 'rules' relating to commas are mainly based on 'natural' pauses. Commas are inserted as follows.

- In a list of items. There is usually no comma before the final 'and' unless the meaning would not be clear without one, eg

  *He needed paper, envelopes, a ruler and a pen before he could start work.*

  but

  *The meeting involved the directors of Marks and Spencer, Sainsbury, and Tesco.*

- In a list of words describing someone or something, eg

  *He was a tall, thin, dark-haired man.*

- To separate clauses not closely linked to each other or which give a contrasting view.

  *He's great fun, but never buys a drink.*

  but

  *She is very lively and a true friend.*

- To separate a distinct phrase or clause in the middle of a sentence. You can test for this because the sentence would make sense even if the clause was omitted. A comma is required both before and after the clause, eg

  *In winter, when it is very cold, many animals hibernate.*
  *Sandra, who only started last week, is joining us for lunch.*

- To separate words such as 'therefore', 'however', 'unfortunately', 'interestingly' and 'consequently' from the rest of the sentence, eg

  *However, many people would not agree with me.*
  *I wanted to go but, unfortunately, it was too far.*
  *It is, therefore, impossible for me to agree.*

- Before a quotation, eg

  *Gracie Allen, a famous American comedienne, once said, 'When I was born, I was so surprised I couldn't talk for a year and half.'*

After inserting commas, the sentence shown on the previous page should read:

*Jo goes on holiday to Ibiza each year, not just because she likes the club scene, but because she also likes to sunbathe, providing she manages to get up whilst it is still daylight!*

## Test your understanding

**1** Identify the difference in meaning between the following two sentences:

*Paul, said Sally, is going to be late.*
*Paul said Sally is going to be late.*

**2** Insert commas in each of the following sentences:

**a** I took with me a woolly jumper an anorak my jeans and a strong pair of shoes.

**b** Mrs Evans who is our Sales Manager will be joining us soon.
**c** Unless you know what to say you are better to keep quiet particularly in a tricky or difficult situation.
**d** Mark Twain said when I was a boy of fourteen my father was so ignorant I could hardly stand to have the old man around. But when I got to be twenty-one I was astonished at how much he had learned in seven years.
**e** Please report to the Personnel Office which is the first building after the main gate at 9 am on Tuesday.
**f** The term 'cyber' which relates to electronic communications and virtual reality has resulted in a new spate of words including cybernetics cyborg cybernaut cyberspace and even cybercafes.

## COMMUNICATION IN PRACTICE

### Test your skills

**1** In the letter below, the office junior has made several errors when keying in the document, none of which showed on her spellcheck! To help you, however, every error is shown in bold. In each case identify

**a** the word that should have been used
**b** the meaning of the word that has been used.

**Deer** Tom

I wanted to **right** to you **formerly** to confirm your appointment **hear** as Computer Operator starting on Monday, 16 October. Please **except** my apologies for not writing to you sooner.

I should be grateful if you would report to the **Personal** Office at 9 am, **wear** you will be issued with your identity card, parking pass and College **stationary** wallet containing items such as your printed business cards.

It is customary for all **knew** staff to **meat** the **Principle** of the College on **there** first day and he will **sea** you at **too** o'clock.

I am **confidant** that you will be very successful and hope that you will enjoy working with us.

Yours sincerely

Mark Adams
**Personal** Officer

**2** At the Riverside Small Animal Centre, John Higgins' niece, Natalie, who is still at school, helps out when she can either after school, at weekends or during the holidays. Natalie always means well but her English skills are atrocious. However, John Higgins is a kind man and simply refers to her as naive! (If you've never met this word before, or do not know how to pronounce it, look it up in a dictionary.) John has asked you to keep an eye on her and to give her the benefit of your experience to help her improve.

Naive Natalie, as she is now known among the staff, has just produced her first letter of confirmation (see Figure 2.6 overleaf) and wants your opinion before she shows it to John Higgins.

**RIVERSIDE SMALL ANIMAL CENTRE**

10 Riverside Place
HIGHTOWN
HG2 8FL

Tel: 01928 620938

JH/DD

Mrs P Harrison
14 Brightside Rd
Hightown
HG3 4AM.

Dear Ms P Harrison

Following your phone call about your cat, Smudge.

I'm pleased to confirm we do do Identichips here. The cost is £28. We fit it in his ear. If you're cat gets lost then anyone who finds him, like the police or the RSPCA, can trace you threw the special number on the chip.

If you want an appointment or to know anything else, give me a ring.

Yours faithfully

John Higgins
Vet

***Figure 2.6*** *Naive Natalie's letter*

**a** How many errors can you find? (Fewer than 17 and you'd better keep looking!)

**b** Now rewrite the letter for her, using the same information. Set it out properly, follow the conventions, and correct all the errors. Rewrite the middle section so that it 'flows' properly when you read it.

## Apply your skills

It had been a very busy morning at Riverside Small Animal Centre. Along with the usual procession of animals needing routine vaccinations, there had been visits from two gerbils, a hamster, four terrapins and two lizards. John Higgins had been operating most of the morning and the two other vets were rushed off their feet in the clinic downstairs. The phone never stopped ringing and to make matters worse, it took Jane until 10 am to distribute all the post.

At lunchtime you were with Jane in the office behind reception as John Higgins stacked some paperwork in a pile and scribbled some notes as reminders for himself. 'Ah, well,' he observed, 'I've always argued pets before paper, but I think we need to spend some time this afternoon sorting things out. Let's see. There's a letter here from Hightown Ladies Circle asking me to confirm if I can definitely give that talk for them two weeks on Tuesday. And James Sandiford, the specialist at Liverpool, has written agreeing to see Henry Scott's dog, Pippa, about that problem with her leg. We need to ring Henry, tell him and then confirm it in writing to both of them. Oh, and I had a phone call from Peter Aspin at Fenlow's this morning. We've now got a meeting fixed with the builder and the county surveyor to go over the plans before we submit them. I said we'd confirm that, too.'

'You'll have to pass me your notes if you want me to reply,' said Jane. 'But I've spoken to Henry Scott already. He rang about half an

1 *Mrs Sue Davies, Events Organiser, Hightown Ladies Circle, 14 Calder Avenue, Edgeworth, Hightown HG8 1SP. Confirm talk on veterinary work, two weeks on Tuesday at 7.30 pm at Riverside Arms. I will arrive at 7 pm as she suggests. I will require an overhead projector.*

2 *James Sandiford, Veterinary Consultant, Liverpool Veterinary Unit, Cross Street, Liverpool L4 7WM.*
*Can see Pippa at 2.30 pm a week on Friday in Liverpool.*

*Check if OK with owner, Henry Scott, 14 Walkden Road, Hightown HG4 2PQ.*
*Then confirm and send map showing route to Veterinary Unit (enclosed with James' letter).*

3 *Peter Aspin, Fenlow and Associates, 16 Grange Road, Hightown HG3 3OS. Wants joint meeting with us + builder and county surveyor - next Monday at 10 am.*
*OK Need parking space booked!*

***Figure 2.7*** *John Higgins' notes*

hour ago to see if we'd heard anything. I told him the basics and said we'd confirm the date and time in writing and send details of how to get there. Didn't James send a map with his letter? Incidentally, there's another thing we must do. Three times this morning we had problems in reception with dogs almost getting into a fight. It's not their fault – it's all these owners who don't bother using a lead. We must put up a polite notice firmly stressing that all dogs must be kept on a lead while they are in reception.'

'If you want a hand,' you found yourself saying, 'I'd be only too happy to help.'

'Oh, that's great!' Jane smiled as John handed his notes to you, 'I can now get on with finishing the newsletter.'

'Good idea,' John remarked. 'And can we have another competition like last month? It was really popular.'

'If you volunteer to do one,' responded Jane, promptly. 'After all, you've been offering for months.'

'OK – I know when I'm beaten,' John observed cheerfully. 'I suppose it's fair shares all round really, I'll do the competition, Jane can get on with the newsletter and it's all thanks to you offering to send off our confirmation letters and do our notice.' With that he grabbed a pen and paper and headed for the door. 'Just a small point', he added, looking back at you. 'When you do the notice for reception, add something about dogs being on a lead in the car park too will you – last week one rushed out into the road after treatment and it's a wonder it didn't have to brought back in again with a serious injury.'

**1** John's notes on the details of his appointments and arrangements are shown in Figure 2.7. Use these to write the letters of confirmation required.

**2** Prepare a suitable notice for reception about keeping dogs on a lead.

Check your work with your tutor.

## WORD WIZARD

This is a word wizard you need to prepare first – but it gives you the opportunity to test your ability to think before you speak!

You need a sheet of white A4 paper (normal letter size) and a set of coloured pencils. Read all of the instructions before you start to write.

**1** You are to write the following words, in any order you wish, several times, across and down the page. Each word should be quite large and using handwriting, not print. The aim is to write each word about five or six times across the page and make about 10 lines of writing.

**2** The words are: black, yellow, green, blue, white, red, orange, pink, brown.

**3** Each time you write one of the words you must use a different colour and you must not use the colour of the word itself. You can therefore write 'black', in any colour but black and so on.

**4** Remember, the order of the words and the colour of each are completely up to you.

When you have prepared your sheet of paper, exchange your sheet for someone else's if you can. However, this is not essential if you are doing this on your own.

Now read the paper aloud but say the *colour* you see and *not* the word you read! This isn't as easy as it sounds and you will feel your brain having to wrestle with the problem. Don't rush and see if you can read the whole page of colours correctly at the first attempt.

# IN THE SPOTLIGHT – MEMOS

In Unit 1, you learned that memos are the internal equivalent of the business letter – which is usually only sent outside the organisation. The word 'memo' (or 'memos' in the plural) is the term you will normally use at work, although the full name is 'memorandum' (singular) and 'memoranda' (plural).

The differences between a memo and a letter are very simple.

- A memo has no external recipient, so there is no need to write an address.
- Memos have a simplified standard layout at the top, which usually includes the following items:
  - TO (after which the name of the recipient is entered – and sometimes his/her designation)
  - FROM (after which the name of the sender is entered – and, in some organisations, his/her designation)
  - DATE (usually typed in full, as in a letter)
  - REFERENCE (usually originator's initials and typists' initials, again as in a letter).

  Bear in mind that the order of these items can vary from one organisation to another, eg FROM on the top line and TO underneath – so be careful to read the heading before you start to enter any information!
- Sometimes the heading SUBJECT then follows. If not, any subject heading is usually typed before the start of the text.
- There is no salutation or complimentary close.
- Memos are never signed in full, but they are often initialled by the sender.
- The 'style' of a memo is normally more informal than a business letter. However, there are exceptions! A memo to a senior executive – particularly about a serious matter or a complex problem – is likely to be written in quite formal terms. Generally, the degree of formality depends upon who is writing to whom. If you are writing to someone at the same level as yourself you will be less formal than if you are writing to someone who is senior to you in rank (eg your boss).

- Usually only one memo is sent on each particular subject or topic. This is to make life easier for anyone who has to deal with the memo or file it! If you therefore need to write to your boss about two different issues, you should normally write two memos, not run both topics together in one memo, which would have to be photocopied to be placed in two separate files. However, do be aware that no two organisations operate in the same way, so find out the normal practice with your own employer.
- Memos are the main form of communications when you wish to write to anyone who works for the same organisation as yourself – whether or not they are in the same building as you. Many organisations have several offices or branches. Communications between branches are still internal to the organisation, and the memo is therefore normally used, rather than a letter.
- You may send the same memo to several people by writing more than one name after the heading TO: and sending a copy to each person you have listed. It is usual to highlight or tick each person's name on his or her particular copy. This also helps to make sure you don't miss anyone by accident.

  Alternatively you may address a memo to someone and send a copy to someone else. This is normally shown by the abbreviation **cc**, which is written on each copy. (This originally stood for 'carbon copy', though today carbon paper is rarely used.) The abbreviation **bcc** stands for blind carbon copy. This is only written on the copy for the person(s) receiving the bcc, and signifies that the other recipients are not aware that this person has also received a copy.

***Figure 3.1***
*A memo*

MEMO

TO Gina Webster, Veterinary Nurse cc Tom Davies

FROM John Higgins, Veterinary Surgeon

DATE 24 May 199-

REF JH/MP

FIRST UK RABBIT CONFERENCE

I have received details of the above conference, which is due to be held in Watford in October. This sounds very interesting as it concentrates on different aspects of rabbit care and disease diagnosis.

Tom Davies is particularly keen to attend the medical discussions and workshops and thought you may like to join him at the conference to learn more about the general area of preventative health care. We would then like you to prepare a short facts sheet for our clients who have rabbits as pets.

I am attaching details of the conference. The centre will obviously pay all your costs. Please let me know as soon as possible if you wish to attend, then we can make the bookings.

Enc

- Because of the difficulty experienced by most people in 'lining up' printed headings to link with a word processing package and computer printer, many organisations no longer use pre-printed memo paper. Instead they save the heading as a template on a computer network or the headings are typed in bold as the text is keyed in.

An example of a memo is show in Figure 3.1. Note that out of courtesy and to keep him informed of the situation, John Higgins has arranged for Tom Davies to receive a copy.

## Composing a memo

Memos are sent for various reasons, such as

- to give information
- to confirm arrangements
- to make a specific request or enquiry

- to ask for or to make comments or suggestions
- to describe the action taken about a certain matter.

When you start to write memos, do remember the KISS principle. If you write five paragraphs when two will do, people will quickly lose interest and, if they are busy, may not even read to the end. Saying what you need to say concisely yet courteously should always be your aim! If you have several points to make, number these to make them easier to read, and quicker to refer back to later.

If you have any doubts about how formal or informal you should be, err on the side of caution and stay fairly formal. Avoid slang, colloquial expressions and abbreviated words. If you find that your organisation is very informal in its internal written communications, it is easier to move 'downwards' later – and you won't have caused any offence by mistake. Bear in mind the following golden rules if you don't want to upset anyone:

- always ask, never command
- stick to the facts – don't give your opinions and views unless you are asked for them
- avoid abbreviations and specialist terms the reader may not know
- keep to the point
- think about the recipient, his/her seniority and job role
- link your facts together logically
- avoid any attempt at humour until you are very skilled at writing and know your organisation (and recipient!) very well indeed.

**MEMO**

**TO** John Higgins, Veterinary Surgeon

**FROM** Natalie Jenkins, Temporary Voluntary Assistant

**DATE** 2 June 199-

**VOLUNTARY WORK**

As you know, I have been helping out here quite a bit at weekends and holidays. I really, really enjoy the work and working with all the animals. I think I'm learning ever such a lot, and although I put my foot in it occasionally, I do try hard, honest.

What I want to know is whether I can work here during my summer holidays. I'll be at a loose end from the middle of July until the end of August and I know many of your staff will be away and I don't want to be just cooling my heels at home. I worked in a supermarket last year but it wasn't a patch on being here.

Please say I can come.

***Figure 3.2*** *Natalie's memo*

## Test your understanding

Natalie has decided that she would like to do voluntary work at the centre throughout the summer holidays. However, rather than ask John Higgins directly, she has chosen to put her request in writing. She has drafted a short memo for him (see Figure 3.2) but is worried that her lack of English skills might make him decide against the idea. She has asked you if you will check it for her.

Although you know she means well you are concerned about the number of slang expressions and colloquialisms she has used. Rewrite the memo for her, removing these and using phrases that you think will be more acceptable to John Higgins.

## SPELLCHECKER 3

In the first part of this unit, you were introduced to the formal word for memo and its plural – memorandum and memoranda. In most English words, the plural form of a noun is easy – you just add an 's'. In some other cases, however, the spelling can cause difficulty.

This Spellchecker aims to improve your spelling of all the different types of plurals you are likely to meet at work.

### PLURALS YOU SHOULD KNOW ALREADY

Check that you can already spell these plurals – and learn those that you can't!

- **Basic plurals, formed by adding 's'**, eg computer/computers, desk/desks, letter/letters.
- **Basic plurals, formed by adding 'es'** because the word ends in *s, sh, ss, ch, x,* or *z*, eg gas/gases, blush/blushes, glass/glasses, watch/watches, box/boxes, buzz/buzzes.
- **Those where a final 'y' converts to 'ies'**, eg city/cities, company/companies, secretary/secretaries, money/monies, penny/pennies. Note that this doesn't apply to all words – boys and monkeys, for instance, both retain the 'y' because it is preceded by a vowel, but these are exceptions to the general rule.
- **Those words where a final 'f' or 'fe' becomes 'ves'**, eg half/halves, knife/knives, shelf/shelves, wharf/wharves. However, again there are exceptions, eg chiefs, beliefs, roofs. Always check in a dictionary if you have any doubts.
- **Those words that have a different plural form**, eg man/men, child/children, goose/geese, mouse/mice, tooth/teeth, foot/feet, woman/women.
- **Those words that are the same in both the singular and plural**, eg salmon, trout, sheep.
- **Those words that have no singular** but are always plural, eg trousers, tweezers, pliers, tights, measles.

### MOVING ON A STAGE

Build on your existing knowledge of plurals by making sure that you would not make mistakes with any of the following:

- Words ending in 'o'. On most occasions you simply add an 's', eg kilo/kilos, radio/radios, halo/halos, piano/pianos, jumbo/jumbos (planes). However, some special words *always* end with 'oes' – and need to be learned. The main ones are potato/potatoes, hero/heroes, echo/echoes, cargo/cargoes, tomato/tomatoes.
- Compound words, such as push-ups, forget-me-nots and vice-chancellors normally just add an 's' to the final part, as in these

examples. However, there are occasions when the *first* part changes to the plural. Examples include: passers-by, daughters-in-law, commanders-in-chief, rights-of-way, runners-up.

- A word ending in 'ful' normally takes the plural by simply adding an 's'. Therefore you say 'mouthfuls' not mouthsful and 'tablespoonfuls' not tablespoonsful!
- Words of foreign origin often have irregular plurals.

  The phrase 'computer data' is plural (the singular is 'datum'), as is 'graffiti' (the singular being 'graffito'). However, many of these words are being anglicised (made more like English) so that we now talk about stadiums, gymnasiums, referendums and exam syllabuses – rather than stadia, gymnasia, referenda and syllabi. Many books now refer to computer 'data' whether they are using the singular or plural. So, over time, things are getting easier!

## WORDS TO LEARN

The following 'foreign' plurals still remain the correct word to use. Learn each of them so that you can say and spell the plural of each. Look up the meanings of any new words and add them to your Wordbank book.

| | |
|---|---|
| addendum | addenda |
| appendix | appendices (or appendixes) |
| bacterium | bacteria |
| basis | bases |
| bureau | bureaux |
| crisis | crises |
| criterion | criteria |
| datum | data |
| formula | formulae (or formulas) |
| fungus | fungi |
| index | indices (or indexes) |
| medium | media |
| phenomenon | phenomena |
| radius | radii |
| stimulus | stimuli |
| stratum | strata |

**DON'T YOU DARE!**

*...write the words 'all right' as one word. Neither must you be tempted to write the phrase 'a lot' as one word (it's preferable not to use it at all!) There is NO such word as 'alright' except on some record titles!*

## TOOLS OF THE TRADE – the importance of tone

If you misjudge the way your words sound when they are read by someone else, you are in grave danger of:

- giving the wrong impression
- not achieving your objective
- annoying, upsetting or even infuriating the other person!

Words play a tune, once they are put together, just like notes of music. The result can be pure harmony or downright discord. Therefore, although your communication may be grammatically perfect and contain no factual errors, it can cause serious problems.

The tone you wish to convey will depend upon your reason for communicating. 'Tone' applies to both verbal and written communications but it is even more critical when you are writing. In this case, you have no opportunity to make instant corrections, because you cannot see the reaction you are getting.

- In a very informal communication you may wish to appear friendly and to communicate on a personal level.
- If you are sending a memo or letter to someone you don't know well, you may wish to be a little more guarded and slightly more formal.
- If you are sending a formal business letter or preparing a report (see Unit 8) for your boss, you are likely to be even more formal and aware that the wrong style would seem impertinent.
- If your boss rewrites your report to submit it to the MD or the board of directors, you are likely to find it becomes even more formal and detached.

In addition to the formality of the type of document, you will also be influenced by your relationship with the recipient. Someone who works with you regularly or with whom you are very friendly would be surprised to receive a very formal communication, unless it was about an important or official matter. Equally, a complete stranger would not expect to be addressed on a personal level.

At the outset you need to decide how you wish your message to sound.

- Do you want to be friendly or impersonal? Do you need to 'distance yourself' from the recipient?
- Do you want to show concern or do you need to be firm?
- Do you know the recipient personally? What is his/her status in relation to your own?
- What are you trying to achieve by sending the communication – what is the purpose of the exercise. What type of messages would provoke the response you require?
- What style is normally adopted by your organisation? If you work for a large enterprise (such as the local council) you are likely to find that letters are relatively formal, as most recipients are not personally known to the writers. If you work with a small creative group who know all their clients personally, you are likely to find all communications much more informal.

## Test your understanding

1 Without any knowledge of the background, how would you interpret each of the following messages from your boss? And how would you feel in each case?

   **a** Please arrange an appointment to see me immediately.
   **b** If you could spare a moment, I'd like a quick word with you as soon as possible.
   **c** I would be grateful if you could see me sometime today.

   Discuss your ideas as a group.

2 You are writing to a customer to remind him about an unpaid account which has not been paid for nearly three months. Which do you think would be the most appropriate tone for the letter – and why? Discuss your suggestions with your tutor.

   **a** We see from our records that you have not yet paid your account for the month of March, despite our reminder of 15 May. At the time we supplied the goods we made it clear that the terms of credit were for one month only. We must inform you, therefore, that unless you settle the amount in full within the next five days, we shall have no alternative but to take legal action to recover the money owing.
   **b** You have still not sent your cheque for the amount you owe for March, even though we reminded you in May. I am sure you know that this amount should have been paid in full at the end of March. We should therefore be grateful if you could let us have your cheque as soon as possible, otherwise we may have to take further action.
   **c** I'm sorry to have to remind you about this, but you still haven't paid the money you owe us for March. We did remind you about this on 15 May but you didn't reply to us. The terms of the agreement meant you were supposed to pay us in full at the end of March and you haven't. If there's a very good reason for this, could you please let us know? Otherwise, could you please arrange to let us have the money as soon as you can.

## MAKING HEADWAY – electronic mail and e-mail messages

Electronic mail is a method of sending messages directly from one computer to another through a 'mailbox' system. The mailbox stores the messages until the user is ready to access them. He or she can then reply, save or delete messages, print them out, forward them to other people with a comment and even, on some systems, check if the messages sent have been opened by the recipient.

E-mail is a common feature in organisations that operate a computer network, where all the computers within the organisation are linked together, and can therefore communicate with each other. If the system is compatible with other software on the network, then the user can attach other documents to an e-mail by using a word-processing, spreadsheet or graphics package. Organisations and individuals with Internet access can exchange messages all over the country and the world.

## The advantages of e-mail

Organisations using e-mail can drastically reduce the number of memos and letters required, as using e-mail is normally a much faster method of communicating. In addition, reminders can be sent quickly and easily.

E-mails are also often preferred to using the telephone for the following reasons.

- Complex information can be sent, or a document can be attached. As the message is in writing, there is less risk of misunderstanding.
- E-mails can be prepared and transmitted at the sender's convenience and recipients can read incoming messages and respond when it suits them.
- A copy can be printed out for the file or for further discussion.

All e-mail systems are protected by a password system and a user ID so that only named users can access mail – unless, of course, they reveal their password to someone else, or leave their computer switched on and in the e-mail system when they are out of the office.

## Using e-mail

The first step is to learn is how the system works in your own organisation. Most systems today are Windows-based, which means that there are graphics as well as text on the screen. You need to know the difference between your 'in' mailbox and your 'out' mailbox and how to move from one to the other. Normally, your incoming mail is displayed in envelopes which 'open' when you read the message. The graphics on your out box may also tell you who has opened your messages and who has not.

You will need to know how to delete messages you have read, reply to messages you have received, send new messages (and copy them to other people when necessary) and print your messages. You will also need to know how to use the other facilities available to you, such as an electronic address book, in which you can store frequently used e-mail addresses or user IDs.

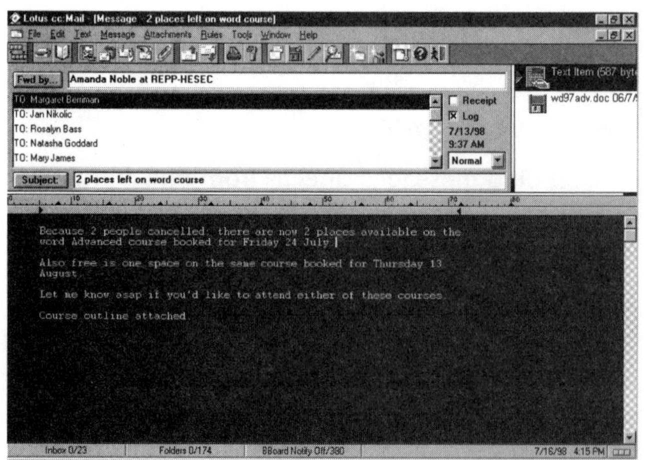


***Figure 3.3*** *An e-mail screen*

## Composing an e-mail message

E-mail is probably the most informal method of written communication currently in use. However, this does not mean that you can make written errors. In fact, the popularity of e-mail has highlighted the English skills of many employees – who would otherwise have used the telephone and kept their lack of writing ability well hidden!

Your computer will automatically put your name and/or ID and the date and time on the top of each message. If you are replying to a message, the name of the recipient will also be entered automatically. You do, however, need to make an entry on your 'subject' line – remember that your message will appear in the list of other messages in both your own mailbox and your recipient's, and it is vital that the subject can be seen at a glance.

When e-mail was first introduced there were few conventions to govern the way in which messages were composed or presented. One or two have since developed, the most important being the use of capitals. Sending a message in capital letters is considered discourteous and is known as 'shouting' – so avoid this. As with all business communications, keep your message short and simple, with good spacing and proper paragraphs or numbered points so that your e-mail is easy to read. As with memos, it is usually better to send a separate e-mail on different subjects.

Finally, beware of one danger. Some people have the mistaken idea that *because* e-mail is informal it doesn't matter how jokey or personal they are or what they say. Never fall into this trap. The simple fact that e-mails can be copied to other people or printed out means that your words will be there for all time – with your name clearly at the top – so any written misdemeanours are easy to see and the senders may be disciplined. You can even break the law if you spread false or malicious gossip about someone by e-mail. You have been warned!

Your messages will be brief and to the point and will be normally more informal to your colleagues than to senior staff. Abbreviated words are quite acceptable and technical terms may be used between internal staff dealing with the same issue, where they are all familiar with the 'jargon' used. E-mails obviously cannot be signed and most people do not put their name at the end, as this merely replicates the information given at the top. But some do, and there is no fixed rule about this. An example of an e-mail screen is shown in Figure 3.3.

**Message 1**

```
From:      Jane Mitchell
To:        (You)
Date:      Wednesday 15 August 199- 09:15 am
Subject:   Health and Safety Group

John and I both wondered if you would be
interested in joining this group, which looks at
health and safety issues affecting the centre. We
both think that you will learn a lot about the way
the practice runs and we are sure you will be able
to make a very useful contribution.

We meet every fourth Monday at 4.30 pm and our
next meeting is next Monday. Please let me know if
you will be able to join us.

Thanks
```

**Message 2**

```
From:      Petra Sinclair
To:        (You)
Date:      Wednesday 15 August 199- 09:30 am
Subject:   Fair exchange is no robbery!

You may remember that I agreed to swop shifts with
you so you could go to your cousin's wedding last
month. Well, I need you to do the same for me, if
you can. I'm down on the rota to do Saturday
morning, 22 Sept but I've got a problem. I
promised Rachel (my sister) I'd go to that new
health and fitness place with her and she's got
her dates muddled up and booked us in for that
date. If we change it we can't get in again for
their special beauty session until the end of
October. Will you swop with me? If you say yes,
I'll check it's OK with John. I'm sure he won't
mind if someone will cover for me.

Please help! I'm desperate.
```

***Figure 3.4*** *Two e-mail messages for you*

## Test your understanding

**1** Find out if your college has an e-mail system that students can use. If not, the system may be available to tutors. Try to arrange for someone to demonstrate it to you and see if you can set up a 'user group' to send messages to each other. Never abuse this privilege by sending discourteous or personal messages – remember that you could be prosecuted as well as disciplined if you do.

**2** John Higgins is a new e-mail convert. The centre uses computers to operate its appointments system and John recently arranged for a friend of his to install e-mail software. When you access your mail this morning you find two messages waiting for you (see Figure 3.4). Reply to both appropriately. Remember to vary your tone between the two – Petra is your colleague but Jane is senior to you, and the topics are very different!

## THE GOOD GRAMMAR GUIDE

### Parts of speech – nouns and pronouns

You probably already know that a noun is a word referring to a person (or animal), place or thing. Did you also know that there are different kinds of nouns?

- **Common nouns** refer to everyday items of which there are many, eg schools, countries, books.
- **Proper nouns** refer to those items of which there is (usually) only one, eg Berwick Grammar School, Australia, Alice in Wonderland.

As you have already seen, common nouns do not take a capital letter, whereas proper nouns do.

Nouns can also be

- **concrete** – relating to things you can touch or see (eg a desk or chair), or
- **abstract** – relating to ideas, emotions or concepts (eg health, wealth and wisdom).

They can be

- **singular** – referring to one item or person, eg the boy, the computer, or
- **plural** – they refer to many items, eg the boys, the computers, or
- **collective** – referring to a group of people or animals, eg class, committee, government, team, flock, swarm.

### Pronouns

A pronoun can be used as a substitute for a noun. The most frequently used pronouns are called **personal pronouns** and are used to refer back to a person or item that has already been mentioned, eg

*Tom is a keep-fit fanatic. **He** visits the gym four times a week.*
*Mary is workaholic. **She** regularly works late at night.*
*The car is due to be serviced. **It** must be booked in tomorrow.*
*The documents are out of date. **They** should be thrown away.*

The pronoun you would choose would depend upon the following factors.

- Whether the pronoun refers to the first, second or third person. In the singular, the **first person** is yourself ('I'), the **second person** is 'you', the **third person** refers to 'he', 'she', or 'it'.
- Whether the person or item to whom you are referring is singular or plural.

- Whether you are using the pronoun to replace the subject of a sentence, to replace the object of a sentence or to indicate possession.

In the examples above, all the pronouns have been used to replace the subject of a sentence. If you had been referring to yourself you would have used the word *I*, and if you had been talking to someone else you would have used the word *you*, eg

*I will phone tomorrow. Will you be at home about six?*

Now imagine you are referring directly to yourself or someone else as the **object** of the sentence. In this case you would use the word *me* but still keep the word *you* for the other person, eg

*Can you phone me tomorrow? If not, I will phone you the day after.*

The table below shows the different pronouns you would choose in different circumstances. Do bear in mind when you look at this that you have probably been using these pronouns for years and years!

| | **To replace the subject** | **To replace the object** | **To indicate possession** |
|---|---|---|---|
| First person singular<br>First person plural | I<br>we | me<br>us | my (+noun), mine<br>our (+noun), ours |
| Second person singular and plural | you | you | your (+noun), yours |
| Third person singular<br><br>Third person plural | he/she/it<br><br>they | him/her/it<br><br>them | his/her/its (+noun), his/hers<br>their (+noun), theirs |

***Figure 3.5*** *Pronouns*

## Test your understanding

Select the correct pronoun from each pair in brackets to complete the sentences below.

**1** (She, her) threw the ball to (he, him) very carefully.

**2** (I, me) collected (us, our) tickets this morning on (my, mine) way home.

**3** Can (he, him) come with (I, me) to help to find the key?

**4** You will have to choose between (they, them) and (we, us).

**5** When Bill opened the door he immediately saw you and (I, me) and only later realised that Sam was with (we, us).

**DON'T YOU DARE!**

*include an apostrophe when you write the pronoun 'its'. It's = it is! Always test whether 'it is' would make sense in a sentence. If not, omit the apostrophe.*

## PRONOUN TRAPS

Although pronouns seem simple, many people make mistakes with them. Here are four of the more common ones.

**1** Traditionally writers used 'he' to refer to a person who could be of either sex. Today it would be considered incorrect to write either of these sentences.

*When an executive returns from a trip, he must complete an expense claim.*
*If a student is late, he must report to the Senior Tutor immediately.*

Unfortunately, there is no pronoun in English that relates to both men and women. Therefore, such sentences are often rewritten as

*When an executive returns from a trip, he/she must complete an expense claim.*
*If a student is late, he/she must report to the Senior Tutor immediately.*

However, this is rather clumsy and the sentence is often better reworded by using the plural form, eg

*When executives return from a trip, they must complete an expense claim.*
*Students who are late must report to the Senior Tutor immediately.*

What you must *not* do is mix the singular and plural form in one sentence, eg *When an executive returns from a trip, they must complete an expense claim.* An executive is singular so cannot become a 'they'!

**2** The further away from the noun you move its replacement pronoun, the greater difficulty there is in understanding what it refers to. This can cause confusion in some circumstances and great hilarity in others! Look at the following sentences as examples.

*Claire told Mary that she would have to go to London tomorrow.*
*The shelf fell on my head because it was loose.*

The solution is to change your sentence around or insert the name of the person to whom you are referring in brackets for clarity, eg

*Claire told Mary that she (Claire) would have to go to London tomorrow.*
*The shelf, which was loose, fell on my head.*

**3** Many people find it difficult to decide whether to use 'I' or 'me' in a sentence – check how successful you were in the exercise above. The rule is to use 'I' for the subject and 'me' for the object. It is easy to check by substituting 'we' or 'us'. If 'we' fits then write 'I', if 'us' fits then write 'me', eg

*Could you help me with this?*

'Us' could be substituted in this sentence, therefore 'me' is correct. (You should have also noticed that 'you' is the subject and 'me' the object in that sentence!)

Another test is to leave out the other person, eg

*Do you think you or I should go?*

You would not make the mistake of using 'me' in this sentence if you left out the other person – 'Do you think me should go' is obviously wrong. Therefore 'I' is correct. Incidentally, don't forget that it is correct to put yourself last, therefore 'Bill and I' – not 'Me and Bill'!

4 Remember not to mix singular and plural pronouns in the same sentence. In other words, do not say

*I apologise for the fact that we sent you the incorrect item.*

Either *I apologise for the fact that I sent you the incorrect item.*
or *We apologise for the fact that we sent you the incorrect item.*

The difficulty arises when you (personally) are writing the letter, but you (personally) did not send the item – which may have been despatched by another department. Try to avoid this problem by changing your sentence, eg *I apologise for the fact that you received the incorrect item.*

## Test your understanding

Correct the errors in each of the following sentences. In any that are ambiguous select the meaning you prefer and make this clear when you correct or rewrite the sentence.

1. Me and John have been playing tennis.
2. Please telephone me if you wish to take advantage of our offer.
3. Frank and Damien argued when Frank said he could no longer go to the match.
4. The dog wagged it's tail furiously, once it realised that Rachel and me were going for a walk.
5. The forest caught fire when it was hot.
6. Just between you and I, its a good thing he's gone away.
7. Each taxpayer must submit his completed form by 30 September.
8. Sarah isn't as keen on sport as me and Kathy.
9. By the time Jan and I left for us lunch the sandwich shop had closed it's doors.
10. Pauline told Debbie that she had to go home immediately.

## POLISH YOUR PUNCTUATION

### Longer breaks – the dash, brackets and the semi-colon

#### THE DASH

Dashes are not very common in formal business correspondence. Often a full stop is preferred. However, dashes can be useful to maintain the flow of a sentence and, often, to give the effect of speech. They indicate a longer break than a comma. They are used:

- when you wish to elaborate on something you have already said, eg

  *The journey seemed to take forever – we didn't arrive until ten o'clock.*

- when you want to change emphasis or break the continuity of a sentence, eg

  *I don't believe it – they've got it right at last!*

- sometimes for a middle clause, instead of commas or brackets, eg

  *The name of the new football club – which came into existence in March, I believe – is Hightown Rangers.*

Dashes are also used to indicate a period of time or a range of some kind, or to link places, eg

- *He was abroad from 1975–1988.*
- *Read pages 23–27.*
- *His route was New York–Washington–Boston.*

## BRACKETS

Brackets are rarely used in formal communications, but when they are used, they must be in pairs! The most usual type of brackets are round ones (), which are called parentheses, but others exist such as square brackets [], brace brackets {} and angle brackets <>. For normal work you only need concern yourself with round brackets and, sometimes, with square brackets.

Brackets are used:

- to separate additional information that would otherwise interrupt the flow of the sentence – if they are used properly, the passage in brackets could be lifted out of the sentence without making any difference to the overall meaning, eg

  *Complete the appropriate form (obtainable from all post offices) and return it to us as soon as possible.*

- to add an alternative version, eg

  *This is written only on the copy for the person(s) receiving the bcc.*

  This indicates that either one person or several may receive a blind carbon copy.

  Note that if the whole sentence is in brackets, the full stop should also be placed in the brackets. If only the final part of the sentence is in brackets, the full stop is placed outside the closing brackets, eg

  *He moved to Zimbabwe (formerly known as Rhodesia).*
  *Paul Brooke started yesterday. (He is the ex-head of Hightown School.)*

- In typescript, square brackets may be used for 'brackets within brackets', eg

  The schemes were devised by the QCA (Qualifications and Curriculum Authority [formerly NCVQ and SCAA]) and the SQA (Scottish Qualifications Authority).

## THE SEMI-COLON

This is probably the most under-used punctuation mark, because most people aren't sure when to use it! There are three major uses (and knowing these is often helpful). These are:

- to join two sentences that are closely related so that you can write one longer, rather than two shorter, sentences, eg

  *On the top floor is a large open-plan office used by twenty employees; on the floor below is the staff restaurant.*

- to separate items in a list, particularly if you need a longer pause than a comma or if you are already using commas, eg

  *I would like to acknowledge the assistance and support of Mary Jenkins, our Sales Manager; Sean O'Connor, Finance Manager; Ben Evans, Graphic Designer and Rachel Naylor, my Senior Administrator.*

- to replace a dash, in more formal correspondence, when you want to indicate a distinctive break, eg

  *I investigated the number of people who use the staff restaurant on a regular basis, and buy full meals rather than snacks; but my findings show that the area is more popular at breakfast time than at lunch time when most people purchase sandwiches.*

## Test your understanding

Punctuate the following passage, inserting commas, semi-colons, brackets and dashes where you think they should be placed. To help, the full stops are done for you!

Maria was panicking the meeting was due to start in ten minutes. She was still collecting her papers together many only copied seconds before and she still had too much to do. The Hazards Working Group a sub-committee of the company Safety Committee had been formed three months earlier. John Brooke formerly Safety Officer in a large firm was the Chairman or Chairperson as he preferred to be called. Maria checked off her list of attendees Mark Bryant Production Manager Jean Pearson Research and Development Sahira Khan Technical Services Julian Smith Warehouse Manager. She tidied the documents agenda minutes and photocopies for circulation. Ready at last she reached for the key to the meetings room and gathered the papers together she just had time to open and tidy the room before John would arrive and if she was lucky he might be delayed.

# COMMUNICATION IN PRACTICE

## Test your skills

**1** Practise your dictionary skills to select which of the words in brackets is correct in each of the following sentences. Then write your own sentence showing a correct use of the word you rejected.

**a** Smoking is not (aloud/allowed) in this building.
**b** I prepared the (draft/draught) document for him yesterday.
**c** Please send the (check/cheque) with the order.
**d** His writing is completely (illegible/ineligible).
**e** The (adverse/averse) weather conditions made it impossible for the plane to land.

**2** A colloquial expression is an informal expression people frequently use in everyday speech. For each expression given below, reword the sentence to retain the meaning but avoid the colloquialism.

**a** He lives *in the back of beyond*.
**b** His estimate was *way out*.
**c** I think I will have *shaken off* this cold by the end of the week.
**d** Will you *just have a think about it*.
**e** She's always *chopping and changing*.

**3** Convert all the singular nouns in the following sentences to plural, spelling every word correctly.

**a** The ship will arrive at the wharf at three o'clock and unload the cargo.
**b** The secretary had the task of assembling the appendix for the report.
**c** The memorandum must be sent to the person concerned.
**d** The basis for the discussion will be the right-of-way for the passer-by.
**e** The thief took the electric piano, the silver penknife and the wineglass.

**4** Many collective nouns are special terms. For instance, you talk about a swarm of bees and a herd of cows. In each of the following examples, you should state (or find out!) the collective noun. To help, the first letter is given for you in each case.

| | |
|---|---|
| **a** directors of a company | B............. |
| **b** those making a decision in a court of law | J.............. |
| **c** people attending a football match | C............. |
| **d** those playing a football match | T.............. |
| **e** those running a ship | C............. |
| **f** those watching television | V............. |
| **g** people watching a particular sport | S............. |
| **h** senior ministers in the government | C............. |

**5** Each of the following sentences contains at least one error. This may be spelling, punctuation, grammar or any other type of mistake discussed so far. In each case, find and correct the error(s). In the case of an ambiguous sentence, select a meaning yourself and rewrite the sentence to state this clearly.

**a** Each resident should complete his own claim form by 15 May and send them to the Town Hall.
**b** Max told Sam he looked ill and should definately go home.
**c** I regret we are unable to help you.
**d** When he asked Paul and I for a referance, we refered it to Mrs Khan.
**e** Any student who hasn't payed his acommodation bill by Monday must see the principle.
**f** Joanne Brightman – formally Joanne Pickup (who works in the general office will issue you with your stationary.

## Apply your skills

Jane Mitchell is having two days' leave. In her absence, John Higgins has been asking you to do certain jobs for him. Today when you arrive for work you find the following memo on your desk from John Higgins (Figure 3.6). When you switch on your computer, you also find two e-mails – one from him and one from Tom Davies (Figure 3.7). Undertake all the jobs you have been asked to do.

**MEMO**

**TO** (You)

**FROM** *John Higgins*

**DATE** (Yesterday)

**URGENT JOBS**

*There are two jobs outstanding and I would be grateful if you could do them for me in the morning. I will be out most of the day, visiting some clients in the morning and then in Leeds during the afternoon.*

1 *Chris Earle, the new RSPCA Inspector for this district, rang me to see if he could call to introduce himself next Wednesday at 2 pm. I said I would have to check. Please write to him at their offices at 14 North Street, Hightown HG1 4MP to confirm this is convenient. We don't want him to forget the posters he promised to bring! Say something like 'I will be interested to see the new posters he mentioned'. This will be a good way of reminding him politely! Say, too, that I look forward to meeting him.*

2 *Please do a brief memo to Jane, telling her that I've agreed that you and Petra can do a Saturday swop for Petra's trip. I know she likes me to confirm these in writing then she can alter her rota officially. You know the dates, please insert them clearly.*

*Thanks*

***Figure 3.6*** *Memo from John Higgins*

To help you, an organisation chart for Riverside Small Animal Centre is shown overleaf (Figure 3.8).

Check all your work with your tutor.

```
From:       Tom Davies
To:         You
Date:       (Yesterday) 6:30 pm
Subject:    National Rabbit Conference

You may already know that Gina and I are attending
this event in Watford. Could you please confirm our
attendance in writing with the organiser, Cathryn
Whiteley (I spoke to her on the phone today).
Confirm we will be attending the conference at the
Moat House Hotel, Watford from Monday 24 to
Thursday 27 October and will require accommodation
(two single rooms with facilities) for four nights
from Sunday, 23 October to Wednesday 26 October.
Please confirm the price - it's £275 per delegate.
I understand she will now send us the full
conference pack and the invoice, but confirm this
politely in the letter, will you, then she won't
forget.

For your information, the price includes
accommodation and the organiser books this - her
title is Conference Organiser and the address is
National Veterinary Association, 14 Harlesden
Court, Blackheath, LONDON, SW3 5MP.

Thanks.

From:       John Higgins
To:         You
Date:       (Yesterday) 7.00 pm
Subject:    Natalie

Sorry - I remembered this after I'd finished the
memo and put it on your desk. Can you do a short
memo to Natalie please, in response to her request
to do voluntary work here during the summer. Please
confirm that she can work here during July and
August provided that she promises to learn how to
use e-mail before then! Ask her to let me know the
dates of her school holidays as soon as she can.
Tell her Jane Mitchell will discuss her exact
duties with her nearer the time.

Oh, and send a copy to Jane please, for courtesy
and to keep her informed. Thanks.
```

***Figure 3.7*** *E-mail messages*

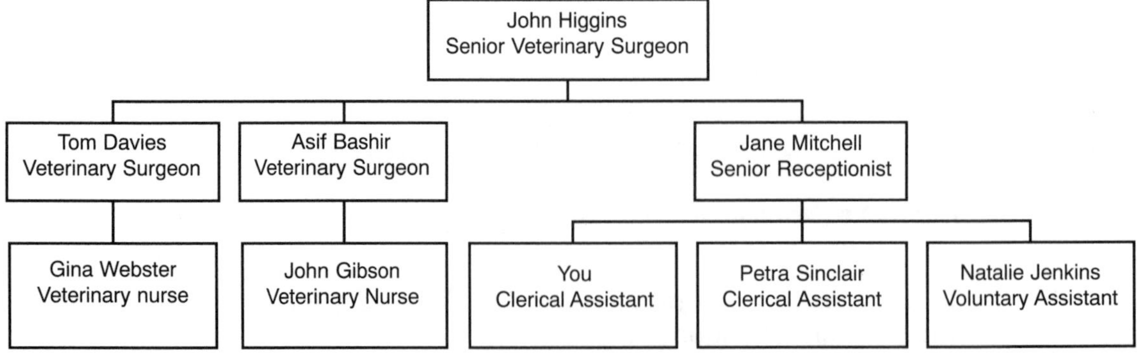


***Figure 3.8*** *Organisation chart for Riverside Small Animal Centre*

## WORD WIZARD

You will have learned about standard collective nouns at school (eg a herd of cows, a flock of sheep), and in this chapter you met some more that refer to people. Some very unusual terms are used for collective nouns – did you know, for instance that people talk about a 'hand' of bananas, rather than a bunch, and a 'kindle' of kittens, not a litter? Very few people use such specialist terms these days, but others have become very talented at inventing a few!

Here are a few *real* collective nouns you may never have heard:

- a string of ponies
- a tribe of goats
- a clowder of cats
- a nest of machine-guns
- a rope of pearls
- a cluster of diamonds.

Now here are a few modern inventions! In each case consider why the collective word has been chosen.

- a configuration of computers
- a cuddle of kittens
- a jotting of journalists
- an embarrassment of parents
- an absence of waiters
- a crush of shoppers
- a wiggle of starlets
- a flood of plumbers
- a fright of ghosts
- a huff of complainants
- a kettle of drums
- a rush of couriers
- a tyranny of dictators
- a mixture of pharmacists
- a spoil of grandparents.

Now it's your turn. Think of different groups of people, animals or things (students, teachers, teenagers, relatives, etc) and try to think of a collective name to describe them. Then compare your ideas with others in your group. Note that if you select a word that starts with the same letter as your final word (eg a jotting of journalists) then this is a use of **alliteration** (repeated sounds), which is often effective, eg *as good as gold* or *Graded grains make finer flour*!

# IN THE SPOTLIGHT – USING THE TELEPHONE

You may be very familiar with using the telephone at home. However, there is a big difference between talking to your friends in an evening and answering the telephone at work – or making a business call. Otherwise, why is it that most students dread having to use the telephone at work? However, this is a key skill expected by every employer. This section aims to make the task much easier and to guide you so that you can avoid making some common errors.

## The skills you need

It may be tempting to think that all you need is the ability to lift the receiver and speak. Unfortunately this isn't true! You need to know:

- how to use the equipment – which may be rather unlike the telephone system you have at home
- the standard terms and phrases to use during a business call
- how to receive a call
- how to record and interpret the information you are given *accurately*
- how to make a call
- how to give a good impression of yourself and the organisation
- how to handle confidential, sensitive or urgent information
- how to keep the telephone bill to a minimum (just like at home!).

No wonder people in their first jobs are sometimes apprehensive when a colleague says, *Just get that call, will you?* You can hardly say, *Er – I'd rather not, thanks.*

In this unit we look at the first four of these skills. In Unit 6, page 105 you will learn the remainder.

### USING THE EQUIPMENT

Large organisations operate a switchboard system so that most calls are received at a central point by a trained operator. Employees have their own telephone on their desks, with specific extension numbers. Today most switchboard systems enable extension holders to make and receive calls without going through the switchboard.

There are likely to be a wide range of facilities available on your extension, such as the ability to divert your calls to another extension whilst you are away from your desk or programming your phone to call another engaged extension automatically when it is free. In your first job, obtain a copy of the handbook usually issued to extension users and look through the available facilities to see which ones would be useful. An important skill is knowing how to transfer a call to another extension without cutting off the caller!

Most organisations also operate some form of automated message system. The most common is a telephone answering machine which receives and stores messages when the office is closed. Another system is known as voice mail. Each extension user has an electronic voicebox in which he or she can record a message for callers, who then leave their own message in reply. With any messaging system, it is essential that someone listens to the calls and responds to them, and one of the first jobs you may be given is to make a note of the calls stored on an answering machine so that they can be dealt with promptly.

## STANDARD TERMS AND PHRASES

Business telephones are not answered with 'Hi', nor are they usually answered by saying the telephone number. If you are answering a central telephone system it is usual to greet the caller properly and state the name of the organisation so that callers can quickly check they are through to the right place. There are several variations on the official company response, but a standard one is:

*Good morning (or afternoon), Parklands College. May I help you?*

If you are working in a specific department, such as Sales, then you should say

*Sales Department, Joanne Wilson speaking.*

When you become familiar with the telephone system you will find that there are different ringing tones for internal calls (from another department) and for external calls (from outside the organisation). Staff who can make the distinction often answer internal calls rather more informally, such as '*Sales, Joanne speaking*'. The best thing to do is to watch, listen and learn in the early days, as every organisation is different.

During the call, try to be aware of informal and slang expressions you may be tempted to use, such as

| | | |
|---|---|---|
| *That's OK, then* | instead say | *'Yes, fine.'* |
| *Well, OK, I'll see what I can do* | instead say | *'I'll do what I can.'* |
| *You'll have to hang on a minute* | instead say | *'Please hold on a moment.'* |
| *You what?* | instead say | *'I'm sorry, could you please repeat that?'* |

Avoiding the use of 'OK' can be difficult at first, but it is worth persevering – particularly when you are speaking to an external caller. Internal callers may be less bothered, but if you are speaking to a senior member of staff, you will need to be more careful.

If you are ending a call you have received, a useful expression to know is

*Thank you for calling. Goodbye.*

This leaves the caller feeling pleased to have spoken to you.

## RECEIVING A CALL

Many people have the mistaken idea that they have to know all about the organisation and the way it operates before they can be of any help to a caller. This is wrong. Obviously it helps if you know who deals with what and have some idea what the caller is talking about. However, it is perfectly possible to be pleasant and helpful on the telephone even if you are answering a call on the first day, within five minutes of taking your coat off! The golden rules for doing this are as follows.

- Always answer promptly, and identify yourself.
- No matter how busy you are when the phone rings, *never* show you are irritated by sounding annoyed with the caller. If your organisation didn't receive any calls or enquiries, it would go out of business and you would be looking for another job. Think of every call as helping to keep you employed!
- Always pick up the receiver with your non-writing hand, and have a pen and paper close by. Saying 'You'll have to wait a minute while I get a pen' makes you sound inefficient at the outset.
- Never answer the telephone if you are eating or drinking. Ask someone else to take the call.
- Find out the name of the caller and either the name of the person he or she is calling or the reason for the call.
- If the call is for someone in the office who is available to take the call, then ask the caller to 'Hold on a moment, please' and explain properly to your colleague who is calling and what the call is about.
- If the person the caller wants is not available, you have four options:
  - see if someone else can help (and ask properly!)
  - offer to help yourself (guidance follows!)
  - take a message
  - ask the caller to ring back later, and say when the person he/she wants is likely to be available.
- It obviously takes a little courage to offer to help someone yourself, particularly in the early days of your career. However, your colleagues will admire you for trying and it is a good way to learn! It will help if you remember that there are only three possible outcomes:
  - you can help immediately, because you know the answer to the query
  - you can help later, because you know how to find out the answer
  - you can't help, because you only know a little (or nothing) about the matter the caller has raised.

  If you can help immediately, then you have no problems – but do make certain that you are giving *accurate* information. No information at all is better than hazarding a guess!

  If you can help later, arrange to ring the person back when you have the information in front of you. Write down the number and repeat it back to the caller to make sure you have written it accurately. Give an estimated time when you will ring back and check that the caller will be available. Don't forget to make the call!

If you can't help at all, then you still deserve points for trying. Either hand the call on to a colleague who will be able to help, or take a message.

### CONFIDENTIAL INFORMATION

There are times when – either on the telephone or face-to-face – you may be given confidential information or told something you should not repeat.

- Never disclose confidential information to anyone without being given permission – no matter how important he or she sounds or what reason is given. Apologise politely and say you have to refer the request to your boss – and do so.
- Never leave a message containing confidential information lying on the top of a desk so that any passers-by can read it. Seal it in an envelope.
- Never repeat confidential or sensitive information you are given over the telephone to anyone except the person to whom it should be given.

## Test your understanding

Read the following telephone conversation between Naive Natalie and a telephone caller. Then make a note of all the flaws you have detected in her telephone (and other) techniques! Discuss your ideas as a group. Finally, rewrite the conversation as you think it should have occurred.

*(Phone ringing ......ringing .....ringing. Natalie is sorting through a pile of customer record cards, obviously looking for something.)*

**NN** 'For heavens' sake, I've only one pair of hands. Wait a minute, will you?' *(picks up receiver)* 'Hello?'

**Caller** 'Oh, good afternoon. Is that Riverside Small Animal Centre?'

**NN** *(distracted by reading a note on one of the cards)* 'Yeah, that's right.'

**Caller** *(more firmly)* 'Can I speak to John Higgins, please?'

**NN** 'Not at the moment, you can't, no. He's doing an operation on a dog what's been knocked down so I can't disturb him.'

**Caller** 'In that case, can you please take a message for me?'

**NN** 'You'll have to hang on while I get a pen. Just a mo.' *(Pause whilst Natalie roots through her handbag and extracts a chewed pencil).* 'Right, OK. What do you want me to say?'

**Caller** 'On second thoughts, I think I'd prefer to call back. What time is he likely to be free?'

**NN** 'Oh, he's never free – he charges for everything! Sorry, just my little joke. What did you say? Oh, yes, well, after the op he's got his surgery to do and that can go on for yonks. You know what people are like about their pets and he listens for ages. I'll have gone home before that. It could be quite late. I wouldn't bother today if it were me. You could always try tomorrow.'

**Caller** *(exasperated)* 'It can't wait until tomorrow. It's important. Look, what would you do if I was a client with a sick animal?'

**NN** 'Oh, that's easy. I'd tell you to come to the surgery tonight and you could see him there, or see one of the other vets. Why? Are you?'

**Caller** 'Am I what?'

**NN** 'Someone with a sick pet, of course. What did you think I meant?'

**Caller** 'Never mind. No, as you ask, I happen to be the architect who is trying to finish the plans for your new extension and I must have his decision on something very quickly.'

**NN** *(helpfully)* 'Tell you what. Why don't you ring him at home? I'm sure he won't bother – he's really soft like that. Anyway it's Hightown 222453. You can catch him any time then.'

**Caller** 'Well, yes, I suppose I'll have to do that, but I really didn't want to disturb him so late. However, you will tell him I called, won't you, and tell him I'll ring him at home this evening if he doesn't ring me back here by 6 pm. My number is Hightown 594833, by the way, and my name is Chris Earle.'

**NN** 'Yeah, course I'll tell him. No probs. Bye.'

**Caller** 'Goodbye.'

**NN** *(replaces receiver and, as she does so, knocks over the pile of cards she'd stacked on the desk. With a huge sigh, she bends down to pick them up).*

## WORDBANK 3 – The numbers game

Everyone knows about telephone numbers. But how much do you know about other number words? There are a great many words in the English language that refer to numbers, but before we look at these, check that you know the basics.

- We write in Arabic numerals, eg 1, 2, 3, 4 and so on. Sometimes you will see Roman numerals used, such as on the face of a clock or in a report, eg I, II, III, IV.
- We say a **cardinal number** in response to the question 'How many?' such as one, two, three or four.
- We say an **ordinal number** to indicate rank or order, such as first, second, third or fourth.
- Some numbers are spelling traps – particularly **forty** and **eighth**. Make sure that you can spell ordinary numbers correctly!

However, in English many **prefixes** denote that a word has something to do with a number. A prefix is the short part sometimes placed at the front of a word, such as **tri** in **tri**plicate or **tele** in **tele**vision. These prefixes occur again and again in different words which are all usually related in some way.

In some cases, the prefix will often tell you the number. For instance

| | |
|---|---|
| **deci** = one tenth | Decimal = in tenths. The word decimate literally means to kill every tenth person. It is therefore wrong to say 'he decimated them' if you mean he wiped them out! |
| **demi, semi** = half | Demi-pension = half board in a hotel, semi-detached = half of a detached house. The prefix semi is also used to say 'partly', eg semi-dark. |
| **sol, uni, mono** = one | Solitary = alone, unicycle = one wheeled cycle, monoplane = a plane with one set of wings. |
| **bi, du, dou** = two | Bicycle = two wheeled cycle, duel = a fight between two people, double-glazing = two panes of glass. |
| **tri** = three | Tricycle = three wheeled cycle, tripod = three legs. |
| **quad** = four | Quadruped = four legs, quadrilateral = four sides. |
| **pent, quin** = five | Pentagon = a figure of five sides, quintet = five musicians. |
| **sex** = six | Sextet = group of six. |
| **sept** = seven | Septuplets = seven children born at the same time. |
| **oct** = eight | Octopus = creature with eight legs. |
| **non** = nine | Nonagon = a figure with nine sides. |
| **deca** = ten | Decathlon = athletic competition with ten events, decade = ten years. |
| **cent, centi** = hundred | Century = one hundred years, centenarian = a person who is 100 years old. |
| **milli** = thousand | Millimetre = one thousandth of a metre. |
| **mega** = million | Megabyte = approximately one million bytes. In addition, the term **mega** is often used to denote a very large amount, particularly in slang words, eg megabucks and megastar. |
| **poly** = many or much | Polygon = a figure with many sides, polymath = a person of much learning. |

Beware of two traps, however:

**1** biannual = twice a year, *but* biennial = every two years
triannual = three times a year, *but* triennial = every three years

Because many people confuse these words, which isn't very surprising, it is safer to write what you mean in full. Similarly, if you wrote 'we will hold the meeting bimonthly' you would probably find that half your colleagues would think it was twice a month and the other half would think it was every two months! For that reason, it is better to avoid words such as 'biweekly' and 'bimonthly'.

**2** We describe a person with a million pounds as a millionaire (although milli = one thousand), but how much money has a billionaire? In England a billion used to be a million million (1,000,000,000,000). Today, most people understand the American definition, a thousand million (1,000,000,000), so this is the most general meaning.

## Test your skills

It is now relatively easy to have an 'educated guess' at the meaning of a word or to build your own! For instance, if you know that 'pentagon' = five sides and 'polygon' = many sides, it is now obvious what the words 'octagon' and 'decagon' mean. Try this yourself by doing the exercises below.

**1** From the list of words given below, select the one that fits each of the following definitions.

**a** three people singing together
**b** a word describing hairdresser's salon which has both male and female customers
**c** six children born at the same time
**d** a person who is between 90 and 99
**e** an insect with a hundred legs
**f** a period of ten years
**g** a period of a thousand years
**h** a person with more than one wife or husband
**i** an athletics contest comprising ten events
**j** able to speak two languages

**i** centipede
**ii** bilingual
**iii** millennium
**iv** unisex
**v** decade
**vi** polygamist
**vii** nonagenarian
**viii** decathlon
**ix** sextuplets
**x** trio

**2** Now find the meaning of each of the following 'number' words. Use a dictionary to help you.

**a** monopoly
**b** octogenarian
**c** pentathlon
**d** decibel
**e** megaphone
**f** monolith
**g** semi-transparent
**h** unilateral
**i** monotonous
**j** biped

**3** Finally, can you find out (or even guess!)

**a** why the month of September is so called?
**b** why the headquarters of the US defence force in Washington is called the Pentagon?

Now enter any new words into your wordbank book and any new spellings into your Spellchecker book. Be particularly careful with 'millennium' – most people get it wrong!

**DON'T YOU DARE!**

*...think that the word 'less' can be used instead of the word 'fewer'.*
*These two words are not interchangeable.*
*Use 'less' if you can't count the number and 'fewer' if you can.*
*There are fewer students in the class this year.*
*There is less space in the office since the new girl started.*

# TOOLS OF THE TRADE – learning to listen

You are in a rush one lunch time when you bump into a friend you haven't seen for a while. You both have lots of news. You hastily exchange the latest gossip and arrange to meet next week. When you get back to the office you can't remember which day you agreed to meet. Was it Wednesday – or was it Thursday? But didn't she say she goes to the gym on a Thursday? If so, could it have been Tuesday?

This problem occurred because you weren't listening to one other! The fact that you were in a rush made things worse. In your private life you can sort out such problems fairly easily over the phone. At work such confusion could cause endless problems, and you would feel rather silly having to call someone back to check the right date for an important meeting. The answer? Learn to listen!

The first thing to realise is that everyone's listening ability fluctuates, depending upon several factors. These include

- their interest in the topic
- the importance of the information
- the degree to which they are 'emotionally involved' with the message
- the length and complexity of the information
- the way in which it is being delivered (eg in a monotone or with humour)
- personal worries and other distractions
- physical discomfort (eg being too hot, cold, having toothache or feeling ill).

Therefore, whilst most of us are likely to 'switch off' during a one-hour lecture on the native habits of tree-dwelling toads, we are likely to listen intently if we are suddenly told that we have won £10,000 in a competition!

Switching off *is* normal – no-one can pay rapt attention to anything for a very long period. Good speakers use a variety of techniques to keep your attention. Humour is a common one – few people in a Billy Connolly audience go to sleep! However, you can hardly expect all your friends, colleagues or lecturers to perfect a comedy routine to keep you entertained – so it is up to you to exert a little effort.

There are two types of listening – active and passive.

- **active listening** is when you are concentrating on the message being given to you by the other person, so that you could repeat the main points afterwards if someone asked you. You may query certain points. You will also be aware by the tone of voice used whether the speaker is pleased, annoyed, impatient, enthusiastic, angry or excited.

- **passive listening** is when you find yourself waiting for the other person to stop speaking so that you can say something yourself. You may be so keen to talk about a new idea while you still remember it that you even interrupt. Passive listening is likely to occur when:

  - you receive information that 'triggers' an idea or reminds you of something you should have mentioned earlier
  - you strongly disagree with or dispute what the other person is saying
  - you are angry and arguing
  - someone criticises you and you feel the need to defend yourself.

## Improving your listening skills

As a start, try to improve your own skills by practising the following.

- Be aware when you are 'switching off' and deliberately 'switch yourself on' again
- Think twice (or even three times!) before you interrupt anyone, and if you do break their flow, focus the attention back on the main topic afterwards by saying something like 'I'm sorry. You were just telling me about last Wednesday.'
- Watch people when they are talking to you face-to-face to try to gauge the 'hidden message' (if there is one) and the emotions behind the communication. You will become more skilled at this when you can spot the different body language used by people in different situations (see Unit 7).
- Make notes of the conversation if it will be important for you to use the information yourself later. Give feedback on all the points you note down to check they are correct. Guidance on this is given later in this unit.
- *Never* start a conversation with someone else when a person is talking to you. Apart from making it impossible for you to listen is extremely ill-mannered.
- Try to avoid external distractions and don't create any yourself by fidgeting or doodling.

Good listeners are highly prized people – by their colleagues, their employers, their customers and not least their friends. In a crisis, everyone wants to communicate with a listener, not another talker!

## Test your understanding

**1 a** Read the following conversations and identify the one in which Peter is

**i** a non-listener
**ii** a passive listener
**iii** an active listener

**b** In each case, state how you would feel and how you would respond if you were Rani.

**A Rani** 'I'm dreading my appraisal interview. I've never had one before, have you? I'm really worried about what might happen.'

**Peter** 'Oh, they're OK. I remember at mine, John Evans tried to talk me into doing another course! As if I haven't done enough already!'

**B Rani** 'I'm dreading my appraisal interview. I've never had one before, have you? I'm really worried about what might happen.'

**Peter** 'I understand your fear of appraisals. I felt the same at first, but John Evans was really nice, there's really nothing to worry about. Do you want me to talk through what happens?'

**C Rani** 'I'm dreading my appraisal interview. I've never had one before, have you? I'm really worried about what might happen.'

**Peter** 'Sorry, what did you say? I'm trying to sort out these invoices before five o'clock.'

2 Ask yourself how good a listener you are and how you would be ranked on a scale of 1–5. Then, if you are brave enough, ask two or three people close to you how *they* would rank you and see if your answers compare. Try to respond positively to what they tell you!

## MAKING HEADWAY – taking messages

A fundamental task that is part of the day-to-day working routine of most people is the taking, sending and relaying of messages to other people.

Many people will give you messages at work. You have three major responsibilities:

1 to note down the message accurately

2 to pass it on promptly in the most appropriate way and,

3 wherever possible, to make sure that the message is received in time to be acted upon.

## Noting down the message

Every type of information will contain both **key facts** and **supplementary information**. When you are taking a message, your first responsibility is to make sure that you record *all* the key facts accurately. Your second, as a good listener, is to note the 'mood' of the caller, your third is to pass on the message using the most appropriate method.

### LISTENING FOR THE KEY FACTS

Professional people who use the telephone are used to stating their business clearly and in a logical order. You may find brisk people rather overwhelming at first, and be reluctant to ask them to slow down or repeat something. Try not to let their manner intimidate you – they would have no hesitation in asking you to repeat your main points if necessary! Conversely, you may speak to a customer who rarely uses the telephone, is perhaps elderly and may be shy or even very garrulous (ie talks a lot!) Whereas a shy person needs coaxing, a garrulous person may be difficult to deal with – and may give you a great deal of irrelevant information that you have to 'separate' from the key facts.

The key facts you usually need include:

- the name of the person and either the name of the organisation or a private address
- the caller's telephone number and local dialling code, plus an extension number if appropriate
- the name of the person to receive the message – if it is known (sometimes you may have to decide who should receive the message)
- the main facts relating to the message, including
  - the reason for the call
  - details of any information requested
  - details of any information passed on

- an accurate record of any dates, times, place names, product names, prices, quantities or other types of numerical data you are given. You can never guess any of these afterwards!

*Always* check that you have understood a message properly by reading your notes to the caller. In particular, check that any figures you have written down are accurate. To the professional caller you will seem efficient and to the unprofessional caller this checking of the main facts will be reassuring – so you cannot lose!

### THE MOOD OF THE CALLER

Extremes of mood are usually very easy to identify. The annoyed caller with a strong complaint will usually leave you in no doubt about his or her feelings – neither will a caller who is ringing to thank you for something. If someone is complaining, listen until the caller 'runs out of steam' – interrupting usually makes things worse. Never try to contradict or correct such a person. Make a few brief notes and then, when the caller has calmed down, check that you have noted the problem accurately and explain that you will pass it to your supervisor immediately. If possible, give a time when someone will call back. Never make vague excuses, put the blame on anyone or make promises you cannot keep. Stick to the facts, record these accurately and treat the call as urgent.

When you become more experienced, you will learn to spot other differences in mood, for instance whether someone is impatient, nervous, anxious or even upset or sad. Listening carefully, checking understanding and paying special attention to the tone of voice can all give useful clues as to how the caller is feeling, and being in a position to pass on this type of information can often be invaluable.

## Relaying the message

The way in which you relay the message should depend upon

- its complexity
- its urgency
- who must receive it
- where the recipient is situated at the moment.

A short, straightforward message can be jotted down and, if the recipient is available, can be passed on verbally and face-to-face. A complex message is always better relayed in writing. This can be done on paper or, in some companies, via electronic mail or even electronic telephone message. However, you still have to know how to word the information!

### WRITING OUT THE MESSAGE

Your own jottings are usually unsuitable for passing on to someone else. Only your closest friend is likely to look kindly on a scrap of paper containing a few scribbles and your latest doodle. In most cases you would be expected to use printed message forms, to write or type the message on plain paper or to communicate it electronically. An example of a form for a short message is shown in Figure 4.1. Such forms are useful as they focus your attention on the key points you must include.

MESSAGE FORM

TO .................................. DEPT. ..............................................
DATE................................ TIME ................................................

CALLER'S NAME ..............................................................
ORGANISATION ...............................................................
TEL NO.......................... EXT NO. ......................................

Telephoned ☐
Returned your call ☐
Called to see you ☐
Left a message ☐

Please return call ☐
Please arrange appointment ☐

**Message:**
..........................................................................................

**Taken by:**................................... **Dept.** ...................................

***Figure 4.1*** *A telephone message form*

Use simple, straightforward words that cannot be misunderstood. Try to vary the length of your sentences so that your message 'flows' properly. Don't forget to convert your pronouns! If you are telling your boss that Jo Bloggs cannot meet him, your message would obviously read 'Jo Bloggs said that *he* cannot meet *you*'. This may seem simple, but many new message takers forget!

Include all the key facts in a logical order and be specific about any days, dates and times. Always give both the date and the day (never say 'today' or 'tomorrow') as the message may be read on a different day from that on which it was written.

Don't forget to include your name (in case the recipient wants to check anything with you) and the date and time of the call. Sometimes this information can be critical, particularly if this caller had several conversations with different people in the organisation during the course of one day.

Be very careful about the tone of your message. A message to your boss must not seem like a direct order! The normal courtesies, eg 'please', 'he would be grateful if' or 'she would be pleased if you could' are just as important in relaying messages as in any other form of written communication.

## Passing on your written message

You may think that you now have nothing more to do than to leave your message for the recipient to read. Yet there are more problems with messages not being actioned than with messages not being received. What can go wrong?

- An urgent message is put in someone's mail tray at 2 pm. The mail isn't distributed again until the following morning.
- An urgent message is put on someone's desk. The desk has dozens of papers on it and the person rushes back from a meeting, drops a pile of papers on top of it without seeing it, then rushes out again.
- An urgent message is put on a clean and tidy desk. But the person concerned is out of the office and won't be back at his/her desk for another two days.
- A message is put on the wrong desk. The person concerned tries to find you to query it but cannot, because you put it there just before you went home.

You can avoid causing these problems by making sure you do the following.

- Mark urgent messages *clearly.*
- Hand them to the person responsible (or a deputy, or another senior colleague) wherever possible.
- If the person required is away from his/her desk at the time, check if he/she is in the office that day. If not, hand the message to someone else. If someone is 'expected back later' check that the message has been received (a quick phone call will often suffice).
- Whenever you are in any doubt, always tell your own boss about the problem and say what you have done so far.

## Test your understanding

**1** The Office Manager, Kay Ogilvie, has her own office some distance from yours. She frequently visits other departments in the company, attends meetings and travels on business. If you received an urgent message for her at 4 pm, what would you do to make certain it was acted upon if she was not in her office at the time?

**2** Copy out the message form on page 71 and complete it accurately from the following information, making sure you include all the key facts.

At 11 am you were in the reception area of the Riverside Small Animal Centre when the phone rang. The caller was a reporter, James Ketchley, from the local evening paper – the Hightown Gazette – and he wanted to speak to John Higgins. As John was out at the time you offered to take a message. James Ketchley is doing a series of articles on animal behaviour and has heard that John Higgins is an expert in this field. He wondered if John would act as consultant by answering reader's letters and queries on their animal problems. The practice would receive free publicity by doing this. He needs to know John's response for a meeting with the editor tomorrow morning at 10 am and would like John to phone him to discuss this as soon as possible. His number is Hightown (01928) 493892, extension 2001.

## ●●●●● *DOUBLE TROUBLE*

In English there are many pairs of words that can cause confusion. For each word listed below, identify the meanings and make certain that you know the difference between them so that you use them correctly.

First – ten doubles!

**a** weigh and way
**b** flair and flare
**c** flea and flee
**d** desert and dessert
**e** wave and waive
**f** cue and queue
**g** story and storey
**h** kerb and curb
**i** here and hear
**j** leak and leek

Now – some threesomes!

**k** peak, peek and pique
**l** vain, vein and vane
**m** aisle, isle, I'll
**n** you, ewe, yew
**o** cent, sent, scent
**p** hair, hare and heir

**q** rains, reins and reigns
**r** site, sight and cite
**s** pair, pear and pare
**t** to, two and too

And a foursome!

**u** write, right, wright, rite.

DON'T YOU DARE!

*...confuse the common threesome of 'there, they're and their.' Remember the difference in this way.*

- *There = a place = here and there (put a 't' in front of 'here')*
- *They're = they are. If 'they are' would make sense instead, then this is the version to use.*
- *Their = something they own, eg their books, their money.*

## Test your understanding

Correct the errors in each of the following sentences. Note that some include 'double trouble' words you have met before. How good is your memory?

**a** Their going to live in the too story building.
**b** Their not going on there holidays until next month.
**c** He was aloud to mend the leek at the building cite.
**d** When we get they're we'll higher a car for the weak.
**e** I think it's rite we pear our expenses to the bone.
**f** She desserted him in a fit of peek.
**g** The local counsel had to pay out a large check in settlement.
**h** It maybe possible to wave the charges as a matter of principal.
**i** She excepts that she will loose her rites to settlement if she signs.
**j** The draught document was written on office stationary.

## THE GOOD GRAMMAR GUIDE

### Pronouns

In the last unit you learned about personal pronouns. However, personal pronouns are not the only ones we use – nor the only type that cause problems. In this section we will look at the other types of pronouns we use and the difficulties these can cause.

- **Relative pronouns.** These are used to start a clause that adds information to a sentence, eg who, whom, whose, which, that.

  Paula is the new girl *who* works in our office
  Mary is only person with *whom* I go to lunch
  This is Gary, *whose* wife had a baby yesterday
  Peter wrote a play *which* was shown on TV last week
  There is the building *that* caught fire recently

- **Reflexive pronouns.** You use these when you want to refer back to a noun or pronoun you have used as the subject of a sentence, eg

I hurt *myself* this morning | Did you cut *yourself* with the knife
He kicked *himself* when he heard the news

- **Demonstrative pronouns.** These are used for pointing out a person or thing. The words we use are: this, that, these and those. If something is close by (either in space or time) we usually use 'this' or 'these', eg

  *This* is my collection.
  *These* are my friends.
  I can't afford *that*.
  I want *these*, not *those*.

- **Indefinite pronouns.** These refer to a person or group of people in general, rather than specific terms. Children greatly annoy their parents when they say

  *Everybody* has one.
  *Anyone* will tell you.
  *Everyone* is going.
  *Somebody* told me.

  Other words in this group of pronouns are: anybody, anything, everything, nobody, nothing, someone, something and no-one. The last word is the odd one out because it is the only one which can be written as two words, with or without a hyphen.

- **Interrogative pronouns.** These are used to ask questions and are sometimes called the 'wh-words'. The main ones are: what, which, when, where, who and whom, eg

  *What* are you doing?
  *When* can you go?
  *Which* club is the best?
  *Where* do you live?

## Pronoun problems

**1** There is often confusion over which pronoun to use, particularly between

- who and whom
- which and that.

### WHO AND WHOM

Use 'who' for the subject and 'whom' for the object, If you can't remember about subjects and objects, look back to page 33.

*Jolanta,* (subject) *who works in Sales, is coming with us*
*Is this the person* (object) *to whom you spoke?*

If you are in doubt, rephrase the sentence, eg *Who spoke to you?*

### THAT AND WHICH

These two pronouns are interchangeable apart from when 'which' starts a clause separated by commas, brackets or dashes in the middle of a sentence, eg

*The car that I drive is red.* or *The car which I drive is red.*
*My car, which is parked over there, was vandalised last week.*

However, problems can occur in relation to people!

- Never use 'which' to refer to people – only to animals and inanimate objects.
- Don't make the common mistake of using the word 'that' when you should say who, eg *It was Brian that forgot the date* is wrong!
- Never use 'what' when you should say 'that', eg *This is the house what I lived in when I was young* is wrong.

**2** A common mistake is to refer to a singular indefinite pronoun as if it were a plural, eg

*Everyone must bring their own lunch.*
*No-one must forget to hand in their form.*

The correct versions would be

*Everyone must bring his or her own lunch.*
*No-one must forget to hand in his or her form on Monday.*

However, remember that it is often better to use the plural (which prevents the 'sexist' problem too), eg *All visitors must bring their own lunch. All students must remember to hand in their forms on Monday.*

**DON'T YOU DARE!**

*...confuse the pronoun 'whose' with 'who's'. Who's = who is or who has. Test if this would make sense in the sentence. If not, write 'whose'.*

## Test your understanding

Rewrite each of the following sentences correctly so that it makes sense.

**1** Someone in the next room has had their bag stolen.

**2** This is the insurance claim form for your car which you must send to the company.

**3** This is the computer what broke yesterday.

**4** The girl was carried by the woman who had broken her leg.

**5** Was it me whom you saw on Saturday?

**6** Janet, who's sister got married last week, is going to America on holiday.

## COMMUNICATION IN PRACTICE

## Test your skills

**1** Read the following telephone conversation and then answer the questions that follow:

**You** 'Good morning, Personnel Department.'

**Caller** 'Oh, good morning, this is Mrs Jenkins here. I've been trying to get through to your Accounts Department but they're engaged and I've got to leave for work myself in a minute.'

**You** 'What I can do to help you, Mrs Jenkins?'

**Caller** 'Well, the problem's my husband Simon. He's in bed and he's hot and clammy – I think he's got flu – anyway, he's certainly not fit enough to come to work today. He's bothered no-one will know why he's off – particularly Keith Bradshaw, his boss.'

**You** 'Don't worry, Mrs Jenkins, I'll make sure Mr Bradshaw is informed.'

**Caller** 'One other thing, Simon's worried because he's got some calculations ready that Keith was taking to an important meeting. He said to tell Keith the file is in the second drawer of the filing cabinet under the heading "Financial Estimates" – he said Keith needs the pink folder, not the blue one.'

**You** 'Fine, Mrs Jenkins, I've got all that – the pink folder, second drawer down, under "Financial Estimates". Tell your husband not to worry, just to get well. Can you please keep us informed of his progress and when he's likely to return?'

**Caller** 'Yes, I'll do that. Thanks a lot for your help.'

**You** 'You're welcome. Thanks for calling. Goodbye.'

**Caller** 'Goodbye.'

**a** If you had answered the telephone in this way and responded to Mrs Jenkins like this, how would you assess

**i** your telephone technique
**ii** your listening skills?

Select appropriate extracts to justify your opinion.

**b** Identify the key facts you would need to pass on in a message.

**c** Write out the message clearly and neatly for Mr Bradshaw.

**d** When you visit Accounts with the message Keith Bradshaw isn't around and no-one knows where he is. One member of staff thinks his meeting is with the MD and is due to start in 20 minutes. What would you do and why? Discuss your suggestions as a group.

**2** Use the definitions below to identify the word required and spell each one correctly. To help, the first and last letter is given in each case.

**a** the person who receives something r.................t
**b** the skill of being tactful and sensitive of others d................y
**c** a person who wants everything to be faultless p.................t
**d** a person you work alongside c.................e
**e** one payment out of several i.................t

**3** Write out each of the following sentences so that there are no errors of grammar, spelling or punctuation.

**a** If you loose any personnel items then you must report the problem.
**b** We recently sent him an invoice for the tyres battery and break linings he ordered but so far he hasn't payed us.
**c** We have visited, many places, including australia singapore and japan.
**d** John Black who is married to my sister directed the play and also drew the design on the cover of the program.
**e** In summery I think you should go as everyone accept alan will be there.

# Apply your skills

You are working on reception today at Riverside Small Animal Centre. You start at 8.30 am. John Higgins and the two other vets are out on emergency calls, and you are busy answering the telephone and dealing with callers.

Your first visitor is Martin Chivers, whose pet rabbit Zebedee had a litter of six a few weeks ago. He wants to know if you can find homes for them. You tell him that the normal procedure is for a notice to be put in reception which includes his phone number – anyone interested must then contact him directly. He tells you he doesn't want any payment for the rabbits – just good homes. He confirms his phone number is Hightown 403948.

As Martin leaves the phone rings. It is Tom Davies on the phone. He asks you to tell John that he is held up at the Hightown Animal Sanctuary and won't be back until lunchtime. His only morning commitment is a visit from Josie Andrews with her labrador, Sadie, at 11 am. He asks if John will see them. Tom tells you he can be contacted on his mobile number – 6019-392829 – if you need him.

Between then and 9 am you receive two further calls. Diane Chan, a friend of Jane Mitchell's, rings to say she will have to cancel their lunch arrangements. You promise you will make sure Jane gets the message as soon she arrives. Diane says Jane can call her back on Hightown 203992.

Your final call is from Jeremy Southwark, the painter and decorator booked for the new extension. He cannot read John's writing on the list of colours he wants – he needs immediate confirmation whether the new reception area is to be painted in egg-shell blue or duck-egg blue. Apparently the difference is quite considerable. He also needs to know if he can start this Saturday – which is only possible if the builders have finished and the plaster has dried. He asks if John can ring him urgently on Hightown 308930. After 10.30 he will be out but can be reached on his mobile number – 6930-309930.

*Mr Higgins,*

*David Hall rang about his rabbit that his son, Ben, fetched in last week. You may remmember, him, he's the one what has the floppy ears and only one front tooth. He said youd promised to wave you're charges because hed overpayed last time or something like that. But his son had to pay £26 for his injec-shuns. He says can you ring him. His phone number is 505093. I think he wants the money back.*

*Natalie*

*(He rang at 6. 30 - just as I was putting my coat on.)*

***Figure 4.2*** *Natalie's message for John Higgins*

At 9 am Petra arrives to take over in reception and you thankfully go into the back office to work. At this point you notice a message Natalie has written for John Higgins which is full of mistakes (see Figure 4.2). You decide to help her by correcting it.

**1** Write out the three messages you have received in an acceptable format for their recipients. Your tutor will tell you whether to copy the message form on page 71 or write each message as a short memo.

**2** Prepare a brief notice for reception to advertise Martin Chivers' rabbits.

**3** Correct Natalie's message and rewrite it in an acceptable form for John Higgins.

## *WORD WIZARD*

Play with number words in this wizard. Start by reading the passage below and see if you can find the 25 'number words' included (look up the meanings of any new words).

Your challenge is then to find 25 other number words yourself (look for their 'roots' in a dictionary) and put them together to make a (relatively!) sensible paragraph. The shorter the paragraph, the cleverer you are.

I have always had a soft spot for old, eccentric uncle Harry who always aimed to be a billionaire. He is now rapidly approaching his centenary but was still starring as a soloist at the Octagon Theatre until he was a septuagenarian, when he sought safety in numbers and joined a sextet. He says he 'semi-retired' last year as he always sang an octave below everyone else. I can well believe it! In his youth he was in the army, but detested being in uniform and was appalled at the scientific advances to develop a megaton bomb. He left after a decade and travelled to America, where he bought a duplex which he said hardly cost a cent! He studied Spanish and Portugese and rapidly became trilingual. He then made a unilateral decision to sail through the Bermuda Triangle in the middle of winter. His sextant failed but he said his lucky pentacle saw him through. He never married, saying he didn't believe in monogamy, and he detested animals, saying bipeds and quadrupeds didn't mix. I haven't seen him for almost a decade but still miss his fascinating monologues – usually delivered from an old armchair under his award for scoring a century in the old quadrangle at York.

## IN THE SPOTLIGHT –

# FAX MACHINES AND FAX MESSAGES

Fax machines vary from small, desktop models to much larger and more automated machines. Devices are available which incorporate a telephone, fax, answering machine, computer printer and copier in one piece of equipment.

Faxes are popular because it is possible to transmit text, graphics and photographs (and anything else that can be copied onto a sheet of paper) quickly, easily and cheaply. In addition, the machines themselves are inexpensive and simple to use. A fax can be sent to Australia in virtually the same length of time as to the next building, meaning that instant communication to distant parts of the globe is now a reality.

Fax machines work by scanning a black and white document and converting this information into signals that are transmitted down a telephone line. When two machines connect there is a brief 'handshake' period during which each machines identifies the other. The slower machine will dictate the speed of the transmission, as will the speed of the modem. A modem is a device through which digital impulses are transmitted. High-speed transmission is obviously better, as the cost of sending a fax is determined by the connection time.

To use a fax, you simply place the page in the document feeder, dial the number of your recipient's fax machine and press the relevant keys. When the transmission has ended the document is ejected and a transmission report is generated. This tells you the time and length of the connection and confirms whether transmission took place satisfactorily. If a transmission is interrupted, the operator must reconnect to transmit the missing pages.

Automated faxes can undertake many operations independently. Frequently used numbers can be stored in memory, with a search facility to aid speedy retrieval, and faxes can be sent automatically during cheap-rate and off-peak transmission times. The machine can be programmed to preface each message with a specially printed cover sheet giving the name of the organisation and sender, and print a previously stored signature if required at a specified point.

## Using a fax

Fax machines are very easy to use, but there are a few basics you need to know before you start. However, if you can use a telephone you should be able to use a fax.

- On the most basic models you insert your document, dial the number and wait for the connection to be made. Most fax machines then transmit automatically. They will also retry a number at regular intervals if it is engaged.
- Knowing how to place your original document in the document feeder is critical – otherwise you are likely to send your message upside down (not too bad) or back to front (disastrous – as a blank sheet of paper may be transmitted)
- Faxes only recognise black and white, so coloured documents must be photocopied first – as should flimsy or important documents which may be damaged by the machine. Remember that the 'sharper' the distinction between the black and white, the clearer the fax at the other end.
- All fax machines automatically print the name and number of the sender at the top of each message. However, this is usually in very small print and not easily seen. For that reason, special fax message forms are often used giving a much clearer 'header' stating the name of the organisation and allowing for other details, similar to those shown at the top of a memo (see Figure 5.1).
- Each page of a fax should be numbered, eg page 1 of 4, page 2 of 4 and so on – so that the recipient can easily check that all pages have been received.

***Figure 5.1*** *A short fax message with a fax header sheet*

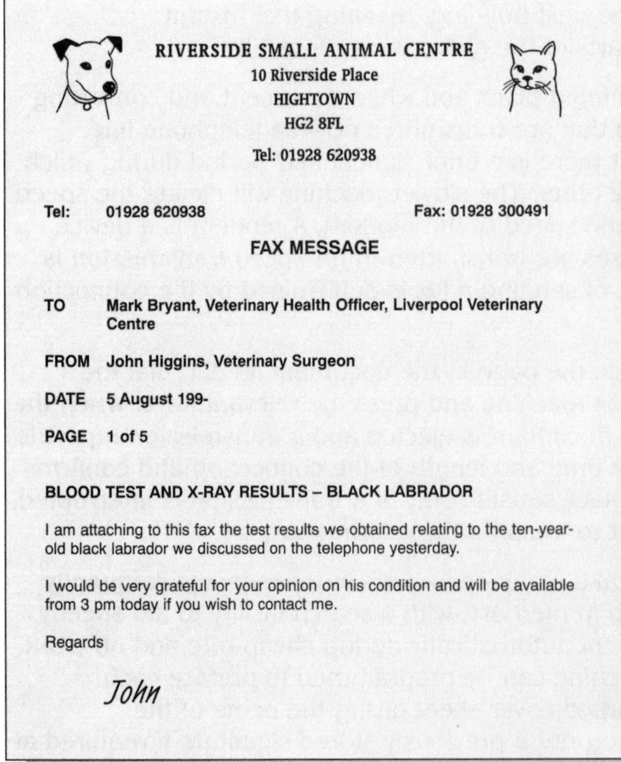

RIVERSIDE SMALL ANIMAL CENTRE
10 Riverside Place
HIGHTOWN
HG2 8FL
Tel: 01928 620938

Tel: 01928 620938 Fax: 01928 300491

FAX MESSAGE

TO Mark Bryant, Veterinary Health Officer, Liverpool Veterinary Centre

FROM John Higgins, Veterinary Surgeon

DATE 5 August 199-

PAGE 1 of 5

BLOOD TEST AND X-RAY RESULTS – BLACK LABRADOR

I am attaching to this fax the test results we obtained relating to the ten-year-old black labrador we discussed on the telephone yesterday.

I would be very grateful for your opinion on his condition and will be available from 3 pm today if you wish to contact me.

Regards

John

- Make sure you transmit the pages in the right order. You also need to know how to stop the fax and cancel the transmission if anything goes wrong – such as dialling the wrong number or running out of paper.
- Fax numbers are given in the UK Fax Book and international fax numbers can be found by dialling 153.

## Receiving a fax

Fax machines are used to transmit urgent information. The benefits are therefore completely wasted if an incoming message is allowed to languish near the machine until the recipient has gone home for the night. All fax machines should be regularly checked for incoming messages, which should be distributed promptly.

## Composing a fax

Fax messages may be typed or handwritten. Their tone can vary considerably – an official or formal letter could be faxed for speed to the recipient. On other occasions faxes are sent between organisations that are already doing business with each other – or between branch offices. In this case the wording is more informal – similar to a memo or an e-mail.

Could you please prepare three faxes for me urgently.

1 I promised the seminar organiser - Jim Parks - that I would confirm my acceptance of the invitation by fax. Please refer to my telephone conversation with him yesterday. Say that I will be pleased to give the talk on separation anxiety on Friday at the Westbury Building on Shooters Hill Road, Blackheath. It will start at 10 am and last one hour, followed by 15 minutes for questions and answers. Tell him I will arrive at 9.30 am and will require an overhead projector and screen. Please end by saying that I look forward to seeing him again.

2 Please fax the hotel and confirm my reservation for one single room with facilities for Thursday night. I will arrive at about 6 pm. I'm staying at Heath View, Morden Road, Blackheath. It's only a small hotel - the owner's name is Mrs Theresa Scott and I made the booking by phone yesterday. Please confirm the rate is £75 for bed and breakfast.

3 Finally, please prepare a fax to Simon Hodgson at Taylor's Veterinary Centre in Banbury. He's an old friend of mine and borrowed some papers which would be useful for the talk. Please ask him to fax me the Watson Study research papers on animal behaviour as soon as possible as I need them for a talk I'm giving on Friday. Tell him I'll ring him later in the week.

If you let me see the draft faxes when you have prepared them, I'll let you have the fax numbers.

Thanks

Asif

**Figure 5.2** *Note from Asif Bashir*

Faxes are often used when someone's response is required to some urgent information that is too complex to read over the telephone. In this case the message is quite short, but several other pages of information may be transmitted (see Figure 5.1). Fax messages are often signed and, particularly when they are being sent externally, usually include the designation of the sender.

## Test your understanding

Asif Bashir is an expert on animal behaviour and has studied separation anxiety of cats and dogs quite extensively. He has recently been on holiday and, on his return home, found an invitation to speak at a seminar in London next Friday. He has contacted the organiser, who is an old friend, and agreed to go. He has now asked you to help finalise all the arrangements as quickly as possible.

**1** Asif's note to you is given opposite (see Figure 5.2). Read this carefully and decide which of the faxes would be the most formal and which would be the most informal. Discuss your ideas as a group.

**2** Draft the three faxes Asif has requested and check your wording with your tutor.

## POLISH YOUR PUNCTUATION
### The apostrophe

The apostrophe is a small, simple punctuation mark (') which probably causes more problems and confusion than all other punctuation marks put together! This is because it has two quite separate uses.

## Indicating missing letters

This is the first use of the apostrophe. It tells us that some letters have been missed out of a word or phrase, eg

| | |
|---|---|
| *can't* (cannot) | *didn't* (did not) |
| *won't* (will not) | *o'clock* (of the clock) |
| *Hallowe'en* (Halloweven) | *ne'er-do-well* (never-do-well) |

The apostrophe is *always* placed at the point where the letters are missing – but remember that contracted words are not used in formal business documents.

Sometimes, when new shortened words are added to the language, an apostrophe is at first inserted to indicate the missing letters, eg 'flu or 'phone. As the word becomes more frequently used, the apostrophe is dropped, which is why we now write flu and not 'flu, phone and not 'phone.

## Indicating ownership or possession

This is the function of the apostrophe that causes problems for many people. You have two decisions to make

**a** whether an apostrophe is needed
**b** if so, where to put it.

### LEARN THE BASICS

An apostrophe is used when we want to show that something belongs to someone, eg

the girl's coat, the dog's dish, the manager's office.

We could therefore have written: 'the coat *belonging to* the girl', 'the dish *belonging to the* dog' and 'the office *belonging to* the manager'. Therefore the 'belonging test' always tells you if an apostrophe is required.

In each of these cases we have *one* 'owner' so there is a *singular noun* – one girl, one dog, one manager.

**First rule to remember**: When there is *one* owner you add **an apostrophe + an 's'.**

Now look at the following phrases:

the members' lounge, the nurses' union, the wasps' nest.

In this case you get 'the lounge *belonging to* the members', 'the union *belonging to* the nurses' and 'the nest *belonging to* the wasps'. They all pass the 'belonging test' so an apostrophe is required.

In each of these cases there are *several* owners and you have a **plural noun** – many members, many nurses, many wasps. In this case you just add an apostrophe.

**Second rule to remember**: When there are *several* owners and a plural noun you just **add an apostrophe**.

In most cases, it is obvious from the noun whether the owner must be singular or plural. If you look at the phrase 'the girl's coat' it *must* refer to one owner (it is unlikely several girls would share a coat!) However, in other cases you cannot tell unless you look at the meaning of a sentence. For instance, the phrase 'the boy's bags' or 'the boys' bags' could both be correct. In the first case there is one boy with several bags, in the second case there are several boys and several bags. The 'belonging test' would sort this out for you, depending upon whether the meaning is 'the bags of the boy' or 'the bags of the boys'.

## MOVING ON A STAGE – SPECIAL PLURALS

The rules you have learned above will solve 80% of your apostrophe problems. The next stage will help to solve another 15% – and they are just as straightforward.

Many nouns change completely when they move from singular to plural, eg child/children, man/men, woman/women, others change their endings, such as thief/thieves, company/companies. In this case the 'belonging test' will still tell you if an apostrophe is required, eg

the children's clothes = the clothes *belonging to* the children
the ladies' room = the room *belonging to* the ladies

We still need an apostrophe, and the **third rule to remember** is as follows:

If the plural does not end in 's' **add apostrophe + s**
If the plural ends in 's' **add an apostrophe**

## SINGULAR NOUNS ENDING IN 'S'

If a singular word ends in 's' then you *may* need to add an apostrophe plus 's', eg

We are going to St James's Park (the Park *belonging to* St James).

However, in many cases, to avoid double or treble 's' endings, the apostrophe is added afterwards, therefore

*Chris's bike* but *Lloyd Bridges' film*!

**Fourth rule to remember**: A singular word ending in 's' follows the 'belonging to' test *unless* it results in an unpronounceable 'iziz' ending.

## THE FINAL TOUCHES

You should now be able to insert apostrophes correctly in 95% of sentences. However, there are a few remaining difficulties.

- Many people forget that units of time, such as days, month and years, can also be possessive, eg

  a year's salary (salary *belonging to* one year)
  three weeks' time (time *belonging to* three weeks).

  The same rules apply. Singular = apostrophe + s, plural = apostrophe after the 's', therefore *one day's time* but *three days' time*.

- You may write a sentence about an item which belongs to two people but only mention it once, eg

  Both John's book – and Margaret's – had the first three pages missing.

In this case you could have written 'and Margaret's book' but this would have been clumsy – anyone who reads the sentence knows you are referring to two books! In this case, when putting in your apostrophes, you treat the sentence as if you had written the word 'book' twice.

- Finally, there are some exceptions that trip everyone up. Did you realise, for instance, that we write Guy Fawkes Day (no apostrophe) but St Valentine's Day? It may be comforting to know that the trend in English is to drop apostrophes in the names and titles of business firms and their products, such as Mothers Pride Bread and McDonalds. It may not be long before Sainsbury's also follows!

**DON'T YOU DARE!**

*...become so keen on apostrophes that you start to include them everywhere, even in normal plural words which are nothing to do with possession! Many people make this mistake – notice how many times you see a greengrocer's sign that advertises potato's or cauli's over the next few months!*

## Test your understanding

**1** Abbreviate each of the following words and phrases and insert the apostrophe in the correct place.

| | | | | |
|---|---|---|---|---|
| shall not | we will | I would | is not | could not |
| it is | should not | who is | you are | she will |

**2** Rewrite each of the following phrases, taking out the words 'belonging to' and inserting apostrophes in the correct places.

**a** the book belonging to the student
**b** the staffroom belonging to the lecturers
**c** the waiting room belonging to the patients
**d** the locker room belonging to the men
**e** the lorry belonging to the driver

**3** Insert apostrophes correctly in the following sentences.

**a** My friends watch has been stolen from her sisters house.
**b** Her mothers birthday is on 8 July and her brothers is on the same day as mine.
**c** The cat refuses to drink refrigerated milk from its dish because its too cold.
**d** 'The jokes on her,' observed Sandra, 'and its about time!'
**e** Music Weeklys feature today was on rock n roll in the 50s.
**f** I ordered a months supply of paper and envelopes and six weeks supply of letter-headed paper from our printers, all of which will be delivered in a weeks time.
**g** All MPs of both parties listen to the Queens Speech when she opens the Houses of Parliament.

# TOOLS OF THE TRADE – speaking clearly

Speaking clearly has absolutely *nothing* to do with sounding 'posh'. It simply means that people can understand what you are saying. If you mutter, speak too quietly, miss the endings off words or run several words together very quickly, then anyone who doesn't know you well will have difficulty in understanding you.

Areas to consider include the following.

■ Your **accent**. Regional accents make life interesting, and a diversity of accents is usual in most workplaces. Problems occur only if your accent is so strong that no-one outside the district can understand you or if you use too many local expressions unknown anywhere else.

■ **Articulation**. This concerns the distinctness of your speech and the degree to which you separate words. 'Hiya', 'D'yuhknow' and 'Waddjadoin'? are examples of words being run together and are probably unintelligible to many people, particularly foreigners trying to learn English! Even if you don't join words together quite as much as this, many people omit or change word endings, particularly '-ing', which becomes '-in' and 'dow' which becomes 'der', or drop the letter 'h' – hence 'I'm openin' winnder, it's 'ot in 'ere.' But do be careful not to speak with unnatural emphasis, which sounds just as bad!

■ Using '**fillers**'. These are words and phrases we use when we are hesitant or are trying to gain thinking time. They include '-er' and '-um' as well as 'you know', ' well', 'I mean' and 'you see'. In a bad case, you can end up with a sentence such as 'Well, er, um you see, what I mean is, you know . . .' – all of which says absolutely nothing and is irritating to the listener.

■ **Pronunciation**. It is important that you know how to pronounce the words you use, otherwise you sound silly. To avoid this problem, practise pronouncing the words you read in each *Say It* box throughout this book.

■ **Pitch, tone, volume and timbre**. These all relate to the sound of your voice. For instance, pitching your voice so everyone in a room can hear you means lifting your head and speaking more loudly and clearly. This is what tutors do when they speak to a large audience in a lecture theatre – otherwise, without a microphone, you wouldn't be able to hear them. It *doesn't* mean shouting!

■ **Cadence and inflexion** versus monotony. Cadence and inflexion both relate to the way someone's voice rises and falls in speech. Normally, we drop our voices at the end of a sentence, but if you do this too much then the listener will not be able to hear what you are saying. Some people use more inflexion than others – Welsh people, for instance, are often described as speaking in a 'sing song' or 'melodic' way. This is far better than a monotone, which is so boring to listen to.

■ **Slang**. The final area of concern is slang – which we all use every day but which is inappropriate in a more formal situation. Expressions such as 'Hi', 'How come?', 'Some hope!' and 'So long' are not standard business phrases! As you have seen, even the use of 'OK' over the telephone to a customer is frowned upon in many organisations.

## Golden rules

- Speak more slowly than normal when you are trying to speak clearly.
- Use the appropriate volume – don't shout or mutter.
- If you are nervous, plan what you are going to say beforehand. This is useful when you initiate a telephone call (see Unit 6) and speak in group presentations (see Unit 12). Take a few deep breaths to steady your nerves.
- Avoid slang or local expressions that other people may not know, or which are inappropriate at work.
- Try to vary your voice, to make it more interesting for your listeners.
- The police force, airline pilots and anyone else who needs to be understood precisely at a distance use the phonetic alphabet to spell out difficult words. In business you can use the telephone alphabet to help you (see below).

## Apply your skills

1 Tape yourself reading or having a conversation with someone. Don't be surprised if on the tape you sound different from the way you *think* you sound – this is normal. Make a note of the 'fillers' you use and any major faults in articulation you need to correct.

***Figure 5.3*** *The telephone alphabet*

| | | |
|---|---|---|
| A – Alfred | J – Jack | S – Samuel |
| B – Benjamin | K – King | T – Tommy |
| C – Charlie | L – London | U – Uncle |
| D – David | M – Mary | V – Victor |
| E – Edward | N – Nellie | W – William |
| F – Frederick | O – Oliver | X – X-ray |
| G – George | P – Peter | Y – Yellow |
| H – Harry | Q – Queen | Z – Zebra |
| I – Isaac | R – Robert | |

2 Practise using the telephone alphabet (see Figure 5.3) with a friend. Note that you don't need to spell out every word – the most usual are names of people or places, and postcodes. B, T and P are probably the most indistinct letters over a telephone. If only a few letters are unclear, say the word as follows:

PAIGNTON – P A I G for George, N for Nellie, T O N.

Now read a name and address to your friend whilst your back is turned (so he or she cannot lipread). If you spell out the difficult letters he or she should have no difficulty understanding your words.

## MAKING HEADWAY – forms, form letters and envelopes

You may consider these are very basic topics to cover, as you have probably been completing forms for many years. You have also probably written many envelopes in your life. However, there are times when forms can be particularly difficult to complete and also very important – such as when you are applying for a job. A variety of forms are used by all organisations and you are expected to complete them accurately the first time and on your own. You may also be expected to prepare form letters which are sent out on routine matters, and to write or print envelopes according to standard business conventions. All this is necessary before you develop your skills so that you can compose complex letters and **design** forms, as well as complete them (see Unit 14).

SAY IT!

Test your pronunciation by saying each of the following words and check with your tutor that you are pronouncing it correctly. Use the guidance in brackets to help you.

- Cello (The first 'c' is pronounced 'ch')
- Charismatic (This is the opposite! The 'ch' is pronounced 'k')
- Facile (The 'c' is pronounced 's', followed by 'i' as in 'mile')
- Ghetto (the 'h' is silent – hence 'getto')
- Malign (pronounced as 'maline')
- Meagre (pronounced as 'meager')
- Pathos (say 'a' as in 'bake', then 'o' as in top)
- Perhaps (don't say 'p'raps' – and pronounce the 'h'!)
- Subtle (said as 'suttle')
- Vacillate (the 'c' is pronounced as an 's')

Now look up the meaning of each word and write it down. Try to use at least four of these words in conversation during the next week.

# FORMS USED IN BUSINESS

Forms vary considerably in their complexity. A well-designed form should be easy to follow, with easily understood questions in a logical order and sufficient space in which to write the required information. Bear this in mind when you start to design forms yourself!

The main reasons for issuing a form are

- to obtain information required
- to ensure information is recorded in a consistent way. This makes it much easier to compare results or to enter the data into a computer.

At work you will probably complete several forms every week. There are forms relating to every single department in an organisation, eg

- Personnel – forms for job applications, interview appraisals, staff appointments, staff appraisals, holiday requests.
- Wages, salaries and expenses – form for payroll, overtime claims, expenses claims, mileage claims, time sheets, petty cash claims.
- Sales – forms for orders, representative reports, visit reports, sales analysis.
- Finance and accounts – delivery notes, advice notes, invoices, credit notes, statements, direct debit forms, receipts.
- Health, safety and security – accident report forms, 'near-miss' accident report forms, security reports.

## Electronic forms

Forms are not just seen on pieces of paper today. Many software packages include a type of form, such as a database where you would enter details such as names and addresses on to an electronic record form.

If you surf the Internet, you will find that many information providers ask you to register on their site. In this case you would complete an electronic form giving details of your name, address and other relevant information.

## Tips on form completion

If the designer has done his or her job properly, completing a form on paper or on screen should be a simple matter – provided you take the time and trouble to read it properly. Otherwise, just as you enter your postcode in the address section you are likely to see there is a special box for it below – and other such disasters! If you do this on a job application form you do little to enhance your prospects of getting an interview!

At work, you may be involved in helping other people complete standard forms, particularly elderly customers or anyone with a visual impairment. If you are familiar with the form then this is usually easy – provided that you remember not to ask people to state personal details in a public area! If you are completing a form you have never seen before, either for yourself or anyone else, it is worthwhile to remember the basics.

- Read the form through *first*.
- Carefully study any guidance notes issued with the form.
- Read any special conditions or other terms which will apply to you if you submit the form. These are often shown in small print at the bottom, particularly if they are likely to be unfavourable!
- Check if there is any expiry date or last submission date.
- If the form is particularly important, obtain a photocopy (or two) and practise on these first.
- Check if the use of a particular type of pen is specified (often 'black ink' or 'ballpoint'). This is likely if the form is in duplicate or triplicate, to make certain that all the copies are readable.
- Note any 'traps', such as the postcode problem above. Note, too, any areas that must not be completed – such as those marked 'for office use only'. Check those questions where optional answers (eg complete A *or* B) are required, or those where you may have to 'jump' a few questions, eg *If you have answered 'yes' to question 4, move to question 8.*
- Check if there are any questions that
  - do not apply to you (in which case enter N/A for 'not applicable' – do not leave any blanks as this implies you haven't read the question)
  - you do not understand (ask someone for help if you cannot work out what it is they want to know)
  - you are unsure about, or need time to find out the answer.
- Take care entering your date of birth (many people write the current year by mistake) and note the format requested (often DD/MM/YY, eg 20/04/80).
- Use block capitals where you are told to do so.
- Write neatly.
- If you have to include an explanation or comment at any point draft it out first, so that you can phrase it to the best of your ability. If the space for

such comments is restricted, then retain all your key facts but reduce the amount of additional information you give. (See resumés and summaries, Unit 10.)

- Check your spelling very carefully. If you have made an error (in ink!) then there are one or two products on the market now that can very cleverly conceal a minor error – but not a major one.
- Don't forget to sign and date the form (if required) and to enclose any other documents necessary.

## Test your understanding

Collect at least three forms such as holiday booking forms (found in the centre or back of all holiday brochures), insurance proposal or claim form, application for a driving licence, mail order form, application form to open a bank or building society account, or a college application form.

Complete these neatly and accurately with your personal details. Score yourself highly if you make no errors. Lose one point every time you reach for the liquid paper!

HIGHTOWN TERTIARY COLLEGE
Barbary Walk
HIGHTOWN
HG1 3ML

Tel: 01928 606060 Principal: Marsha Larraby MA

Date

Dear Student

**LIBRARY BOOKS**

The following book(s) you ordered are now available for collection:

**Title** **Author** **Publisher**

Please note that we will reserve these books for your use for one week from the date of this letter. If you cannot collect them within this time, you are advised to contact the library staff immediately.

Yours sincerely

Marian Delaney
Head Librarian

***Figure 5.4*** *A form letter*

## FORM LETTERS

Organisations may issue a form letter when they have to provide the same type of information on a regular basis. An example would be a standard letter from your college library informing you that a book you have ordered is now available. In this case, the library staff would have a printed supply of form letters and would complete each one with the details, probably in handwriting, as required.

An example of this type of letter is shown in Figure 5.4.

### COMPOSING A FORM LETTER

A form letter is often sent as a reminder or as a response to a request. There is usually a clear heading so that the recipient can quickly identify the subject. There is usually no need for a long introduction – the information is given clearly and simply.

At the outset, identify the information that will be variable in each letter – this will be added later. It may be personal information, dates and times or other specific details.

Bear in mind that even though a form letter may be short, it must still be courteous!

## DESIGNING A FORM LETTER

A form letter is set out according to normal letter conventions. In addition, make sure you

- leave space for the date unless you have been asked to put 'Date as postmark' at the top
- leave sufficient space for the name and address, if required
- make sure you know where to leave any blanks in the text of the letter for specific details, and that you leave sufficient room for these
- check the salutation required. Either leave a blank after the word 'Dear' (where the name is completed in writing) or a use **generic** name. This means a word applying to everyone who would receive a letter. Examples include: Dear Colleague, Dear Parent, Dear Customer, Dear Supporter.

It is normal to include the complimentary close, name of writer and designation as usual.

## COMPLETING A FORM LETTER

If you are completing a form letter by hand, use very neat handwriting, make certain there are no spelling mistakes and check for omissions! Word processors enable many form letters to be held as 'templates' and completed on screen. This is discussed in Unit 8.

## ENVELOPES

The envelopes you will use at work usually come in two colours – brown and white – in various sizes and styles. The main ones you are likely to meet are

- pocket envelopes – where the opening is at the short side
- banker envelopes – where the opening is at the long side
- window envelopes – which have a transparent covering over the address area. These save you the task of printing an envelope as the address on a document will show through the transparency – providing you manage to fold it correctly.

Brown envelopes are cheaper than white ones and are usually used for invoices and other routine mailings of booklets, brochures, price lists, etc. White banker envelopes are usually preferred for letters. DL (de luxe) size enables you to fold a normal A4 document into three (see Figure 5.5) for insertion.

If you are using window envelopes, start with a crease below the address, in line with the bottom of the envelope, and work from there. If you are lucky, the paper may have a small black mark at the left hand side to guide you

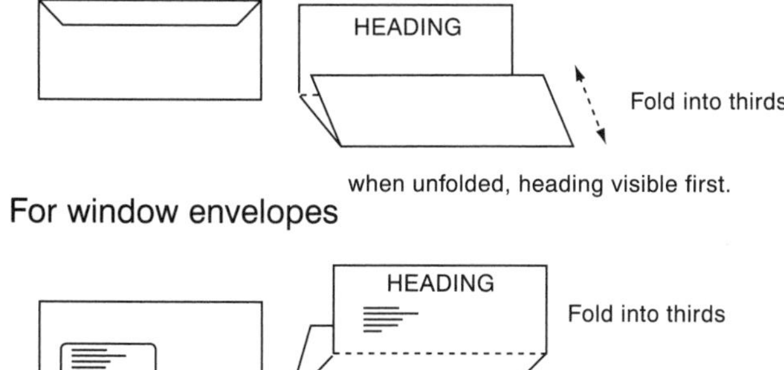


***Figure 5.5*** *Folding A4 paper*

(see Figure 5.5). Otherwise, it's sensible to practise on pieces of A4 paper with a large 'X' marked in the strategic position, before you ruin a beautifully produced letter with fold lines in the wrong places! Remember that it is the bottom fold that is crucial – if the letter is free to move about inside the envelope it is likely that the last lines of the address will disappear when it is handled.

The cheaper types of envelopes are those you have to lick. To remove the need for this unhygienic and unsafe practice (it's easy to cut your tongue), most organisations now use self-seal envelopes. Test for this before starting to seal! Otherwise hunt down one of the special sponges that can be dampened for sealing envelopes, especially if you have several to seal.

## WRITING ENVELOPES

A word processing package will set out and print envelopes quickly and easily. However, there may still be occasions when you have to write an envelope. Check that you are familiar with the correct way to do this.

- Start the envelope half way down and one-third of the way across (the aim is for the address to be in a central position on the envelope).
- Start each line at the same point.
- Always include the name of the addressee and his/her title.
- Start a new line for each line of the address.
- Always put the postal town in CAPITALS.
- Don't use abbreviations (eg St for Street or Rd for Road) apart from official abbreviations for very long county names (eg Glos for Gloucestershire).
- The postcode should be the last item and should preferably be written on a separate line. It must *not* contain any punctuation, neither should your address lines have any punctuation at the end.
- Letters being sent abroad should have *both* the city (or town) *and* the country in capitals. Don't be surprised if the 'order' for the address is slightly different – in some countries the town is shown before the street, or the number is shown after the street name.
- Any special mailing instructions, eg airmail or urgent, should be written at the top left-hand side
- If the item must be marked PERSONAL (or Private and Confidential) then this is written two lines above the address.
- If you are sending a package, it is normal to write the name and address of the sender on the reverse.

## Test your understanding

**1** Many forms ask questions about you using terms you may not be familiar with.

Check your understanding by giving an accurate answer to each of the following questions.

**i** What is your **DOB**?
**ii** Who is your **next of kin**?
**iii** Have you any **siblings**?
**iv** Please state your **forename(s)**
**v** What is your **nationality**?
**vi** What is your mother's **maiden name**?
**vii** Are you the **tenant** of a property?
**viii** Have you any **dependants**?
**ix** What is your **residential address**?
**x** Do you have any **unearned income**?
**xi** What is your **health record**?

**2** You have been asked to address one envelope for the UK and two envelopes for items being sent abroad. Test your copying skills *and* your envelope writing skills by making out an envelope to each of the following organisations.

**a** Canadian Airlines International, 23–59 Staines Road, Hounslow, Middlesex TW3 3HE
**b** Nippon Shoko Kaigi-sho, 3-2-2, Marunouchi, Chiyoda-ku, Tokyo 100, Japan
**c** Camara de Comercio de la Republica de Cuba, Calle 21, No 661/701, Esq Calle A, Apartado 4237, Vedado, Havana, Cuba

## WORDBANK 4

There is a considerable difference between each of the following pairs of words. Look up the meanings and then use each one in a sentence to check that you understand the difference.

**a** dependent and dependant
**b** discreet and discrete
**c** depreciate and deprecate
**d** leased and least

## SPELLCHECKER 4

The following words are all commonly associated with forms – and frequently mis-spelled! Test your ability to spell each one and practise any you find difficult – as well as entering them into your Spellchecker book. Look up any meanings you don't understand.

**a** enrolment
**b** registration
**c** receipt
**d** install/instalment
**e** commitment
**f** appraisal
**g** confidential
**h** initial
**i** application
**j** omissions

## Test your skills

**1** Visit a post office and obtain a passport application form (even if you already have a passport!). *On your own* identify which form you should complete if you were renewing an existing passport and then complete all the details neatly and clearly. List the other items you would have to include if you were sending off the form. Check your completed form and your list with your tutor.

**2** You have recently bought an answering machine for your home. When you purchased it, the sales person advised you not to record a message saying that you were out, but to use some other phrase to indicate you were unable to answer.

- **a** Why do you think it is inadvisable to say you are not at home on a personal answering machine?
- **b** Write out a suitable message you could record on your machine.
- **c** If possible, tape yourself reading this and then listen to it. Evaluate your clarity and tone, and try not to be too distracted by the sound of your own voice!

**3** Select any page from this book (or any other) and tape yourself reading it. Don't be critical about your accent – which you can't help – or the way in which you express the content when you read (you're not entering a drama festival!). Instead, listen to your pace (too fast or too slow?) and your clarity and volume. Having listened to yourself, retape the passage and see if you can improve. Remember to keep your head up and try to project your voice without shouting. (If you have no access to a tape recorder, practise by reading out loud, when there is no-one about, and try to pace and moderate your voice.)

**4** Correct all the errors you can find in the following sentences. The number of errors in each one is shown in brackets afterwards.

- **a** Its long been the case that employer's have prefered to higher staff who show inishative. (5)
- **b** Anyone whom takes a message must rememmber to be discrete when dealing with confidentail information. (4)
- **c** Many organisations prefer to have least cars rather than buy them outwrite because of the deprecation factor. (3)
- **d** John went with Mark to hand in his form and obtain a reciept. (2)
- **e** He's definately got an interview at tescos head office and is confidant itl'l go well. (5).
- **f** Whose taken todays paper and moved it from it's usual place by the window? (3)

**g** There apointment is on 2 febuary. (4)
**h** He said he had many clients that prefered to pay in installments and all aplications were treated in confidance. (5)

## Apply your skills

Jane Mitchell, the Senior Receptionist at Riverside Small Animal Centre, is packing up for the night and so are you. You are both tired and ready for home. John Higgins, on the other hand, is pleased about the success of his new idea to provide a range of items for pet owners, such as engraved identification tags, personalised pet beds and feeding bowls. The following conversation takes place between the three of you.

**John** *(Flipping through the new order book)* Well, six more items ordered today. That is good news. The extra income will be useful – especially as the extension is likely to cost a little more than we planned.

**Jane** *(Putting on her coat)* The problem is that we now have the problem of storing all these items when they arrive and ringing people to tell them to collect them. There seem to be more and more routine jobs every day. So much so, that yesterday I forgot to send the stationery order.

**John** What sort of routine jobs? In this place, apart from appointments, the main focus is on the clients and their pets.

**Jane** Well, for a start there's all the routine vaccinations. We really should have a reminder system for those. Over a twelve-month period people forget – and then their pets are vulnerable.

**John** Yes, I take your point. Has either of you any ideas?

**You** I suppose we could have a form letter for the vaccinations where we simply fill in the details from the computer. We could print out dozens and then fill them in during the last week of the month with all the reminders for the following month.

**Jane** We could do the same thing for the pet items people buy – fill in the details of their order on a standard reminder letter when the items arrive. *(Looks at you)* If I put the main points on a note tomorrow, would you draft out a couple of letters and test them with information from the computer and the order book?

**You** No problem. I'll do it first thing. Can I write in the information or do you want it printed?

**John** Good heavens, no. We might try that later. No, just write it if this is easier. *(To Jane)* What about this stationery order then?

**Jane** I rang Mark at Trivan Supplies and agreed to fax the order tomorrow. *(Looks towards you)* Sorry – could you do that as well? It really should go first thing. If it does, he's promised everything will be delivered by 4 pm.

**John** And can I ask a couple of favours, too? *(He waves an envelope in the air.)* Natalie's tried her hand at envelopes but I've never seen anything like it. Try to straighten her out, will you –

preferably without reducing her to tears! And I've been meaning to do a memo about the items we have on sale here and the discounts for staff. If I give you my notes tomorrow, could you write it up for me?

**You** Yes, but can I have everything fairly early. I'd like to be straight by 2.30 if I can.

**John** No problem. Right – time we were all getting home. Either of you want a lift?

*Please send to all staff under my name. Today's date.*

*Heading: PET SUPPLIES*

*Please say the following.*

- *We have now started selling pet supplies in reception in addition to biscuits and other recommended food products.*
- *Items include collars, leads, litter trays.*
  *Some items can be personalised, such as food dishes and mats, pet beds and engraved name tags.*
- *There is a price list in reception but all staff will get 20% discount on ordinary items and 15% discount on engraved items.*
- *All orders should be given to Jane Mitchell or to yourself.*

*Thanks*

*John*

**Figure 5.6** *John's notes for a memo*

URGENT

```
Mrs Jane Reid
      General manager,
      White swan Hotel,
      High St
      Dawsey Villedge
      Hightown HG10, 6PT.
```

**Figure 5.7** *Natalie's envelope*

**1** Stationery is supplied to Riverside by Trivan Stationery Supplies. Your contact there is Mark Richardson. Prepare a fax which refers to Jane's telephone conversation and to which you could attach the stationery order. Put a clear heading so that Mark can easily identify the reason for the fax. Your order number is S/129/JM. Remind him of his promise to deliver by 4 pm. Note that you will sign it yourself.

**2** John's notes for his memo are given in Figure 5.6. Expand these to produce a short memo for all the staff about the new items on sale in reception. Make sure that you exclude all the comments that are just for you!

**3** Natalie's envelope is shown in Figure 5.7.

- **a** Identify all the mistakes she has made and rewrite the envelope so that she can use it as a model for the future.
- **b** In a brief memo to your tutor, explain how you would talk to Natalie about her mistakes so that she wouldn't become unduly upset.

**4** Jane's notes for the form letters are shown in Figure 5.8. Use these to produce two form letters and check your wording and spaces with your tutor. When the wording is agreed, test that they would be satisfactory by inserting the details of two clients. Note that if you can type these out before adding the details this will give an even better indication of whether the letters would be suitable.

Note that Jane has asked you to undertake one other task for her. Make sure you do this, too!

*Form letters*

*1 Please make the first very short and simple. Leave space for the name and address and the name after the salutation. Head it Vaccination Reminder.*

*First paragraph - please ask them to note that their pet is due for a booster vaccination and general health check next month. After the word 'pet' leave space for the name.*

*Second paragraph - ask them please to telephone the centre to arrange a suitable appointment. Please put my name at the bottom.*

*2 The second I'm sure you can compose yourself. Please think of an appropriate heading. Refer to their recent order - then leave a space for us to write in the items. Please say the items will be kept for two weeks and if they can't collect them in that time to let us know.*

*If you want to test your letters then try the following:*

*Mr J Harvey, 14 Coalbrookdale Avenue, Hightown, HG3 2RM should bring his cat Daniella for her injections next month.*

*Mrs June Stevenson of 14 Willow Close, Hightown 4HG 2SL ordered a dog basket - large size - for her labrador, Spacey, and an identification disk for her cat, Pollux.*

*Incidentally, do you think we need window envelopes for these? In which case, please send a fax to Mark ordering 5,000. If you're quick, he may be able to deliver them with the other order this afternoon!*

*Thanks*

*Jane*

***Figure 5.8*** *Notes from Jane Mitchell*

## WORD WIZARD

For this word wizard you need to be able to read carefully!

**a** Spot the difference between the two identically worded letters
**b** Say why punctuation can be critical!

*Dear Steve*

*I have always wanted a man who knows what loyalty and commitment is all about. You are kind, thoughtful, considerate. Individuals who are not like you admit to being inadequate and worthless. You have completely ruined me for other men. I long for you. I have no feelings at all when we're apart. I can always be happy – will you let me be yours?*

*Susie*

*Dear Steve*

*I have always wanted a man who knows what loyalty and commitment is. All about you are kind, thoughtful, considerate individuals, who are not like you. Admit to being inadequate and worthless. You have completely ruined me. For other men, I long. For you, I have no feelings at all. When we're apart I can always be happy. Will you let me be?*

*Yours*

*Susie*

# IN THE SPOTLIGHT – NOTE-TAKING

The ability to make an accurate and concise set of notes is an invaluable skill – as a student, as an employee and in your private life. It makes most jobs much easier and gives you the potential to master other skills you may have once thought were beyond you. You have already been practising your note-taking skills while studying how to take a telephone message. In this section we will look at more advanced note-taking skills, which are invaluable in a wide range of situations.

You will be expected to be able to make notes:

- when you are being given instructions or information verbally
- if you are involved in meetings or discussions
- if you are asked to undertake any type of research
- if you are asked to attend any type of event and report back afterwards
- if you are expected to summarise or re-arrange any relatively lengthy material into a more concise form
- if you are asked to prepare a fact sheet or other summary document containing only the key information required.

The more advanced applications of note-making will be covered in later units. At this stage, you need to concentrate on learning the basic skills. To learn note-taking you need to exercise control – over your listening and reading skills, interpretation skills, concentration and writing ability.

## The purpose of notes

Understanding the reason for taking notes is important – otherwise it becomes a pointless exercise. The main purpose is to help you to remember what you were told, what occurred or what you read at a particular time. If you are concentrating, then making brief notes helps you to reconstruct the rest of the information later.

A further benefit is that this in itself helps to improve your memory as, in effect, you receive a 'double dose' of the information – once when you make the notes, the second time when you read them or write them. At work, developing a good memory is a major attribute. It saves you time looking for information and makes you an invaluable employee.

PREPARING NOTES FROM A BOOK – LECTURE 10 OCT

Select topic from index

Read first for meaning

Read again - highlight key points (not in library book!)

Decide own title

Decide own headings

Re-read first section

Write key points in own words - briefly - ignore examples/adjectives

Leave space before next heading - for further info if nec.

For revision - use capitals, numbered points, indents to help jog memory

Do all sections - check if complete against original

Reduce again if too long (on to card for presentation aid/easy revision)

Put source of material if useful.

## Good notes and bad notes

Everyone takes notes in slightly different ways – so don't expect yours to look exactly the same as everyone else's. The majority of people write sequential notes, which are lines of writing identifying the main points in the order in which they were discussed. Sometimes these need changing around when they are written up afterwards, as the order may not be the most logical. Some people, however, prefer to create diagrammatic notes, which are more graphic. Which you choose is up to you, provided that your notes pass the ultimate test – that is, that you can understand them and they provide the information you need.

An example of both types of notes is shown in Figure 6.1. Lucy and Dean have both been to a talk on how to make notes from a book. Lucy has written each point sequentially. Dean prefers the diagrammatic approach. See which one you would prefer.

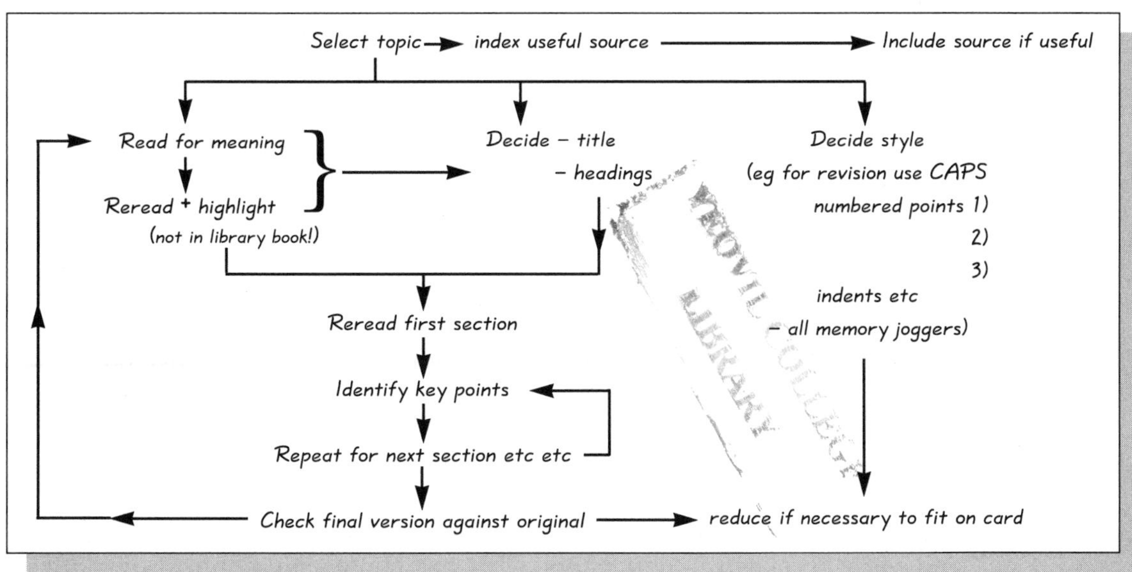




***Figure 6.1*** *Lucy's sequential notes and Dean's diagrammatic notes*

### GOOD NOTES

Useful notes have a clear heading – it is obvious what they relate to – and they are dated. This is very important at work when you may make notes on the same topic on different occasions and need to know which is the latest version. Good notes also have the following characteristics:

- they are brief and don't contain unnecessary or irrelevant information
- they are divided into sections when they are lengthy, under sub-headings, so that information on different aspects or topics can be found easily
- they are clear and easy to read
- they contain all the key facts about names of people and places, dates, and other sources of useful information
- they are organised into a logical pattern.

## Problems with note-taking

People encounter problems when

- they have to take notes under pressure
- they don't understand the subject matter
- the note-taking session lasts a long time
- they lose concentration
- the 'source' of the notes is difficult to follow
- they write too much
- they cannot read or understand their own notes afterwards.

We will now look at each of these potential problems, before you start to practise your own skills.

### OPERATING UNDER PRESSURE

You are more pressurised taking notes while someone is speaking than making notes from a book, when you can take your time and flick back through the pages to check information. It is also more stressful to take notes if you are the only person doing it and you think everyone is watching you, or if your notes must be read by other people. Therefore, the most advanced skill is to be a minute taker at a meeting – and we will slowly build up to this stage.

### THE SUBJECT MATTER

Imagine hearing this announcement on the news. 'Fog caused a series of accidents on the M25 this morning. At least 25 vehicles were involved in a multiple pile-up. Police blamed the high speed of drivers who were not taking account of the conditions. At least seven people are feared dead and over 30 have been taken to hospital with injuries.' You would probably have no difficulty repeating to a friend later 'In that multiple pile-up on the M25 this morning they said seven people died and over 30 were injured.' Similarly, if your friends missed the first 10 minutes of a film, you would probably have few problems bringing them up to date.

In both cases you would have made a 'mental note' of the key facts quickly and easily because you understood what was happening. Contrast this with watching the first 10 minutes of a documentary on Renaissance painters, or

*Today in Parliament,* where you would understandably have more difficulty, unless you are an expert on these areas.

It is, of course, possible to make a brief note about something you do not understand. However, for it to make sense when you write it up or use it later you *must* find out what it means. Equally, you can familiarise yourself with terms you are likely to hear at work by looking through past documents or files – or by asking someone.

## LENGTHY SESSIONS

It is much easier to make notes during a five-minute session than during a meeting which lasts an hour. This is because your concentration must be sustained over a longer period and you are more likely to be distracted. Your notes may become sloppier and then improve a little towards the end, when the session is drawing to a close. The problem is that when you write up your notes afterwards you find that the middle part causes the most problems, as both your concentration and your note-taking skills were at their worst.

Experience is the key here. The more experienced you become, the longer you can sustain your concentration – but this does take some effort as well as practice!

## RETAINING CONCENTRATION

Concentration relates to the skill of 'learning to listen' in Unit 4. It is easier to concentrate if you are fresh and wide-awake, if the topic is interesting, the speaker is entertaining and there are few distractions. You need to make a conscious effort to keep 'switched on' during a lengthy session. If you are making notes from a written source then take a short break if you find your concentration wandering and then return to the task afresh.

## THE DIFFICULT SOURCES

It is much easier to make notes if someone starts by saying 'I have three points to make on this topic. The first is . . . .' If the information seems to arrive in a jumble, you have to sort out yourself. In many cases you will need to re-order and re-write notes in a sensible and logical sequence. Word processing packages have made this task much simpler, as you can easily move text about on screen.

## WRITING TOO MUCH

This is a common fault with new, conscientious note-takers who are worried about missing anything out. The problem is that even if you are successful and write nearly everything down, you have the task of sorting through the pages afterwards to find what you need. Knowing what to leave out is therefore as important as knowing what to write! This is a skill you will develop as you work through this book.

### READING YOUR NOTES

If your handwriting is poor, you are scribbling under pressure and are writing too much then you may have great difficulty interpreting your squiggles afterwards. For this reason, people often develop a personal abbreviation system for writing down common words or technical terms they use regularly. This is fine, as long as you keep to the same abbreviation every time you use a particular word. Serious problems will occur, however, if you are tempted to write an initial letter to represent a word you think you will remember later. 'J going to P on Sat' means nothing! Always write names, places and dates in full.

## Hints and tips

- For a long session use a large sheet of paper (eg an A4 pad) to save time turning over pages.
- Have a spare pencil or pen available, in case something goes wrong with the one you are using.
- Write a clear heading and the date at the top.
- Use appropriate sub-headings wherever they help.
- If you are working from a written source, start by reading the information and highlighting every key point you read (see Figure 6.1 on page 99).
- Leave a gap between each heading, in case you need to add more information later.
- Abbreviate common words using a system you can follow (see below).
- Write in note form, rather than using proper sentences, eg 'Martin visit Luton branch Wed re container prob' rather than 'Martin will visit our Luton branch on Wednesday to discuss the container problem.'
- Disregard superfluous information, eg examples, stories to illustrate a point, unimportant background material
- If someone is speaking, listen for the words that are stressed or information that is repeated.
- In a lecture or presentation, use any visual aids as your focus – these usually summarise the key points.
- Don't panic if you miss something. Keep concentrating on what is happening now.
- If something is said that you do not understand, draw a circle around it to remind yourself to check it afterwards.
- Write up draft notes as soon as possible.

## Test your understanding

1 During a brief session with her boss, an administrator made the following notes. They have been written in note form using simple abbreviations for common words.

**a** Write out the notes in proper sentences putting all the abbreviations in full. KH is Keith Hall, the person who is calling the meeting.
**b** Draft the content of an e-mail notifying staff about the meeting, putting all the information in a logical order.

Metg of safety cmte – room 326 Thur 2 pm. Special metg re new safety regs rec'd last wk. Imp all attend. All must cfm asap + hv with them copy of regs sent by KH thru mail Fri last. Metg shd last 1 hr.

**2** The following notes were made during a telephone conversation. The person speaking did not discuss the topics in a logical order.

**a** Reorder the notes logically, as they should appear in a message.
**b** Write out a suitable message for the recipient.

**Tel call** – 3.15 pm
Query re tel msge he recd
Recd by switchboard op at Trivan Stat Supplies 10 am
Someone here asked to change order for window envs from 1,000 to 5,000
We sent fax 2 days ago – official order no 2038
BUT no window envs in fax msge!
Their tel no 408398
Stat order being despatched 10 am
Cannot incl any wind envs unless we fax proper order
Pse advise asap – caller Richard Blackthorpe ext 251
Msge to Jane Mitchell

**3** Test your listening skills and your note-taking skills! Radio 4 has many speech-based programmes on current affairs. Identify one of these and listen to the first 15 minutes. Make a note of the key items discussed (just main headings will do). Later you can develop your skills to make more comprehensive notes. A useful idea is to do this with a friend and then compare your notes afterwards.

## POLISH YOUR PUNCTUATION

### The hyphen

Hyphens are mainly used to join words together to express a single idea, eg daughter-in-law, half-term and self-help.

Many compound words that were originally hyphenated have now evolved into complete words in their own right without the hyphen, eg teen-age and play-group. However, although the use of the hyphen is declining with some words, with others it is still essential.

It is mainly used in the following cases:

- To separate a prefix, where joining it would result in a different meaning entirely. Examples include

| | |
|---|---|
| re-count (to count again) | recount (to tell or narrate) |
| re-cover (to cover again) | recover (to get better) |
| re-sign (to sign again) | resign (to leave voluntarily) |

- Between letters that repeat and could be confusing or difficult to read, eg co-operation, re-employ, part-time. Negative words sometimes do not take a hyphen, eg uncooperative and uncoordinated.

- To join a prefix to a proper noun, a number or an abbreviation, eg pre-Shakespeare, post-1700 or non-EU countries.
- Where the prefix substantially alters the meaning of the word, eg anti-hero, non-smoker, semi-literate. However, you should check in a dictionary as some words are joined together, eg antifreeze, nonsense, semicircle
- To separate a noun from a preceding letter, eg X-ray, U-turn.
- When a compound word is used to describe someone or something, eg red-haired girl, high-class restaurant, low-calorie diet. But note that if you put the description after the noun, the hyphen is dropped, therefore: The girl was red haired. The restaurant is high class. The diet is low calorie.
- To remove confusion and ambiguity. The most famous example is the sentence 'There were 20-odd men.' This obviously has a very different meaning from 'There were 20 odd men.'

## Hyphen problems

You can check whether a word should be hyphenated or not by looking in a dictionary. However, two areas where you may hesitate and be unsure of the correct procedure is when you are faced with a trailing hyphen or have to split a word at the end of a line.

### TRAILING HYPHENS

These occur when you are typing a list of items, all of which would normally be hyphenated, eg *You have the option of buying a first-, second- or third-class ticket*. Although this is not technically incorrect, in most business documents it is more usual to repeat the noun, eg *You have the option of buying a first-class, second-class or third-class ticket*.

### HYPHENS AT LINE ENDINGS

If you use a computer and a word processing package, you will usually have no need to worry about words at line endings, as the software is designed to justify your right margin if you want it to. This means that it will have a straight, not ragged, edge with all words ending at the same point.

If you are using handwriting, or do not have access to computer justification, you may find yourself having to put a very long word at the end of a line.

- Always try to divide the word so that it will help the reader eg *green-house* (not *greenh-ouse*) and *deter-mination* or *determina-tion* (not *determi-nation*)
- Do not split short words, proper nouns (starting with a capital), abbreviations and figures.

## Test your understanding

Insert all the omitted hyphens in the following sentences.

1. You will need to reestablish communications with them on the spot.
2. He's a self made man but since his accident he's been a non driver.
3. Take the right hand bend at the T junction then move to the left hand lane.

4 The used car salesman strongly promoted the four door saloon claiming it was a once in a lifetime opportunity.

5 There was a dispute at the all party committee meeting between the pro Europeans and the anti Europeans.

6 Non fattening foods are a well known feature of most diets, particularly post 1990.

7 I need an up to date print out of the weekly takings from our self service restaurant immediately.

8 The infra red camera is a recent development, as is ultra sound which has replaced X rays in many cases because it is safer.

9 He was co opted onto the committee because of his first rate knowledge of the subject.

10 The train travels non stop through the two week trip on a never to be forgotten journey of discovery.

## WORDBANK 5

Read each of the following sentences and then say what you are doing – this means you have to establish the meaning of the word in bold. Enter all new words into your Wordbank book.

1 You are acting under **duress**.
2 You are **complacent** about your recent test results.
3 You are **dogmatic** about an issue.
4 You are **empathising** with a friend.
5 You are involved in a **fracas**.
6 You are being **intransigent**.
7 You are **malingering**.
8 You are in a **quandary**.
9 You are **remonstrating** with someone.
10 You are **stymied**.

## MAKING HEADWAY – telephone calls and letters

In the previous units you have looked at answering the telephone and taking a simple message. You have also written some short letters. It is now time to extend your skills by looking at occasions when you will have to take the initiative in these areas.

## Making a telephone call

It is not enough to be able to answer incoming calls. You will also be expected to make calls yourself, both on your own behalf and for other people. Making a call isn't difficult. The secret is to remember the following rules.

- Prepare for the call by noting down all the facts you must mention in a logical order. Leave space alongside to write down answers to questions you are asking or points you are raising.
- Check that you have written down the correct number to call.

- Dial the number carefully.
- When you are connected, check you are through to the right number and then ask for the person (or department) you want to speak to.
- Be prepared to give your own name and that of your organisation – as you will often be asked to say who is calling.
- Greet the person properly and introduce yourself again – in case the switchboard operator hasn't repeated your name or organisation clearly.
- State the facts you need to mention. Don't speak too quickly or gabble the information.
- Make clear notes on the responses you receive.
- Tick each question or fact on your list as you say it, so that you don't repeat yourself or forget anything.
- If you don't understand something you are told, ask the other person to repeat or explain it. Don't assume any lack of understanding is your fault. The person may be using jargon or referring to a complex issue you can't be expected to know about.
- Be aware that, according to telephone etiquette, the person who makes the call should conclude it. Therefore, when you have obtained all the information you need, thank the other person and say goodbye.

## GIVING A GOOD IMPRESSION

Experienced telephone users have one or two other tricks that help to make them sound professional on the telephone. These include:

- using a person's name during the conversation, which makes the other person feel more important
- knowing that if they smile during the conversation this is audible in their voices and makes them sound more friendly and helpful
- saying figures in pairs (eg 24-56-23) because they are easier to understand and note down than figures read in threes (eg 245-623)
- saying 'zero' rather than 'nought' or 'oh' – again because it is clearer
- knowing that if they are cut off during the conversation, the person who made the call should attempt the reconnection
- using the telephone alphabet to spell out difficult names (see Unit 5).

## Test your skills

1 Next time you need to ring an organisation – such as your bank, building society or a retail store – use this as good experience. Prepare properly and make notes on the conversation.

2 You are a student, you left home six months ago and are living in a flat with a friend from another course. This morning you both received a council tax bill for £450. Your tutor says that she thinks you should both have registered with the local council as students and you need a certificate from the college to prove this. She suggests you ring the council immediately.

Make notes to prepare for this call, using the name of any friend you wish! List all the facts you think may be needed and all the questions you should ask.

3 You have the opportunity to go with friends to Greece at the end of August. You are desperate to earn some money and see an advertisement (Figure 6.2) in the paper. Assuming you are preparing to telephone, make notes on the facts you would relate about yourself and the questions you would ask about the jobs. Compare your notes with those of other members of the group.

***Figure 6.2***
*A newspaper advertisement*

*CALLING ALL STUDENTS!*

**SEASONAL VACANCIES – GOOD RATES OF PAY**

Modern leisure complex with friendly staff has limited number of vacancies for lively, extrovert young people who enjoy working with youngsters.

Must be fit and active and willing to work shifts during summer months.

**Ring NOW for information – and to tell us why you would be suitable.**

Marvin Bates, Hightown Leisure Complex, Hightown
Tel: 01928 608585

## Composing a letter

There are many occasions when you have to put something in writing. Most job advertisements specify a written response. You already know that if you make a hotel booking, you are often expected to confirm it in writing. You may often be expected to compose a suitable letter to put facts in writing. This is not difficult if you think first!

### PREPARING TO WRITE A LETTER

There is nothing worse than a staring at blank sheet of paper when you haven't a clue what to write. Two tactics can help you overcome this problem.

1 Plan your letter. This means sorting your information into a logical order and dividing into three sections.

- Your first section will be your reason for writing – it may be in response to a letter, telephone call or personal enquiry. If there is a fact known to both you and the recipient it is usual to start with this. If not, state why you are writing, so that the reader knows the subject of the letter.
- Your second section provides details and relevant information. It is normal to start a new paragraph for each topic you raise.
- Your third section relates to what happens next (if anything). There is often a brief, courteous and relatively standard sentence to end the letter.

| Starting a letter | Ending a letter |
|---|---|
| Thank you for your letter of 29 June 199- regarding…<br>Thank you for your recent enquiry.<br>Thank you for your recent enquiry concerning…<br>Further to your recent letter regarding…<br>Further to your recent telephone conversation regarding…<br>I refer to our telephone conversation yesterday regarding…<br>We refer to the invoice we sent to you recently for…<br>We refer to the appointment you made recently for… | If you have any queries, please do not hesitate to contact us.<br>If you require any further information, please do not hesitate to contact us.<br>If we can be of any further help, please do not hesitate to contact us.<br>We look forward to hearing from you.<br>We look forward to receiving your reply.<br>I look forward to meeting you.<br>I will contact you again within the next few days to discuss the matter further.<br>Thank you for your help in this matter. |

***Figure 6.3*** *Standard phrases for letters*

**2** Practise some standard phrases. Fortunately many standard phrases are used in business letters, particularly at the beginning and at the end. Knowing these can help you to write a letter more easily, and certainly to start writing without too much hesitation.

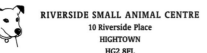

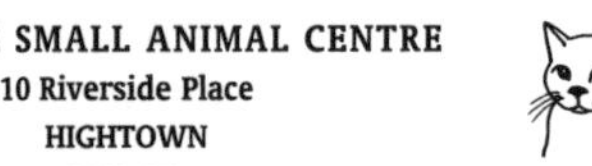

**RIVERSIDE SMALL ANIMAL CENTRE**
**10 Riverside Place**
**HIGHTOWN**
**HG2 8FL**

**Tel: 01928 620938**

16 January 199-

Miss C Sinclair
22 Marydale Road
HIGHTOWN
HG4 1AP

Dear Caroline

**WORK EXPERIENCE**

Further to your recent visit to the centre, we have pleasure in informing you that we are prepared to offer you work experience in the centre for two weeks from 1–14 March 199-. As I mentioned to you, you will be given the opportunity of undertaking both reception and general clerical work, including word processing.

We should be grateful if you would report to reception here at 9 am on Monday, 1 March. Although our permanent staff here work on a rota basis to cover evening reception duties until 7.30 each evening, we are prepared for you to work from 9 am to 5 pm each day, unless you volunteer to work any evenings. Saturday morning working is also optional for students undertaking work experience. You will have one hour for lunch each day, as arranged with Jane Mitchell, our Senior Receptionist.

We look forward to meeting you and hope you will find your time with us both beneficial and enjoyable.

Yours sincerely

John Higgins
Veterinary Surgeon

***Figure 6.4*** *A letter using standard phrases*

The chart in Figure 6.3 shows many of the useful phrases which you can use to start and end a business letter.

There are also many common phrases used within a letter. The more letters you write, the more familiar you become with these.

### DRAFTING THE LETTER

All business letters follow the main conventions you met in Unit 2. A letter using standard phrases to give information in a straightforward way is shown in Figure 6.4. Note that the letter has a clear heading and the order of the information follows the sequence given above.

## Test your understanding

**1** Yesterday, Mrs Joan Barnes called at the Riverside Small Animal Centre with her dog, Sadie. After she had left you noticed that she had left her cheque book on the counter in reception. You tried to telephone her to tell her you had found it but there was no reply. John Higgins suggested you write a brief letter to her, explaining that you have found the cheque book and are returning it to her, and then put it in the envelope.

Draft a short, appropriate letter and check the contents with your tutor.

**2** Your tutor has arranged for a visiting speaker, Mrs Maria Candini, to visit your class. Mrs Candini owns and manages a large employment agency and will tell you about the work carried out there, as well as describing how she first set up the business and how it has grown. You have been delegated to write to Mrs Candini to confirm the arrangements. Your tutor's notes for the letter are shown in Figure 6.5.

```
Name and address: Mrs Maria Candini, Riverside
Employment Agency, Riverside Way, Hightown HG2 3WL

Please put as heading: Talk to Communications Group

Refer to my phone conversation with her yesterday.
Thank her for agreeing to come.

Confirm that the date and time is Wednesday next
at 2 pm. Say you will meet her in reception at
1.30 pm.

Say you have pleasure in enclosing a map which
shows where she can park. Also enclose a visitor's
parking permit (I'll let you have this later)
which must be displayed on her windscreen.

Close by saying you look forward to meeting her.
```

***Figure 6.5*** *Tutor's notes for a letter*

**a** Draft the letter, using your tutor's name where appropriate.

**b** Be careful to extract those comments in the notes that are for you and not for the letter and be careful with your pronouns! There are three people involved – Mrs Candini, you and your tutor.

**c** Check your finished letter with your tutor.

## TOOLS OF THE TRADE – *the communications cycle*

Despite the best attempts of people and organisations to communicate promptly and accurately, things can go wrong. To understand why, it is helpful to study what happens when you communicate with someone – either verbally or in writing.

You have already learned that it is important to

- think and prepare before you communicate
- speak (or write) clearly and unambiguously.

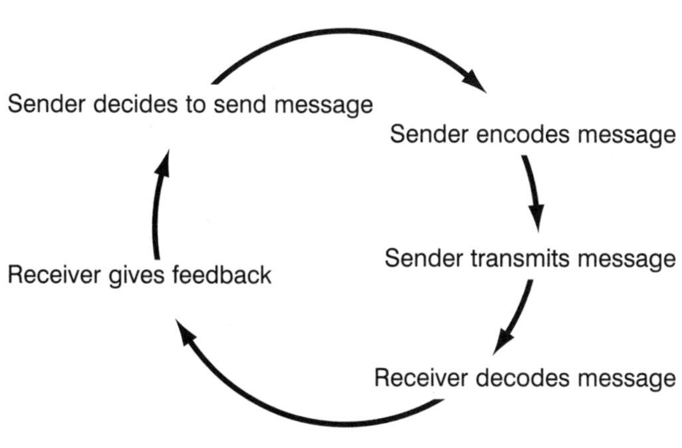


***Figure 6.6*** *The communications cycle*

These two actions relate to the first two stages of the communications cycle, which is shown in Figure 6.6 opposite. At each stage of the cycle, something can go wrong. Knowing where problems can occur means you can take more effective action to prevent them!

### Stage 1 – sender decides to send message

Once you have decided to send a message, you will have problems if you

- do not understand the necessary information
- do not think about how to communicate the message
- have only a vague idea what to say
- have forgotten (or lost) your notes.

**Stage 2 – sender encodes message**

At this stage your message is put into language (or symbols) the other person can understand. This may be written, verbal, graphical or body language. For instance, you may shake your head, and in England this is recognised as meaning 'no'. However, in a few other countries it means 'yes' – so your 'encoding' would be flawed! You must therefore *always* bear in mind the needs of the recipient and the action/response you desire at this stage of the cycle. Problems occur if

- your symbols are unknown to the receiver (eg a foreign language or jargon)
- your symbols are ambiguous, confused, vague or incomplete
- the 'tone' of the symbols is inappropriate for the recipient or situation.

**Stage 3 – sender transmits message**

At this stage you choose the most appropriate communication medium. Problems occur if

- you choose the wrong method for transmission
- your transmission is distorted or interrupted
- the transmission is sent at the wrong time, to the wrong place or the symbols are sent in the wrong order.

**Stage 4 – receiver decodes message**

The receiver has to make sense of the message. Problems will occur if

- the receiver cannot understand the language or symbols
- the receiver stops decoding part way through
- the overall tone of the message is considered inappropriate and these feelings take precedence over understanding the content of the message.

**Stage 5 – receiver gives feedback**

The receiver clarifies understanding by giving feedback. Problems occur here if

- no feedback is given or received
- feedback is sent too late to be useful
- there is no time for feedback.

The cycle may start again here with a further message.

## Developing a conversation

A conversation occurs when the feedback results in the cycle continuing. Some writers liken a successful conversation to a game of tennis, where the ball is passed back and forth between the players. You can't have a conversation unless the other person is willing to keep batting the conversational ball back to you. You will probably have met someone who is difficult to talk to, and answers questions with a few monosyllables, eg

**A** *Have you lived here long?*
**B** *About a year.*

**A** *Oh, as long as that. Where did you come from originally?*
**B** *London.*
**A** *You must find it quite dull here by comparison?*
**B** *I suppose so.*

Eventually A will give up, as the 'ball' never comes back, B catches it and keeps it each time so that A has to find, and throw, another one. A feels like he's banging his head against a brick wall! Compare what happens if B sends the ball back:

**A** *Have you lived here long?*
**B** *About a year. We moved up from London last March. What about you?*
**A** *I was born here, but Sally – my wife – comes from London. She's lived here three years now and enjoys the peace!*
**B** *So do we! It's the crowded train journeys we were glad to leave behind.*
**A** *Oh, I'm sure. Mind you, the traffic around here can be bad, can't it ....*

This is how a conversation develops and how new friends are made. Remember it takes two to make an effort in this situation.

## Test your understanding

Review your understanding of the last five units by deciding at which stage of the cycle communications have broken down in the following situations.

**1** Your brother designs web pages for the Internet. When he tries to tell you about his job, you have only a vague notion about what he really does.

**2** The fax machine cuts out part way through sending a message.

**3** You cannot hear the person who is speaking to you over the telephone because of the roadworks outside.

**4** You have been working hard in your part-time job for a year and were promised a pay review. You start to ask your boss about it just as an important customer walks through the door and shouts her name.

**5** You cannot make yourself understood on an international telephone call.

**6** You have been asked to give a presentation to the rest of your class but didn't allow enough time to find the information you need. As a result you feel that the content was poor.

**7** You annoy a middle-aged customer when you use his first name, despite the fact that you give him some useful information. He tells your boss he considers you presumptuous.

**8** You fail to stop your boss travelling to a cancelled meeting because you found out about the cancellation only after she had left the building.

**9** You forget about the time difference and ring your boss, currently on a trip to San Francisco, as soon as you arrive at work. When you realise how annoyed he is you fail to give him the message properly.

**10** A person you have telephoned complains that she can't possibly remember all the figures you have just read out.

## SPELLCHECKER 5

Each of the following words is commonly used in conversation but also often mis-spelled when it is written. Check that you are confident you can spell all of them correctly. Learn any you are unsure about by heart, writing each one several times. Check, too, the meanings of any words you do not know and write these in your Wordbank book.

| | |
|---|---|
| apparent | alcohol |
| catalogue | controllable |
| disastrous | desperate |
| embarrassed | feasible |
| hazard | infinitely |
| liaison | obedient |
| privilege | queue |
| significant | temporary |
| threshold | transferred |
| voluntarily | wastage |
| weird | withhold |

## COMMUNICATION IN PRACTICE

### Test your skills

**1** Each of the following words has two different meanings, depending upon whether a hyphen is inserted or not. Write down the different meanings in each case

| | |
|---|---|
| **a** recollect | re-collect |
| **b** recreation | re-creation |
| **c** reform | re-form |
| **d** restrain | re-strain |
| **e** redress | re-dress |
| **f** rebound | re-bound |

**2** Carry out a role play with a colleague, choosing one of the scenarios below. Keep the conversation going until your tutor tells you to stop. Any pair running out of things to say has failed! Remember, you have a responsibility to throw back the conversational ball to keep your team in the game.

**a** Your college or school is holding an open night. One of you takes the role of staff representative, on duty to answer questions, and the other takes the role of prospective student.

**b** One of you works for a large electrical retailer and the other wants to buy a portable television for a bedroom.

**c** You are two old friends who haven't seen each other for five years.

**d** You are two strangers who find yourselves standing next to each other at a very boring party to celebrate your aunt and uncle's golden wedding.

**3** Hold a class debate. Divide into two groups, one of which must support the topic and one argue against it. The topic is *The Royal Family gets an unfair press.*

To debate properly you will have to prepare in advance. Each group will need to make notes to support their case. (One of the skills in debating is to argue for something you do not, personally, agree with!) Your tutor will organise the debate and nominate a main speaker for each group. After each main speaker has made his or her case the issue is debated, and the speakers have the right to answer arguments put forward at the end. Then the class votes on the issue. A good debater may persuade you to change your opinion!

Use this exercise as practice in making notes, listening and speaking clearly. Bear in mind that you should make notes when the opposing team are speaking, so that you can challenge some of their points. If anyone misunderstands something, try to think where the communications cycle might have broken down.

**4** Correct any errors in the following sentences and punctuate each one correctly.

**a** The space shuttle is due to reenter the earths atmosphere at two oclock.

**b** Looking forward to seeing you at weston super mare next week.

**c** She was desparate for the job after working on a temporery basis for her last three company's.

**d** The player for liverpool agreed to resign the contact after the board were so complementary.

**e** Some dogs have long and others short haired coats but all should be groomed regularly in addition all dogs enjoy a long walk each day.

*Please can you do me a favour and write a letter to Judith Winters - 14 Beech Grove, Hightown HG3 2MP. Use the model attached as your guide.*

*Tim - her pet - is a golden retriever - aged 7*

*I've booked him in for dental treatment - Thurs 24/11 9 am.*

*Nil by mouth from 2400 hrs Wed because of anaesthetic*

*Est cost £45 unless more work req'd.*

*Please confirm app and send her an info sheet. Shd take 2 - 3 hrs. Tell her she can stay if she would like to.*

*Thanks*

*Jane*

**Figure 6.7a** *Note to you from Jane Mitchell*

## Apply your skills

It is your last week working at Riverside Small Animal Centre. Although you are sad to be leaving you have been offered a more responsible job at Hightown Leisure Complex, where you start next week. The staff have all been very kind to you and you know they intend to take you out on Friday lunchtime for an official goodbye.

In the meantime there are jobs to be done. Jane Mitchell has asked you to write a letter for her and given you a model to work from (see Figures 6.7a and 6.7b). John Higgins has given you a note about two letters he wishes you to write and has asked you to

**RIVERSIDE SMALL ANIMAL CENTRE**
**10 Riverside Place**
**HIGHTOWN**
**HG2 8FL**

**Tel: 01928 620938**

10 October 199-

Mr T Williams
14 Cedar Ridge
HIGHTOWN
HG6 2PN

Dear Mr Williams

Further to our conversation this morning, I confirm that an appointment has been made for your dog, Jasper, to attend the surgery for dental treatment on Tuesday, 24 October at 1 pm. The cost will be approximately £45 unless more extensive work is required.

Please note that as anaesthetic will be given, no food or water should be given to Jasper after 7 am on Monday, 23 October. If you wish to stay you are most welcome, otherwise you will be able to collect him at any time from 4 pm onwards.

I am enclosing an information sheet on the procedure, which will give you other useful information, but please do not hesitate to contact us if you have any further queries or concerns about the treatment.

Yours sincerely

Jane Mitchell
Senior Receptionist

Enc

***Figure 6.7b*** *A model letter to follow*

prepare the letters for his signature (see Figure 6.8). You have also received a note from Tom Davies, written on the bottom of a memo he received from John Higgins (Figure 6.9). You realise fairly quickly that you will have to be tactful when you speak to Mrs Hodgson – as Tom prefers the option of visiting her so that he can see the parrot's surroundings. You will also have to be careful how you ask her about the positioning of the cage. Your preparation for this call will therefore be important.

At present John Higgins is experimenting with a new digital answering machine he has bought. Earlier he asked if you could suggest an appropriate message that could be put on the machine for callers.

Could you please write the following letters for me today.

Letter 1 to Peter Janghir, 14 Manor Drive, Hightown, HG4 3MP.

(For your information, Peter is a sixth-form student hoping to become a vet.)

Please thank him for his enquiry about working on a voluntary basis in the centre over the next twelve months. Then refer to our telephone conversation of this morning and confirm our arrangement for him to visit the centre to meet me and to look around on Thursday morning at 10 am. Tell him to report to Reception and ask him to bring with him his GCSE certificates and his National Record of Achievement.

Letter 2 to Mr J Pickering, 327 North Street, Hightown HG2 1JM. Please refer to the telephone call he made to Jane Mitchell yesterday when he discussed wanting to set up an indoor aquarium. Please tell him that he should really obtain specialist advice as the type of fish he can have indoors will depend upon whether he has cold or tropical water. Also, some fish do not live together very happily so the varieties he selects are important. Tell him the best people to contact are Wetworld Aquatics on Old Bank Road, Hightown, tel 403839. The owner's name is Don Edwards and what he doesn't know about fish isn't worth knowing! (You'd better put this a bit more formally in the letter, please!)

Thanks
John

***Figure 6.8*** *Note requesting two letters*

# MEMO

**TO** Tom Davies

**FROM** John Higgins

**DATE** 7 November 199-

**ANIMAL BEHAVIOUR CONFERENCE, BIRMINGHAM**

As you know, I will be away at the above conference next week. In my absence, would you please see Mrs Tina Hodgson at 3 pm on Wednesday, 12 November, with her parrot, Squawk. It's still losing its feathers and showing other signs of distress. The details you need are in the records – including details of the treatment so far.

If you cannot see her at this time I suggest you ask someone to ring her to re-arrange the appointment – I think it is important she is seen before I return.

Thanks.

*Cannot see her at this time. Pse ring. Either am Thursday or between 5 pm and 7 pm Friday OK. Pse check when you call she has moved cage into lighter area and somewhere where there is more going on – her parrot may be bored! Other alternative – she's up at Bridge End House I think, near the reservoir. I'll be passing there on Thursday afternoon – does she want me to call in? This could be better as I can check the position of the cage etc – see if you can arrange this, could you? Try for about 2 pm if you can!*

*Drop me a note and let me know how you go on!*

***Figure 6.9** A memo with a handwritten note addressed to you*

You want to work as quickly as possible so that you will have time to make some brief notes for Friday, when you will obviously be expected to say thank you and goodbye to everyone. Even though it will be an informal occasion you don't want to be stuck for words and have decided to put a few ideas on a small card you can put in your pocket. You also want to write a personal letter to John Higgins, thanking him for all the help and support he has given to you over the past few months, and for the excellent reference he sent to your new employers.

**1** Write the letter required by Jane Mitchell, using the model she has given you.

**2** Write the two letters required by John Higgins. Be careful to separate his comments to you from the official notes for the letters!

**3** Prepare notes for your telephone call to Mrs Hodgson. If possible, role play the call with a colleague or your tutor. Alternatively, your tutor may ask you to discuss in small groups the best way of communicating this information to achieve your aim.

Mrs Hodgson agrees to a visit on Thursday, but will not be in until 2.30 pm, and also informs you that she has moved the parrot's cage near to the window in the living room. Write a short memo to Tom Davies giving him this information.

**4** Prepare an appropriate message for John Higgins to record on his new answering machine and send this to him as a memo or an e-mail.

**5** Prepare brief notes for your short thank-you speech on Friday. Compare your ideas with other members of your group. Your tutor may wish to select a few speakers at random to give a speech. Remember that in this situation it is not permissible to read from your card – the most you should do is to glance at it occasionally for inspiration!

**6** Write a personal letter to John Higgins to thank him for being so helpful and for giving you such a good reference. Invent other details to make your letter more realistic. Because you will not be using headed paper for this letter, note that you should put your home address at the top right-hand side, using a separate line for each line of the address.

Check your finished work with your tutor.

## WORD WIZARD

Read each of the following 'alternative' definitions and see whether you realise what is clever about each. (It goes without saying that you should also look up any words for which you do not know the *true* definition!)

- adamant — the first insect
- bigamy — the only crime where two rites make a wrong
- bore — a person who talks when you wish him to listen
- censor — a man who knows more than he thinks you should
- desk — a waste paper basket with drawers
- dilate — to live longer
- egotist — a person who's always me-deep in conversation
- fad — in one era and out the other
- impatience — a wait problem
- justice — a decision in your favour
- macadam — first man born in Scotland
- mandate — an appointment with a male
- mayhem — indecision about the best skirt length

# IN THE SPOTLIGHT – READING BODY LANGUAGE

Body language, or non-verbal communication (NVC), is used by every single one of us every waking moment. The way you sit, stand, move and make gestures all reflect your thoughts. Your facial expressions and the way in which you use your eyes are the most obvious indicators – but even where you stand and how you point your feet give valuable clues! 'People watchers' spend hours noticing how people react to a situation and use this to influence the way in which they interpret spoken words. On some occasions, it is possible to tell when someone is saying something he or she does not feel or knows to be untrue.

There are some obvious benefits in appreciating the importance of body language.

- You realise how your own body language is read and interpreted by other people.
- You can use it to improve the effectiveness of your verbal communications.
- You can 'read' other people much better – and adjust your reactions accordingly.

The skill of reading body language is not restricted to your working environment. In your social life you can understand people much better – and the next time you meet someone attractive, you will be able to tell whether he or she is interested in knowing you better or whether you are wasting your time!

Body language can be divided into three separate areas:

1. facial expressions – especially the use of the eyes
2. gestures
3. posture, touching and spatial relationships (ie the distance between people).

Before we study each of these, however, it is useful to note the effect of age on body language. As a general rule, the younger the person, the easier it is to read his or her body language. Young children are particularly transparent, because they haven't yet learned any of the concealing mechanisms we use later in life. If you give a child a present that is a disappointment, this is obvious by the expression on his or her face! When you are in your teens, and the same situation occurs, politeness dictates that you hide your feelings. You try to mask your disappointment and may be able to fool those who don't know you very well, but those close to you will be able to tell how you felt. If you give a gift to your grandparents, however, you may feel exasperated because you cannot tell from their reactions whether they are pleased or not. After years of experience, they can mask their feelings so well that you don't know how they feel unless they tell you!

The same applies to lying. Children who tell a lie cannot resist the overpowering urge to cover their mouths with their hands! In your teens you may partially cover your mouth with one hand, or touch your mouth after telling the lie. As an adult, this is restricted to a brief movement towards the face – or even no movement at all. Those who have to be economical with the truth on a professional basis (eg politicians and lawyers) may have refined their gestures to the extent people cannot tell whether what they are saying is accurate or not!

## Facial expressions

The face is the most expressive part of the body. We smile, frown, grimace, scowl, nod, wink, yawn, blush, blink, stare. We cover our mouths, touch our noses, rub our eyes or ears, scratch our heads, chew our nails, stroke our chins. All these gestures and expressions help to tell a story. And on top of this, we use our eyes. Our eyes are the most expressive part of our body. When we are angry or annoyed our pupils contract; when we are excited or attracted by a person of the opposite sex they dilate. Experienced poker and bridge players have been known to use this to assess whether their opponents have been dealt a good hand or not! You subconsciously look for this signal when you meet a person you find attractive.

We also expect people who are honest to look at us when they are speaking. If they cannot hold our gaze we think they are hiding something. But did you know that where you gaze is also significant? In a business discussion, people will focus above someone's eyes; the lower they focus, the more intimate the gaze. Glancing sideways at someone can indicate interest or unfriendliness. If you glance sideways, slightly raise your eyebrows or smile, you are being welcoming. If you furrow your brow or turn down the corners of your mouth you will appear hostile. The 'come-on' look combines a sideways glance and a slightly intimate gaze. Diana, Princess of Wales was famous for this look, which made her appear approachable and appealing but slightly shy.

Normally, we look at people more when we are speaking to them than when we are listening. This is because we have a natural inclination to watch their expressions to see if they are understanding us and to gauge their reaction. If our listener smiles and nods we take this as approval, and continue. If our listener frowns, coldly stares at us, or narrows the eyes we take this as disapproval. Scratching the head is likely to indicate puzzlement, a wink indicates a joke or empathy, nail chewing (or fingers in the mouth) indicates anxiety, resting the head on the hand indicates boredom, stroking the chin or cheek indicates thinking, rubbing the forehead may indicate acknowledging a mistake whereas rubbing the back of the neck is a 'cover-up' gesture that indicates being annoyed at having been found out in a mistake!

## Gestures

We use gestures for three main reasons:

- to communicate to someone a distance away
- to accentuate what we are saying
- (subconsciously) to echo what we are feeling.

We are all familiar with the 'thumbs-up' gesture – and other gestures that are less socially acceptable! These may be used overtly to give a message to someone with whom we cannot communicate verbally. We also use our hands in other ways. We turn our palms upwards to signal honesty (as with someone holding up a hand when being sworn into a court of law) or to show submission. We point our fingers (or even worse, our thumb) for emphasis. This is normally perceived as being rude – you probably remember being told 'not to point' as a child. We shake hands to signal friendship or acceptance. We rub our hands together if we are cold, but also to indicate glee or expectation. Rubbing the thumb against the fingertips indicates the expectancy of money! We drum our fingers or tap our feet when we feel impatient. We clench our fists tightly if we are under pressure or frustrated and cannot show our feelings. Holding our hands together behind our backs (predominantly a male gesture) signals feelings of superiority. (Think of a burly policeman or security guard in this position, rocking backwards and forwards on his feet.) The front of the body is 'open' in an aggressive stance. Another gesture that implies dominance is putting both hands behind our heads while sitting and leaning backwards.

Conversely, when we feel vulnerable, we cover up our body – by folding our arms and crossing our legs. Some people who are under stress wrap one foot around the back of the opposite calf and sit in a hunched-up position with the head lowered. This is a defeatist position. If we think it would be impolite to fold our arms, we may cover the body with something else – such as a handbag or a file folder – which then acts as a barrier. Someone who can't do this may use a 'disguised' gesture, such as adjusting the shirt cuffs or rubbing the hands together or even playing with a watch strap or bracelet. This enables the arms to be crossed in front of the body – but less overtly.

We adjust the position of our heads according to our reactions. The head is held up and relatively still when we are listening but have not yet made a judgement. If we tilt it to one side we are interested (animals do this as well, particularly if they hear an unexpected noise). If we lower our head we are displeased or feel negative. We often also adjust the position of our body – if you feel excited, nervous or very interested you will lean forwards. Finally, have you ever wondered what prompts you to put your hands on your hips? This is quite an aggressive gesture as it widens your body (your version of a cat puffing out its fur at the sight of a possible enemy!). This pose is often used by models who want to display clothes emphatically, or by men who want to prove their dominance.

It may interest you to know that humans adopt 'courtship gestures' similar to birds when they see someone to whom they are attracted. A man will 'preen' himself by straightening his tie, smoothing his hair, tugging his cuffs. A woman will touch her hair, smooth her clothes, and may toss her hair back if it is long.

## Posture, touching and spatial relationships

If you are interested in something or are feeling confident, you will sit up or stand upright. If you are miserable, depressed or bored you will hunch your shoulders. If you are interested you will lean forwards, towards the object of interest. However, if something threatens you, you may lower your body – showing a subconscious desire to make yourself smaller. This is why bowing and curtseying to royalty is considered deferential. If you lean back you display aggression.

The distance we prefer to leave between ourselves and another person depends upon where we were brought up, how well we know the other person, and the type of situation in which we find ourselves. If someone is a complete stranger then we will try to leave the largest gap – which is why no-one likes being squeezed into a lift or bus with a crowd of strangers. In this situation, we will do our utmost to avoid eye or body contact. If two strangers are alone in a lift they will face away from one another.

The distance we find comfortable depends upon our nationality and whether we were raised in a city or the country. City-dwellers become more familiar with crowded pavements and shops and tend to reduce their distance tolerance, whereas those brought up in a rural area find it more difficult. In Arab or Latin countries, people prefer to stand much closer to strangers than in Britain. If you visited, say, Morocco, you might find yourself constantly moving backwards to maintain the distance you find most comfortable – which your host might interpret as being anti-social!

The more closely two people sit or stand, the more they know or like each other. In this situation their bodies, knees and feet may be angled towards each other. If someone else joins them then they will either 'open up' the circle in acceptance, or just move their heads to look at the person – in which case the interloper feels unwelcome. Similarly, when you are walking and someone stops you, if you like the person and want to talk you will turn your body towards him or her. Otherwise, you will keep your feet and body pointing in the direction you wish to continue, and simply turn your head.

The next time you see two people talking, watch for 'mirror' gestures. This is where one person crosses his or her arms, if the other person does. When one rests his head on his hand, so will the other – and so on. A mirror image shows that the two people are in agreement and in harmony.

If two people constantly touch one another, we often assume they are intimate. However, touching can also be interpreted as displaying feelings of ownership. We touch (or lean on) a new possession we are proud of (such as a new car). If your boss puts his feet up on the desk or your brother has his leg over the arm of a chair, both are signifying the item as their territory (probably because of clothes limitations, women rarely do this!). A man may steer his female relatives by gripping their elbows, or tucking their arm through his – again to denote 'ownership'. Couples may touch each other to prove to their friends that they really have made a conquest! The 'possessiveness' associated with touching is why people often get annoyed if someone is sitting in 'their chair' or using some object of theirs without prior agreement.

## Putting it together

It is impossible to guess someone's feelings by spotting one gesture and trying to interpret this in isolation. But movements made in a 'series' give a more accurate tale. You need to discount obvious physical aspects such as a person being hot, cold or ill, which will also provoke a variety of gestures and movements.

The best way to gain this knowledge is to become a people watcher. In class, in the refectory, at home, at work and certainly on social occasions you can see many movements and gestures – like an unspoken play. Compare your observations with someone else who knows about body language to see if you both come to the same conclusion. Then try to become aware of your own movements at certain points throughout the day. You may notice yourself mirroring a friend, or leaning forwards or back in class. You can be more aware of the gestures and postures you adopt that may be annoying or threatening, as well as be more alert to what the body movements of others are telling you.

## Apply your skills

**1** You visit a supermarket with a friend. How would you explain the following types of body language?

**a** A young girl who works there is being spoken to by an older man in a suit. He has his hands on his hips and is looking at her coldly. She is looking at the floor, head down, and chewing her nails.

**b** Two older women are standing close to them, in the same uniform as the girl. One is looking down and her fists are tightly clenched. The other is standing straight up, looking at the couple, with a slight smile on her face.

**c** A security guard is standing to one side, with his hands gripped behind his back. He stands very erect and is rocking slowly backwards and forwards on his heels.

**d** A man at the delicatessen counter is holding a ticket with a number, waiting to be served. He is continually glancing at the board showing the numbers and drumming his fingers on the counter.

**e** A young trainee manager is standing nearby. He stands straight upright but keeps readjusting his cuffs and touching his watch strap.

**f** Your friend sees a man she knows. She immediately smooths down her skirt and tosses her long hair back as she moves towards him. You see him smoothing his hair as she approaches and lean forward as he says 'Hello'.

**g** Two check-out girls with nothing to do are the mirror image of each other as they sit and chat. Both have one elbow on the counter and are supporting the head with a cupped hand.

**h** An old lady has obviously been parked in a chair, waiting for someone. She clasps her handbag close to her chest and sits hunched up.

**2** Test the distance theory. If you move too close to someone you do not know well, he or she will move away. If you try to talk to a close friend from a distance, he or she will approach you. If you move backwards, he or she will follow! Experiment with this yourself to see it in action.

## *TOOLS OF THE TRADE – proof-reading*

Unless you are a particularly conscientious student, you will be so relieved to have finished a piece of work – whether in writing or typescript – that you will need to summon up every ounce of self-discipline to force yourself to check through it afterwards. The temptation to hand it in (or file it) straight away and move on to something else is almost irresistible.

If you indulge in these habits at work you are likely to encounter serious problems. Why? Because you are human and therefore you make mistakes. This is particularly likely to happen if you are rushed, under pressure or continually interrupted – and all of these situations are typical of a workplace environment.

Checking is both tedious and time-consuming. However, if you are going to be professional, you need to be able to produce professional documents – which means you must stifle any urges to skimp on checking, and think of it as an integral part of preparing a document.

Two skills must be learned if you are to do this properly. One is re-reading, the other is proof-reading.

### Re-reading your work

You re-read your work to evaluate the content and the way you have worded your document. Professional writers prefer to leave their work for a while to 'go cold' before they re-read and correct it. They can then view it more dispassionately. In the first few moments after writing something, you will read what you expect to read – rather than what you have actually written.

### Proof-reading

When you are proof-reading you are looking for fundamental errors, eg mis-spellings, punctuation errors, mistakes that cannot be spotted by your spellchecker (eg 'hid' not 'hide', 'even' not 'event' or 'too' not 'to'). This means you are studying technical accuracy, rather than content.

Some people find it very difficult to proof-read accurately from a computer screen – if this is the case for you, work from a draft print-out. (Setting your printer in draft mode saves money as less ink is used.) Read word by word, rather than reading to understand the content, and check any figures *very* carefully against your original notes or source document. Remember that figures are often the most important part of the document and may be the basis of further calculations or important decisions.

If there are many figures, ask for help. One person can read the document aloud (preferably your helper) and the other person can check from the original. If you have problems keeping your eyes on the correct lines, use a ruler.

Remember, a document that is 99% accurate is not good enough and, if it carries your name, your mistake is advertised in your work. Further, if your boss is willing simply to alter it in pen and sign (or initial) it afterwards, this makes your boss appear kind and you appear sloppy – which is hardly the best impression to create.

## Test your skills

Test your proof-reading skills! Find the errors in the following passage and then write it out correctly. (Fewer than 20 errors and you had better keep looking!)

The increased use of personel computers and the Internet is becoming more widesprread throughout the UK. The result has been a growth in the on-lin services offerred to customers. Many banks, for for instance, offer you the oportunity to control you finances from home, from work or even from abroad, at any hour of the the day or night, simply through the use of a PC and the Internet. Instead of queuing bye a cash machine in the rain, a few clicks with a mice is all it takes to obtain and up-to-the-the-minute balance and to obtain a mini-statement. Bills are paid throough issuing a few simply commands and money can be tranferred between one acocunt and another, quickly and easily. If you are overdrawn in a bad monthe, you can even ask for loan over the Internet, but peraps that is going a little to far!

## WORDBANK 6

Each of the following words, used in the passage above, may be unfamiliar to you. In each case

- look up the meaning of the word
- write another sentence of your own to show that you understand the meaning
- add the word to your Wordbank book
- check that you can spell the word without any problems. Those that commonly cause difficulties are marked with an asterisk (*).

**a** conscientious*
**b** summon
**c** irresistible*
**d** indulge
**e** environment*
**f** horrendous*
**g** tedious
**h** stifle
**i** skimp
**j** integral
**k** evaluate
**l** dispassionately*

## DOUBLE TROUBLE

Each of the following pairs of words appears to be similar, but each word has a totally different meaning. Identify the exact meaning of each word and then use each one in a sentence to show that you understand the difference. Add any words you were unsure about to your Wordbank book.

| | |
|---|---|
| **a** continual | continuous |
| **b** aural | oral |
| **c** assume | presume |
| **d** evolve | involve |
| **e** eminent | imminent |
| **f** delusion | disillusion |
| **g** detract | distract |
| **h** compliment | complement |
| **i** faint | feint |
| **j** assure | ensure |

## MAKING HEADWAY – complex messages

In the first section of this book you were introduced to message taking. You practised identifying key skills in short messages and writing out the 'bones' of the message for someone to understand, using the correct tone as well.

Not all messages you receive will be straightforward. Some will be involved and complex. If you are a professional message taker then you must be able to deal with these and communicate the message accurately. Once you can do this it is only a short step to being able to deal with more complex types of information in other areas, too.

What makes a message complex? Firstly, complexity is not directly related to length. A message is complex if it is

- complicated or involved
- very detailed
- vague and difficult to understand.

## Coping strategies

In the same way as you reduce your reading speed to cope with difficult words or phrases, you must expect to reduce your comprehension speed if a message is complex. No experienced employee would attempt to deal with a complex message at the same speed as a simple one.

It helps if you can get the person concerned to tell you about the background to the message. This improves your understanding and helps you to interpret the information you are given.

A complex message may cover several points or issues relating to one particular topic or situation. In this case, try to get the person giving you the message to give you each point separately – and preferably in a logical order. Another type of complex message covers several topics and situations – in which case you need to know when the subject has changed.

Use clear headings to differentiate the subjects. Use numbered points to list the items mentioned under each subject. Ask questions whenever you are not sure what is meant and check that you have noted all technical terms accurately. Never worry about asking someone to spell a word or to repeat something.

Read your notes back to the person at the end of the conversation and type them up (or write them out) as quickly as possible. Before you start writing, it is useful to read through your notes and put a balloon around any information you wish to move plus an arrow to show where it must go.

Carefully proof-read your finished message against your notes to check that nothing is missing.

## Test your skills

Chloe's boss has a 15-year-old son whose verbal communication skills sometimes leave something to be desired. The following is an extract from a telephone conversation she had with him today.

**Chloe** Good afternoon, Mr Edwards' office. May I help you?

**Matt** Chloe? Is that you? Is Dad about?

**Chloe** Matt? No, sorry, he's in a meeting at the moment and I can't disturb him. Do you want him to call you back later?

**Matt** *(Pause)* No, that's no good. I'm going out. I wanted to talk to him before he goes off on that trip later.

**Chloe** I can give him a message.

**Matt** Oh, great, yes. Well, if you could. Can you tell him I've got the date for that school trip – it's near Perth. Where is that, do you know? I can go on 14 July or 1 August, 'cos two groups are going, but I'd rather go in August 'cos Darren's going then. But if I don't tell Mr Watkins tomorrow it'll be full.

**Chloe** Just a second. Is this a school holiday you're talking about?

**Matt** *(Impatiently)* Yeah, yeah – Dad knows about it. We can go to this outdoor activity centre place for a week and I want to do sailing and it'd be great if I fancied going to Camp America sometime and that reminds me, I can do my Duke of Edinburgh award as well if I want – I've got bronze and I want to do silver but I've got to decide that pretty quickly because they're starting again in two weeks.

**Chloe** *(Laughing)* Just a minute, just a minute. You're going to Perth – it's in Scotland, by the way, look on a map above Edinburgh. And you want to go on the 1 August for a week, because your friend Darren's going then, too.

**Matt** *(Sounds aggrieved)* Yeah, yeah – that's what I said five minutes ago, but I've to tell Mr Watkins and take the deposit tomorrow and I've to tell Mr Adams about my Duke of Edinburgh and I need Dad to tell me if he can take me to Cheltenham on 5 March to play football for the school – I've been chosen for the first XI – Dad'll be dead pleased about that but there's something gone wrong about the coach so I volunteered him to take four of us in his car. *(Slight pause)* He will say yes, won't he, or we're stuck . . .

**Chloe** Slow down, slow down! Am I right that you need your Dad to pay for the holiday? How much is it and how much is the deposit you will need?

**Matt** It's very reasonable, especially as we've all the accommodation and meals and it pays for all the training and activities and . . .

**Chloe** Matt, I'm sure your Dad will realise that. How much is it?

**Matt** *(Quickly)* £295 but then I'll have my certificate and it'll help towards my Duke of Edinburgh's and I could do Camp America before I go to university and get paid for that and . . .

**Chloe** Right, right – I've got all that. Now – how much deposit do you need?

**Matt** I've to take £60 tomorrow but Dad's going away and I don't know how to get it.

**Chloe** If your Dad is happy about it, I'm sure we can sort that out. Now – what do you want me to tell your father about the Duke of Edinburgh award? Is this being run by the school?

**Matt** Yeah – they do it every year. There's nothing much to tell him really, he was hoping I'd do it. I probably will. Yes, I think I will.

**Chloe** Fine, now Cheltenham. Congratulations on getting into the team, by the way. I thought school teams always travelled by coach to away games?

**Matt** They do. There's a problem this time. Dunno what it is. Anyway they want people to go by car. The kick-off's at 11 and it's not that far.

**Chloe** Well, *(glancing at calendar)* the 5th's a Saturday, Matt, so I'll tell him. I don't think he's due to be away that weekend but I don't know what personal arrangements he might have made.

**Matt** I think it's the 5th. Or was it the 12th? Anyway, it's one of those. I've left my fixtures sheet in my locker.

**Chloe** Leave it to me to speak to your father later. He should be free in about an hour. Why don't you call me back about half past four and he can either speak to you then or I'll tell you what he said. If he's happy about the holiday you could always call in and collect the deposit from me in your lunch hour tomorrow. Would that do?

**Matt** That's brilliant, Chloe. You're a star.

**Chloe** No promises, it depends on your Dad!

**Matt** Fine, great. Bye Chloe.

**Chloe** Bye, Matt. Speak to you later ... *(She suddenly realises she is speaking to the dialling tone).*

Quite unintentionally, Matt has given Chloe a complex message. Although the content may not be critically important to the future of the organisation, to Matt and his father it is important.

**TELEPHONE MESSAGE – URGENT**

**TO** Bill Edwards

**FROM** Chloe Jenkins

**DATE** (today)

Matt telephoned while you were in the meeting. He had several items of news and two requests.

1 Matt has found out that the date of his school trip to the activity centre in Perth is 1 August and the all-in cost is £295 for seven days. There is a group going on 14 July but Matt would prefer to go at the same time as his friend Darren – and Darren has already booked for the 1st. If he is definitely going he needs to take a deposit of £60 to school tomorrow. Matt thinks the sailing, in particular, will come in useful in future. He seems to be unsure of the location and I referred him to a map of Scotland!

2 Matt has been given the opportunity to put his name down for the Duke of Edinburgh silver award scheme. He asked me to tell you he is going to do this and his sailing qualifications could count towards it.

3 Matt has qualified to play football for the school's first XI – he thought you would be pleased about this. They have an away match in Cheltenham in early March but Matt is unsure of the date (either 5th or 12th – he knows it is on a Saturday). He wants to know if you will be free to take him and three other members of the team as there appears to be a problem with the coach.

I have arranged for Matt to call back at 4.30 pm to speak to you. If you are not available then, I can speak to him. I could also see him tomorrow lunchtime to pass on the deposit for the holiday, if this would be of help.

*Chloe*

***Figure 7.1*** *Chloe's message*

Look at the message Chloe has prepared (Figure 7.1) and then answer the questions that follow.

**1** Chloe was more informal with Matt than she would have been with a business caller.

**a** Why do you think this was acceptable?

**b** Identify three phrases she used that she would not have used on a formal call.

**2** Chloe struggled to get a clear story from Matt. Identify three occasions on which she reviewed, checked or repeated information back to him.

**3** Compare Chloe's message with the conversation. Discuss as a group how she has arranged her information.

**4** What are the benefits of using numbered points to identify the topics in a complex message

**a** from the point of view of the writer

**b** from the point of view of the reader?

## SPELLCHECKER 6

The suffixes -ible and -able cause a great deal of confusion and many people are unsure which one to write with some words. Often, the only way is to learn the words that have a particular ending. In the two columns below are shown twenty common words – all those on the left have -ible endings and all those on the right end with -able. Learn both lists. Write any words that cause you difficulty in your spelling book. Look up any words where you are unsure of the exact meaning and enter these in your Wordbank book.

| | | | |
|---|---|---|---|
| permissible | plausible | payable | capable |
| collapsible | deductible | agreeable | excusable |
| gullible | inedible | likeable | uneatable |
| forcible | convertible | saleable | acceptable |
| eligible | sensible | noticeable | obtainable |

Many people confuse the two words 'inedible' and 'uneatable', thinking that both describe something that cannot be eaten. If you want to be really precise, you would use the first only if something is unsuitable for eating. Paper is inedible for instance, and so is sand! You would use the word 'uneatable' when something that could normally be eaten cannot because of its condition (eg it is raw, burnt or has 'gone off').

## COMMUNICATION IN PRACTICE

# Test your skills

**1** Replace each use of the phrase 'a lot' in the following passage by a more acceptable word or phrase and retain the same meaning.

Tanya had a lot of work to finish, and not a lot of time to do it in. She looked at her watch – she had been doing this a lot this afternoon. Marion had asked her to be ready at 5 as she had a lot of errands to do on the way home. Tanya looked in her purse. She should really buy some food – she hadn't a lot of food in and had visitors calling that evening. But she hadn't a lot of money on her – unless she called at the cash machine – but there wasn't a lot in the bank, either. Still, not a lot longer and it would be pay day.

**2** Complete the words in the following passage, spelling them correctly.

I have always said I am cap--ble of meeting my com--tments. I am not so gull--ble as to think it would be excus--ble or permiss--ble for me to do anything else. I know that it is both accept--ble and sens--ble to make a defin--te agreement, partic--ly when goods are pay--ble by insta--ments. It is my aim to ensure that my expenditure is contro--ble and I would never wish to be embar--sed by incur--ng any debts.

**3** We use many phrases that relate to body language. State how you would interpret each of the following.

**a** When I saw that film, I was on the edge of my seat.
**b** I'd have felt better if he'd looked me in the eye when he told me.
**c** He's a bit pompous – you'll get on with him if you remember to keep your distance.
**d** She caught his eye at Joey's party.
**e** She's a pain in the neck.
**f** She looked daggers at him.
**g** We don't see eye-to-eye over that.
**h** She turned up her nose at the very thought.
**i** I've a strong leaning towards that idea.
**j** He was rubbing shoulders with the boss last night.

**4** Correct all the errors in the following sentences.

**a** The imminent scientist, whom we all all respected, was a concientious man.
**b** The press were not complementary about his appearance and even said his hairstyle was horrendus.
**c** I want to buy a notebook with faint lines and some other stationary.
**d** Many people, including you and I, are concerned about the enviroment today.
**e** 'I tell you,' said James to his friends. 'The problem is insoluble. I consistantly produce inedible food.'
**f** 'You will never pass your aural french exam if you don't speek clearly,' said his teacher.
**g** The magazine article claimed that worry lines distract from ones appearence.
**h** He is continuously playing the piano and suffers from the disillusion of thinking he is good.

# Apply your skills

You have recently started work at Hightown Leisure Complex. An organisation chart for the complex is shown below. Today, you have been asked to help to organise some interviews. Five candidates are being interviewed for the post of receptionist between 2 pm and 3.30 pm and four candidates are being interviewed for the post of pool attendant between 4 pm and 5 pm. All are being interviewed by May Rodgers, the General Manager.

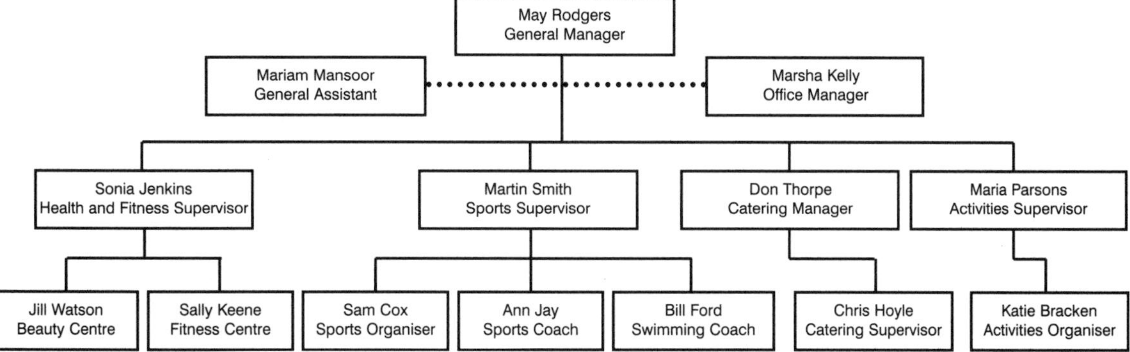


***Figure 7.2*** *Hightown Leisure Complex organisation chart*

I've two sets of interviews to get through tomorrow. Please can you help with the interview arrangements. The receptionist job has 6 candidates – no sorry, 5 – Gwen Watson pulled out last night. I'll give you the names in a moment. Can you produce a brief interview schedule for me as a list – the first one is 2 pm then every 15 minutes until 3.30 – no, it'll be 3.15, won't it? When they arrive they can go to the waiting room next to your office. Between 4 pm and 5 pm we've the interviews for the swimming pool attendant – four applicants for this. Give Bill Ford a call will you and ask him to be available to talk to each of them in my office – he's more up-to-date on life-saving qualifications than I am. Same waiting area please. That reminds me. Can you please ring Sam Jordan, the auditor at Burrough's Accountants. He's due tomorrow to start checking the books. Please tell him I can see him for half an hour at 10.30 am. Oh, and I had a call from Riverside School. They want to hire our sports hall for a special indoor contest for Year 6 pupils next month. Can you please tell Maria and ask her to ring the organiser Ashraf Ali – on Hightown 302983 to confirm everything and to find out what equipment they will need. Oh, the interview candidates. The list for the receptionists is Susan Simpson, Jasmina Jones, Paula Philips, Tanya Thomas and Wendy Southern. Susan is 1 pm – sorry 2 pm – Tanya is 2.15, Jasmina 2.30, then Paula, then Wendy. By the way, Sam's number at the council is 303030. Applicants for the swimming attendant are John Taylor, Martin Mede, Peter Shuttleworth and Hussein Khan. Can I have a separate list of these too please – copy for Bill as well. Sorry – the order for these should be alphabetical – please can you sort it for me. Hope you can understand all this. Thanks.

***Figure 7.3*** *May Rodgers' taped notes*

**1** May Rodgers has left you some instructions on tape. Unfortunately, she was in a hurry and obviously had other things on her mind. Read the script in Figure 7.3 carefully (or, even better, ask someone to read it to you) and make a note of the jobs you have to do. Then rewrite your list in a sensible order.

**2** Prepare the two interview lists required by May Rodgers according to her instructions.

**3** Three of the reception candidates arrive at the same time and you take them to the waiting room and offer them a coffee. From your desk you can see each of them. You notice that

Candidate A, Jasmina Jones, is sitting very still. Her handbag is quite large and firmly gripped in front of her body. She is constantly playing with the bracelet on her right wrist. Her legs are crossed. When you glance at her she looks down quickly.

| | |
|---|---|
| **You** | Good afternoon. Hightown Leisure Complex, may I help you? |
| **Peter** | (*sounds breathless*) Oh, hello. Can I speak to Mrs Rodgers please? |
| **You** | I'm sorry, she's interviewing at the moment and can't be disturbed. Can I help you? |
| **Peter** | (*very agitated*) Oh, have they begun already? The interviews, I mean? I wanted to speak to her before they started. |
| **You** | We've several interviews today. What did you want to speak to her about? |
| **Peter** | Well, I've got a problem. I really don't know where to start. You see, I'm supposed to be having an interview today and it's really important for me to try to get the job but I'm going to struggle to get there on time. |
| **You** | Can you tell me your name, please? |
| **Peter** | Oh, yes, sorry – it's Peter Shuttleworth. You see, I'm fully qualified to be a swimming pool attendant and I was really hoping to get this job as it's just the hours I want, but I can't arrive until later. Would that be OK? My grandmother has to go into hospital this afternoon and I'm the only one with a car, you see, so I'll have to take her. We were having an ambulance to pick her up but there's been some confusion and it hasn't arrived. And now they've rung from the hospital to find out where she is and she's got in a state, and so has my mother, so I'll have to take her, but by the time I've done this I can't possibly be with you at 4.45. Not with the traffic at this time of day. Could I come later do you know, or would that be too late? I'm really desperate, I don't know what to do. Everything's gone wrong at once. (*The caller is talking more and more quickly*). |
| **You** | I'll have to check. What time could you arrive here? |
| **Peter** | (*Slight pause while he thinks*) I'd say the earliest would be 5.30. Would this be OK? |
| **You** | Well, Mrs Rodgers rarely leaves before 6 pm, but there's someone else interviewing with her and I don't know how long he'll be here. There are plenty of payphones at the hospital – I suggest you take your grandmother and ring me from there, and I'll confirm whether you can come here at 5.30. |
| **Peter** | (*Sounding relieved*) Oh, that's a good idea. Thanks very much. You will tell her that it isn't because I'm not interested in the job, won't you? I don't want her to think I'm just messing about. I've been trying to get a job like this for weeks and weeks. I couldn't believe it that everything had gone so wrong at the last minute. |
| **You** | I'm sure she'll understand. Ring me back by a quarter to five and we'll speak then. (*You give him your name*) |
| **Peter** | Will do. Thanks a lot for your help. Bye. |
| **You** | Thanks for calling. Goodbye. |

***Figure 7.4*** *Conversation with Peter Shuttleworth*

Candidate B, Susan Simpson, sits erect, her handbag on the floor beside her. She is looking around at the notices and posters with interest. When you glance at her she smiles at you.

Candidate C, Tanya Thomas, is sitting back in her chair. Her right elbow is on one arm of the chair and she is resting her chin in her cupped right hand. She is not smiling and occasionally she sighs and looks at her watch. When you glance at her, she simply stares back at you.

**a** From your knowledge of body language, how would you assess each candidate's attitude to the job? Discuss your ideas as a group.

**b** Without knowing anything else about them, but realising that as a receptionist the person who gets the job will have to deal with members of the public, which candidate do you think would give the best impression at first glance, and why?

**c** Assuming May Rodgers later asked you for your impression and you gave this, purely on body language alone, how fair do you think this assessment would be? Again, discuss your ideas as a group.

**4** At 4 pm the telephone rings and you receive a call from Peter Shuttleworth, one of the candidates for the pool attendant vacancy. From the script shown in Figure 7.4, write out an appropriate message for May Rodgers. Bear in mind that even though you can't see Peter, his verbal agitation and the words he uses give several indications of his feelings, which might influence May Rodgers' decision if you relay them accurately.

Check all your work with your tutor.

## WORD WIZARD

There are dozens of phrases and expressions related to body language, some of which were given in question 4 on page 128. Now it's your turn!

**1** Fill in the blanks in the following phrases. Each blank relates to a part of the body. Then state what each phrase means..

**a** Jill is head and ............... above anyone else.

**b** She looked really down in the ........... today.

**c** She was all .............. to find out what was going on.

**d** In the race, he was neck and ........... with Jim.

**e** They are living from hand to ......... .

**f** I will fight you tooth and ......... if I have to.

**g** If you want to pass, you'll have to get your ....... down.

**h** Keep your ......... on him for me, will you?

**i** She's hopeless – all fingers and .......... .

**2** Brainstorm other, similar, phrases and expressions. Start with the top of the head and work downwards to the toes. Work in groups of four. See who can come up with the most phrases – repeatable in any company – at the end of 10 or 15 minutes!

# IN THE SPOTLIGHT – THE INFORMAL REPORT

No matter where you work you will find that reports feature highly on the list of written communications you either handle or compose. You will also discover that some reports will be routine and are regularly completed after certain events occur or after a certain length of time has elapsed, whereas others are 'one-off' reports, written for a particular reason. Every report provides information that is required for a reason. The company may be facing a problem on which action must be taken. Unless those making the decisions have the correct information they could make the wrong decision. In other cases, some reports are a legal requirement (such as accident reports). Some examples of both routine and one-off reports are given below.

- **Routine reports** include sales representatives' reports, managers' reports on their departments, production reports (stating target output, actual output, wastage and rejects), maintenance reports, accident reports, safety reports, visit reports, financial reports.
- **One-off reports** give information on a certain matter. A request for one may be made verbally or in writing by a manager. The report may require research and investigation of some kind, with the information obtained summarised in an easy-to-read form. Examples could include: a report investigating why the number of complaints has increased, a report on whether all staff should have Internet access, a report on why staff turnover has increased, a report on why sales are falling in one area.

## VERBAL AND WRITTEN REPORTS

It is, of course, quite possible to be asked to produce a report which you give verbally, as in the following examples.

- Your boss asks you to attend a meeting on her behalf and report back on what took place. You call in her office later and tell her what happened.

- You attend a meeting at which an issue you have been working on is discussed. Your boss asks you to find out some information and give a short verbal report to the meeting the following week.
- A survey of staff, customers or visitors has been undertaken. Your boss asks you for a short report on the results. You add up all the scores and telephone to tell her the response.

For many informal requests a verbal report is very useful. It is a quick way to inform another person about a situation. In fact, you may not even realise you are being asked for a report. '*Tell me what happened*' is a request for a brief verbal report.

The problem with the verbal report is that there is nothing in writing that can be referred to later if there is a query. For that reason, it is often far more useful to have the information in written form.

There are two types of written reports – informal and formal. In this unit we are only concerned with informal reports, which are the most common in business today. Most are only for internal use and will probably be written for your boss or other managers at that level.

## The structure of an informal report

It is normal for a short informal report to be written on memo-headed paper. The report will have three clear sections:

1. An introduction – which states the reason for writing the report. Simply state what it is you have been asked to do.
2. The body of the report – this gives the information you have obtained and states where it came from. This is the most factual section. Clear headings are essential and numbered points are often used to separate different items of information.
3. Your conclusions – this section sums up the information and indicates whether action is likely to be required or not. You may be asked to give your recommendations, which is when you add your suggestions about what should be done.

## How to write a report

Many people feel overwhelmed when they are first asked to write a report. However, because there is a clear structure and because you are dealing with facts, it is not difficult. The key is to be methodical. If you are good at assembling information and arranging it in a logical order, you should have no problems writing a short, informal report. The steps in producing a report are usually the following:

1. Obtain your 'brief'– this means your instructions. You must know exactly what it is you are reporting on if you are to do a good job. It is also important that you find what you can and cannot do to obtain the information. If your boss asks you to 'check last month's photocopying figures' and then finds out you have been asking all the staff for their views on photocopying there are likely to be problems! This is because you have 'exceeded your brief'. If you have good ideas for obtaining additional information, check first if your suggestions are acceptable. Make certain of

the deadline for producing your report, then you know how long you have in which to do the job.

**2** Collect your information. This may be a very simple matter that takes 10 minutes or a much longer procedure. If you are simply referring to details in a log book or a file, then you can study your information and make notes to summarise what you have found. If you are obtaining information from several sources then put it all in a special file folder, clearly labelled. There is nothing more frustrating than finding a critical document has gone missing just when you need it.

**3** Sort your information into a logical order. Group together any documents relating to the same issues. If you are reporting back on a survey, the headings on the survey can be used in the report itself. If you have been asked to find information on three issues, then these issues will be your headings and your groupings.

**4** Draft out your notes. When you become an experienced report writer, you may be able to write your report directly on a word processor from your source documents. At the beginning read each set of information and then summarise what you have found in a few sentences.

**5** Draft out the report from your notes. You will normally find the introduction the easiest part. The body of the report is written from your draft notes. Then think carefully about the conclusions. Avoid the temptation of telling your boss how to do his or her job! Remember that this is a summary section in which you may make one or two suggestions, if you have been asked to do so.

**6** Proof-read your document. If possible, let it go 'cold' over a day or two and then re-read it and make corrections to words or phrases that no longer seem appropriate.

**7** Print out your report and sign it.

## A WORKED EXAMPLE

Mariam works for May Rodgers, General Manager of Hightown Leisure Complex. May received several complaints last week that there was a shortage of towels in the health and beauty centre. According to her figures, plenty of towels are available and they are sent to the laundry twice a week. She has asked Mariam to find out what went wrong and to write a brief report on the matter. She has specifically asked Mariam to make one or two recommendations as to how the problem should be resolved. Figure 8.1 shows the report Mariam produced.

**1** The memo uses the standard headings you have seen in previous memos. However, in an informal report there is *always* a clear heading that provides a title to the report.

**2** The first paragraph clearly outlines the reason for the report. It states

- who asked for it
- when it was asked for
- the reason for the investigation
- how the investigation took place.

# MEMO

TO May Rodgers

FROM Mariam Mansoor

DATE 12 August 199-

**REPORT ON TOWEL SHORTAGE IN HEALTH AND BEAUTY CENTRE**

I refer to your request of 10 August that I investigate the reason for the towel shortage in the health and beauty centre. I carried out an investigation by talking to Mrs Jenkins, the centre supervisor, and with her agreement, each of the six staff who work in the centre. I also checked the laundry records and Mrs Jenkins and I carried out a stock check which I compared to the number of towels listed in the office records.

**Staff interviews**

According to the staff, the following reasons explain the current shortage of towels.

1 Several towels are no longer fit for use by clients. They are old and worn and some have frayed. Staff use some of these when they are clearing up but several have been thrown away. No records are kept of these towels.

2 The centre has been extremely busy over recent weeks. Many clients have visited the centre before going on their holidays. This has meant that more towels have been used each day.

3 The laundry was closed for one week in late July, which created a back-log of dirty towels. On several occasions recently service has been poor. On two days the towels were neither collected nor delivered as promised, despite repeated telephone calls to the laundry. Mrs Jenkins thinks the laundry has recently changed hands and this may be contributing to the problem.

**Laundry records**

The records substantiate the information given by staff. All the records have been completed each time towels have been sent to the laundry and returned, according to instructions. The records show that, on average, it is now taking the laundry an extra day to return the clean towels, which is obviously affecting supply.

1 of 2

**Stock check**

I counted the clean towels currently in stock. When these are added to the number currently at the laundry there is a shortfall of 65 hand towels and 42 bath towels. It would appear this difference is due to the number of towels that have been thrown away, but I have no way of checking this.

**Conclusions**

My conclusions are as follows.

1 There is a definite shortage of towels in the centre at the moment, given the number of clients who visit each day.

2 This problem is made worse by the poor service currently provided by the laundry.

3 The fact that no records are kept when towels are thrown away means that we have no control over this. We also have no routine replacement system in operation.

**Recommendations**

To prevent this problem continuing I recommend the following.

1 We should purchase some additional towels immediately to replace those that have been thrown away and to bring the towel stock back to its former level.

2 We should investigate the services offered by other laundries in the area.

3 We should start a procedure whereby all worn towels can be thrown away only with the agreement of Mrs Jenkins, and clear records are kept. It will then be possible to estimate how long towels normally last and how often they should be replaced.

MM

2 of 2

***Figure 8.1***
*Mariam's report*

**3** You should note that Mariam was particularly careful not to exceed her brief. She talked to Mrs Jenkins first, the Health and Fitness Supervisor, to make sure that she did not make enquiries among the staff without Mrs Jenkins' agreement.

**4** Mariam presented the information she had obtained under three clear headings. For staff interviews, she used numbered points so that each topic could be dealt with separately.

**5** Mariam then gave her conclusions, which are a brief summary of everything she found. These led to her recommendations. In both cases the use of numbered points makes it easier for May Rodgers to refer to the document to find what she needs.

**6** Mariam sticks to the facts. Even when she is asked for her recommendations she bases these on the facts she established. She does not give her personal opinion on what she discovered, nor does she assign blame, make assumptions or jump to conclusions. She takes an objective approach to the issue.

## Test your understanding

**1** A security guard who patrolled the premises of a large organisation would be expected to provide reports both verbally and in writing.

**a** Regular routine reports would usually be given verbally. Why do you think this is the case and what type of information do you think they would contain?

**b** If a particular incident arose, the guard would be expected to submit a written report. Why do you think this is important? What type of incident could be classified as needing a written report?

**2** It is important to collect all relevant information before you start writing a report and keep it safely in a clearly labelled folder. There are two types of information – feedback you have received from other people and relevant documents you have obtained (see also Units 11 and 14).

**a** What documents and other information do you think Mariam might have collected before she started drafting her report?

**b** As a group, decide the type of information you may obtain if you were investigating each of the following topics before writing a report.

**i** Why there is a continual backlog with photocopying at Hightown Leisure Complex.
**ii** Why postage costs have increased considerably over the past few months.
**iii** Why students in your college use the refectory so infrequently.
**iv** Whether it would be feasible to organise a short student trip to Europe.

**3** If Mariam had been less experienced in writing reports she might have drafted the following paragraph. Can you identify:

**a** what is wrong with it
**b** the difficulties that might be caused if Mariam gave it to Mrs Rodgers and sent a copy to Mrs Jenkins.

**Stock check**

I decided to check how many towels we have in stock. Mrs Jenkins was called away so I did this on my own. When I opened the cupboard it was a tip and it took me ages to sort out, fold and count all the towels. One of the staff said it should be tidied every week but they'd been too busy recently. Personally, I don't believe them because the centre was quiet when I went in so they could have been doing it then. It's not surprising we've a towel problem if they are so untidy.

## SPELLCHECKER 7

Each of the following words often causes a spelling problem. Check you can spell each word correctly. Learn those that would cause you difficulties and enter them into your Spellchecker book. Check, too, that you have a clear understanding of the meaning of each word.

| | |
|---|---|
| aggravate | anxious |
| brevity | budget |
| concise | comparable |

| | |
|---|---|
| corroborate | cursory |
| disappointed | excellent |
| essential | emphasise |
| genuine | guarantee |
| hypothetical | incident |
| irrelevant | permanent |
| recommend | valuable |

## THE GOOD GRAMMAR GUIDE
## Polishing your sentences

Even if you are good at grammar it is still possible to write a poor sentence that has a word repeated several times, contains 'waffle' or unnecessary words or, even worse, a double negative which cancels itself out. This section is designed to warn you about such errors!

### Varying the words in a sentence

When you are writing a sentence, try to avoid repeating the same word – unless you do this for deliberate effect eg *Alice was getting smaller and smaller*. Otherwise the sentence sounds very boring

*We were pleased to receive your letter and are pleased to enclose our latest catalogue.*

The sentence would sound much better if there was only one 'pleased' and the other was replaced by another word or phrase, eg

*Thank you for your letter. We are pleased to enclose our latest catalogue.*

or

*We were pleased to receive your letter and take this opportunity to enclose our latest catalogue.*

Make sure, however, that the meaning stays the same

### Redundant words

Avoid words that are unnecessary. If you listen to people speaking, you will be surprised at the number of times they add unnecessary words to a sentence, eg

*I have no children at all.*
*He often visits France and has been there many times.*

Common phrases often contain a redundant word. For instance, have you ever challenged the phrase *free gift*? A gift, by definition, must be free! Other common examples include *advance warning, past experience* and *unexpected surprise*. Try not to use any of these, particularly when you are writing.

## *Positive and negative sentences*

Sentences can be positive or negative. A common way of changing a sentence from the positive to the negative is by adding '-n't' or 'not', although other words in English are also used for this purpose, eg

| | |
|---|---|
| *I do agree.* | *I don't agree.* |
| *She has always been good at spelling.* | *She has never been good at spelling.* |

There are three points to remember in relation to negative sentences.

**1** You already know that in business letters you should avoid using abbreviated words. Write *We regret that we cannot visit you on Monday,* not *We regret that we can't visit you on Monday.* You may find, however, that in memos and some e-mails the abbreviated form is used, because the communication is more informal and only sent internally.

**2** One trap for the unwary is the double negative. In this case the negative words cancel each other out, making the sentence positive, eg

*He never saw nothing.* (He saw something)
*She didn't stay nowhere.* (She stayed somewhere)
*I didn't have nothing to do with him.* (I did have something to do with him)

**3** In business it is usually better to paint a positive picture rather than a negative one. For that reason, you may find sentences adjusted so that the positive form is used. In this case

| | | |
|---|---|---|
| *We regret we cannot offer you an appointment this week.* | becomes | *We are pleased to be able to offer you an appointment next week.* |
| *We do not give discounts unless your order is for £100 or more.* | becomes | *We also offer a discount if your order is for £100 or more.* |

Usually this approach is more likely to please the recipient.

# Test your skills

Each of the following sentences contains one of the above errors. Find the error in each case and correct it.

**1** She never gave me nothing but trouble.

**2** Mr Evans cannot see you until 4 pm.

**3** It is absolutely essential that you attend the meeting.

**4** This parcel must go quickly because it is urgent.

**5** Please state your name and after your name, write your address.

**6** Thank you for replying so quickly and thank you for telling me the situation.

**7** I didn't expect him not to respond.

## DOUBLE TROUBLE

More 'double trouble' words are given below. In each case

- **a** select the word(s) that should be included in the sentence
- **b** write a sentence to show you understand the meaning of the other word.

1. I bought a (chilli/chilly) and some (currents/currants) at the supermarket.
2. We will have to (review/revue) the agreement to (insure/ensure) we are not in (breach/breech) of meeting its terms.
3. Your writing is (ineligible/illegible) and is not even (strait/straight).
4. She was (proscribed/prescribed) some (portent/potent) medicine.
5. If you were a (rational/rationale) person you would acknowledge he is (inept/inapt).

## TOOLS OF THE TRADE – *reading for a purpose*

When you read at home, you will usually be reading for interest. You may enjoy something at that moment but, if you were asked to recall it in any detail later, you might experience some difficulty. This is because the information you received is not retained in your long-term memory, but discarded quite quickly.

Your reading speed will also vary, depending upon how much you read and your vocabulary in relation to the difficulty of the material. If the material is complex, there are many long or technical words, or words you do not instantly recognise, you may find the whole task overwhelming and give up.

Now you are a student, and when you are at work, you should realise that there are different ways of reading, each with its own purpose. Each method is suited to a particular occasion. The methods are:

- scanning
- skimming
- reading for study
- word-by-word reading
- light reading.

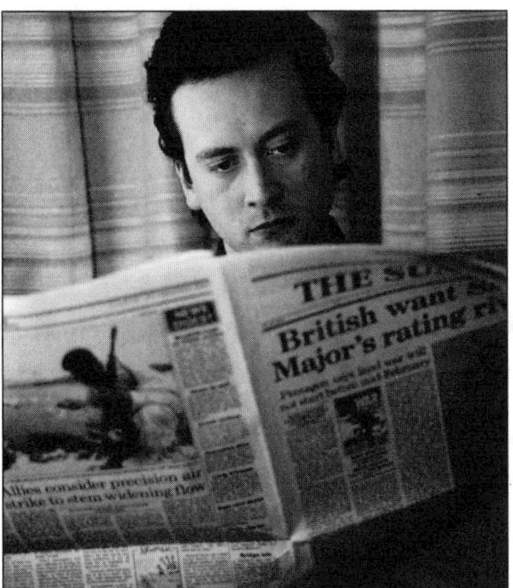


Light reading is the way you normally read newspapers, magazines and novels. Below is a brief description of each of the other methods – and when you should use them.

### Scanning

You 'scan' when you are looking for a person's name in a telephone directory. If you do this correctly, you look down all the entries, for the name or initial you need, ignoring everything else. If you do this correctly it is quite a rapid procedure. If you do this wrongly, you allow yourself to be distracted by other things. Whilst there are few distractions in the average telephone directory, there are several in other things you may need to scan – such as a newspaper for a particular article, a book index for a particular subject or a long article for an item of interest.

## Skimming

The difference between scanning and skimming is that with the former you know what you want to find. When you are skimming you don't. For example, you may skim through a book to see if there is anything interesting in it, or anything relevant to an assignment you are writing. You skim if you are looking through a mail order catalogue to see if there is anything you would like to buy. Skimming takes longer than scanning but you can often reduce your search time by using a particular technique. In a book you could look at chapter headings or glance through the index. In a catalogue you could restrict your skimming to certain types of clothes or other items.

## Reading for study

In this situation you are trying to understand and remember what you read. You can only remember something by making notes and writing down the key points of what you have been reading – over and over again if necessary until you can do it from memory. This is another reason why you need to write down spellings when you are trying to learn them.

## Word-by-word reading

If you invited someone you wished to impress for a meal, you would be risking disaster if you simply skimmed a new recipe and then tried to make the dish! Instead you would need to read it word by word to make sure you didn't make any mistakes. You would follow the same procedure if you were reading the instructions for dyeing a favourite shirt or using a poisonous garden spray.

## Test your understanding

**1** What style of reading did you use when you read the passage above? Test yourself by seeing if you can recall the different methods of reading without looking back! Give your own example of when you would use each one.

**2** Read the passage shown in Figure 8.2 on page 141 *twice*. The first time, read it generally for interest, and to get the sense of the passage. The second time read it much more carefully. Make notes of the key points. Then – without looking back at the passage – see if you can answer the questions below.

**a** What was the title of the passage?
**b** How much faster can computers process information today than in 1960?
**c** If you had a car that ran like this, how far would it go on one gallon of petrol?
**d** In what way can computers be considered a menace?
**e** What name is given to the new, stress-related condition which has been diagnosed?
**f** Write a brief paragraph, summing up the problems that can be caused by too much information.

***Figure 8.2***
*Read me twice*

**Information overload**

The quantity of information that can be collected, processed and analysed by organisations has increased dramatically over the past 30 years. The length of time needed to process one electronic operation by computer has fallen by a factor of over 80 million since 1960! One expert compared this with what a similar advance would mean to the motor industry – the equivalent would be to buy a car capable of doing 15 million miles to one gallon of petrol!

However, computers can be both a blessing and a menace when they are used to process information. The biggest danger is that so *much* information can now be made available that no-one knows how to use it. This is known as information overload.

Pages and pages of data can be produced that are not all relevant, but which some unfortunate manager or administrator has to try to read and understand. When there is too much information, and much of it is irrelevant, this makes decision-making more difficult. So many details are hitting everyone's desk that no-one can cope with all the information, let alone act upon it promptly. In other words, too much information is as bad as too little. It will lead to delays, errors and problems as staff struggle to cope, and has already resulted in a new stress-related condition known as information overload syndrome.

MAKING HEADWAY -
circular letters and tear-off slips


**HIGHTOWN LEISURE COMPLEX**
Castle Road
HIGHTOWN
HG3 4MP

Tel: 01928 309322 General Manager: May Rodgers

August 199-

Dear Doctor

**FITNESS FOR LIFE SCHEME**

We are pleased to inform you that from September we are offering a new range of exercise programmes which have been designed for anyone who has been inactive or who has a specific medical problem or condition. There will be four programmes to choose from.

- GP referral programme – under close supervision by a qualified instructor, for anyone who has a specific medical problem
- Active Living programme – for the over-50s who wish to become more active
- Cardiac Exercise programme – which includes regular consultations with our trained cardiac nurse
- Post-Natal Exercise programme (creche available) – for new mothers who wish to regain their former weight and fitness level.

Full details of days and times are given on the attached leaflet and poster, which we would be grateful if you could place in your waiting room.

We should be pleased if you would bring these programmes to the attention of any of your patients who would benefit. If you would like to consult us about any other fitness programmes you think we could usefully offer, please do not hesitate to contact us.

Yours sincerely

May Rodgers
General Manager

Enc

***Figure 8.3*** *A circular letter*

# CIRCULAR LETTERS

A circular letter is a variation on the form letter you first met in Unit 5. You may remember that a form letter is a letter sent to many people, and that the details are completed for each individual. The letter therefore has blanks for these details to be entered. Where no details need to be entered, but a number of people need to be given the same information, they are sent a circular or standard letter.

An example of a circular letter is shown in Figure 8.3. Note that:

- the letter is written on headed paper
- only the month and year has been shown – as the letters may not all be sent out on the same day
- a generic salutation has been used – to save staff the task of writing in every doctor's name individually
- it is likely that May Rodgers would sign the letter before it is photocopied, to save herself the onerous task of signing hundreds of copies.

**HIGHTOWN LEISURE COMPLEX**
Castle Road
HIGHTOWN
HG3 4MP

Tel: 01928 309322 General Manager: May Rodgers

5 August 199-

Mrs J Stanton
14 Willow Road
HIGHTOWN
HG6 2EZ

Dear Mrs Stanton

**CHILDREN'S BIRTHDAY PARTIES**

Thank you for your recent enquiry regarding children's birthday parties.

We offer parties for children aged between 4 and 12. These can be booked for any afternoon and last for three hours, including the birthday tea. The size of the party is limited to between 10 and 20 children and the cost is £8 per child.

The party starts with an activity session. You can select three activities from the full range shown in the attached leaflet. After this time the children have tea in one of our smaller function rooms. We can provide a special iced birthday cake at an additional cost of £8.50.

All the activities are supervised by our fully-trained staff and each party has its own party organiser. When we confirm your booking we give you the name of your own organiser who will greet your party on arrival. All our organisers are very familiar with the needs of children on these occasions and help them to enjoy their time with us safely.

We have pleasure in enclosing a booking form, which you should complete and return to us with a deposit of 10% of the total amount due. Payment of the balance is due one week before the date of the party. Because of the popularity of our parties I would advise you to make your booking at least three weeks before the party date to avoid disappointment. You can, of course, telephone at any time to make a provisional arrangement. If you require any further information, please do not hesitate to contact me.

Yours sincerely

Maria Parsons
Activities Supervisor
Enc

***Figure 8.4*** *A personalised circular letter*

## Personalised circular letters

You may remember that a form letter is used if the details *within* the letter will be different for each individual or groups of individual. The advent of computers and word processing packages has meant that form letters are used less frequently, as it is now a simple matter to store a circular letter on disk (with or without blanks for variable information), recall this when required, and enter the details before printing it out. This means that the letter has the appearance of being a personalised document. Traditional form letters are more likely to be used in organisations where each person does not have a word processor on his/her desk or where dozens of letters may be sent out each week.

An example of a personalised circular letter is shown in Figure 8.4. In this case, the Leisure Complex keeps on disk a letter giving information about children's birthday parties. The basic letter can be sent to each person who makes an enquiry about the parties. The date, the name and address and the salutation are added and the word processing package merges these into the letter at the points indicated. The result looks like an individual letter.

# TEAR-OFF SLIPS

In some cases, you may wish people to reply to a circular letter, but many people may not wish to be bothered writing a full letter in response. One way to overcome this problem is to include a tear-off form on the bottom of the letter, which people can complete and return easily.

An example is shown in Figure 8.5. Note that:

- the tear-off slip is always at the bottom of the letter (ideally it should end one inch from the bottom of the paper)
- it is separated from the main letter by a line of hyphens running from one edge of the paper to the other
- a clear heading is given on the tear-off slip – in case it is detached before being completed

**HIGHTOWN LEISURE COMPLEX**
Castle Road
HIGHTOWN
HG3 4MP

Tel: 01928-309322 General Manager: May Rodgers

September 199-

Dear Member

**MAKE-UP AND BEAUTY DEMONSTRATION EVENING – 15 OCTOBER 199-**

The Health and Fitness Club is pleased to inform you that we have arranged a special make-up and beauty demonstration at 7.30 pm on 15 October 199-. This will be given by Anita Gerrard, who is renowned in her field. Anita has worked for various model agencies and in television and films. We are therefore fortunate that she has agreed to give us the benefit of her knowledge and experience.

Anita will start the evening with a talk about health and beauty and this will be followed by a make-up demonstration. At least three members of the audience will be offered the opportunity of a free make-over on the evening. They will be chosen at random from all those who have volunteered to take part.

Please note that tickets are strictly limited to one per member and one guest, and cost £5 each. If you would like to attend, we advise you to complete the form below as soon as possible, as demand for tickets is likely to be high. Please return your completed form to reception.

We hope you will join us as this promises to be an evening to remember.

Yours sincerely

Sonia Jenkins
Health and Fitness Supervisor

- - - - - - - - - - - - - - - - - - - - - - - - - - - - - - - - - - - - - - - - - - - -

**MAKE-UP AND BEAUTY DEMONSTRATION – 15 OCTOBER 199-**

Please reserve me ........ ticket(s) for this event. My membership number is ..........

I would/would not* like the opportunity of a free make-over session.

I enclose £5/£10* in payment.

Signed .......................................(Please print name) .............................................

* Please delete as applicable

***Figure 8.5*** *A letter with a tear-off reply strip*

- options are given for the person to select
- because people's handwriting varies in size, one extra space is left between each row of dots.

In some circumstances, a tear-off form may also be added to a memo – again to make it easy for people to respond.

## Test your understanding

**1** Today more and more letters are being personalised on computer, showing the name and address of the recipient. As a group, discuss the advantages and disadvantages of this from the point of view of

**a** the organisation
**b** the person who receives the letter.

**2** You have been given the task of organising a student trip to Alton Towers, to be held on the last day of term. The cost, including coach travel and entry fee, is £10 per person. The opportunity to go on the trip is restricted to four groups of students. For that reason, you have decided to write a circular memo to everyone who is eligible, rather than put up a poster or notice. Knowing students as you do, you will insist that full payment is included with each booking!

Draft a memo to give information about the trip. Add your own details – including the date and approximate times. Then design a tear-off form for the bottom of the memo, which students could complete and return to you together with their payment.

Check your completed work with your tutor.

## WORDBANK 7

In Unit 4 you saw that many prefixes are concerned with number ('deca', 'mega', 'milli', etc). In most cases, these indicate a precise number or quantity. Other prefixes relate to the position of something or to amounts in general. Some examples are given below.

- **pri** = first — primary = first in a series; primeval = first age of the world

| | |
|---|---|
| ■ **ante, fore, pro** = before | ante-room = a room where people wait before going in to the main room: forewarn = a warning before an event; prologue = a speech introducing a play |
| ■ **post** = after | post-operative = after an operation |
| ■ **circum, circu** = around | circumference = the distance around a figure |
| ■ **contra, contro, counter** = opposite or against | contradict = state the opposite view; counterattack = attack in response to an enemy action |
| ■ **pro** = on the side of | pro-European = in favour of Europe |
| ■ **extra, ultra, hyper** = beyond | extraordinary = beyond the ordinary; ultrasonic = sound waves above the human hearing range; hypersensitive = extremely sensitive |
| ■ **hypo** = under | hypodermic = something which goes under the skin (eg a needle) |
| ■ **infra, sub** = beneath | infra-red = waves less than microwaves; subterranean = under the earth's surface |
| ■ **inter** = between | interview = talk between people |
| ■ **intra** = within | intravenous = into a vein |
| ■ **super** = above | supersonic = above the speed of sound |
| ■ **mid** = middle | midnight = middle of the night |
| ■ **multi** = many | multitude = many people |
| ■ **micro** = tiny | microfilm = film containing tiny images |
| ■ **macro** = large | macrocosm = the universe |
| ■ **mini** = lesser or least | minibus = smallest version of a bus |
| ■ **tele** = far off | television = picture from afar |

Knowing what prefixes mean helps you to work out what a new word means, especially when you also know some suffixes – or common word endings. For instance, if you know that sub = under and marine = sea, you can quickly work out what a submarine does, even if you didn't already know!

**DON'T YOU DARE!**

*...confuse the following prefixes:*

- *anti (against, eg anti-aircraft gun) and ante (before, eg antenatal clinic);*
- *for (to prevent or stop, eg forbid) and fore (before, eg forewarn).*

## COMMUNICATION IN PRACTICE

### Test your skills

**1** Each of the following sentences contains a redundant word. In each case, remove the unnecessary word and say why you can do so.

**a** An unknown stranger called this afternoon.
**b** She took her little baby to the clinic.

**c** We will have to postpone this meeting until later.
**d** I ordered a tuna fish sandwich.
**e** If we all join together we will do the job much quicker.
**f** I climbed up the ladder to rescue the cat.
**g** When he wrote my name, it was an exact replica of my signature.
**h** I had an oral conversation with him yesterday.

**2** Visit a bank or a building society and obtain a leaflet about opening an account there.

**a** Read it, looking up any words where you are unsure of the meaning.
**b** Highlight all the key points that would be important to you if you were opening an account there.
**c** State the advantages of this account, as a list of numbered points under a clear heading.
**d** Identify any disadvantages you can think of and list these, again under a clear heading.
**e** Use your notes to give a verbal report to your tutor on what you have found.

**3** Watch a film or television drama of your choice, agreed with your tutor beforehand. Write a brief report on it afterwards. Give your view of the story, how well it was performed and whether it was worth watching. Produce this as a memo with appropriate headings. Finish with two brief sections – your conclusions about the film or programme as a whole, and your recommendations as to who would find it enjoyable.

**4** Improve your word power by replacing each phrase in italics below with one word.

**a** If you make a mistake, comfort yourself with the fact that no-one is *incapable of error.*
**b** The receptionist was dismissed as *not having the ability to perform the job*.
**c** The argument he made in his report was *one which did not help them to arrive at a definite conclusion*.
**d** When the accountant retired, he told his employer that his decision was *one that could not be taken back*.
**e** He is definitely a *person who always looks on the black side*.
**f** This vase is *the same in every respect* to one I have at home.
**g** She is someone who is *able to use both hands alike*.
**h** Her mother was suffering from *a loss of memory*.
**i** He was jailed in South America for *a crime against the state*.
**j** She suffers from *a prolonged inability to sleep*.

## Apply your skills

**1** Hightown Leisure Complex recently paid for you to attend a one-day course on reception skills and dealing with customers. The course was quite expensive – £350 for two days. Before you went, Mrs Rodgers asked you to make notes on what you learned and to let her have a report on your return so that she can decide whether to send other members of staff.

```
RECEPTION AND CUSTOMER LIAISON COURSE

OAKTREE HOTEL

5/6 SEPTEMBER 199-


Course organisation and management

Run by Training Incorporated. Well organised. Greeted on
arrival - recd name badge, course prog and loose-leaf file
for notes. Only 16 of us so received individual attention.

Facilities at hotel good - talks in seminar rooms +
smaller rooms off for workshops. Modern equipment - videoed
on day 2.

Food so-so - choice poor + service slow so pm sessions
late starting both days - but not organiser's fault.

Course content

Day 1 am   Intro
           Importance of first impression
           Verbal comm skills (general overview)
           Personal appearance
      pm   Security and reception
           Reception records
           Customer relationships

Day 2 am   Dealing with difficult situations - emergencies
           and problems
           Dealing with difficult people - awkward/foreign/
           angry customers
      pm   Role plays (video) and feedback
           Plenary session

Suitability/relevance of course

Day 2 better than day 1. Many participants work in orgs
where customers can't wander around (not like a leisure
centre!) so security more relevant. Plus some reception
records not relevant to us. Appearance - would our staff
be insulted? All wear uniform and are v. smart.

Difficult sits session v. gd - wide range of emergencies/
problems covered (we contributed ideas). They did best to
make sits relevant to our jobs. Difficult people session
excellent - gave confidence in dealing with different
needs/probs. Role plays gave practice at coping and
feedback session gd.

Conclusion

In general gd course, but only day 2 really relevant -
therefore expensive.

Recommendations

Wld organiser (or another org) run one-day course just for
us? Not worth sending everyone on this one - too
expensive. Other alt would be to run our own, based on
notes given out on day 2. Could we borrow a video camera?
```

***Figure 8.6*** *Notes made after attending a course*

Figure 8.6 shows the notes you made after you attended. Use these to produce an informal report for Mrs Rodgers under the headings used in your notes. Use numbered points where they will help to make your information clearer and easier to read.

**2** Next month one of the two large sports halls in the complex will be closed for four weeks. It is being redecorated, a new floor is being installed and a climbing wall is being built at one end. This will greatly improve the facilities when it re-opens. In the meantime May Rodgers wants to notify all the members so that they are aware of the situation in advance. The hall closes a week from Friday and opens four weeks later, on the Monday. May Rodgers has decided to send a circular letter containing this information to all members of the Leisure Complex. This will be stored on a word processor and personalised by a mail merge facility, which links the database containing the members' names and addresses with the word processing program.

She has asked you to draft the letter for her, in her name, and to make sure that you mention that the complex apologises for any inconvenience which may be caused to members during this time. Prepare a suitable letter and check the content with your tutor.

**3** Two weeks on Thursday it is Martin Smith's 30th birthday. Martin has worked at the complex for the past two years and is very popular. May Rodgers has agreed that staff can have a social get-together in the bar after 10.30 pm and Don Thorpe has agreed to provide a small buffet. The cost will be £3.50 for each person attending, which will include one free drink. Martin has asked for your help in notifying all staff and finding out how many people would like to attend. Don needs the numbers as quickly as possible so that he can order the food.

Draft out a short, friendly memo to all the staff notifying them of the event. Design a tear-off slip that they can return to tell you if they are interested in attending.

## WORD WIZARD

Many people become word wizards because they enjoy using words. They improve their skills by taking part in word games or quizzes – and by doing crossword puzzles. If these overwhelm you, do the one below with a partner, because two heads are usually better than one! Some hints and tips for doing crosswords are:

- use a pencil (then you can easily erase a mistake)
- do the words you find easy first
- note that the number of letters is given after each clue, to help you
- check the spelling of words you are unsure about
- do the hardest ones last. You may find words 'down' easier to do if you copy the letters and blanks out horizontally.

It is more interesting if you and your partner are allowed to 'trade' answers with other pairs in the class near the end. Then see who finishes first!

As a hint, the crossword below mainly contains words you have met in this book so far – so it also tests your spelling! The key is given on page 313. Try not to look at this until you are absolutely desperate. Then check your spelling as well as your answers!

**Clues across**

1 Person you work with (9)
5 Word or prefix meaning water (4)
8 Send, often electronically (8)
9 Give in when overpowered (5)
10 The opposite of winning (6)
11 To protest or oppose (7)
14 A conjunction which means but, at the same time, or nevertheless (3)
16 Prefix meaning 'beyond' (5)
18 Wary (8)
19 Not many (3)
20 Prefix meaning 'tiny' (5)
21 Title for married woman (3)
25 Allows (7)
26 Middle (6)
27 Not moving (10)
28 Slang for swindle or defraud (3)

**Clues down**

1 A book illustrating products and giving prices (9)
2 Link or communicate with another person (6)
3 Greatly needed, indispensable (9)
4 Disorderly or messy (6)
6 A line of people (5)
7 Specialists who check accounts (8)
12 Abbreviation meaning 'that is' (2)
13 Collective noun for paper etc. (10)
15 Narrow-minded, stubborn, sticking to own views no matter what (8)
17 Belonging to them (5)
18 Bright red (7)
22 Gloss or polish (5)
23 Chooses or selects (4)
24 Prefix meaning 'lesser or least' (4)

# IN THE SPOTLIGHT – GRAPHICAL IMAGES

We are surrounded by graphical images in our daily lives. Advertisements carry pictures and cartoons; newspapers and magazines have photographs, diagrams, charts and tables; so do leaflets, catalogues and brochures. Television and video are predominantly graphical in many ways, much of the information we receive being visual. Indeed, it is possible to say that for every piece of information we receive in text in our lives, we probably assimilate at least twice as many in graphical form.

At first sight, you may think there is very little scope for graphics in business, but you would be wrong. Graphics are not restricted to the organisation's publicity material and advertisements. They are often used to illustrate ideas that would take pages of text to explain, and which people would be loath to read. You saw two graphical images when you studied the organisation charts for Riverside Small Animal Centre and Hightown Leisure Complex. Some further examples are given below.

- **Tables** are used to show mainly numerical information, eg pay scales, interest rates, budgets, accounts, survey results, sales figures, production figures and costs.
- **Pie charts** are used to show proportions, eg sales by geographical region, sales by product, sales to different types of customer, advertising expenditure in different types of media, etc.
- **Graphs** are used to show trends, eg whether sales are increasing or decreasing, whether production is rising or falling, how much is being earned or spent over a period of time.
- **Bar charts** are often used to make comparisons, eg sales at home and abroad, sales of different products, sales made by different representatives, the production rates of different products.
- **Pictograms** are used to show a trend through the use of graphics. They are particularly useful if the audience would not be interested in much detail but needs to be given the basic information.

All these types of graphics can be incorporated into documents such as a letter, a memo or a report on a particular subject. You can save yourself writing many lines of text by taking advantage of the fact that 'a picture speaks a thousand words'.

In this unit, we will examine tables and pie charts in more detail. In Unit 10 we will look at graphs, bar charts and pictograms.

# TABLES AND COMMENTARIES

You can test the usefulness of graphics yourself. At Hightown Leisure Complex, May Rodgers is worried about the staffing rota. Sometimes there is a shortage of staff, at other times there seem to be several staff on duty when areas of the complex are very quiet. She has asked you to provide information on the daily attendance throughout August and then to work out the average attendance on each day of the week. You have to give her this information in a brief report. You have two choices: you can write out the information or produce a table. Both alternatives are shown below. Which would you choose and why?

## THE TEXT VERSION

Attendance at the leisure complex is higher at the weekend. Attendance figures for the health and fitness centre, swimming pool and sports halls show this clearly. Tuesday is the quietest day in all areas – only 92 people came to the leisure complex. Saturday is the busiest day in the health and fitness centre (60 people) and the swimming pool (104 people) but Sunday is most popular for the sports halls (72 people). Monday and Thursday are relatively quiet – there is little difference between the two days (122 people and 125 people respectively). Wednesday is quite busy in all areas (142 people) but attendance increases considerably on Friday (165 people). The busiest area of the three is the swimming pool, which had 506 visitors during the week, as opposed to 298 in the health and fitness centre and 284 in the sports halls.

## THE TABLE

**AVERAGE ATTENDANCE, AUGUST 199-**

| | Mon | Tues | Wed | Thur | Fri | Sat | Sun | **Total** |
|---|---|---|---|---|---|---|---|---|
| Health and fitness centre | 32 | 28 | 40 | 55 | 45 | 60 | 58 | 298 |
| Swimming pool | 62 | 48 | 72 | 42 | 78 | 104 | 80 | 506 |
| Sports halls | 28 | 16 | 30 | 28 | 42 | 68 | 72 | 284 |
| **Total** | 122 | 92 | 142 | 125 | 165 | 232 | 210 | 1088 |

Notes to table:

**1** Main sports hall out of use, Tuesday 13 August.
**2** Attendance includes members and guests.

## WHICH TO USE?

It may seem that the one to use is the one that provides the most information at a glance. This is obviously the table. It is very difficult to provide all the information in text form and, indeed, the writer has missed out a critical piece of information. This is the fact that although Monday and Thursday have a similar attendance overall, the health and fitness centre has Thursday as its busiest day and the swimming pool is quietest. If May Rodgers was thinking of changing the number of staff on duty in these two areas this information would be very important.

But the correct answer to the question is a combination of *both* methods. Unless you have been asked to produce only a table, you should provide a short commentary with it – just a summary of the main points. This is easily done, because you can refer to the table as you write and there is no need to include any figures.

## WRITING A COMMENTARY

Before you can write a commentary you must be able to read and understand a table.

- All tables should have a clear heading explaining what the table is about. Read this first.
- Sometimes a table may have some notes at the bottom. Read these carefully as they are often critical to how you interpret the information. In this case the fact that one sports hall was out of use for a day could severely affect the figures.
- Each column (downwards) and, often, each row (across) has a heading. Check the headings carefully. In particular make sure you know whether the figures are financial (look for the £ sign) or not. In the previous table it should be obvious quite quickly that the table refers to numbers of people.
- If there are totals both across and down, then the right-hand bottom is the overall total box. This is a useful check when you compile a table, because your totals both down and across must always agree! In this table the number of people who attended throughout the week in all areas was 1088.
- Study the entries across. This will show you a comparison of some type. Check whether the figures are increasing, decreasing or staying the same. Sometimes they may go up and down, but try to get a picture in your mind. The first picture you should get here is that attendance is highest at the weekend – and the totals bear this out.
- Compare the entries with each other. This tells you which entries are the highest and which are the lowest. Note if there are any differences between various columns, which show that the amounts may vary under different circumstances or for different entries. In this table you should notice that the swimming pool is the busiest area, the health and fitness centre is next and then the sports halls.
- Make specific comparisons, column by column or row by row. In this case you should see that

  **a** the quietest day overall is Tuesday (but note the closure of a sports hall one day)

**b** Monday and Thursday are also relatively quiet, but the health and fitness centre goes against this trend and has a very busy day on Thursday, whereas the swimming pool has its quietest day and is much busier on a Monday.

- You may now be able to group your information together to make it easier to understand, eg

| | |
|---|---|
| Mon–Thur | Health and fitness centre: quietest day Tues, busiest day Thurs. Swimming pool – quietest day Thurs, busiest day Wed. Sports halls – quietest day Tues (but note closure), busiest day Wed. |
| Fri–Sun | All areas busy, attendance peaks on Saturday except for the sports halls which peak on Sunday. |

You now have enough information to write an appropriate summary of the table.

## Test your understanding

May Rodgers has obtained some statistics on the age range of people who are members of the complex. She is always looking to increase membership and is aware that what appeals to one age group does not necessarily appeal to another. The adult health and fitness centre opened in early 1998 and she considers this had a beneficial effect on membership but is not sure whether it has applied to all age groups.

The statistics are shown in the table below. Read the table carefully and note down the main trends. Then write a brief commentary of your findings.

| Age range | 1997 | 1998 | 1999 |
|---|---|---|---|
| 0–15 | 300 | 350 | 500 |
| 16–30 | 215 | 280 | 355 |
| 31–50 | 185 | 285 | 244 |
| 51+ | 36 | 42 | 54 |
| **Total** | 736 | 957 | 1153 |

# PIE CHARTS

Pie charts give less detailed information than tables but can still be useful for 'see-at-a-glance' information. You probably drew pie charts at school and can remember that they are circles divided into proportional segments. Each segment is shaded or coloured to represent a different area.

It would be an easy matter to create a pie chart showing the membership split amongst age groups at the leisure complex for a particular year. However, you would need to know, or calculate, the percentage for each age group. If you have created a table on a spreadsheet package, this calculation can be done automatically. In addition, you could automatically produce a pie chart. If you are working with paper and a calculator, however, you must be able to work out percentages!

### CALCULATING A QUANTITY AS A PERCENTAGE

You need two numbers, the quantity and the total. For 1999, the quantity of 0–15 year olds is 500 and the total for the year is 1153. Calculate the percentage by dividing the smaller number by the larger one and multiplying by 100. Do this on a calculator by

- entering the smaller number (500)
- pressing ÷
- enter the larger number (1153)
- pressing %.

Your answer should be 43.36, which rounds down to 43%.

Now work out the remaining percentages and compare your answer with those given below.

### PREPARING THE PIE CHART

Firstly, decide on a clear title. Then divide up the segments of your circle to match, as nearly as possible, each percentage share. Note that you will have to colour or shade each segment to differentiate it in some way, and either label the segments or produce a key at the bottom. If you are using a computer then you can produce a 3D pie chart or 'explode' a segment for effect (see Figures 9.1 and 9.2).

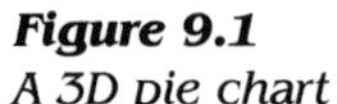

***Figure 9.1***
*A 3D pie chart*

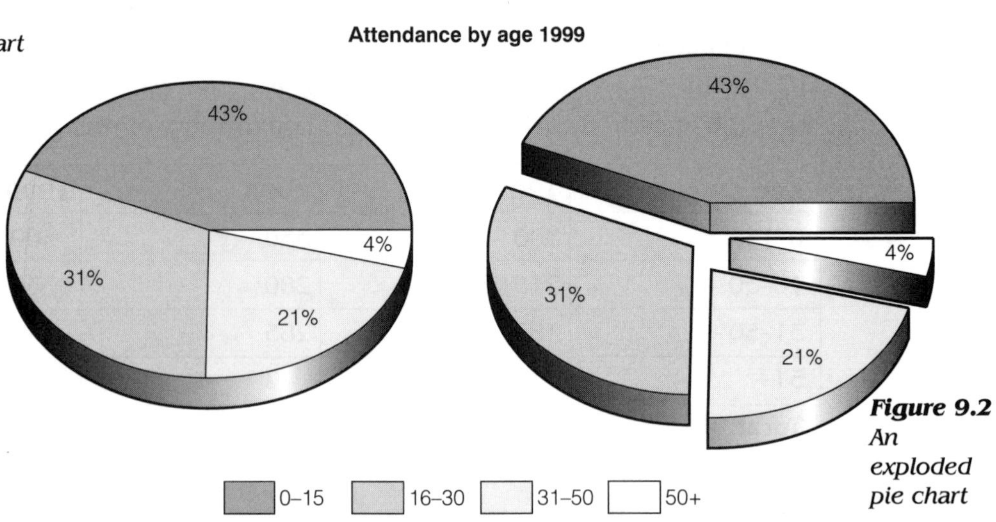


***Figure 9.2***
*An exploded pie chart*

# Test your understanding

1 Prepare your own pie charts for the attendance figures by age given for both 1997 and 1998. Bear in mind you will have to calculate the percentages first. These should give a rapid visual picture of the trends you identified in your commentary.

2 May Rodgers is concerned that more needs to be done to appeal to the over 30s and would like all staff to meet to discuss the problem. She wants them to think about the issue beforehand and then suggest ideas. She has called a meeting for 8.30 am, next Tuesday, in the upstairs function room, and has asked you to send out a memo to all staff informing them of this. Draft a suitable memo on her behalf.

## SPELLCHECKER 8

Appropriately, for Unit 9, none of the words listed has more than nine letters! Yet many are frequently spelled incorrectly. Check that you could write each one of the following 20 words correctly, learn any you are unsure about and enter them in your Spellchecker book. Check the meanings if you are unsure of any, too!

aerial (on the roof, not washing powder!)
calibre
concede
gauge
hygiene
idyllic
psychic
recess
strategy
trolley
amateur
chord
courteous
ghastly
intuition
mileage
qualm
rhyme
syringe
unusual

# THE GOOD GRAMMAR GUIDE

## Verbs

At school you were probably taught that verbs are 'doing words'. You may also remember that some are 'regular' (they follow a pattern) and some are 'irregular'. It is now time to move on a stage. You use verbs dozens of times a day – and in this section we will look at why you say the things you do!

## Types of verbs

While the term 'doing words' describes most verbs, it doesn't really cover all of them. Which words, for instance, are the verbs in the following sentence?

*I must be going home.*

If you look for the 'doing word' then you would identify the verb as 'to go'. However, this is the main verb in the sentence, but it isn't the only one.

There are three kinds of verbs.

- **Full verbs** – which describe an action: to go, to run, to jump, to laugh, etc.
- **Auxiliary verbs –** sometimes called 'helping' verbs. These cannot stand alone in a sentence but can only be used with a full verb. They include the phrases 'need to' and 'be able to' as well as pairs of words such as

  can and could
  will and would
  must and ought
  shall and should
  may and might

- **Primary verbs** – which can operate as either full verbs or helping verbs. There are three of these: 'to be', 'to do' and 'to have'.

Therefore, in the sentence *I must be going home* there are three types of verbs. The full verb is *to go*, *must* is the auxiliary verb and *be* is 'helping' the verb 'to go'.

Auxiliary verbs are useful because they help us to explain whether something is possible, probable or definite. They are used to differentiate between making a request and giving an instruction, together with your tone of voice when speaking. For instance, compare the sentences:

*Can you move this box? Could you move this box? Will you move this box?*

- Using the word 'can' implies the ability to move the box as well as the willingness to do so. The reply may be: '*Sorry, it's too heavy.*'
- All the sentences could be interpreted by the receiver as being a polite request or a command, depending upon
  - the other words you add (or do not add) to the sentence
  - your tone of voice
  - your body language (see Unit 7).

  A polite request to a colleague may be phrased as:

  *Excuse me, but please could you move this box before someone falls over it?*

  An instruction or command from parent to child may be worded:

  *Move this box immediately before someone breaks a leg!*

  Now try reading the sentence *Would you move this box* in three ways. (Add the word *please* where you wish.) Pretend you are speaking to:

  **a** an older person at work whom you do not know very well
  **b** a friend
  **c** your younger brother or sister, with whom you are extremely annoyed.

  Now consider which sentence you should use at work to gain positive cooperation!

## Parts of a verb

There are two further parts to a verb.

- **The infinitive** is the root part of the verb, which usually follows the word 'to', eg *to go, to eat, to sleep.*

  It used to be forbidden to 'split' an infinitive by putting a word in between. *Star Trek* writers were severely criticised when they first used the phrase '*to boldly go*'. Today the rule is not enforced strictly – and there are times when sentences would seem most odd if the intervening word was moved, eg

  *We need to drastically change the rota.* Not *We need to change drastically*

  *I think I have started to really understand how to use this software.*
  *We had to finally abandon our original plans for New Year's Eve.*

  Try to avoid splitting an infinitive if you can, but if you cannot sensibly move the intervening word, let it stand.

- **The participle** – which may be either **present** or **past**.

  **Present participles** are formed with the addition of '-ing', eg *waiting, moving, running*. They denote an action that is currently taking place, eg *I am waiting.*

  **Past participles** are used when an action has been completed. They are formed with the addition of the letters '-ed' with many verbs, eg *cooked,* *worked, shopped*. Irregular verbs have different endings, eg *driven, fought, drank*. The past participle is used, with the addition of the verb 'to be' or 'to have' when a verb is expressed in its **passive** form.

You should note that an infinitive or a participle does not qualify *on its own* as the verb in a sentence as it is not a finite verb – so you must not write a phrase such as *Waiting for your reply* and consider it a sentence. Occasionally, however, you will see an '-ing' word that 'works' at the beginning of a sentence, eg *Smoking is banned* or *Jogging is very popular*. This is because in these examples the words 'smoking' and 'jogging' are used as nouns and are therefore the subject of the sentence.

## Active and passive forms

Knowing the difference between the active and passive form – and being able to convert your sentences from one to the other – is very useful.

Verbs are used mainly in their **active** form, eg *The dog bit the child*. In its passive form the sentence would read *The child was bitten by the dog*. In this case the sentence could be rewritten without naming the dog (which has become the indirect object) to read '*The child was bitten*.' Although we don't know who or what did the biting, the sentence still makes sense.

This can be useful when you want to be deliberately vague about something. If you read the newspapers or watch TV coverage of ministers speaking in Parliament, you will see that politicians often explain an event using the passive form, eg *Benefits must be cut* rather than *I am cutting benefits*.

The active form is more personal and easier to follow. It should therefore be used if you are writing a list of instructions or a notice, as your readers will find it easier to understand and it will appeal to each one of them far more personally.

## Test your understanding

**1** Identify the full verb and the auxiliary verb in each of the following sentences:

- **a** I can help you.
- **b** I will be there.
- **c** I ought to meet him.
- **d** I could go on Tuesday.

**2** Reword each of the following commands to convert it into a polite request:

- **a** Will you hurry up!
- **b** Can you tidy your desk now.
- **c** I shall need to borrow your pen.
- **d** I have to leave early tonight.
- **e** If John Black rings while I'm out, can you take a message.

**3** Convert each of the following sentences from the active to the passive form, so that no blame can be attached to anyone!

**a** I left the lights on.
**b** Farouk lost the file.
**c** Jessica and Ludmilla haven't finish checking the documents yet.

**4** The following instructions has been written in the passive form.

**To change a cartridge in the printer**

The printer must be switched off and the lid opened.
When the cartridge carrier has moved to the central position the spent cartridge can be removed.
This should then be replaced with a new cartridge.
The replacement cartridge must be heard to click into position.
The lid must be closed before the printer is switched on again.

Rewrite this in the active form. To help, the first few lines are done for you below.

**To change a cartridge in the printer**

Switch off the printer.
Open the lid.
Wait until the cartridge carrier moves to the central position.

**DON'T YOU DARE!**

*...write or say any of the following: 'could of', 'would of', 'should of'! This occurs when you have misheard the word 'have' as a child and then keep repeating your mistake. The correct phrases are 'could have', 'would have', 'should have', etc – so forget 'of' altogether in this type of context!*

MAKING HEADWAY –
letters of enquiry, response and acknowledgement


# LETTERS OF ENQUIRY

A letter of enquiry is a letter you send to obtain information or to ask for something. To obtain the right response you need to specify what you require – although the degree of detail required will depend upon the situation.

If you are asking someone to do you a favour this should have a bearing on the tone of your letter – although, of course, all your letters must be courteous. However, there is a considerable difference between asking someone you know well for something and writing to a complete stranger. If your letter is a commercial enquiry – because you may be buying something – you are likely to receive a prompt response because the recipient is interested in making a sale. If, however, you are asking someone to do you a favour, you may have more difficulty. This is why students who write to companies requesting information for a project sometimes struggle.

Your letter should have:

**a** a clear heading, so the recipient can identify at a glance the subject of the letter
**b** a brief introduction, stating the reason for your letter
**c** the specific details of what you require
**d** any essential background information that will help or encourage a reluctant recipient to assist you. If you are responding to an advertisement, this is unlikely to be necessary.

You can close with a suitable sentence. Remember, as always, to keep it short and simple. Remember too, that because you are asking a favour, words such as 'please', 'thank you' or 'grateful' should be included somewhere – but don't overdo it!

24 Sellyoak Avenue
HIGHTOWN
HG3 9MK

14 October 199-

The Publications Department
British Safety Council
National Safety Centre
Chancellor's Road
LONDON
W6 9RS

Dear Sirs

**HEALTH AND SAFETY AT WORK**

I am a student at Hightown College and am undertaking a project with three of my fellow students which involves researching various aspects of Health and Safety at Work.

I understand that your organisation is involved in safety management and accident prevention training and that you publish a monthly newsletter, guides on safety and various information sheets and booklets.

I should be grateful if you could let me have a list of your free publications and leaflets which would give information on safety management and accident prevention, as these would be very helpful for our research. I enclose a stamped addressed envelope for your reply.

I look forward to hearing from you.

Yours faithfully

Joanne Sumner (Miss)

***Figure 9.3*** *A personal letter of enquiry*

## POINTS TO NOTE

- It is always better to write to a specific department or, better still, a named individual – otherwise your letter can be passed aimlessly from one desk to another. If you want someone to do you a favour, telephone the company, find out who should receive the letter and address it to that person. This makes life much simpler if you have to telephone to follow up your letter. Don't forget to check the spelling of the name and the correct designation – nothing is more likely to irritate a recipient than to find his or her name spelt wrongly!
- If you are asking a personal favour of an individual, it is courteous to enclose a stamped addressed envelope (sae). Some advertisements for literature ask for one to be enclosed and sometimes specify the size. Check this carefully if you are responding to such an advert.

A personal letter of enquiry sent by a student undertaking a project is shown in Figure 9.3. Check whether you consider it is courteous and clear and should result in a positive response.

# LETTERS OF RESPONSE AND ACKNOWLEDGEMENT

Whenever a letter of enquiry is sent, someone has to respond to it, preferably by providing the information or item requested or by agreeing or declining to do the favour. In the early stages of your career, you would be unlikely to be expected to write responses relating to complex or highly technical enquiries. However, you can expect to have to respond to straightforward requests.

Letters of response are one of the most frequent and most important types of business communications. They provide a major opportunity for obtaining new customers, which results in more business for the organisation and greater job security for the employees! All organisations are likely to have a range of printed material about their products or services, which can be sent out in response to enquiries. Alternatively, a personalised circular letter may be produced (see Figure 8.4 on page 142). However, because the opportunity to obtain additional business is considered so vital, a personal letter of response is often sent. This is always the case when the enquiry is unusual or individual.

**HIGHTOWN LEISURE COMPLEX**
Castle Road
HIGHTOWN
HG3 4MP

Tel: 01928-309322 General Manager: May Rodgers

10 March 199-

Mr J Thompson
Digital Software Solutions Ltd
Bramhall Way
HIGHTOWN
HG6 2WS

Dear Mr Thompson

**CORPORATE MEMBERSHIP OF HEALTH AND FITNESS CENTRE**

Thank you for your letter of 8 March requesting details of the cost of membership of our Health and Fitness Centre for your employees.

The special rates paid by organisations are determined by the number of employees who are interested in becoming members and the number of times they will wish to visit us each week. Mrs Rodgers, the General Manager of the complex, always deals with these requests personally but unfortunately she is on leave until next Monday, 17 March. As soon as she returns, she will respond to you with full details.

I hope this delay does not inconvenience you in any way. Thank you for contacting us.

Yours sincerely

Mariam Mansoor
General Assistant

***Figure 9.4*** *A letter of acknowledgement*

If an immediate response to the enquiry is not possible it is usual to send a **letter of acknowledgement**. This is a brief, courteous letter acknowledging the request, explaining why it cannot be dealt with immediately and saying when a complete response can be expected. This is much better than a long delay before an official response is sent.

An example of a letter of acknowledgement is given in Figure 9.4.

When you can give more specific assistance or advice, there are six main points you should bear in mind when writing a letter of response:

- it must be helpful
- it must be accurate
- it must be complete
- it must be friendly and courteous
- it should be persuasive
- it must be sent promptly.

## Being helpful

Helpfulness can be measured in degrees – it is not just a case of being helpful or unhelpful. Take an example. You are in the supermarket and looking for lemon grass because you are making Thai food. You have no idea where it is so you ask a girl stacking some shelves. Her possible responses can be measured in degrees of helpfulness as follows:

| | |
|---|---|
| Very unhelpful: | *No idea, sorry.* |
| Unhelpful: | *No, sorry. I don't think we stock it.* |
| Very little help: | *I think we have it – try asking that lad over there.* |
| Just a bit better: | *I think it's down there, third aisle on your left.* |
| Better still: | *It's next to herbs and spices. Do you know where that is? – third aisle on your left from here.* |
| The best: | *Yes – I'll show you, then you'll find it easily next time.* |

The best response impresses you, makes you want to go there again and, what's more, makes an extra sale! When you write a letter of response that is your aim.

It is quite possible to be helpful even if you cannot answer a specific enquiry. Our girl stacking shelves could have said to you *'I'm sorry, we don't stock it at present but I'll tell the manager you were asking. He always likes to know about new lines people want. You can get it from the shop on the corner of Valley Road if you need it urgently.'* Even though you may be irritated, you could not make accusations of unhelpfulness, could you?

## Being accurate

Never guess at the information you put in a letter of response. If you have been asked about a product you sell, a service you offer, for details of dates, times or prices then you must be certain that what you say is accurate. Your potential customers will be more than annoyed if they act on your information only to find they have been misinformed. Always double check the details in your letter and proof-read it carefully.

## Being complete

A letter of enquiry may include several queries and you should make sure that you have answered all of them. The danger is that you include a brochure or a leaflet giving general information but not an answer to some specific queries. In this case you would have to give the answers in your letter.

## Being friendly and courteous

A letter of response is usually quite informal – you want to communicate with your potential customer on a personal level. However, you have to be careful that when you are doing this you don't become too familiar.

## Being persuasive

Being persuasive in a business letter is not quite the same as trying to persuade a friend to do something! You cannot be so obvious. Instead, by sounding positive and giving all the good points you persuade someone to try a product or service. This is like advertising – adverts try to persuade you to buy by making you think you will be better off for the experience! Likewise, you need to 'sell' your service or product.

## Acting promptly

Letters of enquiry should always be answered quickly (or a letter of acknowledgement should be sent in the meantime). Frequently, potential customers will send an enquiry to more than one organisation and if you delay in responding they will go elsewhere. It is also the case that people equate a slow response with inefficiency or lack of interest on the part of the organisation.

126 Grafton Meadows
HIGHTOWN
HG6 2PP

13/11/9-

To whoever deals with enquiries
ASA Ltd
Brook House
Torrington Place
LONDON
WC1E 7HN

Dear Sir or Madam

My name is Natalie Swales and I am writing to you about a project I'm doing at school for my G.C.S.E. I have to find out about advertisments and I know you have something to do with them because if people don't like what they read they can write to you to complain and you will do something about it. Have you any leaflets or things about your work and what you do cos these would help me a lot. I'd be really greatful if you could send me something.

Thanks a lot.

Yours faithfully

Miss Natalie Swales

***Figure 9.5*** *Natalie's letter to the Advertising Standards Authority*

## Test your understanding

**1** You thought you had escaped Naive Natalie when you left Riverside Small Animal Centre. However, a few days ago she tracked you down in the leisure complex, which she visits regularly. She was rather dispirited because, despite writing to several organisations to obtain information for her GCSE project on advertising, she has received little, if any, response. She has brought you a sample letter she intends to send tomorrow (Figure 9.5). Can you help her by rewriting it so that it is more likely to be acted upon by its recipient?

**2** An example of a letter of response sent by Mariam at the leisure complex is given in Figure 9.6.

**a** Check whether you consider it matches all the criteria given above.
**b** Consider the implications if Mariam had given the wrong information relating to Ben's hearing problems. What could have been the result and why? Discuss your suggestions as a group.

**3** Below are shown extracts from five letters. Identify which one is from

**a** a letter of acknowledgement
**b** a helpful letter of response
**c** an unhelpful letter of response
**d** a complete letter of response
**e** an over-enthusiastic letter of response.

**A** We are enclosing a leaflet on our fitness centre which should give you all the information you require. In response to your specific enquiry, we do offer step aerobics every Tuesday and Thursday from 6.30 pm to 7.30 pm.

**HIGHTOWN LEISURE COMPLEX**
Castle Road
HIGHTOWN
HG3 4MP

Tel: 01928 309322 General Manager: May Rodgers

10 March 199-

Mrs J Penny
14 Risedale Walk
HIGHTOWN
HG3 8SL

Dear Mrs Penny

Thank you for your letter of 7 March 199- enquiring about our Tadpoles swimming club for your son, Ben.

The Tadpoles Club is open to children aged from 3–10 years, whether they are beginners, improvers or advanced swimmers. Separate swimming sessions are available for each group on several days of the week and individual coaching sessions can be arranged with specialist staff by appointment. I have pleasure in enclosing a leaflet on the Tadpoles Club which I hope you will find helpful.

In relation to your enquiry as to whether your son's deafness could be a problem, I have consulted our Swimming Coach, Mr Bill Ford, who tells me that this will very much depend upon the cause of his hearing problems. He thinks it is extremely important that you discuss the matter thoroughly with your doctor before you consider enrolling Ben in the Tadpoles Club. Alternatively, Bill would be happy to talk to you about this in more detail if you would like to telephone him. The best time to speak to him is between 9 am and 10 am in the morning or 4 pm and 5 pm in the afternoon, as he has coaching sessions between these times.

I hope you find this information useful. If I can be of any further assistance, please do not hesitate to contact me.

Yours sincerely

Mariam Mansoor
General Assistant

Enc

***Figure 9.6*** *A letter of response from the leisure complex*

**B** I regret we no longer offer karate classes at the complex as there is no demand for them and, indeed, this has been the case for several years.

**C** Yes, we do offer aerobics classes and they're ideal if, like most of us, you want to keep fit or lose weight – so don't delay, start today!

**D** Thank you for your enquiry about reserving the cricket nets for your youth club members between May and September. We have received several requests for this facility and are attempting to provide additional nets this year to meet this demand. We will be able to advise you more precisely on availability in two weeks' time, when we will contact you again.

**E** I regret that we do not offer toning tables at this complex, although you will find that they are available at *Beauty and Fitness* on Riverside Drive. However, we do offer a full range of other programmes which you may find interesting and I am enclosing a leaflet giving this information.

## TOOLS OF THE TRADE – one-to-one interactions

When you are communicating with people, either in writing or verbally, you will always do this more effectively if you can empathise with the other person. In other words, if you are able to look at the situation from the other person's point of view. This is a key aspect of interacting with other people – and if you master this, you are far more likely to get on in life than if you don't. You will also find your own problems easier to cope with, as you can view them from different angles or perspectives.

You interact with other people constantly every day of your life. A brief exchange with someone at home before you leave in the morning, a chat to colleagues in the office, work-related discussions during the day, lunch with a friend, an evening with family or friends. On each occasion you are exchanging views with other people – often on a one-to-one basis, sometimes in a small group, sometimes in a large one. Most of the time these interactions will go smoothly. Many times they are beneficial, amusing or stimulating. Occasionally, however, there are problems. You may disagree with someone, argue, become annoyed or irritated or even have a row. You may both say things you later regret. You may both consider the other is unreasonable and both of you may be too proud or stubborn to apologise.

How well you manage your day-to-day interactions socially will depend, to a large extent, upon your own personality and those of your friends. Two very volatile people are unlikely to stay friendly for long. Indeed it is often said that in every relationship there is a giver and a taker – and two 'takers' are unlikely to remain together for any length of time. In many cases, there can be fundamental misunderstandings because of an inability to communicate with each other. If both talk, neither really listen. Or neither knows how to put his or her feelings into words without upsetting or annoying the other.

You may find some of the following advice useful socially as well as at work. How you manage your working relationships is very important if you are to work happily and productively and to be seen as an asset to an organisation. This is directly related to your ability to communicate – and your ability to appreciate how your communications are received by others. It is also affected by your ability to understand your own reactions when you receive messages. You can hardly row with your boss, sulk or walk out every time you disagree with something! Therefore, your ability to manage your one-to-one interactions means knowing yourself as well as knowing how to communicate.

A communication may be misinterpreted for many reasons, including:

- the situation and the timing – people are too busy or too stressed to listen to what you are really saying
- someone's mood or frame of mind at the time
- the words, phrases and gestures chosen – which are often open to misinterpretation
- the tone used – which may not be the one meant
- the fact that when we are concentrating on ourselves, how we feel and what we hope to achieve by the interaction, we often forget to consider the feelings, perceptions and expectations of the other person.

If you are interacting with a good communicator who has the time and patience to listen, who genuinely understands other people's problems and is a real 'people person' then this person is giving and you are taking during the interaction. Conversely, if you are interacting with someone who is more reserved, who is rushed, stressed or has problems, and who is responsible for achieving a high level of output from staff in the shortest possible time, then you will have more difficulties – unless you are a particularly skilled communicator and a very understanding person yourself!

## Assertiveness, aggressiveness and passivity

Assertiveness skills are invaluable when you need to make a point, but are worried you will upset anyone. You are assertive if you can point something out calmly and reasonably, without attacking or blaming anyone, and simply repeat your point if the other person becomes unreasonable. The difference between being passive, assertive and aggressive is illustrated in Figure 9.7.

Assertive statements are often prefaced by 'I' because you are stating your own feelings frankly. They are made in a cooperative manner which identifies with the other person's feelings, eg *I think this could create a problem.* Aggressive statements are often prefaced by 'you', eg *You can't be serious!* Passive statements often start with phrases such as *If you don't mind* and *It*

| Aggression is | Assertiveness is | Passivity is |
|---|---|---|
| Being selfish and arrogant<br>Wanting your own way<br>Ignoring other people's needs<br>Manipulating other people<br>Being impolite or sarcastic<br>Shouting, losing your temper, arguing<br>Upsetting other people<br>Over-reacting to remarks by being defensive, critical or belligerent | Understanding other people's viewpoints<br>Respecting yourself and other people<br>Being honest but tactful<br>Being open-minded and able to negotiate and reach a compromise<br>Being self-confident<br>Being able to make a point without becoming aggressive<br>Being able to say 'no' nicely<br>Achieving your goals without upsetting other people<br>Feeling good about yourself | Ignoring your own feelings, needs and interests<br>Always putting yourself last<br>Being afraid to say 'no'<br>Always wanting to please other people<br>Never making a fuss<br>Always giving way, no matter how you feel<br>Feeling frustrated, hurt, unhappy or anxious |

**Hostile** ←——————→ **Placatory**

***Figure 9.7*** *Aggressiveness, assertiveness and passivity*

*really doesn't matter*. Body language is also important. Your approach should be non-threatening – hands unclenched and a steady (not raised) tone of voice. Note that if your head is lowered and you avoid eye contact, this indicates you are being passive.

## THE FINAL TOUCHES

Many people can cope with ordinary day-to-day conversations but have problems with three areas – all of which are essential to master if you want to relate to people more easily. Check your own abilities in each of the following areas as honestly as you can.

- Do you accept compliments graciously? Do you say 'thank you very much' and look pleased, or do you negate the compliment in some way, such as by saying 'Don't be silly' or 'It's nothing'. Accepting a compliment to make the giver feel 'good' is a social skill you should learn. It doesn't make you appear conceited, just nice to know!
- Do you say 'thank you' readily when someone does something for you, or do you often forget?
- The hardest of all – do you apologise when you know you are in the wrong or, at least, not 100% right? A useful way to approach this if you're worried about losing face is to make an assertive apology, eg *I'm really sorry if I didn't give you the information on time. I really didn't do it on purpose but I wasn't sure exactly what you wanted. Do you think we could talk about it?* This says how you feel and acknowledges the feelings of the other person. At the very least, it re-opens the channels of communication.

## DON'T YOU DARE!

*...confuse the abbreviations 'eg' and 'ie'. When you use 'eg' you are saying 'for example' – naming several items that belong to a longer list:*

*There are many electronic methods of communication, eg fax, electronic mail and mobile telephone.*

*When you use 'ie' you are saying 'that is', and naming or defining a specific item:*

*To send a message from one computer to another, ie by e-mail, you need to be registered as a user.*

## Test your understanding

For the third time in two weeks your boss has asked you to work late. Tonight is difficult as you are meeting someone, but you are worried about his reaction if you refuse.

**1** From the three approaches below, identify which one is aggressive, which is assertive and which is passive.

**a** You're always picking on me, why can't you ask someone else for a change?
**b** Well, er, it's not really important, but I was wondering if I could leave on time tonight.
**c** I'm sorry, I really would like to help but unfortunately I've made arrangements for this evening and must leave at 5 pm. Is there anything I can do to help in the meantime?

**2** Identify the likely outcomes of each statement.

## WORDBANK 8

Each of the following terms relates to personal relationships. In each case decide the answer to the question and enter any new words and definitions into your Wordbank book.

What are you doing if you . . .

**a** **admonish** someone
**b** find someone an **anathema**
**c** **appease** someone
**d** **concur** with someone
**e** are involved in a **controversy**
**f** do something which is **unethical**
**g** reach an **impasse** with someone
**h** are **impertinent**
**i** **reciprocate**
**j** **refute** an allegation
**k** **reprove** someone
**l** are **reticent**
**m** are **sardonic**

**n** are a **staunch** ally
**o** are **truculent**
**p** are **vehement**

## COMMUNICATION IN PRACTICE

### Test your skills

**1** For each of the following verbs, complete the information which is missing in the following columns. To help you, the first verb has been done for you.

| Verb | Present tense | Present participle | Past participle |
|---|---|---|---|
| to be | am | being | been |
| to begin | | beginning | |
| to choose | choose | | |
| to drink | drink | | |
| to fall | | | fallen |
| to fly | | flying | |
| to forget | forget | | |
| to go | | going | |
| to grow | | | grown |
| to know | | knowing | |
| to ring | ring | | |
| to ride | ride | | |
| to shake | | | shaken |
| to speak | | speaking | |
| to tear | tear | | |
| to write | write | | |

**2** There are 20 spelling errors in the passage below. Can you identify and correct them all without using a dictionary?

Martin had allways been a loner. It was the same at work. He prefered to work seperately from his colleeges. At heart, he was an agreable person. He would never cause trouble and hated arguements. He would conceed to himself that the people he worked with were curteous and helpfull but their noisey laughter and wity remarks often alarmed him. Socail events he found particularly gastly.

His manager was concerned. She didn't have to be psycic to realise how Martin struggled – yet he was a good, consientious worker. Then she had learned someone of the right caliber was needed immediatly for a new research job which required very little liason with other people. Her intuishun told her Martin would find it idilic. Now she needed a stratagy to help him to get the job.

**3** You are hoping to go camping in France this summer with your friends. Six of you will be travelling together. You want to meet to decide when to go and calculate the cost. This morning you collected the following special offer from a travel agent (see Figure 9.8). Study this carefully and then check that you could make an accurate decision by answering the questions that follow.

| Outward travel date | 2 people 6 days | 12 days | 3 people 6 days | 12 days | 4 people 6 days | 12 days | 7th, 13th and 14th nights per party |
|---|---|---|---|---|---|---|---|
| to 14/6 | £ 122 | £ 160 | £ 85 | £ 110 | £ 62 | £ 83 | £ FREE |
| 15/6 to 12/7 | 181 | 284 | 122 | 202 | 95 | 153 | 21 |
| 13/7 to 19/7 | 205 | 320 | 135 | 245 | 108 | 182 | 21 |
| 20/7 to 30/8 | 249 | 429 | 165 | 279 | 131 | 205 | 29 |
| from 31/8 | 122 | 160 | 85 | 110 | 62 | 83 | FREE |

**Notes to table**

1 Prices shown are Folkestone to Boulogne mid-week.
2 Dover to Calais = £5 supplement each way.
3 Fri–Sat inclusive = £6 each way supplement.
4 Personal travel insurance = £15 per person for 7 days' cover.
5 Children under 4 travel free.
6 No cancellation charges apply for 7 days after issue of invoice.

***Figure 9.8***
*Travel agent's information*

**a** How much would it cost for two people to travel from Folkestone for six days, assuming they were travelling mid-week departing on the 24 June and didn't want insurance cover?
**b** How much would it cost for their infant son, aged 18 months?
**c** How much extra would it cost them if another adult joined them?
**d** How much extra would this party (ie 3 adults and one infant) pay if they stayed for a seventh night?
**e** If the six of you wanted to travel from Dover, leave on Wednesday 2 August, stay for 14 nights and you all needed insurance cover, how much would you pay in total?
**f** One of your group would prefer to travel on a Saturday. How much extra would this cost your group as a whole?
**g** When the invoice arrives, two members of the group think they may not be able to go. How long would they have in which to change their minds and cancel if they wanted to avoid paying a cancellation fee?

## Apply your skills

Today you are assisting with several jobs at the leisure complex. There has been a considerable amount of work recently because May Rodgers has decided to change the way in which the fitness centre operates. Demand has increased so much that she has decided to start a fitness club. Members will gain special benefits and everyone has been busy preparing the advertising material. In the meantime you have been given the following tasks.

**1** May has drafted out the details of the membership fees for the fitness club. She wants to see this in a simple, easy-to-understand table. From her draft notes shown opposite (Figure 9.9), prepare the table she requires.

**2** The leisure complex keeps records of the number of participants who choose different activities. These statistics help May Rodgers to identify

FEES FOR LEISURE CLUB

There will be three rates of membership: off-peak, full member and partner (put off-peak last, will you). All rates are for one year. There will be three categories of membership: bronze, silver and gold. I think these had better go across the top. Think up suitable headings, please. The prices for full members are as follows: £200, £250, £300. The partner rate is 25% cheaper and the off-peak rate is 40% cheaper. Can you calculate these for me?

Please put a brief note at the bottom that all fees include a personal assessment at the start with a written report and individual fitness programme. Put a second note too, please, that follow-up assessments are carried out every three months.

Then I'll see what it looks like. Thanks.

***Figure 9.9*** *May's notes on membership fees*

**Participation in activities – 1997–1999**

| **Activity** | **1997** | **1998** | **1999** |
|---|---|---|---|
| Badminton | 1572 | 1428 | 1397 |
| Keep fit | 1176 | 1325 | 1593 |
| Martial arts | 205 | 317 | 524 |
| Squash | 2071 | 1842 | 1653 |
| Swimming | 5294 | 6531 | 7214 |
| Weight training | 426 | 452 | 431 |
| **Total** | **10744** | **11895** | **12812** |

***Figure 9.10*** *Participation figures for the leisure complex*

which activities are the most and least popular and any trends in usage. The figures for the past three years are given in Figure 9.10 below.

**a** Write a short commentary to explain any trends you identify.

**b** Calculate the percentage usage for each activity in 1999 and prepare a pie chart showing this. Include an appropriate heading and an appropriate key.

**3** May Rodgers would like special laminated identity cards to be issued to new members of the fitness club. She understands a good selection are offered by G A Associates Limited, 14 Gordonbridge Road, Hightown, HG2 1PM. She has asked you to write to Mr J Fox, the Sales Manager, asking for details of the ID cards they offer and for information as to whether photographs can be included for security reasons. She has asked you to request a booklet and a price list and to ask for details of how long the cards will take to arrive after being ordered. Draft an appropriate letter for her approval.

**4** Several letters have been received from people who have heard about the fitness club, asking for further details and information. May Rodgers wants to wait until all the advertising literature has been received in the next week or two before responding to these requests with specific details. She has asked you to prepare a brief acknowledgement letter which can be stored on the word processor and personalised for all enquirers. She has asked you to thank people for their enquiry and state that, as yet, all the details have not been finalised, but that she will send each person a leaflet as soon as these are available – probably within the next two weeks. Draft a letter leaving spaces for specific names and addresses to be inserted.

**5** Mrs T Marshall of 15 Heyes Grove, Hightown, HG3 2PH, booked a birthday party for her daughter, Sarah. Yesterday you received a telephone enquiry from her. Apparently her daughter accidentally left two birthday presents in the party room. She has asked if you could look for these and then telephone her so that she can collect them.

Although you have searched and checked the lost property book, nothing has been found. May Rodgers has asked if you will write to

Mrs Marshall explaining the situation and saying that if the presents are found later you will, of course, notify her immediately.

Before you start this letter, consider the phrases you should use, bearing in mind that Sarah is probably upset and her mother is likely to be suffering the consequences!

Check all your work with your tutor.

## *WORD WIZARD*

### FAMOUS INSULTS

It is not suggested you learn any of the following phrases to use with your friends or colleagues! However, some famous word wizards in the past – writers, playwrights and comedians – have been particularly skilled at choosing a particular phrase to express annoyance. Some are particularly acerbic (look up this word!) about other people's communication skills. If you are not sure of the meanings of some of these phrases, ask your tutor!

*She never lets ideas interrupt the easy flow of her conversation.* (Jean Webster)

*She's the kind of woman who climbed the ladder of success – wrong by wrong.* (Mae West)

*Some cause happiness wherever they go; others whenever they go.* (Oscar Wilde)

*He is a self-made man and worships his creator.* (John Bright)

*Nature, not content with denying him the ability to think, has endowed him with the ability to write.* (A E Housman)

*The trouble with her is that she lacks the power of conversation but not the power of speech.* (George Bernard Shaw)

*He thinks by infection, catching an opinion like a cold.* (John Ruskin)

*A gentleman is one who never hurts anyone's feelings unintentionally.* (Oscar Wilde)

*If he ever had a bright idea it would be beginner's luck.* (William Lashner 'Veritas')

*She's the sort of woman who lives for others – you can tell the others by their hunted expression.* (C S Lewis)

*Some folks are wise and some are otherwise.* (Tobias George Smolett)

*I like long walks, especially when they are taken by people who annoy me.* (Fred Allen)

*He is as good as his word – and his word is no good.* (Seamus MacManus).

*An editor is one who separates the wheat from the chaff and then prints the chaff.* (Adlai Stevenson).

# 10
UNIT

## IN THE SPOTLIGHT –
# FACT SHEETS, RESUMÉS AND SUMMARIES

In Unit 8 you first met the term 'information overload'. You may remember that this term describes the vast amount of information that surrounds us today, particularly now that computers are used to prepare, process and analyse data. The article in Figure 8.2, on page 141, referred to the problems that managers and their staff face in reading, understanding and using all this information.

This increase in the quantity of information has meant that it is even more essential to summarise it in some way – particularly for a busy manager.

There are three ways in which this may be done.

- By preparing a **fact sheet**. This is usually a one-page document using the key facts on a particular topic or issue. These are usually written in note form. The sheet is designed to be read easily and quickly.
- By giving a **resumé** – this may be verbal or in writing. For instance, at the start of a discussion, your boss could turn to a colleague and say 'John, you know all about this. Give everyone a quick resumé of what has happened, will you?' At this point John is supposed to summarise what has taken place. He is unlikely to be popular if he 'ums' and 'ahs', includes irrelevant details and takes a long time to do it!
- By preparing a written **summary**. This term is used when a document, or set of documents, is put in a shortened form. In some cases there may be a specific word length that you must not exceed. At work you will normally find you are just asked to make your summary as short as you can without losing the meaning of the original.

You have already learned many techniques that have laid the foundations for preparing these documents. In Units 4 and 6 you learned about identifying the key facts in messages and about making notes. In Unit 7 you learned how to unscramble complex messages and in Unit 8 you looked at writing reports and reading for a purpose.

In this unit we will build on your skills by looking at the tasks you need to undertake to prepare each of these documents and the type of layout you may be expected to use.

# PREPARING A FACT SHEET

A fact sheet is a list of facts about a particular topic, given in a logical order. Sometimes the most important facts are given first, in another case you may find you have to use specific headings or chronological (date) order.

Before you start you must know the following.

- The **exact** topic you are supposed to cover. Unless you know this precisely, you are likely to include irrelevant facts or omit essential ones. Therefore, it is vital you understand what you are being asked to do.
- The type of **material** you are supposed to use to obtain your facts. In some cases, this may be obvious – in other cases it will be less so. For instance, if you were preparing a fact sheet on computers you could do this by visiting a large retailer and collecting literature, or you could spend a long time looking in books, magazines and newspapers, contacting suppliers and talking to specialists. If a topic you are given is very broad, discuss with your boss (or tutor) how wide a search you should make. Sometimes the time limit will be your biggest guide. You can hardly hunt through reams of information if you have only half an hour!
- The **layout** required. If this is not specified clearly, assume you will need a heading at the top, appropriate headings within the fact sheet and itemised or bullet points under each one. Sometimes a form of decimal numbering is used, although today this is usually only in formal documents (see Figure 10.1). The advantage of bullet points over numbered points is that no specific order is indicated. If you use numbered points you imply a degree of order or rank.
- The **style** to use. In most cases you should be brief and to the point. Your opinions and views are *not* appropriate to a fact sheet

***Figure 10.1*** *Examples of numbering systems*

**1** Sometimes a form of itemisation

a) using letters of the alphabet can
b) using numbers in certain cases
c) using arabic numerals is the mos

**2** At other times there may be more use

**1** Sometimes a form of decimal number

1.1 each new item is listed in an ord
1.2 the numbering continues with a

1.2.1 a further level is then ind
1.2.2 the decimal numbers are

1.3 a different point is used when the

**2** In another example the form of itemi

- Whether any **sources of information** are required. These can be useful if someone needs to refer to the sources you have used for further details.

## A WORKED EXAMPLE

At Hightown Leisure Complex many members ask about insurance against injury. May Rodgers asked Mariam to find out about this and prepare a fact sheet that could be kept in reception and in the office. This has been designed to enable staff to answer enquiries about insurance quickly and easily. Read

**FACT SHEET ON INSURANCE FOR SPORTS ACTIVITIES**

**Cover**

1 Comprehensive cover offered by SportsCover Direct, which specialises in providing cover for high-risk activities.

**Risk ratings**

1 Sports are rated according to type of risk and number of accidents/deaths each year.

2 Sports are rated as dangerous, high risk, moderate risk and low risk.

3 Most leisure complex sports are in low risk category.

*Dangerous sports*

1 Most dangerous are hang gliding and paragliding, because errors can cost lives.

2 Annual cover about £77.50.

*High risk sports*

1 These including boxing, bungee jumping, caving, climbing, potholing, polo, ski jumping and ski racing.

2 The only team sport included is rugby as there are more injuries per participant than any other sport.

3 Scuba diving over 30 metres is considered high risk.

4 Cost of cover about £34.50.

*Moderate risk*

1 The only sports which relate to the leisure complex are football, martial arts and weightlifting, as injury rates in all these sports are relatively high.

2 Other sports included in this category are ballooning, ski-ing, horseriding, snowboarding, scuba diving, tobogganing and wrestling.

3 Cost of cover about £29.50.

*Low risk*

1 All other sporting activities relating to the leisure complex are in this category – aerobics, athletics, badminton, basketball, running, squash, swimming, tennis.

2 Other low risk sports include angling, bowls, cycling, cricket, golf, jogging, parascending, pony trekking, roller blading, sailing, skateboarding, snooker, walking, waterskiing and windsurfing.

3 Cost of cover about £26.00 per annum.

(Sources of information: Sportscover Direct and Sports Council Information Centre, 16 Upper Woburn Place, London W1H 0QP)

***Figure 10.2*** *Hightown Leisure Complex fact sheet*

through the fact sheet illustrated in Figure 10.2 and see if you think it is complete, or whether there is too much or too little information. Can you identify any other information that would have been useful?

## Other types of fact sheets – programmes and itineraries

Another version of a fact sheet is a programme for an event or an itinerary for a trip. The aim is to produce the information in such a way that everyone involved can see what happens and when. The events are listed in time order, and it is normal to use the 24-hour clock.

### A WORKED EXAMPLE

May Rodgers has been invited to the opening of a new athletics arena in Hightown. Hightown Council has arranged the event and is delighted that Sean Reynolds, the Minister for Sport, has agreed to formally open the arena. The event will be attended by several local dignitaries, including the mayor, mayoress and local MP.

The programme May has received is shown in Figure 10.3. Note the layout of the programme and the order in which the information has been presented for ease of reference.

Sean Reynolds is staying at the Swan Hotel in Hightown on the night of Wednesday, 14 May. May Rodgers has been invited to meet him at a dinner to be held at 8.30 that evening. At the dinner will be Brian Faraday, the Chief Executive of Hightown Council; the managers of other sports facilities in the area; the mayor, Councillor Vijay Mehta and John Fisher, the Head of Recreation Services at Hightown Council. The following day John Fisher is taking Sean on a tour of different sports facilities in the area. He is collecting Sean from the hotel by car at 9 am and taking him to the council offices to meet various members of staff. The offices are about 15 minutes away from the hotel. Sean is expected to be there about 45 minutes. From there they will take the 45 minute drive to Meadowvale Leisure Centre to meet the Manager, Josie Tyrell, and her staff. Their next stop is at Viewfields Sports Pavilion and Squash Club, where Dana Phillips is Manager. That journey takes about 30 minutes. They then travel to Higher Bank Cricket Ground and Sports

OFFICIAL OPENING OF HIGHTOWN ATHLETICS ARENA

WEDNESDAY, 14 MAY 199-

PROGRAMME

| | |
|---|---|
| 1200 | Arrival of guests |
| 1230 | Opening speech by John Fisher, Head of Recreation Services, Hightown Council |
| 1240 | *Athletics and the Community*, an overview by Marilyn Groves, Chief Coach at Hightown Harriers |
| 1250 | *Hightown and its place in Athletics,* by Councillor Vijay Mehta, Mayor of Hightown |
| 1300 | Official opening ceremony. Arena opened by Sean Reynolds, Minister for Sport |
| 1310 | *Athletics and the future,* by the Right Honourable Tessa Riley, MP for Hightown |
| 1320 | Vote of thanks by John Fisher, Head of Recreation Services, Hightown Council |
| 1330 | Buffet in marquee and tour of facilities for guests |

***Figure 10.3*** *The programme received by May*

Complex to meet Keith Ashton and his staff (another 30 minutes travelling time) and finally to Hightown Leisure Complex to meet May Rodgers and her staff (about 30 minutes from Higher Bank). It is expected that Sean will stay about 45 minutes at each centre or complex and the itinerary has included a one-hour lunch break at the Perch and Pike Restaurant in Waverley Village, near the Viewfields Club, which is just over five minutes away from Viewfields. Finally, John Fisher is escorting Sean to the station to catch the 5.30 pm train to London.

Before you look at John Fisher's itinerary, draft out the events as you think they should be listed. Then check your ideas with the itinerary shown in Figure 10.5 on page 174.

RESUMÉ OF COMMUNICATIONS BETWEEN HIGHTOWN LEISURE COMPLEX AND MRS MARIAN FOULDS

| | |
|---|---|
| 14 March | Mrs Foulds wrote enquiring about birthday parties and cost. |
| 16 March | Standard letter sent in reply, plus leaflet and booking form. |
| 21 March | Letter from Mrs Foulds asking if larger parties could be accommodated. |
| 24 March | Letter from Maria Parsons asking for further details, particularly date and proposed number of children |
| 8 April | Booking form and deposit received from Mrs Foulds. Number of children not completed on booking form. Accompanying letter said 'to follow'. Party booked for 10 May. |
| 12 April | Confirmation pack sent. Letter from Mariam Mansoor asking for exact numbers by 16 April and stating balance required by 3 May. |
| 18 April – 25 April | Repeated telephone calls made to check number and obtain deposit. Letter sent 25 April |
| 7 May | Telephone message received saying 32 children attending. Receptionist taking call said this number would be unacceptable. Mrs Foulds claimed it was by arrangement. Claimed to have posted cheque for balance. Urgent return calls unanswered. |
| 9 May | Staff meeting to discuss arranging sufficient activities – decision to split party into two groups. |
| 10 May | Party held. Mrs Foulds complained facilities cramped and over-crowded. Refused to pay balance of account. |

***Figure 10.4*** *A resumé of events*

# PREPARING A RESUMÉ

Although both the fact sheet in Figure 10.2 and the summary you will prepare on page 175 can be classified as a **resumé**, it is more likely that you will find this term used when you have to list or summarise a sequence of events. The most common type of resumé is the career resumé – which you normally send to a prospective employer. A far more common term for this is **curriculum vitae**, and you will see how to prepare these in Unit 16.

You may be asked to produce a 'resumé of everything that has happened' in a series of business transactions or communications between your organisation and a particular customer. This may be because there has been a dispute or disagreement of some kind and your boss needs a picture of everything that has occurred. Bear in mind that a variety of terms are used for this type of document (see page 186). An example of a resumé of events is shown in Figure 10.4.

### VERBAL RESUMÉS

Having to give a verbal account of something can be quite nerve-wracking at the start of your career – particularly if you are expected to do this in front of several people. This is one reason why many communication lessons include practice on giving presentations (see Unit 12) and speaking in front of other people.

For a presentation you are given prior warning that you must speak in front of a group of people, and you have time to assemble your material beforehand. More informally, you may often be asked to do this on an impromptu basis. This is not something to worry about, as we all do this every day of our lives in one way or another. A friend may ask you what you've been doing all morning, or your tutor asks what exercises you have done so far. Think of these as useful occasions for practising your verbal summarising skills.

## Test your understanding

1 Write a brief resumé of what you have been doing for the past few days. Use each day as your heading and put a brief entry that summarises your activities. If you feel your account is boring or monotonous, feel free to invent one or two events to spice it up a little! The aim is to write enough to summarise each activity appropriately, but not so much that it turns into a 'dear diary' nor so little that it is meaningless.

2 Practise your verbal summary skills. Assume you have been asked to review your week verbally in about two or three minutes. What would you say? Would you stutter and stumble and miss out the most important activity but talk about the least? Or would you focus on the most interesting and omit everything else? Jot down a few notes and then be prepared to give your version when asked to do so by your tutor.

# PREPARING A SUMMARY

The term **summary** is used less broadly than resumé. It refers to a condensed article or account that is sometimes written in continuous prose (ie sentences and paragraphs). Another common format is an itemised summary with numbered points – but less abbreviated than a fact sheet, and not in note form. You may have to make a summary from several different sources but, in the early stages of your career, it is more likely you will be asked to summarise one particular document to extract the key information.

Follow a similar procedure to that for taking notes (Unit 6).

- Check you are certain which format you should use (eg continuous text, numbered points or bullet points). This will usually depend upon why you are being asked to prepare the summary.
- Start by skim reading the document for its overall meaning.
- Highlight or otherwise identify each key point. Do not include examples or descriptions used simply to illustrate a particular point.

**VISIT OF SEAN REYNOLDS TO SPORTS FACILITIES IN HIGHTOWN AREA**

**Accompanied by John Fisher, Head of Recreation Services, Hightown Council**

**WEDNESDAY, 14 MAY**

Accommodation reserved at Swan Hotel, Hightown

| | |
|---|---|
| 2030 | Dinner with Brian Faraday, Chief Executive of Hightown Council, the Mayor, Councillor Vijay Mehta; the managers of various sports complexes and facilities; John Fisher, Head of Recreation Services. |

**THURSDAY, 15 MAY**

| | |
|---|---|
| 0900 | John Fisher to collect Sean Reynolds from Swan Hotel by car. |
| 0915 | Visit to council offices to meet staff. |
| 1000 | Leave council offices and travel to Meadowvale Leisure Centre |
| 1045 | Arrive Meadowvale Leisure Centre to meet Josie Tyrell, Manager, and staff |
| 1130 | Leave Meadowvale and travel to Viewfields Sports Pavilion |
| 1200 | Arrive Viewfields Sports Pavilion and Squash Club to meet Dana Phillips, Manager, and staff |
| 1245 | Leave Viewfields Club for lunch at Perch and Pike Restaurant in Waverley Village |
| 1400 | Leave Perch and Pike Restaurant and travel to Higher Bank Cricket Ground and Sports Complex |
| 1430 | Arrive Higher Bank Cricket Ground and Sports Complex to meet Keith Ashton, Manager, and staff |
| 1515 | Leave Higher Bank and travel to Hightown Leisure Complex |
| 1545 | Arrive Hightown Leisure Complex to meet May Rodgers, Manager, and staff |
| 1630 | Leave Hightown Leisure Complex and travel to station |
| 1730 | Depart Hightown on London train. |

***Figure 10.5*** *John Fisher's itinerary for Sean Reynolds*

- Re-read the document, checking that you have not omitted anything important.
- Write out the points you have identified. At this stage, do not worry about how the information is ordered – follow the original order.
- Re-arrange your information into a more logical order. Group any items of connected information together, regardless of how widely separated they are in the original.
- Check that any important names or other references are included.
- Draft out your summary from your notes – *not* from the original document.
- Select a suitable heading – or use the one from the document.
- Make sure you have kept to the facts – your opinions aren't required.
- Check your English and that your spelling, punctuation and grammar (particularly the tense of your verbs) are correct.
- Read the summary and check that it gives you the same meaning, as near as possible, to the original. Someone reading it should not need to look at both documents to check what was said!
- Include any sources, if these are required. For a book or magazine this should include the title, author's name, publisher's name and date of publication.

Remember that you should not usually write a summary in note form. You would not, therefore, write

*Increase in attendance over last 6 months* but

*There has been an increase in attendance over the last 6 months.*

## Test your understanding

1 The following statements are all given in note form. Expand each one into sentence form and link the sentences to form a connected statement of the points made.

**GET FIT BY MAKING THE CONNECTION!**

Every New Year, one in three of us makes a resolution to improve our health and fitness. By June, most of us have given up our attempts and our good intentions have fallen by the wayside. However, for Hightown residents, there are no excuses in the future following the opening of Fitness Connection – a new private club in the Riverside area opening on 4th January.

Fitness Connection aims to put you back in charge of your life, according to the owner, Don Jenkins. On your first visit, you receive a personal assessment profile of your current health and fitness. There is an in-depth interview including questions on your medical history, any injuries you have received, your overall lifestyle, your diet and your fitness goals. If you are tempted to cover up some of your weaknesses then be assured you will be found out – as the interview is followed with a physical assessment where your heart rate, blood pressure, percentage of body fat, strength, endurance and flexibility are all measured. At the end of all this you are given a personal chart showing your current score and plotting your progress against a target score. My chart was less depressing than I thought it would be, even though it looks as if it will take me several months to reach my goal! Don Jenkins was sympathetic and understanding. 'Too many people', he commented, 'start with unrealistic goals, which they think they can achieve by going mad for a few weeks. This never works. Getting fit through exercise is like dieting – it needs a long-term view and a review of your whole lifestyle. Trying to do too much too soon is not only unsafe but futile. You are far better to work out a programme you enjoy and can stick to, over a period of time.'

So, how much will it cost me to revolutionise my lifestyle? Fitness Connection isn't cheap, but of course, that depends upon how many times I visit each year. There is a joining fee of £25 but this is waived if you pay the annual membership fee up-front – a cost of £350. This entitles you to visit the club as often as you want – I worked out that if I visited twice a week it would cost me about £3.50 a visit. And surely my health is worth that? I could opt for shorter membership – three months costs £120 and six months costs £200. Equally, if I want to take advantage of the discount available for taking out a twelve-month subscription I could pay by instalments – although an additional £20 is added for this service.
A useful bonus is that if I am ill or unable to attend for personal reasons I can 'freeze' my membership for up to four months. I left with a useful set of booklets given to all new members containing information about all the facilities at the club, the times of the classes, a guide to using the gym equipment, safety information and some useful limbering up and maintenance exercises I can do in the privacy of my own home. Add to this a list of contact numbers for the instructors (all of whom seem impressively well qualified) and a healthy eating diet sheet and this makes a useful pack of information to keep me on the straight and narrow for a while. I even avoided all temptation for a quick pizza or bar snack on the way home!

For a limited period only, Fitness Connection is offering new members a tempting offer of a 10% discount. Take advantage of this, and you may be able to make the smug claim that you have kept this year's New Year resolutions!

***Figure 10.6*** *A press report about a new private fitness club*

**a** Most leisure centres open seven days a week now. Opening times vary – most 11 am, some 10 am.

**b** Large increase in Internet use for buying goods. Proper term for this is electronic marketing. Projected sales in 1998 = £8 billion.

**c** Bank cash machines increasing in popularity. More popular with young people. Research by Consumers Association showed two-thirds bank customers use cash machines once a fortnight. Facilities vary. Some give mini-statements and up-to-date balance, some don't. Most machines free, not all.

**2** Yesterday, May Rodgers read a press report about a new private fitness club that has opened in the area. She has asked you to write a summary of the main points relating to the service it offers and its charges.

**a** Read the passage in Figure 10.6 and identify the key facts. Do this by separating all the journalist's comments from those parts of the article that give factual information. Compare your interpretation of the key facts with that of other members of your group and agree these with your tutor.

**b** List your key facts neatly in the order in which they appear.

**c** Re-arrange your facts into a logical order, grouping all related facts together.

**d** Decide upon a suitable heading for your summary, reflecting the brief you have been given by May Rodgers.

**e** Rewrite your facts as a summary:

**i** first in numbered points
**ii** second as continuous prose (at least two paragraphs) with a maximum of 100 words. Give each paragraph an appropriate sub-heading.

Check your completed work with your tutor.

SAY IT!

**SAY IT!**

In Unit 5 you met your first list of 'say it' words. When you are giving a verbal resumé or account, the last thing you want to have to worry about is whether you are pronouncing each word correctly! Each of the following types of words often causes problems. Check you can say each one given as an example and then check you know the meaning of each word. Add any new words to your Wordbank book.

**1** Resumé is a French word where the final 'e' is pronounced like a long a. So are the following:

*crochet cliché cachet buffet croquet protégée*

**2** Other foreign words frequently used in English today include

| | | | | |
|---|---|---|---|---|
| *creche* | *discotheque* | *boulevard* | *gratis* | *entourage* |
| *menagerie* | *garbage* | *largesse* | *guerilla* | *factotum* |

Check you can pronounce them *and* you know what they mean!

**3** Hard or soft 'g'? In the first set of words below, use a hard 'g', in the second set, the 'g' is soft.

**a** *chagrin* (pronounce this 'shagran'), *ghetto* (the 'h' is silent), *meagre* (pronounce this 'meager')

**b** *corsage, lingerie, massage, prestige, harbinger*

**4** The final 'e'. In most English words, a final 'e' affects the sound of the previous vowel (eg mat/mate, bit/bite, cut/cute, dot/dote) but a few words have a final 'e' that is sounded. Listen to your tutor say each one of the following words, then repeat them. Look up the meanings.

*facsimile hyperbole epitome*

# THE GOOD GRAMMAR GUIDE

### *Verbs*

## Tenses and verbs

Have you ever heard the expression 'tempus fugit' – a Latin expression for 'time flies'? You may wonder what this has to do with verbs until you discover that the word 'tense' (which usually means 'taut' to us) comes from the Latin word 'tempus', and relates to the time when an action took place.

An action can occur in the past, the present or the future – and this gives us our three main group of verb tenses, eg

- *He worked* or *He was working* (past tense)
- *He works* or *He is working* (present tense)
- *He will work* or *He will be working* (future tense)

You have two choices for each tense. The first implies that the action relates to a limited time, event or place (eg *He works on Tuesdays, He works in that building, He works as a driver*) and the second that the action is progressive or continuous. You would therefore choose *He is working* if you want to indicate current and on-going activity. This option means using the word 'to be' and the present participle of the verb – the '-ing' form – which you met in the last unit.

You can also use the verbs 'to be' and 'to have' with the past or present participle for other tenses. This gives you further options under our main three headings of past, present and future, eg

### PAST

*He has worked* or *He has been working* (perfect tense)
*He had worked* or *He had been working* (pluperfect tense)
*He would have worked* or *He would have been working* (conditional perfect)

### PRESENT

*He would work* or *He would be working* (conditional present)

### FUTURE

*He will have worked* or *He will have been working* (future perfect)

You probably didn't realise you use so many variations! Consider when you would be likely to use each one. It may help if you think of the type of words you would add to each version to arrive at a complete sentence.

## Verb agreement

By far the most important aspect of verbs when you are communicating is to make sure they **agree** with the subject of a sentence. You already know that

- the subject of a sentence is a noun or a pronoun
- nouns and pronouns can be singular or plural.

The golden rule is that singular nouns and pronouns take singular verbs, plural nouns and pronouns take plural verbs. Therefore *he writes* but *we write, I am* but *you are, the bus was late* but *three trains were delayed.*

For the most part, you will not need to think about this. However, even in a newspaper, you may read a sentence such as *At least one in four cars are likely to be stolen* which is wrong! To guard against this, the main rules you need to follow are given below.

- Titles of organisations, films and books take a singular verb because they relate to one firm or item, eg

  *British Telecom is offering two new services.*
  *Star Wars is still very popular.*

- Indefinite pronouns (each, every, everybody, somebody, neither, nobody, etc) should be treated as a singular noun, eg

  *Each person is to take one.*
  *Neither of us has been to the shop.*
  *Nobody is wrong.*

If some of these sentences sound 'odd', then read the phrase as 'each one', 'neither one' or 'no-one'. The fact that you can include the word 'one' indicates a singular noun.

The word 'none' used to be treated in the same way, but today it is more usual to use a plural verb afterwards because it 'reads' better, eg

*None of the houses were damaged.* (As opposed to *None of the houses was damaged.*)

- Usually, when two nouns are joined with 'and' then the subject is plural and takes a plural verb. However, this does not apply if the two nouns represent a whole unit or idea. Therefore

  *Joe and Tom are colleagues* but
  *Research and Development is a new department.*
  *Marks and Spencer is opening another store.*

- A collective noun, such as team, group, committee or jury, can take either a singular or a plural verb – both are considered correct. However, you must decide which you are going to use – and be consistent! If you are using a pronoun later in the sentence, you must make sure this also agrees with your verb, eg

  *The team has been playing its best all week.* or
  *The team have been playing their best all week.* but not
  *The team has been playing their best all week.*

- The words 'either . . . or' and 'neither . . . nor' both take a singular verb where they separate singular subjects, but take a plural verb when the subjects are plural, eg

  *Either Eileen or Jack has to go.*
  *Neither the drivers nor the inspectors have been to the meeting.*

## DON'T YOU DARE!

*. . . confuse the verbs*

- *to lend and to borrow*
- *to teach and to learn.*

*If I borrow your pen, then you are the lender, or*
*If I am the lender then you are the borrower!*

*If I am the teacher then you are the learner, or*
*If you are the teacher then I am the learner.*

*You would therefore say:*

*Can I borrow your pen?* or *Can you lend me your pen?* and
*She taught me how to do this.* or *I learnt how to do this when she taught me.*

- Deciding which type of verb to use can become more difficult if a phrase is inserted between the subject and the verb. Make sure that you focus on the subject of the sentence, eg

  *The documents, one of which was a fake, were sent to the solicitors.* (Subject = documents) but

  *One of the documents, which was a fake, was sent to the solicitors.* (Subject = one document).

## Test your understanding

Correct the errors in the following sentences.

1 Neither of us have worked for that firm.
2 The Committee has decided that they will meet on Tuesday.
3 Neither the daffodils nor the tulips has flowered this year.
4 The girl, together with several of her friends, are going on the trip.
5 Either Bridget or Marianne have to be there.
6 Everybody who attended the meetings on Tuesday and Thursday are allowed to claim expenses.
7 More staff for Sales and Personnel are the next topic for discussion.
8 The Government is debating the issue when they have studied the report.
9 Marks and Spencer are opening a new store in our area.
10 The examination board are considering the student's appeal at its next meeting.

## DOUBLE TROUBLE

Many words vary their spelling from a 'c' to an 's'. Some examples are given below.

| | |
|---|---|
| ■ practice | practise |
| ■ licence | license |
| ■ advice | advise |
| ■ prophecy | prophesy |
| ■ council | counsel |
| ■ device | devise |

How do you know which one to use?

The answer is that every word with a 'c' is a noun, and every word with an 's' is a verb. Whenever you are in doubt, you can check as follows:

- if an article ('a', 'an' or 'the') can precede the word, it is a noun, so you should spell it with a 'c'
- if 'to' can precede the word, it is a verb, therefore spell it with an 's'.

For example:

**a** *Tomorrow I intend to practi?e for my driving test.* 'to' = 's' = practise
**b** I *have to call at the doctor's practi?e at 2 pm.* 'the' = 'c' = practice

## Test your understanding

Now you practise (note the spelling!) with the following sentences. In each case write out the sentence, inserting the missing letter.

1 She is busy at the moment as she has to coun?el a client.
2 I hope the prophe?y the gypsy made is correct.
3 He hopes to devi?e a new way of doing this which will be much simpler.
4 I would like you to advi?e me how I should do this.
5 There is a meeting of the coun?il this afternoon.
6 I am not psychic, therefore please do not expect me to prophe?y the future.
7 She was busy practi?ing her keyboard skills.
8 I cannot get this devi?e to work.
9 I must pay my television licen?e fee on Monday.
10 Before anyone can sell alcohol they must be licen?ed.

## MAKING HEADWAY – graphs, bar charts and pictograms

In Unit 9 you looked at the use of graphics in a variety of documents, and saw how tables and pie charts can be used to summarise and display different types of information. These are not the only techniques which are available to you if you want to represent information graphically. Other options include:

- line graphs and multi-line graphs
- bar charts and histograms
- pictograms.

Most computer packages will help you to create graphs and charts, but you may not be able to design your own pictograms unless you have access to clip-art and can reduce or increase the size of your illustrations as you wish. It is important that you first understand the type of information represented by each type of graphic.

## Line graphs and multi-line graphs

A graph may have one line or several, in which case it is known as a multi-line graph. All graphs usually show a trend – as the lines go up and down, increases and decreases can be seen at a glance. For that reason they are often used for statistical information such as:

- production increases and decreases
- sales increases and decreases
- population growth and decline
- crime rates
- prices and inflation figures
- profit or income figures.

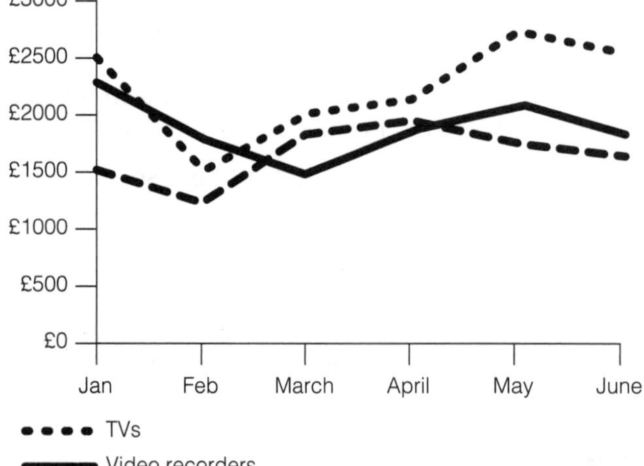


*Figure 10.7* A multi-line graph

In *all* graphs and charts, the vertical axis usually represents quantity and the horizontal axis shows the time period over which the trend has been measured. Both axes must be clearly labelled. The graph should also have an appropriate heading. An example of a simple multi-line graph is shown in Figure 10.7. Note that each line must be drawn slightly differently (unless you are using colour) to differentiate it from the others. In this case you will also need to label your lines clearly or to put a key at the bottom.

### POINTS TO NOTE

There are three main points to bear in mind when you are constructing a line graph.

- Too many lines on one graph make it confusing and difficult to read. It is better to draw two graphs or choose a different type of graphic if necessary.
- The spacings must always be kept even. This is done automatically if you draw a graph on computer.
- The scale of the graph must be appropriate to the information. You do not, for instance, have to start your vertical axis at zero. If you were recording very small differences between, say, 58 and 83, it would be more appropriate to have an axis starting at 50 and going to 90. The differences would then be much clearer than if you had an axis with a scale of 1 to 100.

## Bar charts

Bar charts are a popular method of representing information visually because they are usually both eye-catching and effective. They are more detailed than a pie chart but the information cannot be displayed as precisely as in a graph.

A bar chart can be designed either horizontally or vertically, depending upon the direction in which the bars are drawn. You have the option to

- draw **multiple** bars – usually to make a comparison
- draw **compound** bars – where the bars themselves are divided into different sections, each showing proportional parts.

A variation is a **histogram**, where the area of each bar, not just its height, is related to the amount of information. The bars are often drawn together or joined up.

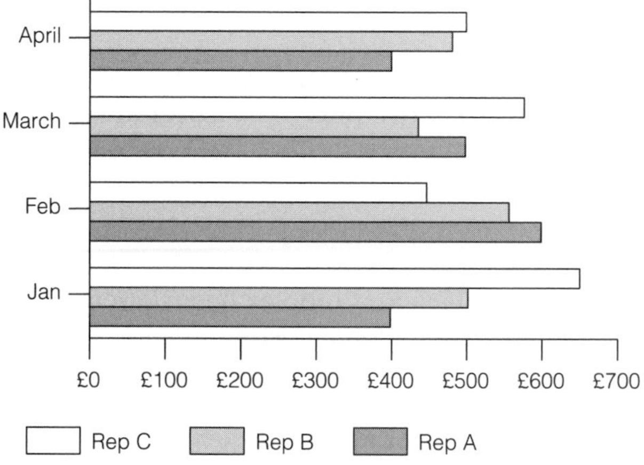


***Figure 10.8*** *A horizontal bar chart*

Examples of all these types of bar charts are shown in Figures 10.8 – 10.10. Note that no matter what type of bar chart you draw, unless you give it a clear heading and key, and label each axis, it will not be understandable!

### POINTS TO NOTE

The points to note are similar to those for a graph.

- Too many bars on a multiple bar chart are confusing and difficult to read. The space they take up also reduces the time period over which you can display the results.

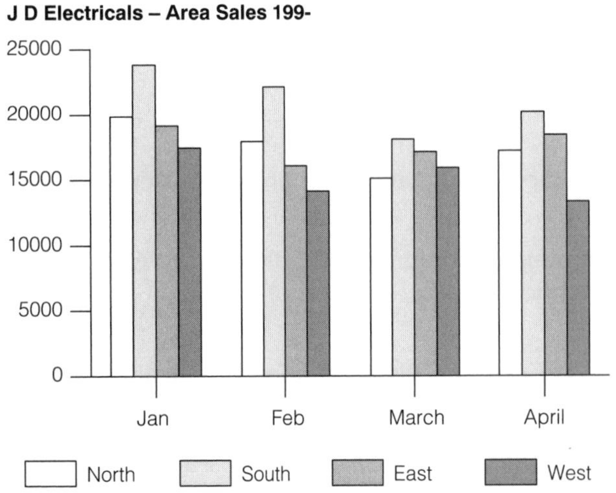

***Figure 10.9*** *A vertical bar chart*

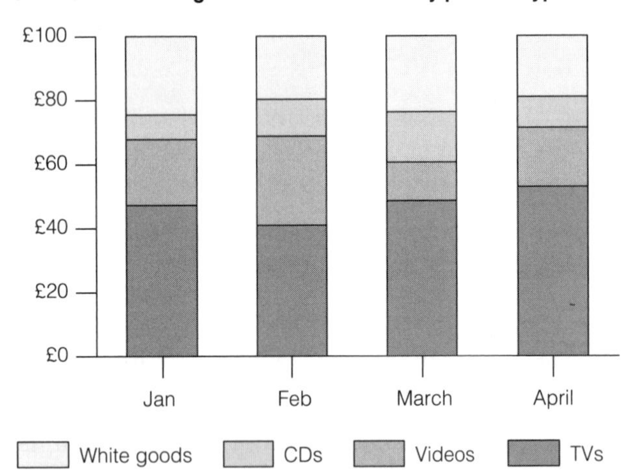


***Figure 10.10*** *A compound bar chart*

- Too many sub-divisions on a compound bar chart make it difficult to read.
- Again the scale is important. It might take you one or two attempts to draw a chart where the bars are of a sensible size. Thinking carefully about the size of the largest and the smallest before you start usually saves time in the end!

## Pictograms

These are very eye-catching and are an ideal method when you want to attract attention but don't need to give much detailed information. Pictures, symbols or other graphics are used to represent a quantity. To show increased quantities, you have the choice of increasing either the size of your graphic or the number of pictures. It is normal to select a picture or symbol relevant to the information being displayed, as in Figure 10.11 opposite.

## Test your understanding

**1** May Rodgers is considering having an open day at the leisure complex to attract new members. She is worried about losing business since the new fitness club opened in Riverside. She wants to produce a short handbook for visitors but to keep the text to a minimum, as she doesn't think people want to spend hours reading about the centre.

For each of the following, decide which type of graphic would be most appropriate (using the options described above plus those covered in the previous unit). Try to select a different option each time. Then do a sketch to test if your ideas would work!

**a** The number of cups won by members of the Tadpoles Club has quadrupled over the past three years.

**b** The cost of membership of Hightown Leisure Complex has fallen over the last five years. However, the average national cost figures for membership of clubs and the price of private fitness club membership have both risen over the same period.

**c** A simple calculation, showing how much it costs for a member per visit if he or she visits once a month, once a week, twice a week and four times a week.

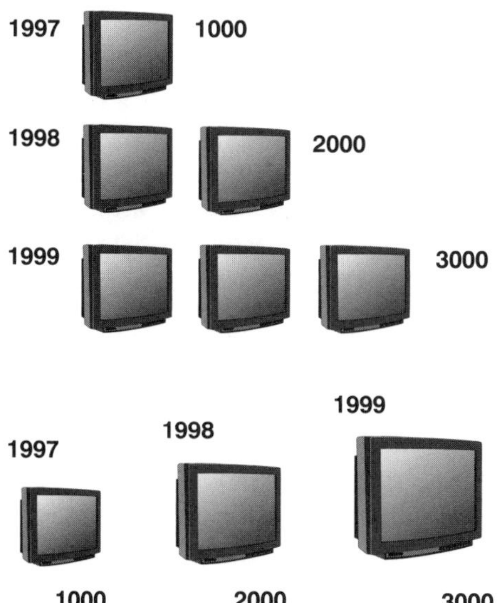


*Figure 10.11* *Pictograms showing sales of TV sets*

d The popularity and usage of each of the six main types of sports activities on offer last year – badminton, keep fit (including aerobics), martial arts, squash, swimming and weight training – shown as a percentage in each case of the total centre use.

e The usage of the health and fitness centre by classification of membership, ie juniors, male (full) and female (full), at six monthly periods over the past three years.

Discuss your ideas and suggestions with your tutor.

2 The leisure complex makes additional income from special activities, such as birthday parties; from catering facilities, such as the cafe area and the vending machines; and from the sale of sports equipment. The income for the past six months for each area is given below. May Rodgers has decided she would like these produced as a graphic. To help you, she has rounded the figures to the nearest £50 in each case.

Select either a line graph or a bar chart as your graphic and produce a clear illustration to show these figures. Decide on an appropriate heading and include a clear key.

| Income area | Jan | Feb | Mar | Apr | May | Jun |
|---|---|---|---|---|---|---|
| Activities | £750 | £650 | £1200 | £900 | £1100 | £1150 |
| Catering | £1250 | £1100 | £1050 | £1450 | £1300 | £1350 |
| Sale of sports equipment | £500 | £650 | £700 | £700 | £600 | £750 |

## TOOLS OF THE TRADE – researching and evaluating information

Researching can involve finding out one basic fact (X's telephone number, what time X & Y close on Saturdays) or finding a variety of information on a particular topic.

## Before you start

1 **Decide what you need to know**. If you have been given instructions, make sure you know the depth and the scope of your investigations. For instance, for the fact sheet shown on page 171, Mariam had to find out about insurance against sports injury, not about insurance in general. She could also exclude sports and activities not undertaken at the leisure complex – such as ballooning or parachuting.

2 **Identify your sources**. These may be given to you or you may choose them yourself. There are three choices:

   **a** People and organisations – including experts on a topic, people who have experience of a situation or those who would be affected by a proposal. Organisations can be local or national. In the example on page 171, Mariam contacted a specialist insurance company and a national sports organisation. Bear in mind that whilst most organisations will give you information for nothing, some may charge.

   **b** Paper-based information – including files, reference books, newspapers, magazines and specialist journals. In addition you may have sales literature and information from leaflets, brochures and catalogues.

   **c** Computer-based information – a vast source of information is the Internet. In this case the problem can be selecting what you want (or finding it) among the millions of documents available. Other computer-based information sources include CD-ROMs and library databanks.

3 **Decide how to obtain your information.** This may include writing letters, making telephone calls, interviewing people or even designing a questionnaire. If you require very detailed information from just one or two specialists it may be better to visit them and make notes at an interview. If you want the views of 50 people, a questionnaire is more likely to be suitable.

4 **Be prepared to re-consider your brief.** This is important if the initial findings of your research show that the original ideas are not useful. As an example, if Mariam had found that most activities undertaken at the leisure centre could not be covered by special insurance, or that no records were kept for some statistics required by May Rodgers, the original idea may have had to be rethought.

## Evaluating your information

One of the most difficult skills to learn when you are surrounded by different types of information is what to include and what to leave out. Often, the more complex the document or the more important the occasion, the more information you have. How do you choose which to use?

Your key rules for selection should be the degree to which your information is up-to-date, accurate, relevant, valid, complete and legally acceptable. We will examine each of these criteria in more detail.

### CHECKING THE DATE

There is nothing more annoying than to spend half an hour writing out the key points in an article and then finding that the whole thing is out of date. In the business world in particular, things change so quickly that you can never guarantee that what you are writing about is current unless you check the date of your source material – whether book, magazine, newspaper or booklet. (Imagine what a five-year-old computer magazine would look like!)

### CHECKING ACCURACY

One of the biggest crimes you can commit is to include inaccurate information. How would you feel, for instance, if you found some of the information in a book to be completely wrong? Let down? Conned, even? You would be reluctant to trust other information given in the same book. Similarly, your boss will be less likely to trust you if you write something that is plainly inaccurate or, even worse, invent something to fill a gap!

The *degree* of accuracy required, however, will depend upon what you are writing about. If you were trying to estimate how many languages people speak in the world, then a rough estimate would do. If you were asked to report your boss's car mileage, you would expected to be far more precise!

## CHECKING RELEVANCE

Information is relevant if it specifically relates to your enquiry. Sometimes, when you are asked to find out information on a difficult topic, it is tempting to write about what you have actually found rather than what you should have found! Always check your information regularly against your brief or instructions. If it doesn't match, then you will have to discard it.

## CHECKING VALIDITY

Whereas accuracy relates to facts (ie they are true or false), validity relates to assumptions. If you are only asked to give the facts then you won't need to worry too much about validity. The time to be concerned is when you are drawing conclusions and making recommendations.

An invalid assumption is one where two or more facts have been linked to draw the wrong conclusion. In this case, the writer has made 2 + 2 = 5 – or even 6! We all do this in our personal lives, to some extent. You pass a friend in the street who ignores you. Do you assume she didn't see you or that she *deliberately* ignored you? Much will depend upon what happened last time you saw her, whether she is moody and so on. But in adding those facts together, you may jump to the wrong conclusion. The trick is not to do this at work, especially when you are preparing formal written documents. If you have a personal involvement or a strong opinion on the matter, there is a great temptation to make the facts fit what you want to say. Try to avoid this!

## CHECKING YOUR INFORMATION IS COMPLETE

In previous units you have looked at the problems that can be caused when messages are incomplete. An extension of this is a report you write or the presentation you give where you 'gloss over' certain areas because you have not covered them properly. If you are concerned that you cannot find any relevant information on an area, then it is better to discuss your problem with your boss rather than hope your omissions will go unnoticed!

## CHECKING LEGALITY

If you are preparing a document and have used other sources for information, you should never claim that someone else's work is your own. This is plagiarism (see page 222).

You must also be aware that if you make any assertions or allegations about anyone then you could be guilty of slander (if you speak it) or libel (if you write about it). This applies whether you are writing a memo, letter, fax, e-mail, report or any other type of document!

## Test your understanding

1 May Rodgers is furious at a headline in the local paper: *Private Fitness Club Trebles Members in Two Months.* When you raise this with Mariam because you are worried it will put the leisure complex out of business, Mariam shrugs and says 'Well, that's easy to do if you only have 20 members to start with, isn't it?'

**a** What does Mariam mean by this statement?
**b** Why would it be far more difficult for Hightown Leisure Complex to triple its members and claim the same headlines?
**c** How would you classify this information – inaccurate, irrelevant, invalid, exaggerated or misleading – and why?

2 Each of the following extracts gives you *part* of an argument or slants the information in a particular way to suit the writer's purpose. A different perspective is put forward in the three matching extracts on page 313. Before you read these, can you identify

**a** what information may be missing or what the opposite view may be
**b** the dangers of using only the information below.

*Extract 1*

*Workers are celebrating following the introduction of new regulations to comply with the European Working Time Directive. The regulations will give millions of workers extra paid holiday rights and also introduce a maximum 48-hour compulsory working week.*

*Extract 2*

*Gender bias in the law profession is obvious. This year the success rate of women applying to be a QC (Queen's Counsel) is 21.7 per cent, whereas the success rate was only 10.7% for men. The Lord Chancellor is obviously showing a definite leaning towards the female population!*

*Extract 3*

*Government claims huge success in slashing the dole queue. According to the Office of National Statistics, there has been a reduction of at least 200,000 benefit claimants in the past 18 months.*

### SPELLCHECKER 9

All the words given below can be linked to reports and summaries in some way. In each case

**a** find the link
**b** check you clearly understand the meaning of each word
**c** learn the spelling!

| | | | |
|---|---|---|---|
| abbreviate | abridgement | abstract | ambiguous |
| ambivalent | assignment | condense | consensus |
| encapsulate | extrapolate | inference | précis |
| prejudice | recommendation | synopsis | |

## COMMUNICATION IN PRACTICE

## Test your skills

**1** Rewrite the following passage, in each case inserting either *was* or *were* in each of the spaces.

Because there ....... a considerable amount of equipment missing, the management team ........... asked to attend a special meeting. When the news ........... given to them, each of the members ........ asked to investigate. It ........ agreed that none of the cleaners ........ to blame and neither ....... the office staff. This ...... because the items .......... stolen on a Saturday, when the only staff on duty .......... the security guards.

**2** Identify the verb form of each of the following words and then use each correctly in a sentence.

| | | | |
|---|---|---|---|
| standard | peace | division | description |
| summary | antagonist | clarity | resolution |
| obedience | wide | critic | |

**3** Each of the following sentences contains at least one error – which may be of grammar, punctuation, spelling or vocabulary. In each case, identify the error(s) and rewrite the sentence correctly.

**a** He has wrote the book at home in his spare time.
**b** The Society explained the new rules to all its members at their meeting on Friday.
**c** The problem with those classes have been made worse through there teacher's absence.
**d** 'I cannot prophecy what will happen when Tesco have opened more stores,' he said.
**e** I asked if I could lend her pen so that I could prepare the draught summery immediately.
**f** Neither of them have renewed their television licenses yet.

## Apply your skills

You arrive at work cheerful and optimistic, but you have been at your desk only a few moments when May Rodgers walks in, obviously frustrated and annoyed.

'I don't believe it,' she exclaims. 'All I asked for was a simple statement giving me the key facts about how much the swimming section had improved and increased its numbers in different areas, and Martin sends me half a book. Just look at this!' May waves the paper in the air, indignantly. 'Do they not understand? For three years now the council has cut our funding and we have done our best to keep our expenditure down and increase our members. All the efforts we made to keep our customers when that new Fitness Club opened! And if I don't make a good case in my annual report for more funding they are likely to cut it even more. And when I ask the staff to help I either get scruffy bits of paper or reams of it – like this.'

You have some sympathy. You know May has the important annual report to prepare and submit to the council before the end of March, and that next year's funding allocation may depend upon some of her arguments. You decide to offer your help. May is delighted.

'I sometimes don't know what I'd do without you. Yes, if you could help me for a while this morning, that would be great. Can you start by trying to make some sense of Martin's memo. Summarise it for me, would you – it's only the key information I want. Do it in numbered points if you find it easier but in the report it will have to be continuous text, so if you could do it as a couple of paragraphs that would be wonderful. Would you also have time to do me two or three graphics? I've worked out the income and expenditure patterns for the past five years – they show quite clearly that the amount of money we've had available for capital items has fallen. This is the money we use to repair and renew equipment, redecorate the place and so on. We never will keep our members if the place becomes tatty and all the equipment is out of date. I could do with two line graphs. Ignore the surplus line at the bottom. On the first, do all income and all expenditure as your two lines – you'll have to work out the total expenditure yourself. On the other, please show all three areas of expenditure. Sort out some suitable headings please. I've also got the figures for usage of all our main areas over the same period. These show an increase of about 50% overall. A bar chart of some kind would show that off well, I'm sure. Round the numbers to make life easier for yourself. Oh, and Sonia Jenkins has still to give me the information I requested relating to the health and fitness club. Write a brief memo to her – put it in my name – giving her a reminder and saying I must have it by next Wednesday. Oh and I understand we now hold six times as many birthday parties as we did three years ago! Can you sketch a graphic I could use to illustrate that? Not in the report – it's too formal for that kind of thing – but for a new leaflet we're thinking of producing advertising the parties.'

You stop scribbling notes for a minute as May puts down the papers on your desk. She looks over your shoulder at everything you have written.

'I'm sorry. There's such a lot, isn't there? And on top of everything I've still to sort out the arrangements for Jim Jackson's visit here a week on Tuesday. You may remember he's the Sports Council representative I told you about. I've promised to take him to meet John Fisher, Head of Recreation Services in the morning at 10. Jim's staying at the Highbury Lodge Hotel and I'll collect him from there at 9.30 – that should give me time to drive to the council offices and park. We'll probably stay about an hour and then I'll bring him here – that'll take about 30 minutes, depending upon traffic. We'll stay until lunch – rather than eat upstairs I've booked a table for lunch at the Puffin Inn on Wellington Place for 1 pm and John Fisher is joining us there. In the afternoon Jim wants to visit Meadowvale Leisure Centre to see Josie Tyrell – that drive will be about 45 minutes and we'll probably stay about an hour. I've told Josie we'll probably arrive about 3 pm. Then we're going back to the council offices to meet Brian Faraday, the Chief Executive, at 4.30 pm and I'll take Jim to the train station for his train back to London at 6 pm. Is there any chance you could do me a sensible itinerary for the day? Please try your best – if I can get that report off and everything else sorted by Friday lunchtime, you can have the rest of Friday off!'

Eager not to lose any time, you settle down to work.

1 From the notes given above, list the tasks you have to carry out and note down the key points you must remember in relation to each one.

2 Figures 10.12 and 10.13 are the papers to which May referred during the conversation. Use these to carry out your tasks.

Check your completed work with your tutor.

***Figure 10.12***
*Martin's memo to May*

# MEMO

TO May Rodgers

FROM Martin Smith

DATE 15 March 199-

**SWIMMING ACTIVITIES**

In response to your request for information on the increase in swimming activities and membership of the various swimming clubs, I talked at length to Bill about this. As our swimming coach he obviously knows most about all this and he has said that he will be pleased to talk to you about any of the activities if you want more information. Incidentally, just a point you may not be aware of – we also employ five part-time members of staff now to assist in the pool area (last year it was only three). All are fully-qualified and have gold medals for swimming and life-saving.

The Tadpoles Club (for 3–10s) has been really successful and membership has more than tripled in the last four years. Last year we won a huge number of cups and medals – more than any other swimming club in the county. The League Club (10–18) is also popular. Sean Davies, one of our swimmers, is in the county team and if he continues at this rate he could be swimming for England before too long. He's really dedicated and travels to Marsbury to practise in their Olympic-sized pool nearly every day. His mother gets up at 6 am to take him before school! The exact number of the Tadpole members at 28 February was 110. This time last year it was 75, the year before 60 and four years ago it was 36. We really can't expand it any more without additional staff. The League Club is now up to 46. There are always fewer in this group as many young people drop out when they start doing GCSEs or start work.

1 of 2

The Waterbabies Club for mothers and children is also very successful. It meets three mornings a week now. There is a maximum of fifteen in each class, otherwise we need another instructor. All the classes are full at present and there are seven names on the waiting list. This club is run by Wendy Smythe, one of our part-time instructors, who also has a youngster herself so she can empathise with the mothers and gets on really well with them. I'm sure this has been a key factor in its success.

Our early morning swimming sessions have been very popular. We now open three days a week (7.15 am–8 am) rather than two. Our Serious Swimmers sessions have also increased from two days to three days (32 members) and our weekday and Saturday life-saving classes are full (24 members).

New classes we have introduced this year have been Swimfit (twice a week), Active Improvers (twice) and Lunchtime break (three days). Only the latter hasn't caught on – I think we are a bit far from the town centre for people who haven't a car to come during lunchtime. Sometimes, as well, there has been a slight delay in using the pool, which is unacceptable for this group. Bill and I are looking at this problem. We may decide to offer it on only one day but at present cannot work out which would be best.

Finally, we also have our disabled sessions twice a week (24 members) and our Nifty Fifties sessions (30 members). These are as popular as ever.

Bill and I are currently discussing ideas for the next year. If you need details of these please let us know.

Hope this is what you want.

*Martin*

2 of 2

**Leisure complex income and expenditure**

| | 1995 | 1996 | 1997 | 1998 | 1999 |
|---|---|---|---|---|---|
| Income – all sources | £ 300,000 | £ 320,000 | £ 330,000 | £ 350,000 | £ 360,000 |
| Expenditure<br>– capital items<br>– staffing<br>– consumables | <br>20,000<br>180,000<br>90,000 | <br>45,000<br>185,000<br>88,000 | <br>42,000<br>194,000<br>92,000 | <br>18,000<br>220,000<br>110,000 | <br>15,000<br>230,000<br>114,000 |
| Surplus | 10,000 | 2,000 | 2,000 | 2,000 | 1,000 |

**Leisure complex usage**

| | 1995 | 1996 | 1997 | 1998 | 1999 |
|---|---|---|---|---|---|
| Health and fitness centre | 837 | 1025 | 1584 | 1722 | 1945 |
| Swimming pool | 3803 | 4006 | 5294 | 6531 | 7214 |
| Sports halls | 1560 | 1620 | 1795 | 1800 | 2000 |
| Squash courts | 2200 | 2149 | 2071 | 1842 | 1653 |
| Total | 8400 | 8800 | 10744 | 11895 | 12812 |

***Figure 10.13***
*May's tables*

## WORD WIZARD

Read the following report of an event carefully. Then decide how many of the statements below are factually accurate and undeniable. To save arguments, the answer is printed on page 314.

*The grey-haired security guard rubbed his hands together as he walked round the yard. It was time they got someone else for this job, he thought. Ten years was enough for anyone. An owl hooted in the trees. The guard wandered on around the building, lost in thought. He was tired and weary. His head down, he never noticed a light in the corner of the yard. Suddenly he knew no more.*

*The policeman standing over him was new – Tom had never seen him before. 'You've had a lucky escape,' he observed. Tom struggled to his feet. A pile of broken glass, debris and a hammer lay in the corner behind him. 'They broke this window to get in,' said the policeman, 'and seem to have cleared the place out.'*

*'I've been saying something like this would happen for years,' said Tom, shaking his head. 'But would they listen? Old-fashioned they are, and mean. It's time we had proper security around here. Well, they asked for it, now they must live with the consequences.'*

**1** Tom is a security guard.
**2** The security guard is old.
**3** The security guard wears a uniform.
**4** The security guard had worked for the firm for 10 years.
**5** The security guard heard an owl.
**6** The burglars had a torch.
**7** The burglars knocked out the security guard.
**8** The burglars had a hammer.
**9** The burglars knocked out the security guard with a hammer.
**10** The burglars broke the windows with the hammer.
**11** Tom is poorly paid.
**12** The policeman is young.
**13** The policeman is in uniform.
**14** It was cold.
**15** The attack took place at night.
**16** Tom wanted to leave the firm.

# IN THE SPOTLIGHT – ADVERTS, NOTICES AND LEAFLETS

We are surrounded by promotional messages every day of our lives. On hoardings and in magazines, on television and in newspapers, on buses, in the cinema and on the radio we are bombarded by dozens of advertisements. In the post each day we may receive brochures, catalogues and sales letters to tempt us to buy a particular product or service.

Organisations do not just advertise to consumers. They 'advertise' to their own staff when they want to inform them about internal functions and events – such as a training course. They also advertise to prospective employees when they need new or replacement staff.

The messages they send to promote their products and services are not just restricted to advertisements. Other methods of promotion include

- posters
- notices
- leaflets
- brochures and catalogues
- sales letters.

Large organisations usually employ the services of an advertising agency to prepare professional advertisements for customers, such as those you see on television and in the press. Smaller organisations are unlikely to be able to afford this and probably only advertise locally in a morning or evening newspaper. They may employ a local printer to produce their catalogues, brochures and any large posters they need. Items such as notices and leaflets may be designed by staff and printed internally, as modern technology has made it much easier for these to be produced 'in-house' by non-specialist staff. Certainly, it is usual for staff notices, advertisements for staff and sales letters to be prepared within organisations.

## Creating promotional items

The acronym to remember when you are preparing promotional items is **AIDA**. These four letters stand for **attention, interest, desire, action**. In other words you must

- capture the **attention** of the readers
- gain – and hold – their **interest**
- make them **desire** what you are selling or offering
- tell them how to take **action** to obtain it.

If you watch or read advertisements with this acronym in mind, you will probably be able to spot the techniques used at each stage.

You can link AIDA with the two aspects of promotional material, ie

**1** the display and layout
**2** the information and wording.

### DISPLAY AND LAYOUT

The display must be eye-catching so that people who see it pause to read it. Often graphics or illustrations are used for this purpose. 'White space' makes the display easier to read, because too many words or too much text is off-putting. The most important points should be highlighted in some way – by using larger letters, emboldening or colour.

### INFORMATION AND WORDING

The information must be accurate, complete and easy to understand. A catchy or interesting heading and the use of words such as 'free', 'bargain' and 'sale' attract attention. The rest of the message should be worded in such a way that readers want to continue reading to the end. There should be no technical errors of grammar, punctuation or spelling, and if you miss out an important piece of information – such as the day, time or place of an event – the whole exercise is useless. For that reason, you should always check that you have included details of **what, where, when** and **how**. If any of these are missing, it is unlikely anyone can take action, even if they want to!

## ADVERTISEMENTS

You must not say anything untrue in an advertisement, or make misleading claims. In many cases this is not only unethical but also against the law. Advertisements can be divided into two types

- those that are mainly factual
- those that are mainly persuasive.

Usually, persuasive adverts are the type you see in magazines and on television, where the message is linked to the perceived benefits of using a product. This why you are never shown people eating breakfast cereals in an old dressing gown on a wet Monday morning! Instead, the weather is always sunny, families look happy and carefree, everyone is dressed in bright clothes and looks attractive. The hidden message is that breakfasts in your house will be like this if you simply buy the cereal!

Informational adverts, on the other hand, are designed and written to give you factual information. A job advertisement is an example and so are advertisements about college courses, houses for sale and financial services. Words and phrases are used to promote these positively, and sometimes there is a strong mix of both persuasion and information in an advertisement.

As an example, think of car advertisements that sell the perceived benefits of having the car and also provide technical information.

## Designing an advertisement

The biggest mistake made by amateurs preparing an advertisement is trying to include too much information. This is overwhelming to the reader and ruins the visual effect. The amount of information that can be included effectively depends on the size of the advertisement. If you are preparing an advert for a newspaper, be aware that space costs money! The same applies to classified advertisements if you want to advertise a personal item, where the cost is usually calculated by each word or line. In a larger display advertisement you will usually pay per column centimetre (ie the number of columns across multiplied by the number of centimetres down).

A useful method is to:

- identify the **key points** – critical information you *must* include
- add any details you would like to include if you have space
- think of an eye-catching heading linked to the message you are trying to get across
- space out the information effectively (use bullet points, asterisks or numbered points where appropriate for clarity)
- consider your wording carefully – it should be accurate but 'sell' the benefits
- embolden, underline or emphasise any key items of information.

Finally, show your draft advertisement to at least one other person. Ask for *honest* feedback. Don't become defensive if the reader doesn't understand something – change it. If this person cannot understand it without an explanation then other people won't either.

***Figure 11.1*** *Two advertisements for the same job*

**PUBLISHING TRAINEE**

**required by**

**national magazine publishers**

The successful applicant must have

- excellent keyboarding and communication skills
- good English writing skills
- an eye for detail and the patience to proof-read carefully
- the ability to use own initiative and work as a member of a team

No previous experience required, as full training will be given. Good starting salary.

Interested? Please send your CV with a covering letter to:
Sarah Scott, Portland Publishers Ltd, 35 Princes Street, London W1R 7RG

---

**PUBLISHING TRAINEE**

required by large national magazine publisher

**NO PREVIOUS EXPERIENCE REQUIRED**

If you have excellent communication skills, the patience to proof-read carefully, good written English skills and are adept at keyboarding then you could be just the person we need! You must be able to use your own initiative and work as a member of a team.

GOOD STARTING SALARY

Please apply in writing with your CV to Sarah Scott,
Portland Publishers Ltd, 35 Princes Street, London W1R 7RG

## Test your understanding

1 The following is a classified advertisement your friend has written. In trying to keep the number of words to a minimum she has omitted a crucial piece of information. What is it?

*Exercise bike – excellent condition. Unwanted Xmas present. Ring Hightown 308920 after 6 pm.*

2 Figure 11.1 shows two examples of a job advertisement for the same job. Both use exactly the

same information. Which do you find the most attractive and why? Discuss your ideas as a group.

3 Obtain a copy of your local paper on 'jobs night' and look through the advertisements for jobs. Look at other advertisements, too, for local products and services. Collect *four* advertisements which appeal to you and be prepared to say why. Try to find at least *two* advertisements that you don't find appealing. Compare your ideas with other members of your group.

# POSTERS AND NOTICES

The term 'poster' is usually reserved for large A1 or A2 advertisements for an event, such as those you are likely to find on your college notice board, in shop windows and on some billboards. These are often produced on coloured paper, frequently include graphics and are usually designed and printed by specialist printers or print shops. A notice, on the other hand, is usually a smaller 'internal' document. There are unlikely to be illustrations, unless the creator has access to a computer with a graphics or clip art package. If you wish to tempt people to stop and read your notices you need a clear heading, good display and to keep the amount of information to a minimum. For that reason, your summarising skills again come in useful!

You first met notices in Unit 1 – but these were simple notices with only one or two sentences. Some notices need more detailed information – a notice about an internal job vacancy, for instance, would be similar to a job advertisement in your local paper.

Most organisations have notice boards on which a variety of internal notices can be placed. However, unless these notice boards are well managed, and out-of-date notices are removed regularly, the board can be over-crowded and off-putting. The most successful and appealing are those that:

- have clear headings so that information on different topics can be grouped in different areas (often divided by coloured tape)
- are routinely tidied and updated – with existing notices re-arranged so that people are tempted to study the board regularly to see what is new.

Even then, you cannot guarantee people will read your notice. For that reason, notices are used for information of general interest, rather than of critical importance.

## Designing a notice

The style and layout of the notice will depend mainly upon the formality of the message and the amount of text that has to be included. Graphics are suitable on some informal notices – so, too, is informal language. Both may be out of place on a formal notice relating to a change in company policy or procedures (such as the introduction of a no-smoking policy). Some basic rules, however, apply to all notices.

- Keep the notice as short as possible. People will not want to stand for long to read it. If the text is relatively long, break it up into smaller chunks by using headings and bullet points.

- Use terms that everyone will understand. This is particularly important if you are writing a notice issued by a specialist department (such as Computer Services) which will be read by non-specialists.
- Remember the AIDA principle – you need to attract attention with your headline, even if this is factual.
- Use two or (at most) three colours if this will be appropriate and you have the facilities, and different sizes of print and display effects. However, remember that too much of a mixture looks childish, rather than professional. Usually the minimalist approach is more effective.
- It is normal to put the name of the person issuing the notice and the date at the bottom. This also makes it easier for people to tell when it is out of date and should be removed.

## Test your understanding

1 Check one of your college notice boards and note how many notices and how many posters you see. Identify the main differences between them and the type of information each contains.

2 Two notices are shown in Figure 11.2. Which would you find the easiest to understand and remember – and why? Discuss your answers as a group.

3 Discuss the type of layout, style and wording that would be appropriate for each of the following notices. In particular decide which would be the most formal and which the most informal.

   **a** An announcement that the company has increased its mileage allowance for employees using their own cars on company business.
   **b** An appeal for helpers for the staff children's Christmas party.
   **c** An announcement that a member of staff has become a father.
   **d** An update to the existing Fire Regulations.
   **e** A notice about an Internet training course for staff.

4 The terms and conditions of the company pension scheme are about to change. Personnel have produced a pack of information to explain the

***Figure 11.2*** *Two notices giving the same information*

**VISITOR PARKING PERMITS**

A new procedure has been introduced for issuing Visitor Parking Permits to improve flexibility and security. This will be effective from next Monday, 14 May. From that date, there will be two categories of Visitor Parking Permits. The first will be for regular callers who have been cleared by security. These will be GREEN and valid for one month. The second will be for casual callers. These will be RED and valid only for one day (normally date of issue).

Red Permits can be obtained in advance for pre-arranged visits through reception (although the day of the visit must be clearly specified beforehand). Applications for Green Permits must be sent to Bill Jones, Head of Security, at least one week before they are required.

Only visitors with a company permit will be allowed to park in the company car park. Visitors who are calling to obtain a permit must park in one of the temporary bays by reception until the permit has been issued. All visitors must display their permits clearly in the windscreen whilst parked on site. Security reserve the right to clamp any cars not displaying current staff or visitor permits.

Lani Webster, Personnel
10.5.9-

**VISITOR PARKING**

**NEW PROCEDURE FROM MONDAY, 14 MAY 199-**

TWO types of Permits now available

**RED PERMITS** – for casual callers. Valid for **one day** only. Can be obtained in advance from reception staff.

**GREEN PERMITS** – for regular callers. Valid for **one month**. Apply to Bill Jones, Head of Security and allow one week for issue.

**Permit holders must**

- park in temporary bay by reception until permit has been issued
- display permit prominently in car windscreen when on site

Note that cars in the company car park without a valid staff or visitor permit could be clamped.

Lani Webster
Personnel
10.5.9-

changes. They are also holding information sessions in the staff restaurant each lunchtime this week from 12.30 to 1 pm. This will consist of a brief talk outlining the main changes and a question-and-answer session to respond to staff questions. The changes take effect from the first of next month and it is important all staff know about them.

**a** How appropriate would a notice be to convey this type of information? What other alternatives could be considered? Discuss your ideas as a group.

**b** Assuming it is decided to notify staff by a variety of methods, *including* a notice, draft a notice on A4 paper which effectively and attractively summarises this information.

Four page leaflet (A4 paper folded once)

Six page leaflet (A4 paper with 'gate' fold)

Six page leaflet (A4 paper with 'three-way' or 'concertina' fold)

***Figure 11.3*** *Folding methods for A4 leaflets*

# LEAFLETS

A leaflet is a useful and relatively cheap method of conveying information to a large number of people. They can be handed to people, left in a public area for people to collect, sent through the mail or delivered to people's homes with newspapers and magazines. There are various styles. Some are printed on one side of A5 paper, some on both sides. Some leaflets are made from A4 paper folded once, to produce a 4-page leaflet, or twice, to produce a 6-page leaflet – and there are two ways of folding card or paper to produce this type of leaflet.

## Designing a leaflet

All leaflets should be designed bearing in mind the AIDA principles. Divide your information so that the key features which will **interest** and **attract** are on the front cover of a multi-page leaflet and displayed clearly.

Within the leaflet, the information should be divided logically, using techniques such as headings, sub-headings and bullet points. The number of continuous text lines should be kept to a minimum. These pages are the ones on which you must retain your reader's attention. The 'action to take' is normally left until last. Some contain a tear-off portion to be completed by the reader, sometimes with a reply-paid address label printed on the reverse.

The back page or back cover should contain the least important information. In some cases this is even left blank, or the organisation's name and address, logo and telephone number are inserted in the centre and towards the bottom of the page.

HIGHTOWN COLLEGE

**FREE COURSE**

***Introduction to the Internet***

**Saturday, 14 October for 3 weeks**
**10 am–12 noon**

**Has modern technology left you behind?**
**Do your children (or grandchildren) know more than you?**
**Would you like to buy your own computer but don't know where to start?**
**Have you heard about 'the Net' and want to know what you are missing?**

***THEN THIS COURSE IS DESIGNED FOR YOU!***

The course features

- a basic introduction to computers and the Internet
- the equipment you need to 'surf the Net'
- how to find your way around Windows
- accessing the Net using Windows Explorer
- searching and finding information
- book-marking useful pages
- printing, saving and storing information to keep your connection costs to a minimum

The course can lead to further study, either additional qualifications relating to the Internet or courses on web page design and HTML – the language in which web pages are written.

**LEARN BY DOING – ALL TUITION IS 'HANDS-ON' USING THE LATEST EQUIPMENT . . .**

To book your place contact Bridie Jones, Hightown College
Tel 01928 373839.

***. . . BUT HURRY – PLACES ARE STRICTLY LIMITED***

***Figure 11.4*** *A leaflet advertising a course at Hightown College*

# Test your understanding

**1 a** Read the leaflet in Figure 11.4, designed to advertise a course at Hightown College. Identify which features relate to each aspect of AIDA.

**b** The course organiser has decided that the information would look better on a folded A4 leaflet. Decide which type of folded leaflet you would prefer and divide up the text so that it fits appropriately on your pages.

Check your completed work with your tutor.

**2** Collect some leaflets and compare the styles and designs. You will usually find them freely available at tourist information offices, at exhibitions, museums and in some supermarkets. You will also find examples arriving through the post and in newspapers and magazines. Assess these for their ability to attract your attention and interest you.

**3** As a group, you have decided to raise money for charity, by holding a 'good as new' fair. Your aim is to collect any suitable items from householders (books, toys, CDs, unwanted presents, etc) and to hold the fair one Saturday in college. You need to inform as many householders as possible – about the date and time of the fair – and that you will be going around the district collecting suitable items. You have decided that clothing will be accepted only if it is in very good condition.

You have decided to communicate the information in a leaflet, which you can put through people's doors a week before you start collecting. Name your own charity and your own date and time for the fair. Add any other details that you think would be useful and would help your appeal. Select your own style and format for the leaflet.

Design your leaflet and compare your ideas with others in your group.

## SPELLCHECKER 10

Check you can spell correctly each of the following words, which you may want to use in promotional literature. Learn any you are uncertain about and enter them in your Spellchecker book.

achievement
benefited/beneficial
competent
convenient
incomparable
indispensable
irreplaceable
potential
successful
unequalled
appropriate
colossal
connoisseur
especially
indestructible
ingenious
judgement
prestigious
undoubtedly
warranty

## TOOLS OF THE TRADE – *the art of persuasion*

Until this unit, you have mainly been involved in preparing *factual* business communications – your memos, letters, reports and summaries have all been composed from factual information. However, as you probably discovered when you were designing notices and leaflets, certain business communications require the art of persuasion – and this involves a rather different method of communicating.

## Telling versus selling

You are more likely to achieve your aims if you can communicate persuasively. Frequently we have a choice – if we choose to 'tell' someone something we are factual, we use unemotional words and we may speak in a relatively 'flat' tone. If we are 'selling' something we are more emotive, our vocabulary changes, we speak enthusiastically and we emphasise important points. Normally, if you want someone to do something for you – or to see something from your point of view – you will have greater success if you 'sell' your message in some way.

## Persuasive situations and communications

In business, certain situations and certain types of communications give greater opportunities for persuasion than others. Examples include:

- meetings and discussions – when you want to persuade someone of your point of view
- all forms of advertising and promotion
- interviews – when you want to persuade a prospective employer you would be the best candidate to employ
- certain types of letters, such as letters asking someone to do you a favour and sales letters (see page 200)

- internal communications when you want to persuade staff to do something
- presentations, when you are trying to 'sell' an idea or product and convince your audience that you know what you are talking about.

## Persuasive words

If you can learn to write persuasive material well, then you have a future – as a copywriter in advertising, a speech writer for a politician, a fundraiser for a charity or even as a spin doctor, to name but a few occupations linked to this art! Various techniques are employed to achieve the desired effect.

- **The personal approach** – the use of the second person (you) not the third person (they) and the use of active not passive speech. In other words, say

  *You can join today* not *It is possible to join today.*

- **Asking a question** – this actively involves the reader or listener and is useful to gain attention, eg

  *Wouldn't you like to lose weight for summer?*
  *Like to know more?*
  *How can we help?*

- **Appropriate repetition**. 'Speed skills – kill your speed' is a typical example of effective repetition in a poster. In a written document you may find this put rather differently, eg

  *We can help you to save money. We can help you to save time. We can even help to save you the job of rushing out to the shops to buy one.*

  or

  *We can help you to help others and help yourself at the same time!*

- **Visual imagery**. This means using words and phrases that paint a picture or are designed to 'excite' your audience or reader, eg

  *This private and exclusive hotel is set in peaceful surroundings in the heart of England.*

*This exciting new product will revolutionise the way you work for years to come!*

*Farmhouse cooking – wholesome, nutritional food with natural ingredients, each dish individually prepared to order.*

*Soothing, refreshing, ultra-smooth after-sun lotion – the perfect end to a perfect day.*

## Test your understanding

**1** You have an urgent job to finish. Your colleague is getting ready to go home. You want to persuade her to stay an additional ten minutes and help you. What words would you choose? Discuss your suggestions as a group.

2 There are three free places remaining on the college's Saturday Internet course, illustrated in the leaflet in Figure 11.4. You are very interested in attending as you think the experience will look good on your CV when you apply for a job. Several other people in your group want to attend so your tutor has asked each of you to put your request in a short memo. Write a memo applying for a place and use a few persuasive arguments to support your request.

## WORDBANK 9

People with a good vocabulary find it much easier to select the correct words for a situation. Identify the correct meaning of each of the following words by giving a simpler word or phrase to replace each one. Enter any new words into your Wordbank book together with their meanings.

| | |
|---|---|
| commiserate | extenuating |
| facilitate | fortuitous |
| hypothetical | inadvertently |
| infringe | meticulous |
| mitigating | negligible |
| optimal | panacea |
| placatory | preclude |
| pristine | tardy |

## MAKING HEADWAY – *promotional and sales letters*

Virtually all commercial organisations and charities send sales letters. Today these are more commonly known as 'mailshots', and computers have enabled them to be targeted more cleverly and more accurately than ever before. Large national organisations can either buy or create their own database of thousands of potentially interested customers, and then send a promotional or sales letter. These can be targeted specifically to those individuals who will be interested in the product or service being promoted.

- Superstores who issue loyalty cards match sales against card numbers and then notify customers of new products in which they will be interested. The data is taken from previous purchases made by each customer.
- Banks and financial institutions maintain databases of individuals who are in a particular income bracket and inform them of new investment opportunities or offer to lend them money to cover new purchases.
- Charities exchange databases so that people who regularly donate to charity often receive appeals from other charities.
- The age range of customers can be noted on computer so that organisations can target their mailshots. Saga, for instance, will write to customers over 50 with details of insurance policies, and some nightclubs routinely write to local people about to have their 18th or 21st birthday, telling them about their hiring rates for parties and celebrations.
- Individuals who have insurance policies due for renewal are likely to find they receive mailshots from other insurance companies offering them cheaper rates. Those who buy a car may find they receive information from

the car company on deals to help them renew or replace their car after a year or two, and so on.

The preparation and mailing of sales and promotional letters is now big business and is far more sophisticated than it was in the past. However, the cost of writing to thousands of potential customers is considerable – and it is the skill of the letter writer that is important when customers open and read the letter. Obviously, the more customers respond positively to the letter, the more cost-effective the mailshot has been.

## Planning a promotional letter

Promotional letter writing combines all the techniques of letter writing you have learned so far with all the sales techniques you learned in the first part of this unit. Such letters follow the AIDA principles as well as being written in a personal and persuasive way.

Before you start you need to identify:

- exactly what you hope to achieve by sending the letter
  - **a** how do you want the customer to respond?
  - **b** how can you achieve this response?
- the 'market' or type of customers to whom you are writing
  - **a** are they private consumers – and what are their interests and age range?
  - **b** are they commercial organisations or industrial companies?
- the potential benefits of your product or service to that particular market – ie
  - **a** what are their 'needs' and how can you fill that need?
  - **b** what words and phrases will appeal to them?
  - **c** are there any special offers you can make that will encourage them to try your product or service?

You also need to know all the relevant facts that apply to the product or service about which you are writing. In particular you need to know any special selling points. These are often called USPs or 'unique selling points'. Having a USP can make all the difference between effective promotions and ineffective ones.

## Drafting your promotional letter

There are three basic stages to writing a good promotional letter.

1. Assemble all your facts relating to the product or service you are promoting.
2. Identify the main benefits for users and any special offers you are using for the promotion. Focus on any USPs. Note down all the other 'selling points' in a logical order. Any adverse points are normally left out of the letter but may be written in small print on one of the accompanying documents, such as a booking or application form. (This is why you should always read the small print carefully before accepting any offer!)
3. Order your benefits and facts against the AIDA sequence and check you have information that links to each stage.
4. Write your letter using persuasive words and phrases.

**BIRTHDAY PARTIES AT LEISURE CENTRE – FACT SHEET**

Age range 4–12

Afternoons only – start time 1 pm–6 pm. Last 3 hours

Numbers participating 10–20

Cost – £8 per child

Choose any 3 activities from following list: swimming, kwik cricket, football, aeroball, volley ball, trampolining, roller skating, roller blading, short tennis, table tennis.

Birthday cake (iced with candles and child's name) – £8.50

Experienced, trained party organiser.

Pay 10% when booking, balance a week before party.

Cancellation fee if less than 7 days' notice given.

***Figure 11.5*** *Mariam's fact sheet*

## A WORKED EXAMPLE

May Rodgers is concerned that demand for birthday parties at Hightown Leisure Complex has declined. She has decided to send a mailshot to see if she can improve the situation and has obtained a database from Hightown Council giving the names and addresses of all parents in the area whose children go to Hightown schools. The postage charges will be considerable and she therefore wants an excellent letter.

Mariam is working on the letter. Her fact sheet for the birthday parties is shown in Figure 11.5.

She and May have a brief planning session to discuss the letter.

**May** I think the main benefit to working mothers and fathers is not to have the worry and hassle of holding a children's party at home. No preparation, no mess afterwards. Bring them here and let us worry about it.

**Mariam** I agree, although I think the cost sometimes puts people off.

**May** Yes, I've been thinking about that. The new ice rink has started offering children's parties. They say from £6 a person, but note the word 'from'! You get very little for £6, but it makes ours seem expensive. I wondered about dropping the charge to £7 'for a limited time only' to see if that will tempt people.

**Mariam** Well, it might, but it's unfortunate if your child's birthday isn't until after the offer ends!

**May** That's true. What do you suggest?

**Mariam** Well, I had a different idea. Wouldn't it be a nice touch if we gave a free birthday cake – which actually works out cheaper for us than dropping the price?

**May** I like that idea, but I'd also like something to encourage people to respond promptly. I need to get our bookings up quickly! What about a £10 voucher, valid against any party booked in the next three months?

**Mariam** That sounds like an excellent idea. We can enclose the voucher and a booking form with each letter. Do you want me to draft something for you to look at?

**May** Yes, please. By the way, don't forget to point out that if children come here they can choose from a range of activities and actually do three. At the ice rink they are stuck with the same thing all afternoon.

**Mariam** That's true. I also thought I'd mention the fact that we are experienced at organising parties, how professional our staff are – that sort of thing. Parents can have confidence in us.

**May** That sounds good. Don't forget flexibility too – we run the event the way they want it. Rather than give too many details in the letter, why don't you enclose an explanatory leaflet? Then you can just concentrate on the selling points when you are writing.

**Mariam** Leave it with me, I'll see what I can do.

## Test your understanding

**1** From the discussion above, list the benefits and key selling points Mariam should now include in the letter. Then check these against the AIDA principles. Compare your finished list with Mariam's in Figure 11.6 below.

**2** Consider the wording you should use to appeal to your potential customers. Remember all the points made on pages 198–199. Then try drafting your own sales letter for May Rodgers. Compare your draft version with the one Mariam produced, shown in Figure 11.7 below.

Don't be disheartened if you think Mariam's is much better – instead, note the differences. It may be that you have thought of one or two useful points or effective adjectives that she hasn't!

***Figure 11.6*** *Mariam's list of benefits and key selling points*

**BENEFITS AND SELLING POINTS OF PARTIES**

**USP – £10 voucher and free birthday cake**

**Get attention**

1 No hassle, mess, time spent planning and preparing a party

2 You are free to put your feet up whilst we look after your children

3 Take advantage of this special offer and save money at the same time!

**Create interest**

4 Parties for between 10–20 children (tailor-made to suit group)

5 Wide range of popular activities to choose from + tea and free cake

6 Experienced, well-trained party organisers

7 Flexible start time – between 1 pm and 6 pm any day

**Create desire**

8 Mention our experience and facilities – build confidence

9 Enclose leaflet giving details

10 £10 voucher for all parties booked in next 3 months (state date voucher expires)

**Take action**

11 Enclose booking form – complete and return.

**HIGHTOWN LEISURE COMPLEX**
Castle Road
HIGHTOWN
HG3 4MP

Tel: 01928 309322 General Manager: May Rodgers

October 199-

Dear Parent

**£10 OFF YOUR NEXT BIRTHDAY PARTY**
**+ A FREE BIRTHDAY CAKE**

Do you dread the thought of organising your child's birthday party? Do you worry about how to keep everyone entertained, and all the work clearing up afterwards?

Let us do the work for you! Our special offer gives you the chance to put your feet up this year and save money at the same time.

We can offer you:

- a tailor-made birthday party for between 10 and 20 children
- a wide range of popular activities to choose from, all supervised by experienced staff
- a scrumptious birthday tea and FREE birthday cake, iced with your child's name and complete with candles
- your own personal party organiser to run the event the way YOU want it
- a flexible starting time from 1 pm–6 pm on any afternoon.

We have been organising successful parties for over ten years and have the experience and the facilities to give your child a birthday party to remember. We are enclosing a leaflet which gives you full details of all the activities and other events from which you can choose.

In addition, if you make a booking with us before the end of January, you can use the enclosed voucher to reduce the cost of your party by £10!

All you have to do is to complete the form and return it to us – we will do the rest!

Yours sincerely

May Rodgers
General Manager

Enc

***Figure 11.7*** *Mariam's draft sales letter*

### Adjectives

Adjectives describe or modify nouns and pronouns. This means that they give a more precise meaning to the noun or pronoun.

The use of adjectives enables you to say something more descriptively and knowing when and how to use them effectively can improve your persuasive communications. As an example:

*Take advantage of our offer to visit our gymnasium* is a correct sentence but it is hardly interesting or persuasive.

*Take advantage of our special offer to visit our large, fully air-conditioned gymnasium* is far more tempting!

In addition to promotional literature, there are other occasions when the use of adjectives helps you to explain something more precisely. Read the following two extracts from an accident report:

*I fell in the corridor yesterday morning.*

This gives us only a sketchy idea of what occurred. However, you could have written:

*I fell in the corridor because the tiled floor is uneven, with some tiles cracked and others peeling away at the edges. In addition, the floor was slippery after being cleaned yesterday morning yet there were no notices stating this fact.*

This time your report is more detailed and gives a more accurate description of what happened.

## Positioning adjectives

Most adjectives **describe** an object or a person, and they are usually placed immediately before the noun, eg *the black cat; the tall, dark stranger; the tiled floor*. However, they can be placed after the verb in the sentence, eg *The floor is uneven; the stranger was tall and dark*. Some are always put in this position. You wouldn't, for instance, write *The afraid child* – you would always put *The child is afraid*. Conversely, some adjectives are always used before the noun. Therefore you would say *That's a tall order* but never *That order is tall*!

You need to note those occasions where the position of the adjective changes its meaning. *Will all staff concerned contact Personnel* has an entirely different meaning from *Will all concerned staff contact Personnel* – so be careful in this situation.

## Types of adjectives

In addition to being **descriptive**, adjectives can also tell us about **quantity** – both definite and indefinite.

*There are eleven players in the team.*
*We met several people we knew.*

The words 'eleven' and 'several' are both being used as adjectives.

## Comparative and superlative

Most descriptive adjectives can be compared in three ways – to a higher degree, to a lower degree, or to the same degree, eg

*Tom's car cost as much as Ben's* = a comparison to the same degree
*Tom's car cost less than Ben's* = a comparison to a lower degree
*Tom's car cost more than Ben's* = a comparison to a higher degree.

Many adjectives use the addition of the words 'less' or 'fewer' if you are comparing downwards and 'more' or 'most' when you are comparing upwards, eg

*The group have shown less/more interest in travelling abroad this year.*

With some words, however, you add the suffix 'er' or 'est' at the end instead.

*Tom is older than Ben* (not 'more old'), and
*Tom is the oldest boy in the group* (not 'most old').

### THE RULES TO FOLLOW

When only two people or objects are being compared use -er or 'more'. This is called the **comparative** form, eg

*We offer more options than they do.*
*Our products are better and cheaper than theirs.*

When more than two people or objects are being compared use -est or most. This is called the **superlative** form, eg

*We offer the most options.*
*Our products are the best and cheapest in town.*

Note that some adjectives have completely different words for the comparative and superlative eg

*He is bad. She is worse than him. Tim is the worst boy I've met.*
*He is good. She is better. Tamila is the best girl I've met.*
*He has many friends. She has more. He has the most of all.*

Beware of **absolute** adjectives, which cannot be qualified in any way, eg *perfect, unique, excellent*. You may see the sentence 'She is totally perfect' or 'That was absolutely excellent' but both are technically wrong, given that if perfection wasn't total it wouldn't be perfect, and excellence must be absolute! This is similar to the 'redundant words' you studied earlier.

## Test your understanding

Film reviews often contain adjectives to tempt you to see the film. In the following passage, identify all the words that are adjectives. Can you also find the two absolute adjectives placed next to each other?

*This fast-paced, mystery thriller, based on the popular TV series, mixes rapid action and tense drama. Add a witty script and a star cast and the result is a superb remix of an old favourite! In the film, our intrepid hero meets a mysterious woman on a night flight to Hong Kong. Her turbulent life involves him in unexpected encounters and totally impossible and daring escapes from one of the world's most lethal assassins. Not to be missed!*

## ✱✱ DOUBLE TROUBLE

Several adjectives are often confused and can cause problems. For each of the adjectives below:

**a** select the right word from the options in brackets
**b** write a sentence containing the remaining word(s) to show you understand the meaning.

**1** She was prosecuted for living off (immoral/amoral) earnings.

**2** That was a very (inflammable/inflammatory) remark and I am not surprised she was annoyed.

**3** He has recently bought some (invincible/invisible) ink so that he can write secret messages to his friends.

**4** Tomorrow it will be the (official/officious) opening of the new theatre.

**5** He asked me to agree a (definite/definitive) date for the presentation.

## ●●●●● COMMUNICATION IN PRACTICE

### Test your skills

**1** In certain expressions the adjective always follows the noun. A list of examples is given below. Some you may know, but may have never thought about (have you ever wondered why newspapers don't advertise 'vacant situations', for instance?) In each case look up the meaning of the phrase and then write a sentence to illustrate its meaning.

**a** heir apparent
**b** attorney general
**c** situations vacant
**d** president elect
**e** poet laureate
**f** time immemorial
**g** court martial
**h** paymaster general

**2** Test your spellings to date. All the words listed below have appeared in previous units. 10 are spelled correctly and 10 incorrectly. Can you identify the incorrect words?

| | | | |
|---|---|---|---|
| agravate | alcoholic | awfull | calibre |
| colleegues | committment | courteous | cursory |
| excellent | embarassed | feasable | guarantee |
| hypothetical | infinately | initiative | livelyhood |
| millenium | prefered | sincerely | valuable |

**3** Select one personal item of your own and assume you would like to sell this through the classified advertisement section of your local paper. There is a special offer at present – advertisements of 20 words or fewer are free.

Word your advert so that it will be appealing to readers and contain all the relevant information.

**4** Below are 28 nouns. In each case identify the corresponding adjective. Write two paragraphs to go into a brochure about short holidays in the British countryside. Try to include at least 10 of the adjectives you have identified.

| | | | |
|---|---|---|---|
| adventure | energy | nation | sun |
| attract | fire | nature | thought |

| | | | |
|---|---|---|---|
| autumn | giant | north | variety |
| beauty | industry | oak | Wales |
| business | life | peace | water |
| comfort | melody | picture | winter |
| distance | mountain | silk | wool |

**5** Identify the errors in each of the following sentences – which may be punctuation, spelling, vocabulary or grammar. Rewrite each sentence correctly.

**a** Barbara and me had an exciting day at the Pleasure Beech last week.
**b** They made a definate comitment to except him at the athletics club as he ran more fast than Mark.
**c** I don't know who's idea it was to revue the finishing time but I think staff will be adverse to the idea.
**d** The local counsel advertised there new purpose built acommodation for the elderly.

## Apply your skills

Unfortunately, Mariam has flu and is absent from work. She is expected to be away for a while and May Rodgers has asked you to do several jobs for her. As May will be away herself at a conference for the next two days, she has left you instructions in a memo (Figure 11.8) which you found on your desk this morning.

Read this carefully and prepare all the documents she needs.

Check your completed work with your tutor.

***Figure 11.8*** *May Rodgers' memo to you*

# MEMO

TO (You)
FROM May Rodgers
DATE 17 October 199-

I have listed below all the jobs I would like you to do. If you can have all the draft documents ready for me to look at when I return I would be grateful.

1 As a result of Mariam's absence I have arranged for a local doctor to visit the complex on 26 October at 2 pm. He will give anti-flu vaccinations to all staff who want to receive one. There is no charge to staff – the complex will pay. Anyone who can't attend can ring the surgery and make an appointment to attend at any time within the next three weeks. After that time they would have to pay. The doctor's name is Jane Burrows and the surgery number is Hightown 200389.

   Can you please draft out a notice for the staff noticeboard. Try to make it as persuasive as possible – the more people have the jab the fewer absences we are likely to have this winter.

2 Mariam has drafted the letter to promote the birthday parties but we still need a leaflet to go with it. I think you will find most of the information you need in her letter and the notes she made to prepare this. I think the leaflet should be capable of standing alone – it should make sense even without the letter. This means that we can have a supply on reception for people, and perhaps do a mail drop through the local paper. In addition, if anyone loses the letter, the leaflet would tell them all they need to know. Don't, however, include information on the special £10 offer – as I want the leaflets to be usable after the offer has ended. However, you can include information about the free birthday cake.

1 of 2

   I will leave the design and layout up to you. Please put Maria Parsons, the Activities Supervisor, as the contact on the leaflet. I don't want everyone ringing me up instead!

3 I have now obtained agreement that we can have another receptionist, so we need to write an advert for the Gazette. I want the usual attributes included – must be of smart appearance, good with people, etc – I'm sure you can decide what to include. It's important that you mention candidates must be prepared to work some evenings and weekends on a rota basis. Hours per week are 37. Salary will be negotiable, according to age and experience. If you draft a display advertisement then I'll have a look at it. Don't make it too large, however, as the Gazette rates aren't cheap!

4 Finally, Sonia Jenkins and Bill Ford have got together and devised something new called Splash Aerobics. Apparently it combines swimming for fitness with aerobics. The sessions will be held on a Monday evening from 6.30 to 7.30, obviously in the pool area. Those who attend must be able to swim, but beginners at aerobics are welcome. The cost is £2.20 for members, £3 for non-members.

   Sonia has a list of health and fitness members who she thinks may be interested. Could you draft a short, punchy sales letter she could send to them promoting the sessions. As the sessions start in January there's no mad rush, but you might like to think of themes such as getting fit for the New Year and that sort of thing!

Must rush. Please do your best with all these and we'll finalise them on my return.

Thanks

M R

2 of 2

## WORD WIZARD

Have you ever tried product spotting? Or working out why the things you buy are called what they are?

- Many products linked to your teeth have the syllable 'dent' in their name – why? (Steradent and Pepsodent, for instance – the word 'dental' should give you a clue!)
- Many cleaning products give the impression of 'speed' (Jif and Flash, for example).
- Cat food is called Whiskas or Choosy, and dog food is Pal or Chum – why?
- Many chocolate products are named after outer space (Mars, Galaxy, Milky Way, etc).

Today there is the added pressure of global marketing, where a company needs a name that can be used without problems in a wide variety of languages. This is why:

- a Ford Anglia car became a Ford Escort – now to be a Ford Focus
- Marathons became Snickers
- Treats became M & Ms
- Opal Fruits became Starburst

Some translation efforts for slogans and names have gone dreadfully wrong:

- Kentucky Fried Chicken's slogan 'finger-lickin' good' translated in Chinese to 'eat your fingers off'
- The Nova car name was changed to Corsa when it was discovered that 'no va' means 'won't go' in Spanish
- Pepsi's 'come alive' slogan translated in Taiwanese to 'Pepsi will bring your ancestors back from the dead'!

## Your turn!

Decide on your product – it could be a chocolate bar, cold drink, shower gel or other consumer product. As a group, hold a brainstorming session to decide on an appropriate name.

Remember that:

- a brainstorming session should be limited to 15 to 20 minutes
- all suggestions should be written down, no matter how absurd they first appear
- no criticisms of suggestions are allowed
- the ideas of one person should spark off another
- you call a halt to the session at the appropriate time and start to refine your ideas.

UNIT

# 12

## IN THE SPOTLIGHT – MAKING PRESENTATIONS

Unless you are very unusual, you are unlikely to be overjoyed when you are asked to make a presentation to a group of people – even if you know them well. It is an interesting phenomenon that whereas students become familiar with watching dozens of presentations made by their tutor, the request that they actually give one creates a variety of reactions from dumb-struck terror to blind panic. Some even go to great lengths trying to persuade their tutors to forget the whole idea!

The reason for asking students to give a presentation is usually three-fold:

1 You will normally be asked to give a presentation as a member of a group, particularly when you first start. This gives you useful practice in working as a member of a team. This ability is vital for your working life, as few people ever work completely alone. However, there are advantages and disadvantages to working in a team, as you will see on page 215.

2 Preparing for and delivering a presentation brings together virtually all your communications skills – particularly if you are also asked to produce a brief report on the subject. Your oral skills, written skills, graphical skills and body language can all be assessed at the same time.

3 You would be unusual if, during your working life, you were *never* asked to give any type of presentation at all. In some cases, you may even be expected to give a short one at an interview. Certainly you can expect to have to speak in public (even if only to a small group of visitors) at some point in your career. Although the idea of giving a presentation at college may seem horrific, this does give you the opportunity to develop your self-confidence before you are being paid to give a professional performance!

The best way to calm your nerves is to prepare well and to be extremely well organised. A checklist for doing this is given below.

# PRE-PREPARATORY STAGE

Check your brief carefully. In particular you need to know the following.

- The *exact* topic on which your presentation must be based. Make sure you have received detailed instructions and you clearly understand them. Otherwise you will waste a lot of time researching or preparing irrelevant material.
- The date and time of your presentation – so that you can work out how long you have to prepare. If possible, find out where it will be held so you can check out the location, space and equipment available.
- The length of time the presentation must last. It is very amateurish to over-run and you will impress your audience if you finish spot on time!
- Whether you are expected to make the presentation on your own. If not, you need to get to know the other members of your group (see also page 215).
- Whether you will be expected to answer questions on your presentation afterwards.
- Whether you are expected to give out written information to supplement your talk.
- Who will be watching the presentation. If your audience are experts on your topic then you will have to make sure you are very well prepared, but you could use jargon without having to explain every term. If your audience knows very little about your subject matter then you will need to keep it straightforward and avoid terms and abbreviations they would not know.

# PREPARING YOUR MATERIAL

Your presentation will need a beginning, a middle and an end. If you are working as a member of a group it is normal to divide the material to share the load. A common error is to neglect to join up the segments so that it is disjointed between one speaker to the next. In a good presentation the sub-divisions should appear deliberate – not accidental!

## Obtaining your information

The next stage is to obtain your material, and this is where good researching skills can be very useful. Obvious sources include the following.

- Printed information – in books, newspapers, magazines, business journals, leaflets and catalogues.
- Written information – such as that found in your printed course notes. At work you would have access to office files and previous reports or other documents on the topic.
- Verbal information – from people who know about the topic and who can help to give you useful, practical advice from their own experiences. Often this can help to make your presentation more up-to-date and relevant.

However, do be careful not to include other people's assumptions or prejudices – only use facts that can be proved!

- Graphical information – illustrations, cartoons, drawings, graphs, charts and photographs. Sometimes you can use some of these ideas in your visual aids (see page 218).
- Electronic information – from computer reports, library databanks, CD-ROMs and the Internet, for example.

If you are working as a team, you need to decide whether each person will find out about his or her own part of the topic from each source, or whether you are each going to research from a particular source and then pool all your information.

## Selecting your information

It is often the case that, if you have worked hard to obtain information, you end up with more than you need rather than too little. At this point you need to work out which you need to keep and use and which you should discard. The key rules for selection discussed on page 184 are relevant here. You should check whether it is up to date, accurate, relevant, valid, complete and legally acceptable.

Now decide the order in which you will be presenting the information and group your information into batches to link with each step of the presentation. Useful techniques include:

- seeing if the main topic will divide into logical sub-divisions
- seeing if chronological order would be best
- deciding whether giving the arguments for and then against a particular course of action would be appropriate
- working out whether you have to sell an idea and persuade your audience – in which case you may wish to work to the AIDA principles.

Agree which information is essential, and which should only be used if you have enough time. Then divide it into batches.

If you are working in a team, by the end of this process you should only have material relating to your own part of the presentation in your hand – which should make your task seem a little easier.

## Preparing your information

Read your information carefully, highlighting key points and important information. Do not include anything you do not understand. Make notes where visual aids would be useful (see page 218). Summarise your main points and then prepare a detailed summary – to equate with what you are going to say. Finally, you will need to shorten it again so that you can remember it! This point is discussed later on page 214.

## Team preparations

Once each member of the team has reached this stage you need to meet again to agree the following.

- The visual aids needed and who will prepare them. You need to use the same style for each one – if each person does their own your presentation may look ragged and disjointed.
- Who will introduce the team and the topic.
- How the presentation will start.
- How hand-overs will be made from one person to another.
- Who will conclude.
- How the team will handle questions.
- Whether a report or summary is needed, how it should be prepared and when it should be given to the audience.

These issues are closely related to the sequence of events during a presentation, which is usually as follows.

- A brief introduction – of the team members and the topic, eg *Good afternoon. My name is Salma and these are my colleagues Tom, Rashida and Patrick. We are going to give you a short presentation on the Effect of Modern Technology on Business Communications.*

- The opening. A good presentation always attracts the audience's attention (think of AIDA again). There are various techniques you can use at the beginning of a presentation to get attention, including:

  - giving some facts and figures, eg *In 1990, only 30% of the population owned a computer, only 20% owned a mobile phone and only 10% had heard of the Internet. By the year 2000 it is forecast that 70% will own a computer, 50% will own a mobile phone and 90% will have heard of or use the Internet.*

  - asking a question, eg *I would like to start by asking you a question. How many people in this building do you think own a computer, use a mobile phone or know what is meant by the Internet?*

  - painting a verbal picture, eg *Imagine an office in 1980. There are three typewriters and one phone with a dial, linked to a switchboard. The post room is used for mail sent within the UK and abroad. Now imagine the same office in 2010...*

  - using a quotation, eg *According to the magazine, Software Weekly, 'By 2010 most communications will be between computers. . . .'*

- Developing the theme according to the most appropriate sequence. It is important that you keep your audience with you throughout. The best way to do this is by

  - pausing at the end of a particular section
  - repeating the main points at the end of your section
  - identifying clearly when you are moving onwards.

  For example, *This summarises the points I have made about telecommunications,* – pause – *Rashida will now explain how the Internet has affected business communications.* (Gesture towards Rashida so the audience can quickly identify who will be the next speaker.)

- Ending the presentation should be done decisively – it is better to end on a high point than to let your presentation drift to a standstill. If you cannot find one useful, interesting point to make at the end then prepare two or three summary sentences either summing up the whole purpose of the presentation or pointing towards the future, eg

- *And, of course, if Bill Gates has his way it is likely that in the future our computers will be doing all our communicating for us!*
- *There is no doubt that the workplace of tomorrow will include a wide array of communications equipment.*

■ You and/or your team may then be expected to answer a few questions from those who have been watching. It is sensible to prepare for these in advance in the same way that you have been preparing your other notes and materials:

- think about likely questions
- think about the answers you could/should give
- decide who will answer question on which area
- be prepared to ask someone to repeat a question if you do not hear it properly
- be prepared to ask someone to rephrase a question if you do not understand it
- be honest if you do not know the answer and offer to find out later, eg *I'm sorry, my research didn't include that, but if you would like me to find out for you and tell you later, I will.*
- be prepared to help out a team member who is stuck with a question if you know the answer – but don't leap in too quickly before your colleague has had time to think!

■ You may, of course, have been asked to produce notes or a brief report to supplement your presentation. Do bear in mind that this should not be a copy of your script! It is often useful to use this to:

- summarise your main points
- expand your points with statistics and other details you might have found difficult to remember.

You can try to second-guess some possible questions from your audience and put the answers on this paper. The trick then is to give out your paper just before the question session – so you can refer your audience to key points on the paper in answer!

A final piece of advice – do not give out your papers at the beginning of the presentation. Otherwise your audience may be reading these rather than listening to you!

# PREPARING YOURSELF

Researching your topic well, summarising your notes properly, preparing good materials and visual aids (see page 218) and thinking through the sequence of your presentation will all help to reduce your nerves. However, there are several other aspects to think about if you are to do a professional job.

■ Your image is important. A pair of scruffy jeans, trainers and a tee-shirt give the wrong impression. Whilst you shouldn't look as if you are going to a wedding, it is important you should be well groomed and dressed smartly.

■ Your body language should imply you are confident, even if you don't feel it! Take deep breaths beforehand to steady your nerves, stand up straight with your feet slightly apart and hold your head up. This will prevent you from talking at the floor! Be prepared to meet people's eyes (don't glare solidly at the back wall of the room or stare glassy-eyed at one person) and start by smiling – if you look welcoming your audience will respond to you more positively from the very beginning.

- Your voice should be as steady as possible and loud enough for everyone to hear. Say your words clearly – don't mutter. Avoid the temptation to speak quickly to get it over – you will 'lose' your audience. Try to project interest, enthusiasm and variety into your voice and slightly stress important points you want your audience to remember.
- Treat this as a formal occasion – no matter how well you know some members of the audience. Over-familiarity is very embarrassing, and so too is any direct reference to a particular member of the audience. The only occasion when this is permissible is if you are giving a short talk or explanation to a group of colleagues – in which case you could then, during the question and answer session, call on expert advice from a particular person.
- Your memory may desert you when you need it most! You need to use a technique to help you to remember what to say. You should note that it is *never* acceptable to read from pages of notes, nor is it feasible to think you can remember them all. Even if you did manage to learn to say them parrot-fashion, this would sound very artificial. Instead, prepare cue cards (postcard size) or visual aids with key words which will prompt you to remember your notes. How to do this is described in more detail on page 218.
- Keep calm! The value of having a few rehearsals (either on your own in front of a mirror or as a group if you are giving a team presentation) cannot be over-emphasised. This enables you to identify and remedy any possible teething troubles and to fine-tune your timing. Be prepared to cut some material if you are over-running, rather than pressurise yourself. Develop a technique of placing your cue cards where you can see them at a glance – just in case you 'dry up'.

## PREPARING YOUR VENUE

On the day itself allow yourself plenty of time to check the room before you are due to start. You need to make sure that:

- it is tidy
- there are sufficient chairs
- you have space for all the materials and visual aids you need
- you have any equipment you need and it is working
- you can plug in your equipment without falling over any trailing wires
- you know how to work the blinds if you need to shut out the light
- you have sufficient space to move around freely at the front.

Set everything out appropriately and neatly. At this stage you have done all you reasonably can to prepare yourself – and you are likely to find that the ordeal is not as dreadful as you perhaps feared!

**TALK ASSESSMENT FORM**

Names of presenters ..........................................................................

Topic ..........................................................................................

Date of talk ..................................................................................

1 **DELIVERY**

Appearance/dress
Confidence
Mannerisms
Eye contact/body language
Pace/enthusiasm

2 **INTRODUCTION**

Did it create interest?
Was it clear?

3 **PRESENTATION**

Was it well structured?
Was it clear?
Was it organised
Was it appropriate for the audience?
Was it the right length?

4 **TEAMWORK**

Did the first person introduce the talk properly?
Was the work equally shared?
Was the handover done properly?
Did the team support each other?

***Figure 12.1*** *Tutor's assessment form for a presentation*

## Test your understanding

Work in pairs to research and prepare a short talk on a topic that you have agreed with your tutor. Topics you might like to consider include:

- new developments in business communications
- the value of persuasion in communications
- the growth and popularity of the Internet
- the importance of body language
- health and safety at work
- the growth of mobile phones
- the importance of listening skills
- formal and informal methods of communicating.

Prepare your talk to last for four minutes, talking for two minutes each. At this stage, no visual aids are required, neither will you be expected to handle questions.

Practice listening to each other to assess each other's style, delivery and timing. Then deliver your talk to the whole group and ask your tutor to assess you using the form in Figure 12.1. Finally, book a tutorial session with your tutor where you can discuss the tutor's assessment with you privately. Then you can work on any areas needing improvement.

## TOOLS OF THE TRADE – teamwork

Today, many job advertisements include statements such as *'must be a good team player'* and *'must be able to work as a member of a team'*. Why is this attribute considered so important – and what does 'teamwork' mean?

Very few people operate completely on their own at work. Most people prefer to work with others as this makes working more enjoyable and adds a social dimension. However, there is a big difference between working with other individuals and operating as a member of a team. This is because when you are part of a team each member depends upon the others for a successful result. You only have to think of a sporting team to realise that this is true. One good player in a football team will never succeed if he is surrounded by ten players who ignore him and never pass him the ball. It is the *combined, linked* and *mutually supportive* efforts of all the members that allow the team to succeed.

Working in a good team can be a very enjoyable experience. You can share the work, rely on other people for help and support, laugh together, comfort

SAY IT!

## The 'ed' problem

In most words in English the final syllable 'ed' is not pronounced. Think of words such as *called, named, housed* and *telephoned.*

However, in certain words this syllable *is* pronounced – such as in the word *naked, wicked, jagged, sacred* and *wretched*.

There is another group of words where you alter the meaning if you pronounce the syllable 'ed'. This group is given below. In each case check that you know the meaning of each word for *both* pronunciations – so that you don't say the wrong one by mistake.

| | **'ed' NOT pronounced** | **'ed' pronounced** |
|---|---|---|
| *aged* | = has the age of (eg she is aged two) | = very old (eg he is an aged man) |
| *beloved* | = when replacing 'loved' (eg he was dearly beloved) | = when used as an adjective (eg my beloved friend) |
| *crooked* | = past tense of 'to crook' (eg he crooked his finger at me) | = dishonest (eg he has always been a crooked man) |
| *cursed* | = past tense of 'to curse' (eg I cursed him for being late) | = when used as an adjective (eg it's that cursed song again) |
| *dogged* | = past tense of 'to dog', meaning to go after (eg he dogged me all day) | = tenacious (eg he works on a problem doggedly until he solves it) |
| *learned* | = past tense of 'to learn' – although 'learnt' is also commonly used | = very knowledgeable (eg he is a learned physician) |
| *ragged* | = past tense of 'to rag' (eg he ragged me about my new haircut). | = rough or torn (eg his clothes were very ragged). |

each other on the bad days, talk over new ideas together. A bad team can be dreadful. People argue, let each other down, and some may even enjoy seeing other people get into a mess. There is little, if any, communication so no-one knows what is happening. Just *one* disastrous team member can create havoc for every single member. This is why 'teamwork' skills are often covered very thoroughly in job interviews!

## Team building

Some organisations spend many thousands of pounds on team building exercises for staff. The aim of these is for

**a** individuals to improve their individual teamwork skills
**b** teams to function more effectively.

Often the team will be given a problem and then expected to solve it. They are then assessed not on *whether* they solved it successfully but *how* they went about it. A team where one person took charge from start to finish, shouted everyone else down and got the answer right would be considered less successful than one that worked productively together but perhaps failed to reach the right conclusion.

If you are expected to work as a member of a team – to give a presentation, for example – then you are being given a 'team problem' to solve. On some courses, how each team member relates to the others and how the team performs together may be assessed to the same extent as the final presentation.

## Teamwork skills

A good team member is one who:

- puts the goals of the team before his/her own needs
- keeps his/her promises
- communicates with other members honestly but tactfully
- is open-minded about new suggestions
- is supportive and helpful
- is prepared to go along with a decision for the good of the team
- can be relied upon to produce high-quality work by an agreed deadline
- is punctual and has a good attendance record
- is prepared to trust other team members
- knows when to talk and when to listen
- is loyal
- will help to solve team problems constructively.

This last point is very important. Teamwork is much easier when life is simple. When it becomes stressful or pressurised there is a very human tendency to blame other people. If team members start accusing each other every time something goes wrong then the team will rapidly disintegrate.

### SPELLCHECKER 11

All of the following words represent a characteristic you would not want to find in any of your team members! In each case, can you spell the word correctly *and* say what it means? Add any new words or words that cause you difficulty to your Spellchecker or Wordbank book.

| | |
|---|---|
| aggressive | antagonistic |
| biased | humourless |
| hypocritical | impressionable |
| incoherent | incompetent |
| inflexible | ingratiating |
| irresponsible | mischievous |
| monotonous | obdurate |
| opinionated | presumptuous |
| uncontrollable | whingeing |

## MAKING HEADWAY – preparing and using visual aids

We receive information through all our senses but the most dominant by far is our sight. This is why television has a much greater impact than radio. We are more likely to remember something we see and hear than something we only hear.

For this reason, visual aids are a common feature of many business situations. A presentation without any visual aids can seem drab and lifeless, unless there is a particularly talented or witty speaker. A meeting to discuss several complex issues can seem confusing unless there is some visual evidence to assist everyone.

If you are considering visual aids you need to consider:

**a** the type of information that is suitable for representing visually
**b** the range of equipment and facilities at your disposal, as this will limit your choices.

## Type of information

Visual aids can be overdone. If you start a presentation and almost every word you say you write on a whiteboard or read off an overhead transparency, you will rapidly lose the interest of your audience. The use of visual aids will depend on the topic and content of your presentation, but think in terms of:

- using pre-prepared visual aids to 'jog' you on your key points – OHTs (see below) are particularly useful
- using visual aids of pre-prepared graphics – charts, graphs, tables – which illustrate the point you are making quickly and effectively
- using visual aids to add interest or even humour – statistics can be illustrated with a pictogram; a drawing or cartoon (which may be photocopied) can lighten a relatively tedious section; a poster (bought or made) can summarise or draw attention to a particular point
- using visual aids to illustrate something that is difficult to describe in words.

## Range of visual aids

Each type of visual aid has its own strengths and weaknesses – and you are unlikely to have every option available. Whatever you do, don't even think of using more than about two in a single presentation!

Your choices are likely to include the following.

- **An overhead projector** on which you can put pre-prepared overhead transparencies (OHTs) containing text, drawings, charts or even photographs. OHTs can be prepared by hand, using coloured pens; on a photocopier or on a computer printer. They can be used more interactively if you leave spaces on an OHT and then write in information or overlay another OHT that fills in the gaps as you are talking. However, you should practise this type of more advanced technique carefully first.

**Do**

- make sure your text is large enough to be read from the back of the room
- write neatly and clearly – preferably, print it
- use colour for effect
- focus and check the projector with a test OHT beforehand
- check *each* OHT is positioned correctly, with all the text showing, before you start to talk about it
- point to items on the OHT itself as you are talking – not at the screen

**Don't**

- put your OHT on the screen upside down or back to front.
- block the screen by standing in front of it
- talk to the screen instead of the audience
- leave on the projector when you have finished.

## ■ A blackboard

These are being replaced by whiteboards (see below). You will be familiar with the purpose of a blackboard from your schooldays!

**Do**

- write clearly – if you are not used to using a blackboard then use print, rather than joined-up writing
- write in a straight line – most people move downwards as they move to the right
- use good quality chalk
- clean the board afterwards

**Don't**

- press too hard – your chalk will break
- lean against it – especially if you are wearing dark clothes
- turn your back on the audience whilst you are writing and speak to the board.

## ■ A whiteboard

These are more versatile than blackboards and, indeed, are the only type of board allowed where there are computers (as chalk dust could damage them). You will use a whiteboard more effectively if you build up your diagram or key points one by one, as you are talking.

**Do**

- use colour for effect
- make your writing large enough for everyone to see
- practice beforehand so that your writing is neat and clear (again, printing helps)
- clean the board afterwards

**Don't**

- face the board as you write – try to learn the art of writing whilst you are standing sideways and facing forwards!
- use the wrong pen by mistake – whiteboard pens are designed to rub off after use, so if you use an indelible pen in error you will have to plead with your caretaker to remove your marks with special solvent!
- leave the top off your pens, or they will dry out and become unusable.

## A flip chart

These consist of large (A1) pads of paper screwed to the top of an easel. You can either prepare a pad in advance or use a flip chart to write key facts during your presentation. Each sheet can be flipped over or torn off when it is full. One useful technique is to draw a large diagram in pencil on a flip chart page and then ink it in during the presentation. Your audience won't be able to see your pencil marks, and will be impressed by your skills!

**Do**

- check you know how to fasten a pre-prepared pad at the top beforehand and check you can reach
- check there are sufficient clean pages, if you are using an existing pad
- decide in advance whether you are going to flip over or tear off each sheet
- make sure you tear along the perforation if you are choosing the latter
- make your writing large enough and clear enough for everyone to see
- use colour for effect.

**Don't**

- write facing the flip chart, or even worse, talk to it!
- use the wrong pens
- over-use a flip chart – they are useful for summarising facts but have a limited role in presentations.

## Video equipment

If you have a short, *relevant* video clip then this may be appropriate. However, bear in mind that during presentations you are supposed to be speaking, not someone else. The clip should highlight or illustrate a point you are making, not replace it.

**Do**

- learn how to use the equipment beforehand
- set the tape in the right place
- check the volume level.

**Don't**

- spend ten minutes introducing it – it is better to introduce it quickly and then make your relevant points afterwards, when the audience knows what you are talking about
- speak again until it has finished – or until it has been switched off
- make technical adjustments when people are watching

## Computer-based presentations

These should only be used if you are computer literate and know your equipment backwards! Otherwise, you are in danger of experiencing technical problems that will be very nerve-wracking. Their advantage is in the fact that you can prepare extremely well in advance and can then rely on your materials to present your case for you. The disadvantage is that you have to think about two things simultaneously – giving your talk and moving on each frame at the right time.

**Do**

- give careful thought to the screens you will show
- make sure the projection is large enough for everyone to see

- proof-read your screens carefully
- prepare a set of OHTs as a back up
- test the equipment beforehand and rehearse your timing.

**Don't**

- expect the equipment to do all the work for you
- prepare too many screens so that they become a distraction rather than an aid
- talk to the screen, rather than your audience.

### ■ Props, posters, maps and models

A presentation can often be made much more interesting if you devise your own, personal visual aid that is different from the run-of-the-mill items. This technique is particularly effective if your presentation is being assessed against other people's, and you want to create an impact. A group of students once scored very highly when giving a presentation on the layout of a reception area because they had mocked up a model to illustrate their ideas.

Other ideas can be obtaining pre-printed posters (put these up in advance), obtaining samples of a product or different products, or having a human model to demonstrate something (such as a first-aid technique).

**Do**

- check the cost and time implications beforehand
- link your model or aid to the overall theme – it should enhance it, not distract from it
- make sure it (or they) are in perfect condition.

**Don't**

- volunteer a human model without his or her prior agreement
- overdo this idea – otherwise your presentation will look gimmicky
- be too ambitious – your creativity may be greater than your artistic talent.

## Test your understanding

1 Check the type of equipment and visual aids available in your college. Ask a technician to demonstrate how to focus and adjust an overhead projector, and see if you can change a flip chart pad without dropping it on the floor!

2 Practise writing on a blackboard or whiteboard. You may get a shock! Write a line of text and then walk to the back of the room and appraise it. Now try writing just as neatly but facing the audience while you do it.

3 Prepare an OHT on a topic of your choice. Do not use more than two colours. Write (or print) in different styles and different sizes and then check which looks the clearest.

4 See if you can watch a computer presentation and discuss its strengths and weaknesses as a group.

5 Watch any type of television programme where facts and information are being presented. Assess the type of visual aids used and the type of information contained in them. Try to spot the way in which complicated information is reduced to a few key facts or one graphic.

## POLISH YOUR PUNCTUATION – QUOTATION MARKS

### Single and double quotes

Quotation marks – otherwise known as inverted commas, quotes or speech marks – are always used in **pairs** and can be formed in two ways:

- by the use of single quotation marks, ' (which is the same as the apostrophe on a keyboard)
- by the use of double quotation marks, ".

In the business world it is more normal to use single quotes than double, unless you work in the media, when you would need to check the policy of your particular organisation.

### Speech marks

The standard use for quotation marks is when you are writing dialogue or a quotation, as they denote that the words enclosed between them are those that someone has said. This is the reason they are sometimes called speech marks. You will be familiar with this use from books you read or from magazines or newspapers reporting an interview with someone, or quoting from someone's statement. The writer is repeating the actual words used by a person – known as direct speech.

Although you will be unlikely to use quotation marks in general business correspondence, it is worth noting that when you are writing speech the quotation mark follows the final punctuation mark at the end of each period of speaking.

*'What time are we setting off?' asked Mary.*
*'About three o'clock, I think,' replied Steve.*
*'That's too late. We'll never arrive in time for the start,' cried Angelo. 'How do they think we're getting there – by helicopter?'*

You may need to include quotations in written work yourself – for instance, if you are referring to a passage in a book and are repeating the words exactly. Never do this and pretend they are your own words. This is normally quite obvious to the reader, because the writing style changes. Trying to pass someone else's work off as your own is known as plagiarism – and is considered a very serious offence. If you are ever asked to write an assignment or a report with quotations, indicate these properly and also state the source. You may find that in business, a report which refers to a particular source of information does the same thing, eg

> *According to the Health and Safety Executive, 'Medical evidence shows that using display screen equipment is not associated with damage to eyes or eyesight; nor does it make existing defects worse.' Health and Safety (Display Screen Equipment) Regulations 1992 – Guidance on Regulations page 41.*

In a report you may find that the quotation is marked at the end by a small raised number in the text[1] and listed, under this number, as a footnote at the bottom of the page or in a reference list at the end. Book sources are usually given in the following order: title, author, publisher, year of publication, page number.

## Short titles

Quotation marks are sometimes used to identify the titles of short works, such as an article, lecture or a speech. In this case the quotation mark comes *before* the final punctuation mark. Longer titles are usually printed in italics, rather than in quotes, eg

The title of his talk was 'Among the Natives'.

I enjoyed the story 'The Dangerous World of Relationships', which I read in Peter Ustinov's book *Laughter Omnibus*.

## Highlighting special text or terms

The most frequent use of quotation marks at work is to

- identify special terms or phrases
- show that words have been used in a different way from normal – in case the reader misinterprets this, the particular words or phrase are shown in quotation marks
- to highlight and separate a word or phrase to show it is like a miniature quotation, rather than the writer's own words
- to identify slang or cliches – because this particular phrase must be quoted in the context, and not because the writer cannot think of the correct word to use!

In all these cases, if the final quotation mark relates to the last word, put this first, before the final punctuation mark, eg

*He said Mark is 'vertically challenged'. This appears to be the phrase Americans prefer rather than the word 'short'!*

## Quotes inside quotes

Occasionally you might find yourself in the situation when you have already placed something in quotes and then need to put another statement in quotes inside it. Simply use the other type of quotation marks than the one you started with. In most cases, you will be using single quotes for your work. A quotation inside this therefore goes in double quotes. Make sure you have

---

[1] This is an example of a footnote. There is always a line separating any footnotes from the rest of the text on the page.

closed each pair of quotation marks at the end and be very careful where your punctuation is placed if it is the last word of a sentence which is in double quotes. This is shown in the example below.

*'Have you any idea,' Greg asked, 'what our word processing tutor means by the terms "orphans" and "widows"?'*

## Test your understanding

1 Identify three technical terms or phrases you have used in a subject you have studied. Write sentences containing each of these, putting the term or phrase in single quotes in each case.

2 Convert at least one of your sentences above into direct speech and illustrate how you would use quotes inside quotes in this case.

3 Select a brief passage from this book and write a short paragraph in which you quote the passage. Punctuate this correctly and write the source afterwards as a footnote.

# *COMMUNICATION IN PRACTICE*

## Test your skills

**1 a** In groups of three, decide whether each of the following words should have the 'ed' stressed or not stressed. Solve any disagreements through negotiation rather than argument! Then compare your answers with other groups.

| | |
|---|---|
| belatedly | decidedly |
| embarrassed | level-headedness |
| self-centred | hurriedly |
| markedly | unreservedly |
| deservedly | advisedly |
| tiredly | allegedly |

**b** On your own, look up the meaning of each word and write a sentence to illustrate this for any *six* of the words listed.

**2** Each of the following can be expressed by a single word. What is it? The first has been done for you.

**a** relating to the teeth *dental*
**b** to show sympathy
**c** concerning the hands
**d** loss of memory
**e** to cast a spell on
**f** relating to the nose
**g** to make pure
**h** to put in prison
**i** concerning the face

**3** The following notes have been written for a presentation but all the punctuation marks, apart from full stops, are missing. Insert these correctly.

### Electronic commerce – or Ecommerce

Ecommerce is new term relates to shopping on the Internet. Not just groceries but also buying travel houses books cars etc. Extension of electronic banking. Some companies have set up web departments and employ cyber commanders and web wizards.

World Trade Organisation says that in principle all goods and services which can be digitalised can be transported over the Internet such as extracts from databanks music film documents medical diagnostics lectures and classes stocks and bonds and much more.

WTO also predicts number of Internet users will increase from about 4.5 million in 1991 to 300 million by the year 2000 and value of ecommerce will climb from virtually zero to about $300 billion. But survey also says Internet not user friendly.

Survey by Shelley Taylor & Associates concluded most business have failed to respond to the opportunities presented by the Internet. Don Tapscotts book Growing up Digital says this is often because senior managers control the organisation and young ones understand the technology.

**4** Rewrite the following passage, correcting all the spelling errors.

Paula was desparate. The presentation was likely to be disasterous unless they develloped a proper stratagy for working together. Sam was really difficult to work with. She was very inflexable and obdurrate and could never be disuaded from her own ideas. She often critisised the others and had been really scathing about Peter's visual aids. Peter had been so dissheartened he had asked to be transfered to another team yesterday. Paula sighed, gave her notes a final, cursery glance, and put them in her bag. She was now regreting turning down an invatation to Sarah's birthday celabrations to finish the work.

The next day, to her suprise, hardly anyone arrived for the final rehersal. Graham Scott, her tuter, arrived looking harrased. 'It seems like everyone who went out with Sarah to that new Italian place has food poisening,' he announced, 'so I've had to re-think the presentations. Peter, Paula, you liase with Jim and Sue now. Your topics are broadley similar. Sam is one of those who's ill, I'm afraid.' Paula looked across at the other pair. She tryed to force herself to think charatable thoughts about Sam. At least now, she decided, they stood a chance of being succesful.

**5 a** Test your proof-reading skills! The following article has been prepared for your boss but there are 14 errors in it. Can you find them?

**b** The junior who typed it asks you to explain the meanings of the following words. Can you help her?

**i** inaugural  **ii** strategy  **iii** debriefings

How well teams perform under stress was measured in the BT Global Challenge Race organised by Sir Chay Blyth's The challenge Business, were racing yachts have crews comprising one proffesional skipper and 13 amaturs. In the inaugural race, held in 1992–3, they found many skippers lacked leadership qualities and were impatient with the the new recruits. In the 1996–7 race more time was spend on training the leaders. How the teams performed had a direct results on their final place in the race. Good teams pulled togeether and this helped them to relate positively to each other-particularly when they had to manaage with very little sleep and cope in apalling conditions. The best crew's had a clear strategy, everyone was involved in making decisions, they held regular debriefings and never thought the basics – such as as saying 'please' and 'thankyou' were beyond them.

## Apply your skills

A leading national company, Speakeasy Digital Communications, is opening a communications centre in Hightown. The centre will market mobile phones to young people on a national basis. Speakeasy is offering a wide variety of well-paid jobs and has liaised with your college to offer the opportunity for a guaranteed interview to students who have the right skills and abilities. It has advertised this in a series of notices on the college notice boards (see Figure 12.2).

***Figure 12.2*** *Speakeasy's notice advertising job opportunities*

**WELL-PAID JOB OPPORTUNITIES**

**with mobile phone company**

Speakeasy Digital Communications is moving to Hightown in the spring and will require staff for its new communications headquarters. Job opportunities exist in the following areas:

- receptionists
- word processor operators
- administrators
- sales staff
- accounts staff.

The company enjoys a reputation as being the leading mobile phone company chosen by young people and sees continued growth in this area. It prides itself on knowing and understanding the needs of those with a dynamic, mobile and active social and working life.

If you feel you can contribute to our continued success then we need to know you share our vision for the future and can communicate this to our customers. We assess this by asking you to make a brief presentation, as a member of a group of 3 or 4. Your contribution to the planning process, ability to work as a member of a team and communication skills are judged as well as the content of your presentation.

**All students who succeed in the presentation session are guaranteed an interview with the company in the area of their choice.**

If you are interested, full details are available from your tutor, including the times and dates when the presentations will be held.

Speakeasy Digital Communications, Westwood Way, Hightown HG4 9PS

Westwood Way
HIGHTOWN
HG4 9PS

**Presentation Brief**

**BACKGROUND**

Today 25% of people in the UK own and use a mobile phone regularly. In Scandinavia and some other countries the figure is much higher. In Britain it has been estimated that the number of mobile phone users will increase from around 6 million people (1996) to 12 million people by the year 2000. However, forecasts show that this will not be because of increased use by businesses, but because **young people** see a mobile phone as an important part of their lives.

**THE FUTURE FOR MOBILES**

Modern developments are enabling us to produce more sophisticated mobile phones. Portable videophone technology is now possible. Call charges are falling and phone companies can sell direct only to consumers. But competition is fierce and to appeal to young people in the future, Speakeasy needs to know what they want. For instance

- is there a future for portable videophones?
- will young people in their first homes prefer to use a mobile rather than have a landline phone installed?
- what features would they want on the phone itself?
- what is their lifestyle and how will a mobile help them?
- to what degree is their buying decision based on the cost of the equipment and the cost of the calls?

**YOUR TASK**

If you can help us to answer some of these questions you could have a future with Speakeasy. Your task is to devise a 10-minute presentation as part of a group of 3 or 4, with appropriate visual aids, telling us how you see the future of mobile phones and how Speakeasy can tailor-make their product to appeal to young people. Be prepared to answer a few simple questions – as a group – at the end.

Specific teams and the times and dates of the presentation will be given to you by your tutor.

***Figure 12.3*** *Speakeasy's presentation brief*

You are very interested in applying to work for the organisation and therefore want to take advantage of the opportunity. You approach your tutor for a presentation brief (see Figure 12.3).

Use this brief to prepare the presentation required by the company. Your tutor will give you further details of the location, date and time of the event, as well as allocating particular teams. It is up to your team to find out any relevant information you feel would be useful, to allocate roles to each person and to prepare suitable visual aids.

## WORD WIZARD

**Different definitions revisited**

Following on from the definitions you saw in Unit 6, can you say what is clever about each of these – and can you say you know the true definition in each case?

| | |
|---|---|
| ■ atheist | a man who believes himself to be an accident |
| ■ boy | a noise with dirt on it |
| ■ claustrophobia | fear of Santa |
| ■ diode | what happens to people who don't die young |
| ■ dishonest | ethically disorientated |
| ■ hamlet | a little pig |
| ■ lawyer | someone who prepares a 10,000 word document and calls it a brief |
| ■ network | what fishermen do when not fishing |
| ■ neurotic | self-taut person |
| ■ optics | fleas with very good eyesight |
| ■ locomotive | a crazy reason |
| ■ positive | mistaken at the top of one's voice |
| ■ poverty | having too much month left at the end of the money |
| ■ quadruplets | four crying out loud |
| ■ sarcasm | quip lash |
| ■ stick | a boomerang that doesn't work |
| ■ tact | making a point without making an enemy |
| ■ volcano | a mountain with hiccups. |

# IN THE SPOTLIGHT – BUSINESS MEETINGS

It has been estimated that some managers spend up to 65% of their working week in meetings. Why are so many meetings held and what is their purpose?

Meetings are a particularly useful method of face-to-face communications between a group of people who may meet to:

- share, discuss and exchange information
- benefit from each other's views and opinions
- decide upon the best action to take
- analyse and solve problems
- talk about planned new developments and exchange ideas and suggestions for action
- link together the activities undertaken by a number of people
- discuss issues of mutual concern
- exchange up-to-date information to make sure that all are aware of current events and developments.

However, a meeting will only be useful if it is well organised and if those attending know why it is being held and what is meant to be achieved. In this case, the benefits include:

- an exchange of current information so that each person learns from his or her colleagues
- time saved – as important issues can be debated with everyone concentrating on the same item at the same time
- increased understanding and appreciation of the views of other people
- the best possible conclusion being reached, because of the exchange of views and information
- gaining the commitment of those present to the decisions reached.

A wide range of meetings are held by most organisations. Some of these may be very formal, others very informal. A list of these is shown in Figure 13.1. Meetings are **formal** when there are set rules and procedures that must be followed and a complete written record must be made. In some cases, holding these meetings is a legal requirement. Meetings are **informal** when there are no official rules (unless some have been devised by the organisation itself) and a written record or notes *may* be made, but this is for reference and is not a legal, or even an organisational, requirement.

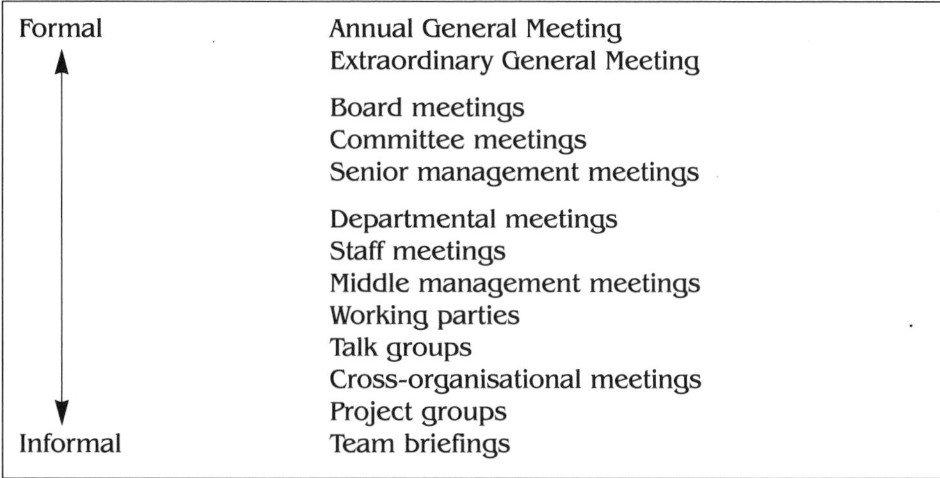

Formal
Informal
Annual General Meeting
Extraordinary General Meeting
Board meetings
Committee meetings
Senior management meetings
Departmental meetings
Staff meetings
Middle management meetings
Working parties
Talk groups
Cross-organisational meetings
Project groups
Team briefings


***Figure 13.1*** *Types of meeting*

# MEETINGS DOCUMENTATION

No matter how informal the meeting it is unlikely that it will have no paperwork at all. Even if no notes are made, it is possible that everyone will need a list of the items to be discussed and that information circulated at the meeting will have to be photocopied in advance. As an example, if your group was holding a series of meetings to decide on a student visit, you would start obtaining information on different venues and prices, and so become involved in meetings documentation.

There are some specific meetings documents you need to know about. All of these serve a useful purpose.

- They tell people where and when the meeting will be held – so they have a written notification of the event. For an informal meeting, notification may be sent in an e-mail or memo. For a formal meeting it is done by issuing a **notice of the meeting**.
- They tell people what will be discussed – so they can consider the issues likely to be raised. Sometimes there may be paperwork to read in relation to these issues. The list of items to be discussed is called an **agenda**. It is usually incorporated into the **notice** or memo calling the meeting to save time (and paper!)
- They help the chairperson to run the meeting more efficiently. In some cases the chairperson may ask for a special **chairperson's agenda** to be prepared. This lists the items to be discussed with additional useful information and space for noting down what has been agreed. These are usually only required for formal meetings, and some chairpersons don't use them at all.
- They record what was discussed and the action people agreed to take – both for future reference and as a reminder of what they promised to do.

For an informal meeting the record may be given in a brief memo, but for most meetings **minutes** are prepared according to a special format (see page 234).

# CALLING A MEETING

If you are preparing a document to inform people about a meeting, remember they need to know four key facts:

1. **where** it will be held
2. **when** it will be held
3. **what** will be discussed
4. **who** else will be there.

**MEMO**

**TO** All sales supervisors

**FROM** Jack Pearson, Manager

**DATE** 23 February 199-

**NEW CASH REGISTERS**

On 14 March, new cash registers are being installed at the store. Training will be given to all staff as the method of processing sales will be different.

In order that we can decide the best way to implement this training, I would like you to attend a brief meeting in my office at 9 am on Monday, 27 February. I expect the meeting to last about half an hour. Please let me know immediately if, for any reason, you are unable to attend.

***Figure 13.2*** *A memo about an ad hoc meeting*

## Informal and ad hoc meetings

People who regularly attend certain types of meetings will know from the name of the meeting group who else will be attending. They will also know what kind of meeting it is. An ad hoc meeting – called for a special, one-off purpose – is a little different, and people won't know what to expect unless you tell them! An example of a memo about such a meeting is shown in Figure 13.2. Check that it gives those involved all the information needed.

## Semi-formal meetings

Although the information is broadly the same for a formal meeting, it is set out in a rather different way. For a semi-formal meeting, you can expect the notice and agenda to have wording similar to that shown in Figure 13.3. Look at this now and note the following points.

- The meeting is comprised of **standard** items of business included each time (apart from the very first meeting held).
  - **Apologies for absence.** Those who cannot attend should have notified the person who called the meeting in advance. This means the chairperson can check at the start who is expected and who is not.
  - **Minutes of the previous meeting**. This is normally a brief item where the chairperson checks that everyone present agrees the minutes or record taken of the last meeting are correct and do not contain any factual errors.

HIGHTOWN COLLEGE

HEALTH AND SAFETY COMMITTEE

The next meeting of the Committee will be held in Room C406 at 1600 hours on Thursday, 17 March 199-

AGENDA

1 Apologies for absence

2 Minutes of the previous meeting

3 Matters arising

4 New Fire Regulations

5 Planned electrical rewiring work

6 Any other business

7 Date and time of next meeting

Pat Nuttall
Health and Safety Officer

3 March 199-

***Figure 13.3*** *A notice and agenda for a semi-formal meeting*

- **Matters arising**. This is the point at which members comment on or query any action taken since the last meeting. In other words they discuss any matters that have arisen in relation to the minutes which have just been checked and agreed.
- **Any other business (AOB)**. This is for *minor* issues not included on the agenda but which may be of interest to the members. New major issues would be kept until the next meeting.
- **Date and time of next meeting.** This is when arrangements are made for the next meeting. This item may be brought forward if someone has to leave early.

■ The meeting also has **specific** items to be discussed. These are the main reason for calling it in the first place – if there is nothing to discuss then the meeting would be postponed. In this case there are two specific items of business, the new Fire Regulations and the proposed electrical rewiring work. This is the main business to be discussed at the meeting.

If you are asked to prepare an agenda, it is useful to know that there should not be too many items of specific business – otherwise the meeting will run out of time before everything has been discussed. It is useful to put the most important item first, and then work downwards, so that if time is short only the less important items will have to be deferred until the next meeting.

## Formal meetings

The most formal meetings are those that are a legal requirement. An example is the Annual General Meeting of a public limited company (plc). The notice and agenda is sent to all shareholders by the company secretary and the wording is very formal. An example is shown in Figure 13.4.

# RUNNING A MEETING

Although the procedures to be followed will vary, depending upon the type and formality of the meeting, all meetings must be well organised and efficiently run. Therefore, there are some similarities in the ways all meetings are chaired and administered. At this stage we will concentrate on those meetings that are held daily in most organisations, rather than very formal meetings such as the AGM, where large numbers of people may attend.

**NOTICE OF MEETING**

NOTICE IS HEREBY GIVEN that the sixty-sixth Annual General Meeting of the Westchester Building Society will be held at the Main Office of the Society at Carr Hill, Westchester, on Thursday, 24 April 199- at 7 pm for the purpose of transacting the following business.

A G E N D A

1 To receive the Directors' Report, the Annual Accounts and the Auditors' Report thereon for the year ended 31 December 199-.

2 To consider and, if thought fit, to pass the following Ordinary Resolutions:

– That JDK Audit plc be reappointed as Auditors
– That Jane B Smedley be re-elected as a Director
– That Martin T Smith be re-elected as a Director.

By Order of the Board of Directors

*Peter Marsden*

Peter Marsden
Group Secretary

28 February 199-

***Figure 13.4***
*A notice and agenda for a formal meeting*

## Common features of effective meetings

- They are chaired by an experienced chairperson who:
  - is good at managing people
  - understands the issues being discussed
  - starts the meeting on time
  - introduces any new members to each other
  - keeps to the agenda
  - encourages participation from all present
  - keeps discussions to the point at issue

**Meeting** Health and Safety Committee
**Date/time** 17 March 199-, 1600 hours
**Place** C406, Hightown College

| AGENDA ITEM | NOTES |
|---|---|
| **1 Apologies for absence** | 1 |
| Jean Coupe in Singapore until June. | |
| **2 Minutes of previous meeting** | 2 |
| **3 Matters arising** | 3 |
| Questions may be asked on results of recentfire drills | |
| **4 New Fire Regulations** | 4 |
| Effective from 1/5/9-<br>Copy circulated to members<br>Fire officer's letter attached | |
| **5 Planned electrical rewiring work** | 5 |
| Scheduled for July/August<br>Contractors: J D Electrical<br>Computer suite first, then<br>A, D, B and C floors<br>Staffrooms = first two weeks Aug | |
| **6 Any other business** | 6 |
| **7 Date and time of next meeting** | 7 |
| Suggest 19 April to avoid<br>Easter break | |

***Figure 13.5***
*A chairperson's agenda*

- stops anyone taking over the meeting or talking too much
- sums up each discussion at the end
- insists that all participants address the chairperson, rather than talk to each other – so that order is kept and the chairperson can follow the discussion
- keeps order when there is disagreement between members
- checks everyone is clear what has been agreed
- ends the meeting on time.

To help, he or she may use a chairperson's agenda. An example is shown in Figure 13.5.

■ All those present participate positively in the meeting with the common aim of achieving a satisfactory outcome. They:

- send their apologies promptly if they are not able to attend
- arrive on time
- remember to bring with them any paperwork they have been sent beforehand plus their copy of the agenda
- have read the paperwork in advance, so they can contribute knowledgeably
- put their point of view forward clearly, tactfully and succinctly (ie in few words)
- are prepared to consider and discuss the opinions of others
- carry out any duties they have been given before the next meeting
- are loyal to the chairperson and to the other participants.

■ There is a clear system for notifying people about the meeting in good time, for recording apologies and for keeping a record of what occurred at the meeting. A formal meeting, such as of the Board of Directors, may have a meetings secretary. At more informal meetings the duty of notifying people and keeping a record may be rotated amongst those who attend.

**Figure 13.6** *A memo recording an informal meeting*

**MEMO**

**TO** All sales supervisors

**FROM** Jack Pearson, Manager

**DATE** 28 February 199-

**TRAINING FOR NEW CASH REGISTERS**

Further to our meeting yesterday, please find below a summary of the points we agreed.

**1 Information session**

Staff should be informed about the change as soon as possible. Mahandir Jackson to summarise head office instructions and memo in a simplified form for staff, issued by 4 March.

**2 Staff queries/training session rota**

A short meeting of all staff will be called and held in the staff restaurant at 08.30 am and 5.30 pm on 7 and 8 March. The four sessions will enable all full-time and part-time staff to attend.

**3 Store closure for training**

The store will not open until 11 am on 15 March to enable key staff to be trained between 0830 and 1045 on that day. Jim Blackstone to put up notices in store informing customers by 4 March.

*JP*

# KEEPING A RECORD

At a very informal meeting no record may be kept. The problem with this approach is that there may be disagreement later over what was decided. There are normally some written notes, if only to remind everyone what happened! As an

**HIGHTOWN COLLEGE**

**MINUTES**

Minutes of the Health and Safety Committee Meeting held in room C406 at 1600 hours on 17 March 199-.

PRESENT

| | |
|---|---|
| Pat Nuttall | Health and Safety Officer (Chairperson) |
| Jim Edwards | Administration Officer |
| Nasreen Hussain | Staff/Student Welfare Co-ordinator |
| Petra Morrison | Departmental Representative |
| Ken Taylor | Estates Manager |

1 APOLOGIES FOR ABSENCE — ACTION

Apologies for absence were received from Jean Coupe who is currently working in Singapore.

2 MINUTES OF PREVIOUS MEETING

The minutes of the previous meeting were taken as read, agreed as a true and correct record and signed by the Chairperson.

3 MATTERS ARISING

Ken Taylor queried whether the recent fire drills had resulted in an improved evacuation time. The Chairperson reported that the results had been excellent in all areas except the outside workshops where the alarm could not be heard. An alarm extension was being fitted in this area to rectify the problem.

4 NEW FIRE REGULATIONS

These would be effective from 1 May 199-. Members agreed that all staff must be informed of the implications. It was decided that the Chairperson would ask the Principal for the opportunity to address all staff at the next Staff Training Day scheduled for 3 April. PN

5 PLANNED ELECTRICAL REWIRING WORK

It was proposed that this would be undertaken by J D Electrical during July and August to minimise disruptions to classes. All staffrooms would be rewired during the first two weeks of August when no computer equipment would be operational. It was planned to start with the computer suite, then A floor, then D, B and C. Ken Taylor pointed out that the greatest disruption would be in the catering and hairdressing areas. Both were on B floor and therefore should be done earlier to ensure they were completed promptly. It was agreed he would discuss this matter with Jack Knowles, of J D Electrical, and report back at the next meeting. KT

6 ANY OTHER BUSINESS

Nasreen Hussain reported that there had been staff complaints that when the photocopiers had been re-sited recently on D floor, the appropriate fire extinguishers had not been moved to that area. Petra Morrison agreed to investigate this, as the rooms concerned were in her department. PM

7 DATE AND TIME OF NEXT MEETING

It was agreed that the next meeting should be held at 1600 hours on Thursday, 19 April 199-

Signed *Pat Nuttall* (Chairperson) Date *20/3/9-*

***Figure 13.7***
*Minutes of a committee meeting*

example, a memo confirming what was agreed at the informal meeting about staff training (see Figure 13.2) is shown in Figure 13.6.

In the majority of cases a special type of record is kept, called **minutes**. There are different types of minutes for different types of meetings. **Minutes of narration** tell the story of a meeting – although very concisely. **Minutes of action**, on the other hand, list only the conclusions and the action agreed. These must not be so abbreviated that no-one can understand them! **Minutes of resolution** are produced for very formal meetings, such as an AGM.

The format of minutes can vary from one organisation to another. Many companies have a standard template for minutes on a computer network and specific details for each meeting are entered. A standard format for minutes is given in Figure 13.7. Note that this includes the following.

- The name of the organisation.
- The type of meeting.
- When and where it was held.
- The names of those present. The chairperson is listed first and the meetings secretary, if any, last. The other participants are listed in alphabetical order (to save any arguments!) and anyone who has been invited for a specific reason is also listed.

- The items are discussed in the same order as they appeared on the agenda.
- An action column giving the initials of all those who promised to do something before the next meeting.
- Space for the chairperson to sign and date the minutes.

## Test your understanding

**1** Your tutor is holding a meeting for the course team to review various student issues. The meeting will be held a week on Thursday, in room G22 at 10 am. It is expected to last for thirty minutes. Student issues to be discussed include work experience, student visits and examination entries.

**a** Write a short, informal memo, addressed to the Course Team, calling the meeting and mentioning the items to be discussed.

**b** Your tutor has also asked you to book coffee and biscuits for six people. Write a brief memo to your Catering Manager asking for these items to be brought to the room at 10.15 am.

**2** You are an active member of your Student Union and have often helped the Secretary on an informal basis this year. This week, the Secretary is away ill and you have been asked if you can help to produce the Notice and Agenda for the next meeting to be held two weeks on Tuesday at 12 noon in the Student Union office. In addition to the standard agenda items, Tom, the Chairperson, has asked you to include one special item: the arrangements for the Valentine's Ball.

In addition, he has received the following agenda items from members of the committee.

- Sanjay Scott wants to discuss the proposed increase in tuition fees.
- Andrew Sullivan has asked that the issue of student common rooms be included. He has asked you to note, however, that he will not be able to attend the meeting until after 12.30.
- Riaz Khan would like to discuss the problem of student parking on the campus.

Prepare a notice and an agenda for the meeting for the members.

## *WORDBANK 10 – Meetings terms*

Many specialist words and terms are used in meetings. Some of these are foreign words and phrases. Learn the definitions below so that you understand what is meant when someone uses these terms.

| | | |
|---|---|---|
| *ad hoc* | – | for a particular purpose |
| *adjourn* | – | to postpone or put off with the intention of resuming later |
| *casting vote* | – | the decisive, final vote cast by the chairperson |
| *convene* | – | the formal term used to call a meeting |
| *ex officio* | – | describes a person entitled to attend a meeting because of the importance of one's position |
| *nem con* | – | with no-one voting against – but some may have abstained (ie not voted for or against) |

| | | |
|---|---|---|
| *nem dis* | – | with no one dissenting, ie a unanimous decision |
| *proxy* | – | someone entitled to vote on another's behalf |
| *sine die* | – | 'without date' – used in relation to an adjournment |
| *unanimous* | – | everyone in favour. |

**DON'T YOU DARE!**

*...confuse the two words 'cancel' and 'postpone'. If a meeting (or other event) is cancelled it will not be held. If something is postponed it will be held at some time in the future. The formal term for this is 'adjourned'.*

## TOOLS OF THE TRADE – contributing to a discussion

You hold a class meeting to discuss your ideas for an end-of-term trip. Which of the following parts would you play?

- The leader – determined to control the discussion.
- The mouse – quiet and shy, too scared to voice your opinions.
- The follower – anything for the quiet life, you'll go with the herd.
- The realist – you'll agree with a suggestion if it's sensible.
- The pessimist – it'll never work, you can't see any point in the discussion and anyway, if you do go, it'll be a disaster.
- The ideas person – full of suggestions and bright ideas.
- The controller – you'll be annoyed if people don't agree with you.
- The listener – willing to listen first and suggest later.
- The enthusiast – you think everything's a great idea and really want it to work.
- The diplomat – always tactful, tries to keep harmony among the group.
- The helper – full of suggestions as to how ideas can be put into practice.
- The sulker – if they don't agree with you, you'll opt out.
- The talker – rarely keeps quiet, likes to be seen and be heard.
- The interrupter – can't wait to say his/her bit, and chips in when other people are speaking.

Any of these? None of these? How honest dare you be?

Some people are a delight to have at a meeting. They prepare for the discussion in advance, participate purposefully, don't upset other people and fulfil their commitments afterwards. Others are a pain. They arrive late and unprepared, either don't participate at all or never shut up, ruffle other people's feathers and then forget to do what they promised afterwards. Wherever possible, colleagues will try to arrange meetings when such a person can't be present. Most of us keep quiet at the start. Later, if we know what is expected of us and how we should behave, we try to become an asset on these occasions, rather than the person everyone dreads!

This section looks at the behaviour expected of you when you are involved in informal discussions – which are excellent preparation for more formal meetings you may attend later in your career.

## Preparing for the discussion

Generally, you will be expected to contribute something to a discussion, otherwise there is no point in being there. It no use grumbling afterwards that you don't agree with what was decided if you never spoke. However, saying something useful is different from opening your mouth just for the sake of it – and you will be much more helpful and constructive if you have thought about the issue to be discussed in advance.

On some occasions, little formal preparation is required. Simply thinking about the issue means that you have some good ideas. Try to take this one stage further by considering how some of your ideas might be received, what objections could be raised and how you could answer these. For other discussions you may be expected to prepare more thoroughly. This would be the case if you were asked to find out about something in advance and tell everyone about it. This would mean obtaining the information, making brief notes summarising the main points and talking to people. It is often helpful, if the information is fairly long, to produce a copy of the key points for each person.

Check the date, time and place at least twice and gather together anything you must take to the discussion in good time. Remember to take a notebook and pen. It is impolite to be late and you would then have to start off by apologising.

## Positive participation

Be prepared to take brief notes of other people's suggestions so that you can refer back to them later in the discussion if you wish. This is where your skills of listening, note-taking and reading body language all come together! If you watch people's reactions you will be able to assess how they feel about different ideas and opinions – as well as noting what they say.

If you have a specific 'slot' in which to make your contribution speak clearly but don't speak for too long. Otherwise what you say will lose impact. In other discussions you have to pick your moment. If you have a particular suggestion you wish to be considered it is sensible to say this fairly early in the discussion. If you have not, listen to other people's ideas first before you make your comments. If someone tries to interrupt or contradict you, don't raise your voice in reply, otherwise a shouting match can result. Simply ask them to wait until you have finished.

Give support to other people's ideas when you think they have made a good point. They will be grateful and more likely to support *you*. Even if you don't agree entirely with someone's suggestion, praising it first before you suggest one or two amendments is more tactful than openly contradicting it. If you make an enemy by being hostile, over-bearing, rude or sarcastic, this will be remembered long after the meeting has ended!

Don't be frightened to question other people about what they mean or to investigate a possible suggestion further. However, don't make this an inquisition, and try to frame your questions politely – *'Sorry, but can you just tell me what you mean by...'*

Unfortunately, some people have very fixed views, others are excitable, some people sulk if they can't get their own way, others become aggressive. If you have someone controlling the discussion, such as a leader or chairperson,

then it will be his or her job to keep any in-fighting to a minimum and to control difficult members. However, this is not an easy job and it is the responsibility of the participants to get along together constructively!

This means that you must be prepared for disappointment on occasion. You will never have all your ideas accepted in their entirety. This is a good thing – the whole purpose of a discussion is that 'many heads are better than one' – but it also means that you have to be prepared to lose a few battles without taking it personally. Most group decisions are something of a compromise.

## Test your understanding

Each of the sentences below is not likely to obtain cooperation or harmony!

**i** State the likely result of someone saying each one.
**ii** Rewrite sentences 1–5 in a more acceptable format.
**iii** Discuss as a group your ideas for controlling a discussion which appears to be getting out of hand.

**a** Any idiot can see that we could never afford to go there.

**b** If somebody would give me a chance to speak, I've got one or two ideas of my own, you know.

**c** I wish you'd all shut up a minute, this isn't getting us anywhere.

**d** Oh, I don't care where we go. What time does this finish?

**e** If you think I'm going along with that, you must be mad.

**f** I can't think why you bother coming. You never say anything sensible.

**g** OK, OK, have it your own way. I'm not interested anyway.

### SPELLCHECKER 12

How accurately do you spell the following words – all of which may be used in minute taking? Check that you wouldn't have any difficulties with any of these words – or learn them and enter them in your Spellchecker book. Check, too, that you know the meaning of each one or look it up and enter it into your Wordbank book.

| | | | |
|---|---|---|---|
| committee | compatible | consistent | criticise |
| debatable | deference | demurred | exercise |
| inadvisable | preceding | preliminary | prominent |
| resolution | statutory | terminate | warranted |

# MAKING HEADWAY – writing minutes

Most people are understandably nervous when they are first asked to produce a set of minutes. They are worried that they won't understand what is being discussed, will not be able to make clear notes that they can read afterwards, or will struggle to compose the minutes properly.

The obligation to produce a document for several other people to read can seem quite overwhelming. However, minute-taking is a skill that no-one can expect you to learn in five minutes. In the early days at work, therefore, it is sensible if you attend meetings with an experienced minute writer so that you don't have sole responsibility. You can produce a draft set and check these against the experienced writer's set. Another option is taking notes and recording what is agreed at very informal meetings, where there is less pressure to produce a precise document.

## The skills you need

You will find the task much easier if you have the following.

- Skills as a note-taker and an established set of abbreviations to help you (this was first covered in Unit 6).
- A fairly good mastery of the English language – improved by the grammar and punctuation exercises in this book.
- A good vocabulary and understanding of the technical terms, jargon and abbreviations that may be used in the meeting.
- Word processing skills – so that you can amend your minutes as you wish.
- Summarising skills (see Unit 10).
- Knowledge of how to use reported speech – this aspect of minute-taking is covered on pages 242–244.
- A kind chairperson who will help and guide you in the early days. It also helps if he or she keeps to the agenda, summarises each discussion and is willing to check your draft minutes.
- The sense to recognise the type of comments you are expected to record, and those you are not. A heated debate between two members is not usually recorded in detail!

## Preparing for the meeting

You can help to overcome your nerves if you prepare well beforehand. This means doing the following.

- Read through previous minutes for the same group to check the layout, the amount of detail you are expected to record and the style of the minutes.
- Check you know the names of those who will be attending. Learn their initials, as this is the quickest way of noting who is speaking.
- Get together the appropriate stationery. You will need an A4 pad (this is better than a shorthand notebook as you don't have to turn over pages so

often). Divide the page into two columns, a narrow one for initials and a wide one for remarks.

## At the meeting

- Make sure that you are not expected to serve coffee and make notes at the same time.
- Try to sit near the chairperson and to obtain his or her notes afterwards (which may be scribbled on the chairperson's agenda). These may help you if you are stuck at some point.
- *Concentrate* on what is being discussed. This way your memory may also come in useful. If necessary, refresh your memory about listening skills in Unit 4!
- If you are worried about something you have written, or didn't understand it when it was discussed, make a note in the margin and query it the moment the meeting ends. This is better than interrupting a chairperson in full flow. Never keep quiet if you think you have a problem – no chairperson wants to have to recall what was said three days' later – it is much better to check any doubtful points as soon as possible.

## After the meeting

- Type up your notes as soon as you can.
- Ask your chairperson to check your draft when you have finished. If you find that your written English is also regularly corrected, make a vow to improve it. Don't be surprised, however, if some of your phrases are changed – the chairperson will be aware of who may read the minutes and the views they may hold on certain matters.
- Correct and edit your minutes as required. After the chairperson has signed and dated them, send a copy to each person who attended and any absentees.

## The technique of minute-taking

Certain conventions apply to writing minutes.

- Minutes are *always* written in the third person, past tense and using reported speech. You should therefore never write 'I', 'we' or 'you'! The past tense is used because the meeting has now ended – so you are writing about a past event. Reported speech is also logical, as you are reporting what people said. This means that you never use quotation marks (see page 222).
- Slang and colloquial expressions are not written in minutes. Neither are strong adjectives, expletives or exaggerated statements! For all we know, at the Health and Safety Committee meeting reported in Figure 13.7, Ken Taylor's reaction to the proposed re-wiring rota could have been '*What idiot decided on that sequence? I bet it was that clot at J D Electrical. Heaven knows why we're using them again, they were a disaster last time.*' For many reasons (including possible libel!) such remarks are not recorded. At the most you would have been expected to write '*Ken Taylor queried the proposed rota.*'

- Good minute writers avoid repetition. This means that they don't write *Ken Taylor said that . . . then Nasreen Hussein said that . . then the Chairperson said that . . . ..* Other phrases can be used in this situation to introduce some variety.
- The grammatical construction of your sentences, your spelling, punctuation and proof-reading skills must all be first rate.

## Test your understanding

**1** As a group identify as many alternatives as you can for each of the following words. If necessary, use a thesaurus to help you.

**a** asked **b** said **c** urged
**d** told **e** declared **f** discussed

**2** Re-read the minutes shown in Figure 13.7. Try to envisage the type of discussions that resulted in these minutes.

**3** Nominate four members of your group to read the discussion between Tom, Sarah, Andrew and Riaz shown in Figure 13.8. Make *brief* notes, using appropriate abbreviations, to record the main points.

**Notes of discussion at Students' Union meeting**

**Tom** We really need to sort out where and when we will hold the Valentine's Ball. The 14th February is on a Sunday this year, so that's no good. What about the Friday before or afterwards?

**Sarah** I think the Friday afterwards is pointless. No-one will be in the mood then.

**Andrew** I agree. But I think it would be better on a Thursday. Most people have other commitments on a Friday, and many people are working in part-time jobs.

**Sarah** That doesn't matter. They could come to the Ball after work.

**Andrew** Well, I couldn't, for one! I work until 11.30 most Fridays. I think most people would prefer Thursday.

**Riaz** I'd prefer Thursday, and so would most of my friends.

**Tom** OK, Thursday it is then – the 11th. Now where? We could hold it at Merridale Heights or The Barn. Merridale Heights is free – they are happy with the bar takings – but we have to provide our own DJ. The Barn will cost us £80 but that includes the DJ.

**Andrew** I like The Barn for atmosphere but their DJ is awful. Can we have the place without him?

**Tom** Apparently not. The other point is, do we have a good alternative DJ?

**Sarah** Oh, come on – Billy and Dom could beat The Barn DJ hands down. What about them?

**Andrew** We'd need to know if they were free that evening. What would they charge us?

**Sarah** I don't know. They may be prepared to do it for nothing.

**Riaz** Not if I know Billy they won't. Anyway, they may be good but their music is pretty specialised. The Barn DJ will have a broader appeal.

**Tom** Look, we can't keep discussing this forever. Sarah, you find out whether Billy and Dom are free on that night and how much they would charge. I'll need to know tomorrow. Unless we get a definite commitment from them I suggest we book The Barn before we lose the opportunity.

**Andrew** I agree. I think we go for the cheaper option. But if we can get Billy and Dom that would be great. Can I make another point? I think the word 'Ball' is too formal – people will think they have to dress up for it and it'll put them off.

**Sarah** I quite like it, it sounds romantic. We could have red roses everywhere.

**Andrew** At that rate the tickets would cost a fortune! What about Valentine's Vamp?

**Riaz** You're joking! 'Vamp' is so old fashioned it's unbelievable. What about 'Rave'?

**Tom** No. Raves went out 10 years ago. Let's settle for Valentine's Night at The Barn – or something similar. What do you think?

**Andrew** I like that, apart from the fact it won't actually *be* Valentine's Night, will it?

**Tom** I don't think that will make any difference. Sarah? Riaz? What do you think?

**Sarah** If you must, but I preferred the word 'Ball' myself.

**Riaz** No, I'll go with Tom, it's straightforward and to the point.

**Tom** OK. So that's settled, and I'll check if Billy and Dom are available, how much they will charge and then make the booking. Riaz, will you sort out the tickets and posters if I give you the information? What do you think we should charge?

**Andrew** I don't think we can decide that until we know about the cost. Why don't we meet again on Thursday to discuss all the outstanding issues?

**Tom** Can you all manage 12 noon – it's the only time I'm free.

**Andrew** I can – how about you two?

**Sarah** Yes, good idea. I'm free then providing we finish by one o'clock.

**Riaz** I'll have to change round a couple of things but yes, go on, count me in.

**Tom** OK. 12 noon here on Thursday. I'll get the minutes out for today as fast as I can to help speed things up.

***Figure 13.8*** *Notes of discussion*

Compare your notes as a group and assess whether you listed all the key points or omitted some. You may find it helpful if the 'actors' re-read their parts again to allow you to improve your skills further.

## THE GOOD GRAMMAR GUIDE

### Reported speech

There are two ways in which you can give an account of what someone said. Newspapers, magazines and books (particularly novels) often use **direct speech**. In this case they quote the actual words the person used, eg

*'It hasn't been a good year for us,' said Jim Fox, the manager of Hightown United.*

Direct speech is rarely used in business communications. Instead, the words people use are normally recorded in **indirect** or **reported speech**.

If we convert the passage above into reported speech we would write the following:

*Jim Fox, the manager of Hightown United, said that it had not been a good year for the team.*

The rules for converting from direct speech to reported speech are not complicated, although there are one or two problem areas you need to note.

#### PRONOUNS

The first person (I, we, my, we, us, our) usually changes to the third person (he, she, they, their). This is because the person reporting the speech is not the person who said it.

Be careful if you really are reporting what *you* said – as in this case you would retain the first person, eg

*'Has this type of accident occurred on other occasions?' I asked*
is converted to
*I asked him if this type of accident had occurred on other occasions.*

Be careful, too, if substituting a pronoun would result in ambiguity. In the example above, Jim Fox's pronoun 'us' has been changed to 'the team', which is more precise.

#### VERBS

Present tense verbs change to the past tense because the person spoke before your written report. Therefore:

We think – they thought
We are going – they were going
We do not know – they did not know
We were hoping – they had been hoping
We have been there – they had been there

If the speaker refers to something in the future, then you cannot say for certain whether this will occur. Use the conditional tense or the word 'intended', eg

We shall go – they would go (or they intended to go)

We shall be visiting – they would be visiting (or they intended to visit)

- **'Always true' statements.** There are occasions when the use of the past tense is inappropriate. Take an obvious example:

  *'The world is round', announced Christopher Columbus.*

  It would not be correct to record this as:

  *Christopher Columbus said the world was round*

  This is because you have implied that the world could now be a different shape! Therefore it is correct to write:

  *Christopher Columbus said the world is round.*

- **Time statements.** In direct speech we refer to time using words such as 'today', 'tomorrow', 'yesterday'. The listener or reader can quickly work out which day we are referring to. In reported speech this is not possible because you don't know when your report will be read – so 'today' could be any day!

  This problem is solved by replacing these words with some standard phrases:

  now = then
  today = on that day
  yesterday = the previous day
  tomorrow = the following day or the next day
  last week = the previous week
  next week = the following week or the next week

- **Place statements.** If I say to you 'He's coming here tomorrow,' you know where I mean because we are both 'here' when I say it. But someone else would not have a clue where we were unless we told them!

  It is usual, therefore, to specify the place the first time you mention it. After that, you can change 'here' to 'there' and your reader will understand you.

  Similarly, if you are referring to a particular thing in a certain place, remember that 'this' becomes 'that' and 'these' becomes 'those'.

- **Questions that aren't questions.** The correct term for these is **rhetorical** questions. Picture the scene. A regular late-comer is late for class again.

  | | |
  |---|---|
  | Teacher: | *Wendy, this is the third time this week. Where have you been?* |
  | Wendy: | *Sorry, miss. My alarm clock didn't go off and then I spilled coffee all over my tee-shirt and by the time I'd found a clean one I'd missed all the buses.* |
  | Teacher: | *You don't honestly expect me to believe that, do you?* |

  The first question the teacher asks is a real question. She expects and wants an answer. The second question is rhetorical. No answer is expected! Instead, she is giving her opinion of the explanation she has received. People use rhetorical questions to imply disbelief, incredulity, annoyance and sarcasm.

  If you were writing this statement in reported speech you would be expected to convey the meaning of the sentence, not just record the statement. Therefore it would be wrong to write:

*The teacher queried whether the pupil expected her to believe the explanation.*

It would be more accurate to write:

*The teacher responded that this explanation was difficult to believe.*

- **Informal to formal.** People who are speaking often use slang, colloquial expressions and abbreviations. These should not be converted into indirect speech – instead, you have to find a more appropriate way to report what they said.

## Test your understanding

1 Convert each of the following sentences into reported speech. Convey the meaning properly and to avoid any ambiguities.

**a** Mr Evans said, 'Next year we are hoping to buy two more machines for the new factory.'

**b** 'This year our sales have increased dramatically,' said the Chairperson.

**c** 'It is important that you attend the conference in Edinburgh next week,' said Maria to the sales manager.

**d** 'Can you sort out this problem immediately, please?' the store manager said to the cashier, obviously annoyed.

**e** 'You've no hope of seeing Jack Evans next week,' said Adam to Sarah. 'He won't be there as he's going to Australia.'

2 Go back to the notes you made following question 3 on page 241. Now write these correctly as minutes, using reported speech. Check your completed work with your tutor.

## POLISH YOUR PUNCTUATION

### The colon

There are three main uses of the colon:

1 It is often used to preface a list, eg

*I have ordered four items: staples, paper clips, floppy disks and mouse mats.*

2 A further use is as a punctuation mark before a clause that explains the previous clause. In this case it replaces a comma, semi-colon or dash, eg

*The fire drill resulted in several recommendations: more wardens are required and louder alarms are needed in the motor vehicle workshops.*

*He is constantly late: on Tuesday he arrived at 9.30 am and on Thursday it was 10.45 am before he reported for work.*

3 The final use is before quoted information, titles and other types of references, eg

*The Chairman said: 'I would like to thank you all for coming today.'*
*I suggest you look in the book Technology for All: Second Edition*
*The chance of winning is apparently 13:2 against.*

You may like to note that some organisations insert colons in Memo headings after To: From: and Date: although today this is considered rather out-dated.

## COMMUNICATION IN PRACTICE

### Test your skills

**1** Several foreign expressions are commonly used in everyday speech.

**i** Find out the meaning of each of the following.

**ii** Write a sentence to show you understand the meaning of each.

**a** au fait
**b** bona fide
**c** carte blanche
**d** de rigueur
**e** deja vu
**f** faux pas
**g** per se
**h** persona non grata
**i** in lieu
**j** avant garde
**k** tete-a-tete
**l** status quo
**m** ad infinitum
**n** vice versa

**2** Punctuate the following sentences correctly.

**a** for the examination mr hunter said we would need the following items a calculator pen ruler and pencil
**b** i asked him to bring several groceries butter eggs bread and cheese
**c** he has visited several countries in the far east malaysia singapore and indonesia
**d** when you send in your vehicle licensing form you must submit the following a valid insurance certificate a valid MOT test if applicable and the correct fee
**e** john marsh looked at the assembled delegates and said thank you for coming here today to join us on this auspicious occasion

**3** Match each of the following words ending in '-ance' with the correct definition below:

**i** vigilance
**ii** tolerance
**iii** pittance
**iv** abundance
**v** instance
**vi** nuisance
**vii** arrogance
**viii** alliance
**ix** appliance
**x** performance

**a** a piece of equipment
**b** a willingness to accept and respect the views and beliefs of others
**c** to give an example of something
**d** a great amount or surplus
**e** an action that is annoying or potentially dangerous to others
**f** an overbearing and superior attitude to others
**g** a dramatic or musical entertainment
**h** an agreement to join or cooperate
**i** a very small amount of money
**j** the act of being watchful or alert

I'd be very grateful if you could produce a notice and agenda for the next meeting. We'll hold this in the Community Centre in Hightown as usual, starting at 7.30 pm. Please put in the usual items plus three additional items – plans to establish a community woodland, the restoration of the nature trail at Westbury and publicity for the Greenwatch group. There are some other items of business I've received from committee members – can you include these, too, please?

Thanks

*Mark*

***Figure 13.9*** *A note to you from Mark Chapman*

*Mark*

*I'm really concerned about the closure of some local footpaths. Can we raise this as an issue at our next meeting please?*

*Thanks*

*Sammy*

*Mark*

*Can we talk about putting pressure on the council for more bottle banks in the area please? Can we also discuss the council's policy on recycling?*

*Cheers*

*Bill*

*Mark*

*A group of volunteers would like to look at cleaning up the canal towpath at Bridge End. It's a disgrace and there are many hazards for walkers. As I represent this group, can we discuss whether we could anything about this at the next meeting.*

*I'll obviously let them know the outcome of the discussions.*

*Claire*

***Figure 13.10*** *Agenda items received from committee members*

## Apply your skills

You have always been interested in environmental issues and your friend has persuaded you to join a voluntary group that has been formed in your area. But you were not too pleased when you found that she had volunteered you as general assistant/meetings secretary because of your communication skills! When you tried to refuse, the Coordinator, Mark Chapman, persuaded you to help for a month. He has now asked for your assistance with the following tasks.

**1** The next meeting of the Greenwatch Group Committee is two weeks from today. Mark has asked you to prepare a notice and agenda. His note to you is shown in Figure 13.9 and the requests for agenda items he has received are shown in Figure 13.10.

**2** Mark is unsure of the council's policy on recycling and decides to write to his local councillor in advance of the meeting to find out. He also wants his councillor to confirm the number of bottle banks in the area – or to let him know where to find this information. He would like you to draft a letter he can send. His councillor's name is Mrs Judy Burrows, 14 Westacre Road, Hightown, HG3 9EP. Write the letter of enquiry.

**3** The local paper – the Hightown Gazette, 15 High Street, Hightown, HG2 3MP – has written to Mark offering to support Greenwatch and to sponsor their efforts by contributing £1 for every £3 raised from other sources. They wish to publicise the group in the paper and would like to send a reporter and a photographer to the next

**DISCUSSION AT GREENWATCH GROUP COMMITTEE MEETING**

| | |
|---|---|
| **Mark Chapman** | As you are aware from the press session earlier, the Hightown Gazette is now sponsoring the Greenwatch Group. They are prepared to donate £1 for every £3 we raise from other sources. They are writing an article from information I have given them, to go with the photograph they took earlier, and this will appear in their paper next week. They've also now asked me to prepare an advertisement to state the aims of the group. |
| **Claire Tidbury** | We need to include our slogan – 'Tomorrow's world for the children of today'. |
| **Sammy Jones** | We could do with a good logo. A friend of mine is an artist – do you want me to ask him for a few suggestions? |
| **Mark Chapman** | That would be good. But I have to send them the draft advertisement by next Wednesday. |
| **Sammy Jones** | That's OK – I'm seeing him tomorrow night – I'll have his ideas with you by Friday. |
| **Mark Chapman** | I won't have time to bring them back for general approval. Does that matter? |
| **Claire Tidbury** | Well, there are only six of us and most of us live nearby. Could we not hold a quick ad hoc meeting this weekend? |
| **Mark Chapman** | What do the rest of you think? You could come over to my house on Sunday evening at about 7 pm if you like. |
| | *(Unanimous approval for this suggestion)* |
| **Bill Andrews** | What about the text? I'd like to see it focused as an appeal for more volunteers. |
| **Emma Botur** | I agree. Something along the lines of 'prove you care for your environment'. |
| **Claire Tidbury** | I think that's a bit heavy. I think we need to include some information about our current projects – the towpath, for instance, the nature trails, more bottle banks – most of the items on this agenda, in fact. |
| **Mark Chapman** | I like that – but we also need to tell them what to do if they want to join. Could they contact you Claire, as Membership Secretary? |
| **Claire Tidbury** | No problem – either write to me at home, 15 Risedale Walk, Hightown, HG3 6MP, or ring me on 01928–303029. |
| **Emma Botur** | Could we say something like 'an hour of your time could result in years of benefit for your children'? |
| **Sammy Jones** | That sounds good. We need something short and snappy to appeal to them. |
| **Mark Chapman** | Right, I think we've enough to go on now. Thanks for all your ideas. (*Turns to you*) Could you please try drafting the advert for us, based on all this? And please leave space for the logo. Could you bring the draft with you on Sunday night? That's brilliant, thanks. Now let's see what's next on the agenda. |

***Figure 13.11*** *Part of the committee's discussion*

meeting. Mark wants to cooperate with them but does not want them to report any discussions at the meeting without his approval. He therefore wants the press session to take place between 7 pm and 7.30 pm – before the meeting is due to start. He has asked you to draft a brief letter to the editor of the paper, Jim Butterworth, thanking him for his support and stating the time of the press session and the place where the meeting will be held. Draft the letter required.

**4** Figure 13.11 outlines part of the discussion at the meeting of the Greenwatch Group. From this information:

**a** write brief minutes to cover the discussion with an action column alongside

**b** prepare the draft advertisement for the Hightown Gazette.

## WORD WIZARD

Some word wizards have used their skills to highlight the ambiguities in the English language. Here is an example. As you read it, try to find clues to the nationality of the author:

**Crazy English** – Richard Lederer

Let's face it: English is a crazy language. There is no egg in eggplant or ham in hamburger, neither apple nor pine in pineapple.

English muffins were not invented in England or french fries in France. Sweetmeats are candies, whilst sweetbreads, which aren't sweet, are meat.

We take English for granted. But if we explore its paradoxes, we find that quicksand can work slowly, boxing rings are square, and a guinea pig is neither from Guinea nor is it a pig. And why is it that writers write, but fingers don't fing, grocers don't groce and hammers don't ham? If the plural of tooth is teeth, why isn't the plural of booth beeth? One goose, 2 geese. So, one moose, 2 meese? One index, two indices? Is cheese the plural of choose?

If teachers taught, why didn't preachers praught? If a vegetarian eats vegetables, what does a humanitarian eat?

In what language do people recite at a play and play at a recital? Ship by truck and send cargo by ship? Have noses that run and feet that smell? Park on driveways and drive on parkways?

When the stars are out, they are visible, but when the lights are out they are invisible. And why, when I wind up my watch, I start it, but when I wind up this essay, I end it?

Now I know why I flunked my English. It's not my fault; the silly language doesn't quite know whether it's coming or going.

# IN THE SPOTLIGHT – FORM DESIGN

You first studied forms in Unit 5. If you have had to complete many different types of forms you will realise that some forms are better designed than others. They introduce each item in a logical order, are easy to follow, give plenty of space (but not so much that you think you have missed something out), there are no difficult instructions or terms you do not understand, and so on.

It is easy to criticise a form someone else has designed, but it is far harder to design a good one yourself! Yet this might be essential, for a variety of reasons:

- you may need to ask people for information that has never been required before
- a form may be out of date, and need updating or revising
- it may be decided to reduce the number of forms in circulation by combining information on some of them
- people may be having difficulties with a particular form, and it is decided to simplify it.

## Basic considerations

The first thing to consider is what you are trying to achieve, ie what is the purpose of the form. The next stage is to think about the questions you need to ask to obtain the necessary information. It is always annoying to have to complete a long form if a short one would do just as well. It is also inconsiderate to ask people for personal information unless this is essential. Therefore, check:

- why the form is needed (this will help you decide on an appropriate title)
- what information will be required
- what format must be used

  **a** for the form itself (some organisations like all their forms to follow the same format)

**b** for the information you are obtaining – the computer department may need dates of birth to be recorded as 21/04/82.

- who will be completing it. This will affect the language level of the form and the way in which the instructions will be worded.

## Planning the form

Start by listing all the information you have to obtain. Then decide a suitable order for this.

Think very carefully if you are asking people to choose options. There are various ways in which you can do this, eg

- put a tick or cross on a dotted line or in a box
- delete the option that does not apply
- write 'yes' or 'no' as appropriate.

Try not to mix these styles in one form.

Another problem for form designers is when they reach an 'if . . . then' situation. In this case you are saying something like '*If the answer is YES, go to question 9, if NO go straight to question 10.*'

If you have only one or two of these you may have no problems. If you have several then it is sometimes difficult to work out the most logical order. It is very important that you draft out this type of section and ask someone to test it for you before you incorporate it into the form.

Decide how much space people will need to answer each question. Leave rather too much space, rather than too little, if you wish the form to be easy to read when it is returned.

## Drafting the form

- Put the name of your organisation and the title of the form at the top.
- Decide what instructions are required for people at the start. Are you going to ask them to complete it in block capitals, for instance? Or to use black ink because you will need to make multiple copies? Remember, too, that you must clearly state what people should do with the form once it has been completed.
- Think about the mistakes people might make and how they should correct them. Some forms give an example of how errors should be corrected.
- If you need a considerable amount of information, decide whether it would be better to divide this into different sections or sub-sections. For instance, you could have a section on personal details, a section on financial information and so on.
- Decide whether you will want people to sign the form at the end (and possibly print their names too) and date the form.

Printed forms can be produced easily using desktop publishing packages and some word processing packages. In this case it is normal to produce the form with dots for the information lines. It is also usual to use double spacing, to allow enough room for handwritten entries.

## Testing your form

It is usual to test your form by asking a few volunteers to complete it when you have produced a draft version. Be prepared to make any amendments in line with their suggestions. It is also sensible to check there are no problems when your form is first being used more widely. If an instruction is ambiguous or a space is too small then you will soon find out – and you should take the necessary steps to remedy the problem.

### A WORKED EXAMPLE

Your friend's father is keen on renovating vintage cars. Some years ago he purchased an old, white, convertible Rolls Royce and the car now looks immaculate. When he became semi-retired a year ago his wife suggested he put the car to good use offering it for hire for weddings. He quite enjoys the role of chauffeur and, to his surprise, his small business enterprise has rapidly become more and more popular.

Unfortunately, his expansion has been marred by one or two administrative problems over the past few months. On two occasions either the wrong details or insufficient information were obtained about bookings. Your friend knows you are learning about form design and has asked if you can help. She considers that the solution would be for all bookings to be recorded on a form and then transferred into a diary. In most cases, the booking forms would be sent to the enquirers, who would complete them with the correct information.

You decide to start by talking to her father about the type of information he needs for each booking. He answers you as follows.

'Well, let's see, the most important details I need are the date and the time of collection – as well as the pick-up or collection point. This is usually the bride's home – but not always. I also need to know how long they want to hire the car. The phone number would be useful in case there's a problem. I need to know the names of the people I'm collecting. Really all this comes under the details of the hirer, which could be your first section. I usually wait at the church or registry office, drive them to the reception and then leave, but not always. Perhaps we could do with the route details as the next section. We normally decorate the car with white ribbons and flowers, but it's worth checking if they want these – people vary, you know. Finally, I need to know to whom – and where – I should send the bill. I suggest you draft out a form from this information and then I can try it for a few weeks to see if it works. Oh, one thing – I suggest you put clearly at the top that all telephone bookings must be confirmed by completing the form within 14 days, and that forms should be returned to this address, ie Classic Wedding Cars, 15 Grosvenor Court, Hightown, HG3 5PM.'

## Test your understanding

1 From the information above, discuss as a group the headings you would use on the form and how you would design it. Compare your suggestions with the sample form in Figure 14.1, shown on the next page.

2 Turn back to Unit 5 and refresh your memory about how to complete standard forms and the terms commonly used.

3 In groups of three or four, collect about four forms. (Alternatively you could

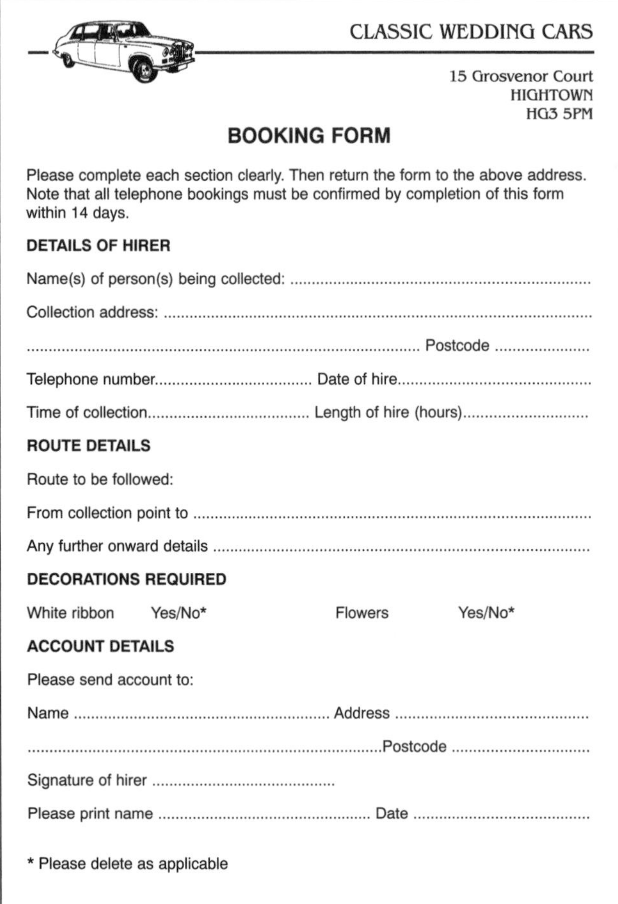
CLASSIC WEDDING CARS

15 Grosvenor Court
HIGHTOWN
HG3 5PM

**BOOKING FORM**

Please complete each section clearly. Then return the form to the above address. Note that all telephone bookings must be confirmed by completion of this form within 14 days.

**DETAILS OF HIRER**

Name(s) of person(s) being collected: ..........

Collection address: ..........

.......... Postcode ..........

Telephone number.......... Date of hire..........

Time of collection.......... Length of hire (hours)..........

**ROUTE DETAILS**

Route to be followed:

From collection point to ..........

Any further onward details ..........

**DECORATIONS REQUIRED**

White ribbon Yes/No* Flowers Yes/No*

**ACCOUNT DETAILS**

Please send account to:

Name .......... Address ..........

..........Postcode ..........

Signature of hirer ..........

Please print name .......... Date ..........

* Please delete as applicable

***Figure 14.1***
*A sample booking form*

re-use some of the forms you collected as part of the exercise in Unit 5, page 89.) These could be a holiday booking form, a mail order form, a job application form, a driving licence form, an application to open a bank account or any other type of form. As a group, score each one out of 15 as follows:

Clarity of design
(maximum 5 points)
Ease of understanding
(maximum 5 points)
Appropriate space for entries
(maximum 5 points)

As a class, discuss the features you have identified that make a good form, and those that make a bad form.

**4** Several groups of students are being visited next week by a speaker from a local employment agency, who will provide details of temporary vacancies for those who wish to work during the summer. He has told your tutor that if any students are interested, they should provide him with appropriate details.

Your tutor has decided that it would be a good idea if everyone interested completed copies of the same form, which the speaker could take away with him at the end.

**a** As a group, discuss the type of information each student would need to provide in order to be considered for one of the vacancies. Put this into a logical order.

**b** Individually, design and produce a form that could be issued to students on the day of the talk.

**c** Compare your finished forms and score these (as for Question 3 above) to decide which are the best.

## SPELLCHECKER 13

One of the spelling rules most people remember is 'i before e except after c'. We could add 'and when the word says 'ay''. Following these rules enable us to spell all the following words correctly:

**i before e**

convenience
grievous
incipient
lenient
recipient
shield
thief
proprietor
experience
mischievous
medieval
patience
piece
sieve
niece
relieved

**e before i after c**

receipt
perceive
conceited
deceive
receive
conceive

**e before i when the word says 'ay'**

reign
beige
veil
weigh
feint
feign
neighbour
vein
deign
feign

**Exceptions!**

Unfortunately, there are several exceptions to these rules. Common words which you need to learn include the following.

**e before i rulebreakers**

caffeine
eiderdown
fahrenheit
forfeit
heir
seize
surveillance
counterfeit
either
foreign
height
leisure
sovereign
weird

**i before e except after c rulebreakers**

ancient
conscientious
efficient
glacier
science
sufficient
conscience
deficient
financier
proficient
society
species

Check you could spell all the words given above correctly. Practise any you are not sure about and enter them into your Spellchecker book.

## TOOLS OF THE TRADE – *tact and diplomacy*

You first studied tone in Unit 3. Using the correct tone is the first stage of communicating tactfully and diplomatically. In the last unit you looked at contributing positively and constructively to discussions – and this is another aspect of tact. However, it is relatively easy to tell people what they want to hear, and far more difficult to raise a topic about which they have strong feelings, particularly when these are different from your own. Equally, it is easy to be courteous and polite on a good day, when things are going well, and far more difficult on a bad day when you are feeling stressed. Being tactful and diplomatic means that you consider the reaction of the recipient, try to prevent any feelings of hurt, distress or annoyance, provide information in the most appropriate manner and enable people to 'save face' whenever possible.

Developing your tact and diplomacy skills means that:

- you can cope with difficult situations more easily
- you will find it much easier to practise your assertiveness skills (see Unit 9)
- you will rarely cause offence with your colleagues and friends
- you will be popular with customers and able to generate more business for your employer
- you will be able to extend your communication skills to respond effectively in sensitive situations covering a broader range of topics.

The development of these skills doesn't happen overnight – which is why very difficult or sensitive communications are often handled by senior staff in an organisation. It is no coincidence that a professional who deals with these situations on an international level is called a diplomat.

# SITUATIONS REQUIRING TACT AND DIPLOMACY

Some of the most common examples are given below. You should note that whereas these skills are important in both verbal and written communications, in the latter they are even more critical. You may remember that when you are writing you cannot change your tone quickly to adapt to the receiver's response. In addition, if you cause serious offence, there is a permanent record of what you have written!

Difficult situations include those where:

- you need to find out personal information from someone
- you wish to refuse a request or an invitation
- you have to point out that someone else has made a mistake or an error of judgement
- you have to acknowledge that either you or your colleagues are responsible for a mistake or a problem
- you have to give unwelcome news or information
- you have to remind someone of something they have not done (particularly someone senior to yourself).

## Finding out personal information

It is usually easier to ask for personal information in a form than during a face-to-face interview. This is because it is seems more impersonal on a written document. Many people, for instance, will complete their date of birth on a form or enter their current salary, but would be affronted to be asked verbally how old they are or how much they earn. It always helps if you explain the reason for asking, eg *It will help us to process your application more quickly if you tell us your current salary.* This is a far wiser approach than suddenly asking *'How much do you earn?'*

Other personal details that people are often reluctant to give include their weight and their clothes size. In some cases, you may find your respondent giving a flattering estimate rather than accurate information. It takes a very high level of skill and diplomacy to ask them to reconsider!

Three other factors also influence the type of details people will confide to you. First, the reason for your discussion. A person applying for a bank loan will expect to be asked about financial affairs, but someone applying for a job will not. Second, whether or not the interview is in private or the form is confidential. Third, their perception of the situation. Some people are far happier about discussing personal details than others. Such individual differences, you will find, affect reactions to many sensitive situations.

## Refusing a request or an invitation

Your aim should be to phrase a refusal in such a way that you do not cause offence or upset anyone. This was mentioned under assertiveness skills in Unit 9. In this section, we shall also look at declining more official requests and invitations, often in writing.

It always helps to have a good reason and to state what this is. *'I really would have stayed late tonight but unfortunately I've made arrangements to go out at 7 o'clock'* is far more acceptable than responding *'Sorry, I can't'* or – even worse – *'You must be joking!'*.

Written invitations can be in a letter or more formally in a printed invitation – such as for a wedding. You are expected to respond in the same style. It is usually much easier to phrase an acceptance letter than a refusal. It is both tactful and sensible to give an acceptable reason – and not imply that you are doing something far more interesting on the day or evening in question!

## Pointing out an error

Just as it is tactless and insensitive to point out someone's typing mistake at the top of your voice, neither is it acceptable to accuse a customer of making an error. A better way is to put the burden of responsibility on yourself, eg *'I'm sorry if I didn't explain this clearly but the goods aren't due to be received by us until the 15th.'* This helps the customer to save face, whereas saying *'You must have misunderstood when the goods were due'* obviously doesn't.

In cases where a dispute may arise, you should state the facts impersonally and accurately, eg *'We regret you thought the goods were due to be delivered on the 10th September. As you will see from the acknowledgement of order we sent you last week, the expected date of delivery is shown as the 15th.'*

## Acknowledging an error

It is never sensible to fudge a problem or pretend that it is not your fault if a mistake has been made. It is also 'not done' to put the blame on anyone else. No-one is perfect and it may take some courage to own up to making a mess of something, but people will respect you for it – particularly if you offer to make amends. *'I'm sorry, I've been very busy lately and forgot you wanted the report for today. I'll start it immediately and let you have it this afternoon'* – this is a far more mature and responsible approach than pretending your printer broke down or your pet rabbit chewed up the paper.

When you respond to a complaint made by a customer, you may have to acknowledge a mistake on behalf of your organisation. In this case, being honest, not making spurious excuses and trying to remedy the situation are far more likely to result in a satisfied customer than any other course of action. Writing this type of letter is discussed on page 258.

## Unwelcome news and information

You have two issues to consider when you are imparting unwelcome news or information. The first is how your message will be received. The second is how to phrase it so that you make your message as positive as possible. In other words, you are using your persuasive and sales techniques to try to make the information as acceptable as you can.

One way of doing this is to see the problem as a potential opportunity. For example, assume your friend bought a new outfit and you consider the style doesn't suit her. She asks for your honest opinion! Rather than blurting out what you really think, or lying through your teeth, a more diplomatic approach is to change the focus of the conversation, eg *'It looks fine. But do you know the outfit of yours I've always loved is . . . . .'* If nothing else, this gets you out of a tight spot and, if your friend thinks about it afterwards, it does give a little guidance.

In a business letter you may have to give unwelcome news such as the fact that an item will be delayed or can no longer be supplied. Again, keep the information factual and unemotional – but express your regrets if the problem has caused inconvenience. Focus on any positive aspects – such as any future assistance you may hope to provide. If the company is giving really bad news it may be offering compensation of some kind. In this case, this is the opportunity you should stress. Always try to think how you can phrase information or bad news so that the disappointment is minimised.

## Sending a reminder

Just as you are not perfect, neither is anyone else. If you have to remind a member of staff about something he or she promised to do or remind a customer to pay a bill, always start from the premise that it has been an honest mistake. Point out the facts in a friendly manner. Only if you find that repeated reminders are required should you become more formal – but this does not mean being tactless or insulting!

# PLANNING A TACTFUL COMMUNICATION

You have several issues to consider, preferably in the following order.

**1** Think first, respond later. Good planning is essential in this situation.
**2** Consider the viewpoint of the other person and the likely reaction to the message.
**3** Decide what information you should include – and what you should not.
**4** Consider your wording very carefully. For instance, how to 'angle' the message and the type of phrases that would please or annoy.
**5** Draft your communication and ask for someone else's opinion before you send it.

## Test your understanding

Discuss as a group how you should phrase each of the following messages to cause the minimum offence

**a** verbally
**b** in writing.

Prepare a written response to two messages of your choice.

**i** A message to your boss that the reason a member of staff did not arrive for a meeting was because your boss gave him the wrong room number.
**ii** A message from your boss refusing permission to a member of staff to leave early next Tuesday. His official reason is because of pressure of work on that particular day but you also know that he is annoyed about the number of requests he is constantly receiving from that particular person.
**iii** A message to your boss that the Managing Director wants this month's sales report within the next two days. The MD is annoyed that for the third month in succession the report is late.
**iv** An explanation to your boss about why you mistakenly opened a letter marked 'personal and confidential'. The letter is from his bank and is a request for an immediate interview to discuss his overdraft, which is over the agreed limit.

## *DOUBLE TROUBLE*

Check that you know the difference between each of the following words by

**a** selecting the correct word in each sentence
**b** writing a sentence that clearly illustrates the meaning of the other word.

**i** We are hoping to clinch/clench the deal on Tuesday.
**ii** He is a real extrovert/introvert – always laughing and joking with everyone.
**iii** I hope you will be able to elicit/illicit the information when you see her next week.
**iv** You will not be able to flout/flaunt the rules when you start work.
**v** An unruly hoard/horde of football fans descended on the shopping centre.

**vi** She is foundering/floundering in her new job but, to be fair, has had little guidance.

**vii** I would be loath/loathe to agree to that course of action.

**viii** That is a moot/mute point that we will need to discuss further.

**ix** He said that if the situation continued he would be forced to prefer/proffer his resignation.

**x** He is a bad influence and has reeked/wreaked havoc in his group ever since he arrived.

**DON'T YOU DARE!**

*. . . confuse the two words affect/effect and enquiry/inquiry.*

*1 Effect is a verb and a noun, eg*
*The effect (ie the outcome or result) was startling.*
*I wish to effect (ie bring about) a change.*

*Affect is a verb which means 'to influence or have a result on', eg*
*Too little sleep affects your performance.*

*2 Enquiry is generally used in relation to queries or investigations, eg*
*Our customer enquiry department is open every day.*
*Inquiry is used mainly for government or formal investigations, eg*
*A public inquiry was held into the Hillsborough disaster.*

## MAKING HEADWAY – letters of complaint and adjustment

When people are annoyed or disappointed with a product or with the service they have received they may write a letter of complaint to the organisation concerned. Even the best-run organisations receive letters of complaint, because it is impossible to guarantee that nothing will ever go wrong. The organisation will send a letter of adjustment. Sometimes this is known as a letter of apology, but 'adjustment' is a better word, as sometimes action or compensation is offered to help to 'adjust' the situation. An apology on its own may not be enough.

You should be capable of writing both types of letters. You may need to complain about a service or product your organisation has received. Equally, you may have to answer a letter of complaint you have received. This section is concerned with giving you the basic skills to compose both types of letters.

# LETTERS OF COMPLAINT

Why might you (or a customer) write a letter of complaint? Normally, you would do this when you feel that:

- there have been unacceptable problems or delays processing your order or request

- you have had an unpleasant experience, eg been given incorrect information on several occasions, been sold unsatisfactory (or incorrect) goods, have been treated discourteously by someone in their organisation
- you have been treated unfairly or unjustly, eg sent repeated reminders to settle an account you have already paid, or given different terms from those you were originally offered
- you have lost money through the action of someone else, eg your supplier's delay or inefficiency has prevented you from making a sale to a customer.

To write an effective letter of complaint you first have to decide:

**a** what it is that you are complaining about
**b** what problems have been caused
**c** what you want in return.

The last point is very important. For instance, do you want a simple apology, a straightforward replacement, your money back or financial compensation? If you do not know what you want, and do not specify your request clearly, then you may be dissatisfied with the reply. Equally, do not expect to be compensated out of all proportion to your loss! If you bought a chicken that was not fit to eat, you would hardly expect the supermarket to give you a free trolley run to compensate. But if your holiday of a lifetime was ruined, you would be silly to accept a £5 voucher!

## The structure and tone of your letter

The structure of a letter of complaint is similar to any other letter.

- Start with an introduction, which clearly sets out the background to the problem or complaint.
- The main section should give further details to support your case. These should be factual and accurate.
- Your conclusion should tell the recipient the action you think should be taken to compensate you.

Your tone should be courteous but firm and authoritative. You are not asking a question or asking for an opinion, you are stating your case. *Never* let your emotions affect your judgement or become rude or threatening. Equally, do not ramble on about the problem – keep your letter as focused as possible.

## Test your understanding

1 The following are four excerpts from a letter of complaint. Only one is acceptable. Decide which one and identify the problem with each of the others.

**a** We have ordered photocopier paper from your company for many years. Indeed we order many items of stationery from you. Your representative, Mr Thomas, is normally very helpful and informed. However, the last batch of photocopier paper we ordered from you didn't work properly. We checked we had put it in properly but it still didn't work, no matter what we did.

**b** We have ordered photocopier paper from you for many years but the last batch of paper is, quite simply, a disgrace. It isn't fit for lining our rubbish bin. I cannot think why your representative recommended it unless he gets a better commission for this paper. If he thinks it is fit for use then he needs his head testing.

**c** On 13 March we took delivery of a large amount of photocopier paper. We regularly order large amounts from you because we use the machine almost incessantly. We often operate to tight deadlines and need to be certain that our copies are clear and produced with few difficulties. However, this batch has caused us considerable problems to the point where it has been impossible to keep up with our workload.

**d** On 13 March we took delivery of 200 reams of photocopier paper. This was a new type of paper which we purchased on the advice of your representative, Mr Thomas. Despite checking carefully that we were using it according to instructions we have had continual problems. In particular the paper regularly jams in the machine, which creates delays. To solve our immediate problems we have had to buy an emergency supply of paper from a local supplier.

2 You recently saw a superb guidebook for Canada advertised in a magazine. You ordered it for a friend's birthday present as she is planning to visit Canada soon to see some relatives. When it arrived it had very poor binding and the moment you opened it several of the pages fell out.

**a** You want to return the book. Decide what compensation you want (eg a replacement book or your money back).

**b** Draft a short letter of complaint outlining your problem and the action you wish the firm to take. Invent appropriate factual details yourself, including the date you ordered and received the book, the cost, and the invoice number.

# LETTERS OF ADJUSTMENT

There are three categories of letters of complaint:

- those relating to a serious problem or difficulty
- those involving a minor issue
- those that are unjustified.

Many organisations have specific policies for dealing with letters of complaint and it is important you know what these are and follow them. In many cases, all letters of complaint are handled centrally by a Customer Services Department. Some organisations are very reluctant to lose a customer, and may have a policy of replying promptly to even trivial complaints and offering some small token as compensation. Others may only be so helpful with regular or long-standing customers. A few may offer little compensation, unless the customer persists!

The letter of adjustment may therefore be dictated more or less by company policy and produced by a central department. If you work for a smaller organisation you may be expected to prepare them yourself. Do make sure, however, that you check carefully before you make any offer to a customer on behalf of your firm – and never assume that a customer's allegations are accurate until you have checked the facts.

Finally, it is not good policy to keep a customer with a complaint waiting for a reply. For that reason, if it will take you some time to establish what happened, it is sensible to send a short letter of acknowledgement in the meantime. This should simply state that the letter has been received and the complaint is being investigated.

## The structure and tone of your letter

Again it is important your letter has a clear structure.

**a** The introduction should thank the customer for his or her letter and express regret that the problem has occurred or that the customer has been inconvenienced. This is important even if you are going to refute some of the claims. The fact that the customer *feels* inconvenienced is enough!

**b** The main part of the letter should state the action that has been taken to investigate the matter and the results of this. You should then describe the action you are taking to remedy the problem.

**c** In the last part of the letter it is normal to restate the apology and then to express your hope that the customer will continue to do business with your organisation.

Of course, it is much easier to write a letter of adjustment when you are offering something! If you are refuting an allegation then it is more difficult. In this case:

**a** start the letter in the same way

**b** continue as before, describing the investigations and their results, then state, clearly and factually, why it is not possible to make an adjustment on this occasion

**c** end the letter positively and in a friendly way. Do not anticipate trouble!

## Test your understanding

**1** A senior tutor in your college has sent the letters shown in Figure 14.2 in response to two letters of complaint. In each case identify:

## DON'T YOU DARE!

...*confuse should/would, shall/will or could/would. Note the following carefully:*

- *'I' and 'we' are followed by 'should' or 'shall' unless you want to indicate a specific intention. Therefore I shall be pleased to see you but I will send you a replacement next week.*
- *Use either shall/will or should/would in a sentence but don't mix them, therefore*

  *If you will attend to this request immediately I shall (not should!) be grateful.*
  *I should like to see you on Tuesday if you would (not will) be available.*
- *Could = able to; would = willing to. Therefore*

  *I could retype this for you if it would help but*
  *Would you allow me to leave early on Friday?*

> Dear Mrs Evans
>
> I understand that you recently tried to arrange for your daughter to attend this college to take a beginners' typewriting course. I have also been informed that, although your daughter is still at school, you were advised that she could be accepted on the programme provided she had a letter of agreement from her Head Teacher.
>
> I regret that you were misinformed on this occasion. The policy in relation to students under 16 changed some time ago and we are no longer able to accept students who are under the age of 16 years.
>
> I apologise for any inconvenience you have been caused and would assure you that, once your daughter attains the age of 16, we will be only too pleased to offer her a place on the course.
>
> Yours sincerely

> Dear Miss Jackson
>
> I understand that you have recently had problems trying to establish the correct night for your new course to start and, in fact, made two fruitless journeys to college as you were wrongly informed about the actual start date.
>
> The reason for this error was a mistake on the computer listing sheet which showed this course lasting for 36 weeks. In fact, it actually does not start until the 23 September and runs for 32 weeks.
>
> Please accept my sincere apologies on behalf of the college for the inconvenience you have been caused through this error. As some degree of compensation, please find enclosed our cheque for £4 to reimburse you for your bus fares.
>
> I would add that mistakes like this are relatively isolated and we do make every effort to ensure that students are given the correct information. Unfortunately, occasionally, something can go wrong, as in this instance.
>
> I very much hope that you enjoy your course and successfully achieve your qualification at the end of the year.
>
> Yours sincerely

***Figure 14.2*** *Two letters of adjustment*

**a** the degree of honesty that has been expressed
**b** phrases which denote tact and diplomacy on the part of your tutor
**c** how the writer has concentrated on accentuating the positive, rather than the negative aspects
**d** how you would feel if you were the recipient.

**2** Your boss is on holiday when you receive a letter of complaint from an important customer, Mr Benjamin Peters, Purchasing Manager of Westwood and Griffiths Ltd, Dale Road, Hightown, HG3 4SP. The letter is complaining about the late delivery of letter-headed paper, which was urgently required over a week ago. You are aware your boss handled this order personally and you are not sure how to respond. Given she will be back next Monday you decide to send a short, courteous acknowledgement letter to Mr Peters. Draft the letter required.

**3** When your boss, Julia Waters, the Sales Manager, returns from holiday she investigates the matter of the late delivery further and finds that the original batch was rejected by Printing Department because of a fault with the printing machine, which wrongly aligned the colours in the heading. The Printing Department notified her by e-mail but this was not read nor acted upon because she was away. She has asked you to draft a letter to Mr Peters apologising for the problem and for any inconvenience caused. As a gesture of goodwill she is deducting 20% from the invoice.

As a group, discuss the type of phrases you will use in composing your letter. Then, individually, draft the letter and check your finished work with your tutor.

## WORDBANK 11

Each of the following sentences is from a letter of complaint. Can you say what the writer means in each case? Look up any of the words in bold type which you do not know and enter them in your Wordbank book.

**1** Our recent trip to Ireland was a complete **fiasco**.

**2** With **hindsight**, I realise that I should have checked the documents more carefully.

**3** This has caused **irreversible** damage to the machine.

**4** The experience was extremely **traumatic**.

**5** There was **blatant** inefficiency on the part of your staff.

**6** I do not wish to be **pedantic** about the terms of our agreement but I feel you have definitely **breached** it on this occasion.

**7** Your representative seems **oblivious** to our needs.

**8** I received a **tirade** of abuse from the staff member to whom I complained.

**9** Please **instigate** a **rigorous** investigation.

## THE GOOD GRAMMAR GUIDE

### Adverbs

You have already learned that adjectives tell us more about a noun or a pronoun. Adverbs do the same thing – only with other parts of speech. They usually describe a verb, but they can be used with adjectives and other adverbs. Just as adjectives help us to be more precise, so do adverbs.

Consider each of the following sentences.

*He left slowly.*
*He left quickly.*
*He left hesitantly.*
*He left suddenly.*
*He left with great sadness.*
*He left yesterday.*
*He left very early.*
*He left here recently.*
*He left for a holiday.*

Each is completely different – but only because of the addition of an adverb or an adverbial phrase. An adverb that describes an action is one word, whereas an adverbial phrase is a group of words that does the same thing.

## Types of adverbs

Adverbs and adverbial phrases answer a question. They describe **how, when, where, why, how long** or **to what extent** something is done.

### ADVERBS OF MANNER DESCRIBE 'HOW'

These are the adverbs used in the first five sentences above. In each case the adverbs describe the way in which the subject left – slowly, quickly, hesitantly and so on.

Sometimes people mistakenly believe that all adverbs end in 'ly'. Many do, but words such as *sideways* and *backwards* can describe an action and are often used as adverbs. In addition, there are some 'ly' words that can be used as adjectives, eg *It was a heavenly day. He is a very friendly person.*

A phrase can also be used adverbially to describe behaviour. In the examples above *with great sadness* is used for this purpose.

### ADVERBS OF TIME DESCRIBE 'WHEN'

'Yesterday', 'very early' and 'recently' all described *when* he left. These are therefore all adverbs. Other words commonly used to say 'when' include *then, now, sometimes, later, afterwards.* Phrases can also be used, such as *in good time, for a few minutes, before me, since then, about five minutes ago.*

### ADVERBS OF PLACE DESCRIBE 'WHERE'

We often use words like *here, there, somewhere, anywhere, indoors, outdoors, upstairs, downstairs* to describe where someone is. Equally, we could use a phrase such as *in my office, in his office, at his house.*

### ADVERBS OF REASON DESCRIBE 'WHY'

We may decide to explain why something happened. *I dropped the vase accidentally* differs from *I dropped the vase deliberately*! It indicates the purpose behind an action. In the examples above, the phrase '*for a holiday*' is used to describe why he left.

### ADVERBS OF DURATION AND NUMBER DESCRIBE 'HOW LONG' OR 'HOW MANY'

If somebody asked you the question *Has he left already?* or *Has he left yet?* they are trying to establish how long he has been gone. In this case, the words *already* and *yet* are both adverbs. Other common words and phrases we use include *still, any longer, any more, no longer*. We use numbers in the same way, eg *He saw him twice.*

### ADVERBS OF DEGREE DESCRIBE 'TO WHAT EXTENT'

In this case we use adverbs to say how certain we are about something or to what extent it occurs. We also use adverbs in this category to say how frequently something takes place. In this case we normally put the adverb before the main verb, eg *He **always** leaves at 4 pm, He **rarely** leaves this* *late, He will **definitely** leave at 2 pm, He will **perhaps** leave at 6 pm, He **frequently** leaves early on a Friday.* Other words we use in this way include *often, never, a lot, seldom, probably, certainly.*

### ADVERBS THAT ASK A QUESTION

A final group of adverbs are those that ask questions relating to where, when, how and why, such as ***When** did he leave? **Why** was he leaving? **Where** was he going? **How** was he getting there?*

## Why use adverbs?

You may wonder why you need to know about adverbs if you have been using such words quite easily for years without thinking about them. There are several reasons:

1 When they are speaking, many people often omit the ends of adverbs, eg *I'll do it as quick as I can.* Knowing about adverbs will improve your oral skills.

2 Many slang words and expressions can be used as adjectives and adverbs. Recognising them helps you to avoid using them in formal communications of any kind – examples include *He's dead mean* or *That's real good* or *I clean forgot*.

3 You need to know how to compare adverbs properly. Adverbs are compared in a similar way to adjectives, using the comparative form 'more' and the superlative form 'most', eg

*She writes more neatly than I do.*
*He argued most forcibly against the proposal*

However, irregular adverbs are different. Some examples are given below:

| | | |
|---|---|---|
| *He did badly.* | *John did worse.* | *David did worst of all.* |
| *He lives far away.* | *John lives even farther.* | *David lives farthest of all.* |
| *He did well.* | *John did better.* | *David did best of all.* |

4 The position of an adverb can change the meaning of the sentence. You should always place an adverb near to the words it is meant to modify, otherwise you give the wrong impression, eg

| | | |
|---|---|---|
| *Happily, she agreed.* | = | It was fortunate (in the circumstances) that she agreed. |
| *She agreed happily.* | = | She was happy to agree. |

## Test your understanding

1 The following words also add 'ly' but the spelling changes slightly, eg heavy = heavily; gentle – gently. Convert each of the following adjectives, spelling the adverb correctly in each case.

easy, wary, automatic, clumsy, full, hungry, visible, true, frantic, greedy.

2 Write the comparative and superlative of each of the following adverbs:

cruelly, early, carefully, recklessly, confidently.

3 Identify the errors in each of the following sentences and rewrite the sentence correctly.

**a** He left so sudden I never saw him go.
**b** I can do it quick if you give it to me now.
**c** I need this checking very badly.
**d** They arrived more early than me.
**e** The report showed that fewer than half the first-aiders helped someone who had collapsed quickly.
**f** Please arrive prompt at nine and report to Personnel.
**g** You've spelt that word wrong.

**DON'T YOU DARE!**

*...over-use meaningless adverbs such as: actually, definitely, really, surely. I actually knew him means nothing more than I knew him!*

## COMMUNICATION IN PRACTICE

### Test your skills

**1** Reword each of the following tactless or undiplomatic sentences into one which is more acceptable!

**a** 'You've put on weight since I last saw you.'
**b** 'I can't believe you're as old as that.'
**c** 'There are three spelling mistakes in that letter you're typing.'
**d** 'I can't work late on Tuesday, I'm going out.'
**e** 'It's your fault I put the wrong date, you definitely said Tuesday.'
**f** 'I didn't understand what you wanted, did I?'
**g** 'He said he can't come to your meeting, he's too busy.'
**h** 'It's not my fault it's not done, I've only one pair of hands.'
**i** 'You don't look ill to me.'

**2** Replace each of the following phrases in bold with a single word that means the same thing.

**a** Because they were losing money, they called in a **specialist to give advice** for his opinion.
**b** I have asked both teams to **work in association with one another**.
**c** He has asked me to take down his statement **word for word**.
**d** I understand he lives in a **district adjoining a town or city**.
**e** The newspaper report said that she had married a **gymnast who practises violent twisting postures**.
**f** Yesterday I bought **an instrument for measuring atmospheric pressure**.
**g** He has recently obtained employment as **a person who visits customers on behalf of his organisation**.

**3** 'Only' is a dangerous adverb – it is often misplaced. For each of the following sentences, identify what the writer is saying (which may not be what he or she really meant to say!).

**i** Only I want to read my book for a while.
**ii** I only want to read my book for a while.

**iii** I want only to read my book for a while.
**iv** I want to read only my book for a while.
**v** I want to read my book only for a while.

**4** Rewrite each of the following sentences to correct any errors.

**a** Neither of the letters were in the file.
**b** I shall be able to consider your request for a refund if you would return the item to us.
**c** In my report I said that I definitely saw her there at 7 o'clock and I was really surprised she was there.
**d** He moved from 22 Osborne Drive on 3 March which has been empty ever since.
**e** He said I had to carefully and consienciously check it.
**f** This medicine effects me by making me sleepy.
**g** He acted very mischeivous when he stayed with us.

## Apply your skills

*Figure 14.3* *Memo to you from Graham Palmer*

You have recently obtained temporary work with an express delivery company – Speedlink UK Ltd, 10 Granby Walk, Hightown, HG2 4PH.

**MEMO**

**TO** You

**FROM** Graham Palmer

**DATE** Yesterday

I'll be out at a meeting all morning. Whilst I'm away can you sort out the following for me.

1 I've had two complaints from customers about the late delivery of packages they sent through us. Both of these we subcontracted to Alpha Couriers Ltd, 14 Adelcott Road, Hightown HG3 2PM. The first complaint is from Mrs Linda Taylor of 10 Cliveden Road, Hightown HG1 3WO. She asked us to send a package from here to Wetherby using the express service on 1 May – the package was collected at 10 am. The package didn't arrive until 3 May – despite the fact it's only 50 miles away. She had to send a duplicate package and this cost her £25. We'll have to reimburse her this money and apologise. The second is from Ravinder Singh of Risedale Publications, Juniper Street, Hightown HG1 3DE. This is more serious in that Ravinder is a Graphic Designer and uses us a lot. He sent some drawings to Manchester which were very urgent and had to arrive later that day. These were again collected in the morning of 1 May – about 9.30 – and had to arrive in Manchester that afternoon. In the event the firm there, Layton and Cox Ltd, didn't receive them until the *following* afternoon. Can you send Ravinder a brief acknowledgement letter please, saying we're investigating this matter, as I'll have to look into what happened in more detail for him.

2 Can you draft a letter of complaint to Alpha Couriers giving them the details above. Send the letter to Trevor Stevens, the Sales Manager. Please ask him for a full report on what went wrong in both cases. Stress, please, that we offer a quality service to our clients and that we obviously cannot continue to sub-contract work to them if they cannot fulfil their commitments to us. Please say we need information as soon as possible so that we can respond to our own clients. I'll sign the letter.

3 I've a complaint here from Judy Griffiths of 12 Cheyne Walk, Hightown, HG5 3SD. She alleges that when she phoned us two days ago to find out if we could express a parcel to Edinburgh she rang for ages before the phone was answered, then was passed from one person to another and kept holding

1 of 2

on for five minutes while the right person was found, and that the member of staff who eventually spoke to her was very abrupt. She thinks the person concerned was called Tanya. It sounds like this is the new girl who started two weeks ago. Can you do a memo from me to her supervisor, Joan Symmonds. Ask Joan to investigate the matter and report back to me. Be careful how you word it – Joan is very protective of her new staff, but obviously if this girl needs further training we will have to organise it. Second, please write a memo to Bill Tyler, Administrative Officer, and tell him there appear to be problems on the switchboard. The call was made about 12.15 – so it could have been the lunchtime relief operator. Please ask him for his comments.

4 Next, please send a letter to Judy Griffiths, apologising for the poor service she received. Explain that we were short staffed at the time because of the flu epidemic but we regret she was treated in such an offhand manner. Normally all our staff are given comprehensive training before they deal with general enquiries but, because of the staffing difficulties, less well-trained staff were helping out at the time. Enclose a booklet on our services and a price list and say that we would welcome the opportunity of proving the efficiency of our delivery service to her – or something like that.

5 Finally, I think it would be useful if our couriers delivered a form with the parcels, which checked customer satisfaction with the service. Customers who are unhappy will probably return it promptly and those who are happy will probably throw it away – but we can but try! It needs our heading and address at the top. We need customers to write their name and address, a brief description of the parcel and the condition it was in. We also need to know whether it arrived earlier than expected, on time or later. I'd also like a section about the person who delivered it – I think some of these contract people are a bit surly. Check if the delivery person was pleasant, asked for a signature, was smartly dressed, that sort of thing. Try to think of one or two ideas yourself – you must have received a parcel or two! Just draft down some ideas for me please and I'll have a look at it when I return. Don't make it too long, or people won't be bothered to fill it in. Don't forget to say where they should return it. Use our Freepost address, so that it won't cost them anything, please.

Thanks

*Graham*

2 of 2

The organisation delivers letters, packages and parcels by bike or van nationwide. There is guaranteed two-hour delivery within a 40-mile radius and guaranteed 12-hour delivery to any city in Britain using the fastest service. The normal service guarantees delivery in 24 hours. The organisation will also quote for an express courier service to any destination. Most of the bikes and vans are owned by the company but when they are very busy they sometimes sub-contract the services of other private couriers to help them.

Your boss is Graham Palmer, the Customer Service Manager. Your task is to help him to cope with a backlog of enquiries and correspondence he has received over the past month, when several of his staff have been absent because of a flu epidemic. When you arrive for work this morning you find the memo shown in Figure 14.3 on your desk. Prepare the documents Graham Palmer requires.

## WORD WIZARD

### Colour blind

In this Word Wizard you have to participate. You will enjoy this more if you compete in several teams – and see who comes out best. You can also swop your ideas later.

We frequently use colour words to express ideas or describe a person or situation, eg *we're in the black* when we have money and *in the red* when we haven't, *in the pink* when we're pleased but *see red* when we're not.

Below are 22 words. Each one results in a commonly used expression when it is combined with one of the words in the following colour list:

**COLOUR LIST**

black, white, blue, yellow, purple, red, green, grey, brown

**WORD LIST**

carpet, sheep, wash, herring, list, moon, elephant, mail, patch, light, fingers, blood, nose, eye, comedy, letter day, lie, streak, market, print, matter, neck.

**YOUR TASK**

The winning team is the one that pairs up all the words correctly with their colours most quickly *and* can give the meaning of each expression!

# 15

UNIT

## IN THE SPOTLIGHT – FORMAL REPORTS

In Unit 8, you learned how to write an informal report. You may remember that this is produced as a memo and gives a brief introduction, the results of the investigation, the conclusions and the recommendations. If you have forgotten about informal reports, refresh your memory by re-reading pages 132–135 and the report illustrated in Figure 8.1 on page 135.

Today, most reports are informal. However, it is sometimes necessary to produce a more formal document. This is often the case if the report will be presented to senior members of an organisation (such as the Board of Directors or Board of Governors) or to an external organisation. Examples include:

- a request by your College Principal to the Health and Safety Officer to produce a summary of current health and safety issues for a Board of Governors' meeting
- the requirement for a Research and Development Manager of an organisation to prepare a report for the Board of Directors on developments each year
- an investigation into new marketing opportunities for an organisation by a firm of management consultants who prepare a report for the senior managers
- an assessment by a firm of surveyors of the work required and cost of renovating a run-down factory building for an organisation interested in purchasing the premises.

In all these cases a more formal report structure is used than for routine, informal reports. In some cases the organisation may have a 'house style' for reports. In either case, you are likely to find a standard report structure is used.

## The standard structure – investigative reports

All reports should start with a clear title. They are then divided into sections under specific headings. The headings normally associated with formal investigative reports are as follows:

**1 Terms of reference**

This states the reason for writing the report.

**2 Procedure**

This states how the information contained in the report was obtained.

**3 Findings**

This is usually the main part of the report, giving the results of the investigations.

**4 Conclusion**

This is a brief section summarising the main points outlined in the findings and pointing the way to the final section.

**5 Recommendations**

This gives the writer's views about the action that should now be taken.

A list of appendices – documents included to support the report – follows. These would be mentioned in the report, numbered sequentially and placed at the back.

***Figure 15.1***
*A checklist for report writing*

**Report checklist**

**The brief**

1 What is the reason for writing the report?

2 Do I clearly understand this?

**The recipients**

1 Who will read the report – one person or several?

2 How important are they?

3 Do they already have some knowledge of the topic or not?

4 Must I be careful not to upset anyone in particular?

5 Will some of them hold strong views and opinions already?

**The content**

1 Do I have to state purely the findings and conclusion or have I also to make recommendations?

2 Must I stick to the facts or have I been asked to give a personal opinion?

3 Is the report just factual or should it be persuasive as well?

**The procedure**

1 What methods can/should I use to obtain information?

2 Is the report confidential and will that affect how I can find out information?

3 Is information available in documents or files or will I need to interview people as well?

4 Will I have to undertake any research or obtain permission to use any information?

# REPORT WRITING MADE SIMPLE

There are certain 'golden rules' for report writing which make the task much simpler.

## At the start

- Check that you are clear about your brief or terms of reference. Use the checklist shown in Figure 15.1 to help.
- Plan the structure of the report. This will help you to decide
  - which information should be classed as relevant and what is irrelevant
  - which information you already have and what you need to find out

- the best methods to use to find out what you need
- the most appropriate headings to use.

If you have any doubts at this stage, it is sensible to clarify your ideas with the person who has asked you to write the report.

## During its preparation

- Be neat and orderly, particularly if you are dealing with a large quantity of information. File everything methodically. It is often useful to note the source of a document and the date at the top right, so that you can refer to these easily.
- Make sure your report is logically ordered, so that your reader can follow what you have written. Bear in mind that managers are busy people and brief summaries, clear headings and succinct writing are valuable skills.
- Write in an acceptable style. This means being objective, using the third person and reported speech (see Unit 13, page 242), sticking to the facts and keeping it short and simple.
- Use diagrams and tables to reduce the amount of continuous text where you can. This is particularly useful in a long report and makes it much easier for the reader to refer to key data. Don't forget, however, that all such statistics should also have a clear commentary to go with them (see Unit 9).
- Use a clear layout, with decimal or numbered points for sub-headings. Use bold type, italics or different sizes of type to differentiate between main, sub- and other headings. (As an example, check the way that the headings vary in this book, and yet are consistent from one unit to another.)

## When you have completed your first draft

- Check it carefully. First read it for sense, then check that everything is presented clearly and logically.
- Check your spelling, punctuation and grammar carefully. Never rely on your spellchecker!
- Make sure that you have included any footnotes required or made clear references to any appendices.
- If you have obtained information from any books, journals or official statistics, make sure you have identified the source in each case (see page 223) and included these in your footnotes or bibliography.
- If the report is a long one, prepare a title page giving the title, your name and the date prepared.
- Print out the report on good quality paper.

## A worked example

You are working on a temporary basis in the regional office of a firm of accountants in Hightown. During the last few weeks there have been two attempted break-ins at the premises and three incidents where personal

SECURITY REPORT NOTES

**Staff comments**

1 Reception counter often left unattended, office staff in back office supposed to cover reception area during breaks and lunch-time. Cannot watch counter all the time so visitors could enter undetected.

2 Office doors never locked – most staff haven't keys so cannot enter locked offices, therefore everyone leaves doors unlocked for ease.

3 Staff nervous if leaving car park late at night and in the dark. Several large trees overhang the car park.

**Your observations**

1 Staff often leave personal belongings lying about – handbags on desks, jackets on chairs.

2 When visitors arrive to visit a partner there is no check when they have left. In your last place of work, visitor badges were issued which were handed in when each visitor left. You think such a procedure would be useful in your present firm.

3 In your last organisation, too, all general offices could be entered by using a master key. Every member of staff had a master key for these rooms so could lock and unlock doors as necessary. Directors' offices were double-protected by an individual key as well, with restricted holders. You feel, again, that this could be adapted for these premises.

**Crime Watch Officer observations**

1 Back door can be entered from car park. This should be a no-entry door and used as emergency exit only.

2 Door from reception area to main offices could be adapted to open only when released to do so by receptionist. This would prevent unauthorised entry.

3 Several windows have no security locks. This is likely to contravene insurance requirements and locks should be fitted to all windows.

4 Main driveway and car park should have security lights.

***Figure 15.2*** *The information you have obtained for your report*

items have gone missing from the offices. The Senior Accountant, Pamela Bates, has asked you to investigate the problem and to recommend any security improvements that may be required. She thinks you may be able to view the situation more objectively as you are a relative newcomer. However, she has told you to obtain help and guidance from a security consultant if necessary – she understands that a Crime Watch Officer from the local police may be able to help. She has asked for your report to be formal so that she can present it to the senior partners at head office.

You start by interviewing staff. You also make your own observations. Finally, you telephone your local police who arrange for an officer to visit the premises. During this visit you make notes on his comments. The information you obtain is detailed in Figure 15.2.

You now have the task of assembling all this information into a report for Pamela Bates.

A version of the finished report is shown opposite in Figure 15.3. Before you read this, however, you may like to consider what you would have written under the five standard headings given on page 270.

## POINTS TO NOTE

**1** This report has been written in the third person. If the writer had wanted to refer to himself/herself, this would be done by saying 'the writer' and not 'I'. In some reports you may be able to use the first person, which is often easier – it usually depends upon how formal your report must be and who will be reading it. A useful guide is to check with the person who has asked for the report.

**2** The report may seem repetitive in places. However, the layout means that it is easy for a reader to find information easily. In particular, the recommendations could be discussed at a meeting of the senior partners without people having to hunt for them throughout the report.

**3** The report should end with your name and the date on which it was prepared unless, of course, it is a long report with a separate title page.

DAWSON, PICKLES AND MARSDEN, CHARTERED ACCOUNTANTS

**REPORT ON SECURITY SITUATION AND REQUIREMENTS AT HIGHTOWN OFFICE**

**TERMS OF REFERENCE**

To investigate security arrangements and make recommendations for improving security, following two recent attempted break-ins and three reports of missing staff items, on the instructions of Mrs Pamela Bates, Senior Accountant, on 16 June 199-.

**PROCEDURE**

1 Interviews were held with staff working in the Hightown office.

2 Observations were made during a tour of the building and from a study of visitor procedures.

3 The local Crime Watch Officer visited the premises and made a verbal report.

**FINDINGS**

1 **Staff concerns**

1.1 The reception counter is usually unattended during breaks and lunch-time. Although staff in the back office are responsible for monitoring visitors this is not always possible because the reception desk cannot be seen clearly from the back office.

1.2 Office doors are normally left unlocked because of the inconvenience to non-keyholders when they are locked.

1.3 The car park is very dark at night and several overhanging trees would give cover to anyone watching the building.

2 **Other observations**

2.1 Many staff bring personal belongings to work and leave these in unattended offices. Handbags are left on desks and jackets left on chairs.

2.2 There is no procedure for registering the arrival and departure of visitors.

3 **Observations by Crime Watch Officer**

3.1 The car park gives access to the back door, which is usually left unlocked and unattended.

3.2 Several windows have no security lock. The officer queried whether this contravened insurance requirements.

3.3 The main driveway and car park are not illuminated.

3.4 There are no measures to prevent unauthorised access from the reception area to the main offices.

**CONCLUSIONS**

1 There are several security risks in relation to the location of the premises and access to the office areas.

2 There are few internal security procedures.

**RECOMMENDATIONS**

1 **Premises and access**

1.1 The back door should be for exit only, to prevent access from the car park.

1.2 The driveway and car park should be illuminated at night.

1.3 The door from reception to the main offices should operate on a release mechanism controlled from the reception desk.

1.4 All office doors should be locked when not in use. Staff should be issued with master keys. Restricted access to certain areas is possible by fitting a second lock with keys issued only to senior staff or the occupant of the office.

1.5 Window locks should be fitted to all windows.

2 **Internal security procedures**

2.1 There should be a clear procedure for registering the arrival and departure of visitors. This can be achieved by issuing visitor badges on arrival and collecting these on departure.

2.2 Staff should be given advice on personal security and the storage of personal items.

*Your name*

*Date of report*

***Figure 15.3*** *A finished report*

# Test your understanding

You work for a local firm of recruitment consultants who are about to move offices. Your boss, Carolyn Brooks, is keen that the new reception area should be welcoming and inviting. Most clients arrive in reception and may have to wait for a short time before seeing a recruitment consultant. A full-time receptionist also has to answer a small switchboard and direct incoming calls. She is delighted about the move as the existing reception area is cramped and rather drab. Carolyn Brooks wants to persuade the Directors that spending money on the new reception area to give it a modern image and make it attractive to clients will result in increased business. She has asked you to investigate the issue and to make recommendations about the way in which it should be furnished and set out.

**1** As a group, discuss how you would find out the information on which to base your report. In other words, what *procedures* would you follow?

**2** If you honestly felt that most of the existing furniture would do if it was moved to the new premises, and wrote this in your report, what do you think would be Carolyn Brooks' reaction and why?

RECEPTION REPORT NOTES

**Interview with receptionist**

1 Clients without an appointment may have to wait up to 20 minutes during busy times. Nothing to distract them. Should have range of modern magazines – daily paper would be a bonus.

2 New clients need to fill in a registration form – need to have a table to write on. Existing coffee tables too low.

3 Chairs don't match at present, makes area look uncoordinated and second rate. Not enough chairs – can seat only eight people at present.

4 A payphone would be useful. Many people ask to use the phone if they are delayed.

**Ideas from magazines**

1 Colour important. Red can make people restless, black is depressing, white too stark. Need restful colours such as blue or green.

2 Distractions for waiting visitors include magazines, fish tank, pictures, noticeboard on company and staff.

3 Coat stand and umbrella stand useful.

4 Need to decide image. Can be traditional – implies reliability (eg all wood furniture), futuristic – implies trendsetter (eg metallic furniture) or just functional.

**Your own ideas**

1 Company literature useful.

2 Flower displays or plants would make area look attractive.

3 Chairs with arms take up more room but are more comfortable.

***Figure 15.4*** *Your reception notes*

**3** As a group, decide the main headings and sub-headings you could use to organise your information.

**4** Assuming your findings are those given in Figure 15.4, write the report required. With the agreement of your tutor, you could add to any of the ideas given in Figure 15.4 – but you are advised not to make your report too complex or lengthy.

# THE GOOD GRAMMAR GUIDE

## Prepositions

The job of a preposition is to link a noun or pronoun with a verb, eg

*She ran* ***across*** *the field.*
*He spoke* ***to*** *the visitor.*
*The dog is* ***behind*** *the door.*
*We must arrive* ***before*** *nightfall.*

Many prepositions comprise one single word. These are **simple prepositions**. Others consist of two or three words and are known as **complex prepositions**. Some examples are given in the table opposite.

You will normally have few difficulties using simple prepositions when you are speaking or writing. There are, however, three areas where you need to take care.

**1** Sometimes a preposition must be repeated to avoid ambiguity in a sentence. Compare the following sentences

*I have been talking to Paul and Bill about this.*
*I have been talking to Paul and to Bill about this.*

In the first sentence you imply you talked to both at the same time. In the second sentence you imply you talked to both of them, but not necessarily together.

| **One word prepositions** | **Two word prepositions** | **Three word prepositions** |
|---|---|---|
| about, above, across, after, against, along, among, around, at, before, behind, below, beneath, between, beyond, by, down, during, except, for, from, in, inside, into, of, off, on, onto, out, over, round, since, through, to, towards, under, until, up, upon, with, within, without | ahead of, apart from, because of, close to, except for, instead of, near to, next to | as far as, by means of, in accordance with, in addition to, in front of, on behalf of, with reference to |

**2** Many prepositions are used in standard expressions we use every day, eg

*Even when I was* ***off colour*** *and* ***under the weather*** *I was* ***up to my eyes*** *in work.*

*We'll* ***meet up*** *later when I've* ***finished off*** *this report as we don't want to* ***miss out****, do we?*

It is not normal to use such expressions in formal communications. This is mainly because such phrases are often difficult to understand if read literally.

**3** If you are referring to a person, it is often correct to use a different preposition from the one you would use to refer to an article.

| **A person** | **An item, event or thing** |
|---|---|
| You agree with | You agree to |
| You are annoyed with | You are annoyed at |
| You are disappointed with | You are disappointed in |
| You part from | You part with |

**4** People are often told not to end a sentence with a preposition, eg

*Is that the person you were talking to?*

They argue it is much better to write:

*Is that the person to whom you were talking?*

To most people, however, the second version sounds very formal and is virtually unheard in everyday conversation. Today, therefore, there is no official rule about prepositions. But you should try to avoid them when they appear 'stranded' at the end of the sentence. Try rewording your sentence or adding a phrase at the end.

| **Instead of saying** | **Say** |
|---|---|
| *Who do I report to?* | (formally) *To whom should I report* or *Who should I see?* or *Who is the best person to see when I arrive?* |

| | |
|---|---|
| *It's something you'll get used to* | *You'll soon get used to it.* |
| *He owned nothing to speak of* | *He owned very little.* |
| *Which room are you in?* | (formally) *In which room are you?* or<br>*Where is your room?* or<br>*Which room is yours?* |

You may like to know that several word wizards have objected to the rule about never ending a sentence with a preposition. According to the *Guinness Book of Records*, the longest sentence containing prepositions was one spoken by a boy whose father had chosen for bedtime reading his least favourite book – one on Australia. When the boy saw the book he exclaimed: 'What did you bring that book, that I don't want to be read to from out of about Down Under, up for?'

Winston Churchill similarly showed his disdain when one of his books was edited clumsily to remove such a sentence. He allegedly scribbled on the manuscript: 'This is the sort of English up with which I will not put.'

Today, the main rule is to write a 'natural' sentence, but if you can avoid 'odd' prepositional endings, it is usually better to do so.

## Test your skills

Reword each of the following sentences so that it is more acceptable in a letter or memo, and/or correct English.

**1** What do you want another copy of the manual for?
**2** We fell out with those suppliers and broke off the agreement.
**3** I agreed to Harry's suggestion and fell in with his idea.
**4** I was disappointed in Brenda's performance last week.
**5** I get on with all my colleagues.
**6** We came out of that dispute very well.
**7** Please let me know who you spoke to.

**DON'T YOU DARE!**

*...say (or write) 'different than', eg Your accent is different than mine. This is incorrect.*

*In formal English it is often considered better to use the phrase 'different from', although when we talk we often say 'different to', eg*

*Your way of working is different from mine. (Formal)*
*You do that a different way to me. (Informal)*

Communications become more complex and difficult to write when

**a** you have a great deal of information to include,

**b** they deal with difficult or sensitive issues.

In the first case you have the task of organising all the information so that it is included logically and nothing is omitted. In the second case you have to be particularly careful about the way in which you phrase your communication, so that you do not cause offence or disclose confidential information by mistake. When you have to think about both at once, it may take you several attempts before your final draft is acceptable.

In this book you have learned all the skills you need to be able to cope with these situations, but it is helpful to review the issues you must consider.

**1** Deal with the content *first*. If you have a large amount of information to include then either highlight the key points or list these.

**2** Double check you have not omitted anything.

**3** Decide upon the structure of your communication – the beginning (which must include an introduction to the topic), the middle (which has the main body of information within it) and an appropriate ending.

**4** Be prepared to sub-divide your middle section into different paragraphs or use numbered points for clarity. If the information is very long and complex then separate sub-headings may be necessary.

**5** Group your information into your chosen sections.

**6** Order your information logically within each section.

Now decide whether there are any particularly contentious, difficult or sensitive aspects you must consider. These may relate to:

- the recipient – eg his/her frame of mind, previous knowledge, possible reactions to the information
- the information itself – eg if anything is confidential or too technical to be included in its present form
- the reason for writing – in particular, what you are trying to achieve?

## A worked example – complex content

Tim Gregson is Marketing Director of Imagine Software plc. He is due to leave on a business trip to the United States with Bill Sutton, the MD, tomorrow morning. He receives an urgent call from the MD's Personal Assistant, Alison Moores. She has just noticed that Bill was booked to give a presentation at a business seminar in Birmingham next week. As neither Bill nor Tim will be able to attend the seminar, she askes Tim to find someone else who can do it instead – the MD doesn't want the slot given to one of their competitors, and has suggested Tim's deputy might enjoy the challenge. Alison agrees to e-mail the details. Tim, meanwhile, is left with the task of finding and briefing a stand-in. To his dismay, Sarah Trimble, his deputy, is out of the office all day. It is at this point he calls you into his office and gives you the background information.

*'I suggest you write a memo to Sarah – mark it urgent – she can clarify any further details with yourself or Alison Moores. Stress to Sarah that the MD asked for her personally and has great confidence in her ability to do a good job – that should encourage her. The e-mail gives the details of times*

*and so on, but I've also got Bill's scribbled notes here about what he wanted to say. She'll never read all these – but basically they cover the main issues you can put in the memo. First, he wanted to focus on the problems firms have had with the 'millennium bug' – the fact that many organisations had to spend thousands of pounds upgrading their computers to cope with the year 2000. He then wanted to lead into the fact that this is because there is a distinct lack of planning in many organisations – firms blindly react rather than plan systematically. Planning relates to forecasting – finding out what the future is likely to hold and then working out what to do about it. Also, considering investment costs, what equipment will need replacing, what new products are on the market. This will lead to the final section of the talk on our new software product – PlanWare – which enables firms to forecast and plan more easily – not just IT requirements but for all aspects of their organisation. There's all the literature on PlanWare in the marketing cupboard, plus some glossy posters. Tell Alison to help herself. She may also be able to use the OHTs that Jim Barnes prepared for the sales seminar on PlanWare last month. Otherwise, if she needs one or two more, can you please help her. Tell Alison to confirm with the organisers that Sarah will be attending in Bill's place, so they get the name right on the programme. She'd better ring them so that she can clarify any other points with them about the equipment available for visual aids, etc. Alison has put the name of the organisers on the e-mail and the contact name and phone number. Finally, you'd better give a copy to both myself and Bill of the memo.'*

```
From:      Alison Moores
To:        Tim Gregson
Date:      Tuesday, 16 June 199-
Subject:   Business Seminar, Birmingham

The seminar is at the Imperial Hotel, Birmingham
on Thursday, 25 June. It has been organised by the
Midlands Computer Federation. The contact name is
Mohammed Raza at 15 Queensway Street, Birmingham
B2 4DP - tel 0121-398-3939, fax 0121-398-2008.
He's on e-mail too - mohammed@comfed.co.uk.

The seminar lasts all day - Bill's slot is 11 am
until 12 noon (lunch). He was driving there in the
morning and then driving back after lunch.
However, if Sarah wants to stay overnight the
evening before then I can arrange this - ask her
to let me know. The focus of the seminar is IT in
the Millennium, and Bill's slot is entitled
Planning for Success. Hope this helps.

Alison
```

***Figure 15.5*** *E-mail from the MD's PA*

## POINTS TO NOTE

**1** A copy of the e-mail from Alison is shown in Figure 15.5. Read this carefully.

**2** The memo needs to be written in six sections:

- **a** introduction and background to the request
- **b** basic details about the seminar
- **c** the MD's ideas for the talk
- **d** additional details and information (eg relating to literature and assistance)
- **e** further action required
- **f** closing paragraph.

Using each of these sections as headings, note down the information you would include in each one from Tim's instructions and from the e-mail. Check your ideas with the suggested outline shown in Figure 15.6 on page 280.

**3** Draft out the memo required from the original documents, but following the outline in your notes. A useful hint: often, when you are given complex instructions in writing, you can copy some of the statements and wording used. Just make sure that your tenses agree throughout!

**4** Check that your memo broadly agrees with the example shown in Figure 15.7 on page 280. If it varies substantially, check whether this is because you omitted anything or you simply changed the order of the information. As long as your order is logical and your memo is courteous and 'flows', this is acceptable. As a final check, discuss your completed work with your tutor. One further point – whether you refer to senior staff by their first names, their full name or their formal titles will depend upon the organisation and your own status within it. In the example shown, informal styles are used for all staff except for the MD, but this is a suggested style only.

## A worked example – sensitive content

Tim Gregson has one more request for you before he leaves. This one is much shorter but concerns a potential problem with a customer. The information he gives you is as follows:

*I need you to write a letter to Jane Ireland, Technical Manager, Imaging Solutions Ltd, 14 Derby Road, Linchester, LC4 3WM. The situation is complicated. Clive Webster has spotted a problem with our DeltaWare accounting software when it's installed on certain machines – the type they have at Imaging Solutions. Jane hasn't mentioned any difficulties, but Clive thinks it may not be noticeable until they reach their financial year-end. Basically, I want to call and chat to Jane when I get back – though she may wonder why. The best thing may be to say that I'm in the area at the end of next month, and would like to talk to her. Time to suit her – I don't want her saying she's too busy to see me. You could mention that a free upgrade to certain products she has installed has just become available. This may interest her and I can bring details. Tell her my schedule that week is fairly flexible. I would telephone to follow up the letter myself but I shall be abroad – could you do this for me, please? The main thing is to get the appointment – I don't want her to find out about the problem before I've talked to her, so don't mention anything about it in the letter. Incidentally, start it 'Dear Jane' and end it 'Kind regards/Yours sincerely' will you? Thanks.*

### POINTS TO NOTE

1 In this situation Tim has made it clear what you should include in the letter and what you should not. As a brief check for yourself, make a list of the points you *are* allowed to mention.

2 Tim has also been helpful in suggesting possible ways to obtain the appointment. In real life you may be asked to suggest these yourself! Also, your boss may not be so explicit about what you can mention, and you may have to use your own judgement on occasion. In this situation *always* check if you are unsure. Now put the points you have listed in a logical order.

3 Draft your letter, using a suitable tone and style. As you have to be careful not to say too much, it is sensible to keep your letter relatively short. As a group, you may wish to suggest how you should phrase the letter.

4 Check your finished work with the suggested version in Figure 15.8 on page 281 and with your tutor. Then, as a group, discuss the best technique you could use when you make the telephone call. It may be good practice to role play this – with your tutor (or a partner) in the role of Jane Ireland.

1 Introduction and background to the request

- MD booked for seminar – now has to visit US
- Has personally asked for Sarah to take over – has confidence in her ability to do a good job

2 Basic details about the seminar (see e-mail)

- Where and when held
- Seminar and talk titles

3 MD's ideas for talk

- Problems of the millennium bug caused by lack of planning
- Links to general lack of planning in organisations
- Planning and forecasting linked – find out what future may hold then work out plan
- Includes considering investment costs and replacing equipment
- Includes finding out what products are on the market
- New software product – PlanWare – designed to assist all aspects of planning

4 Additional details and information

- Literature on PlanWare + posters available
- Jim Barnes' OHTs may be suitable
- I can prepare more, if required

5 Action to be taken

- Contact organisers and state replacement/check equipment
- Alison will book accommodation previous evening if required

6 Closing paragraph

- If any further help and assistance required, let me know.

***Figure 15.6*** *Suggested outline of memo*

## MEMO

**TO** Sarah Trimble cc Bill Sutton, Tim Gregson

**FROM** (you)

**DATE** 16 June 199-

**URGENT – BUSINESS SEMINAR, BIRMINGHAM, 25 JUNE**

As you may be aware, both Bill Sutton and Tim Gregson are leaving for the States tomorrow. Unfortunately, Mr Sutton has just found that he had agreed to give a talk at a business seminar in Birmingham next Thursday, and has specifically asked if you could stand in for him at this event as he considers you have the ability to do it well, and may even enjoy the challenge! He appreciates that he is asking you to do this at the last minute and hopes you find the following information helpful.

The seminar has been organised by the Midlands Computer Federation and will be held at the Imperial Hotel, Birmingham. It is a one-day event entitled 'IT in the Millennium'. Mr Sutton's slot is at 11 am and he is scheduled to speak for one hour. The title of his talk is 'Planning for Success'.

He has drafted several ideas for his talk, which are listed below:

1 He proposed to start by talking about the problems of the millennium bug, explaining that many of these had been caused by a lack of planning. This resulted in organisations spending thousands of pounds to upgrade their computers to cope with the year 2000.

2 He then intended to lead into the fact that there is a distinct lack of planning in many organisations. In many cases firms blindly react to situations rather than systematically plan for the future.

1 of 2

3 He then wanted to discuss how planning relates to forecasting – finding out what the future may hold and then working out the plan.

4 In many cases this includes considering investments costs and deciding what equipment will need replacing.

5 In addition, it is important to find out what new products are on the market and how they might help.

6 The final section of the talk was to be focused upon our new PlanWare software which enables firms to forecast and plan more easily – not just for IT requirements but for all aspects of the organisation.

I understand that there is a stock of literature on PlanWare in the marketing cupboard plus some glossy posters and other materials. You are free to take as much as you require. Tim Gregson suggested that you may be able to use the OHTs that Jim Barnes prepared for the sales seminar on PlanWare last month. However, if you need any new ones I will be pleased to help you.

Tim also suggested that you should contact the organisers to state that you are replacing Mr Sutton so that the programmes can be changed. You may also wish to check what equipment will be available for visual aids. The contact name and address is Mohammed Raza, Midlands Computer Federation, 15 Queensway Street, Birmingham, B2 4DP. Tel: 0121–398–3939. Fax: 0121–398–2008. E-mail address is mohammed@comfed.co.uk.

Finally, I understand that Mr Sutton intended to drive to Birmingham that morning and return after lunch. If you wish to travel down the previous day and would like accommodation to be arranged, Alison Moores will be happy to arrange this for you.

If you require any further assistance please let me know.

2 of 2

***Figure 15.7*** *Example of the finished memo to Sarah*

16 June 199-

Ms Jane Ireland
Technical Manager
Imaging Solutions Ltd
14 Derby Road
LINCHESTER
LC4 3WM

Dear Jane

I find that I will be in your area during the last week of July – with a fairly flexible schedule. As several free upgrades have just become available for certain products you have installed, I thought you may be interested in the details. I will be pleased to call at any time to suit you.

Unfortunately, I will not be able to confirm the exact appointment with you personally as I am leaving for the States tomorrow. However, in the meantime, I have asked my assistant, (*your name*), to telephone you to agree a convenient date and time.

I look forward to seeing you again.

Kind regards

Yours sincerely

Tim Gregson
Marketing Director

***Figure 15.8*** *A suggested version of the letter to Jane Ireland*

## SPELLCHECKER 14

### – one letter or two?

Frequently words are misspelled when an 'ending' has to be added and the writer is unsure whether any letters are then doubled or not (eg *shop/shopping* but *install/instalment*.)

Check that you would have no difficulties with each of the following. Check also that you would spell the root (basic) word correctly in each case.

| **Double the consonant** | **Do not double the consonant** |
|---|---|
| appal/appalling | benefit/benefited |
| begin/beginning | budget/budgeted |
| control/controlled | centre/centred/centring |
| deter/deterrent | enrol/enrolment |
| enthral/enthralled | focus/focused |
| input/inputting | install/instalment |
| level/levelled | offer/offered |
| omit/omitted | relax/relaxing |
| quarrel/quarrelling | rivet/riveting |
| remit/remittance | target/targeted |
| travel/travelled | market/marketing |

# TOOLS OF THE TRADE – *figuratively speaking*

The Word Wizards in this book have already shown you that some people can use words expertly. Whilst this is a skill that is normally achieved only over time, certain 'tools' can be used to help you to express your thoughts and ideas well. Some of these you have met already. In Unit 1 you learned about synonyms and antonyms. You have learned about colloquialisms, slang, cliches and jargon. You have seen how advertisers can use alliteration for effect (see Unit 3). Hyperbole (over-exaggeration) was mentioned in Unit 10. These are not the only ways in which you can express ideas. This section concentrates on other techniques used by writers to put forward their ideas.

## Analogies and similes

An analogy is when a writer draws a parallel between his or her own idea and something else which is, in all other respects, dissimilar. A simile is a figure of speech that compares one thing with another. In both cases we are looking at words and ideas being used in a comparative sense.

Examples of similes include: *as cunning as a fox, as busy as a bee, as fast as light*. Many similes are little more than clichés and are used only in informal conversations.

An analogy can be used to illustrate an idea very effectively, because it gives the reader a comparison. This can be used to help understanding or to add wit and humour to a situation. An example should help you to understand the concept more easily.

Many years ago a sociologist called Ernest Goffman compared our social skills to learning the lines in a lifelong play. In his view, we learn to play various 'parts', depending upon our 'roles'. Therefore, when you are in the role of son or daughter you act and speak in a different way than when you are in the role of 'friend on a good night out' or 'employee who can be trusted to be responsible and adult'. Speaking the wrong 'lines' in a situation can be disastrous. Goffman was not the first to make this type of comparison – William Shakespeare wrote *'All the world's a stage, and all the men and women merely players . . .'* in *As You Like It*.

## Euphemisms

We all use euphemisms – although we may not be aware that we are doing so. A euphemism is a word or phrase that is substituted for an expression that is unacceptable because it is distasteful, cruel or stark. Subject areas where euphemisms abound are toilets, ill health and death. In these cases people prefer to use a roundabout expression instead of being blunt, eg instead of saying *'I am going to the toilet (or lavatory)'* they say *'May I use the bathroom?'* or *'I think a comfort break would be welcome'* – and many others.

Rather than saying *'He died'* or *'He is dying'* we say *'He passed away'* or *'He's not expected to be with us long.'*

Rather than saying they are making half the workforce redundant, managers will use expressions such as *'downsizing', 'restructuring', 'slimming down'* and *'rationalisation'*.

## Idiomatic expressions

An idiom is an expression that cannot be understood literally – it therefore causes considerable consternation if you use an idiomatic expression when you are talking to a foreigner. Examples include: *'the grass is greener on the other side', 'he's a dark horse', 'the straw that breaks the camel's back', 'let the cat out of the bag'* – and dozens of others.

## Metaphorical expressions

Whereas a simile is a comparison, a metaphor is better described as imaginative substitution. A modern example is *'glass ceiling'*. Ceilings aren't made of glass but they do prevent people moving higher. The word 'glass' suggests an invisible barrier.

There are different types of metaphors. A **dead metaphor** is one that is so common it is accepted as a routine part of the language, and the origin is no longer considered, eg *'the bottleneck is caused by that machine'*. Other metaphors are used by imaginative writers to create a new image, eg *'he's our golden boy', 'the Tiger economies'*.

Sometimes you may find a metaphor you don't understand! Many people were perplexed when they first read about a computer (or printer) 'footprint'. This metaphor has been invented to describe the space taken up by the machine.

## Puns

A pun is a play on words. Used selectively and cleverly a good pun can be very funny. Over-used, the technique rapidly loses its appeal. You will find puns in many situations:

- in newspaper headlines: *Off the rails* (an article on problems experienced by Railtrack), *High rollers* (an article on a bid to buy Rolls Royce)
- on notices: *We dispense with accuracy* (chemists), *Our business is developing* (photographer's shop)
- in general conversation and 'one-liners', eg *a committee is a group that takes minutes and wastes hours.*

**DON'T YOU DARE!**

*... mix your metaphors. A mixed metaphor is when two (or more) inconsistent metaphors are crammed together, eg 'She'll be flogging a dead horse if she keeps burying her head in the sand' or 'He's gone over the top exploring every avenue.' They normally cause a certain amount of mirth!*

## Test your understanding

Identify whether each of the following is an analogy, simile, euphemism, idiom, metaphor, mixed metaphor, or pun. To help, there is one of each!

**1** He went as red as a beetroot when Paula entered the room.
**2** She has a reputation for being rather light-fingered and economical with the truth.
**3** Mr Brown caused a storm in a teacup by barking up the wrong tree.
**4** Oil drillers have a boring occupation.
**5** Jenkins scored a hat trick in the game last Saturday.
**6** Learning to write effective communications is rather like driving a car. The handbook alone never works – you need to practise, practise, practise.
**7** 'I'll sit between you,' she said to her uncles, 'A rose between two thorns.'

## WORDBANK 12

The ending 'ly' is an example of a suffix. A suffix is the opposite of a prefix, which you first met in Unit 4. It is a group of letters giving a particular ending to a word. In the same way as a prefix can help to give you the meaning of a word, so can a suffix. For example:

| | | |
|---|---|---|
| **-arch/archy** | = | head or chief, eg monarchy (rule by a monarch), oligarchy (rule by a few powerful people) |
| **-cide** | = | killing, eg infanticide (killing an infant), suicide, insecticide |
| **-gon** | = | angle, eg polygon (many angles), pentagon (five angles) |
| **-graph/gram** | = | written, eg diagram, pictogram, autograph |
| **-less** | = | absence of something, eg fearless (no fear), harmless (no harm) |
| **-naut** | = | traveller, eg astronaut, argonaut. An exception is juggernaut which comes from the Hindu word for massive. |
| **-ocracy** | = | a form of government, eg aristocracy, bureaucracy |
| **-oid** | = | resembling something, eg humanoid, spheroid |
| **-ology** | = | the study of something, eg astrology, sociology |

| | | |
|---|---|---|
| **-phile** | = | love, eg Anglophile, bibliophile |
| **-phobia** | = | fear, eg claustrophobia, arachnophobia |
| **-phone** | = | sound or voice, eg megaphone, telephone |
| **-scape** | = | like a picture, eg seascape, moonscape |
| **-meter** | = | a measure, eg barometer, speedometer, milometer |
| **-ware** | = | a manufactured item, eg earthenware, silverware |

## Test your understanding

Many new words are added to our language by the addition of a suffix, eg journalese, stress-free, user-friendly, streetwise.

From these examples, and those shown above, can you identify the word for each of the following from the list alongside:

**1** the language used by computers
**2** fear of open spaces
**3** having no friends
**4** a form of government where the people or their representatives rule
**5** a device to measure temperature
**6** the study of the weather
**7** someone who loves books
**8** an object that resembles a cube
**9** a manufactured computer program.

**a** bibliophile
**b** thermometer
**c** cuboid
**d** democracy
**e** computer-speak
**f** software
**g** friendless
**h** agoraphobia
**i** meteorology

## POLISH YOUR PUNCTUATION
### Miscellaneous punctuation marks and other devices

With a number of punctuation marks, you may hear the names mentioned, or see them used, without realising exactly which term relates to which sign or mark. The list below includes both English marks and some common foreign ones that you may be expected to use. It also revises some of the more unusual terms you have met earlier in this book:

Acute accent (´) This mark is used over letters in some languages to denote the letter must be pronounced. In particular, it is often used over a final 'e' which must be pronounced 'ay', eg paté, resumé.

Ampersand (&) The & key is correctly used only in names of firms, such as Potter & Keys Ltd. It should *never* be used to replace the word 'and' in normal text.

Asterisk (*) This symbol usually indicates a footnote (see Unit 12). Alternatives are a dagger (†) and double dagger (‡).

Backslash (\) This mark slopes from left to right. See also slash or oblique. The backslash is commonly used in computer commands, eg c:\ or http:\.

Caret (‸) This is a mark used in a manuscript or draft typescript to indicate that letters or words must be inserted.

| | |
|---|---|
| Cedilla (ç) | A sign under a 'c' in French words indicates the 'c' is soft (pronounced 's') and not hard, eg garçon. |
| Ellipsis (...) | This is a series of full stops used to indicate an omission of a word or several words (see Unit 1). |
| Emboldening | **Bold** type is often used for important words or special terms. |
| Grave accent (`) | This sign is placed over a letter in some languages to indicate the pronunciation, eg à la carte. |
| Hash (#) | Used in computer programs, this symbol also often indicates a number, eg '#5' rather than 'version 5'. |
| Italics | A sloping type face is usually used to imply *emphasis*. |
| Parentheses | This is a term sometimes used for round brackets. These were discussed in Unit 3. |
| Period | This is the American term for a full stop. |
| Slash (/) | This term is often used for an **oblique** or mark that slopes from right to left. Examples of its use include:<br>■ to indicate alternatives, eg *You will need a certificate and/or exemption form*<br>■ to indicate time periods, eg *The accounts for 1998/9 are enclosed*<br>■ in some abbreviations, eg a/c = account, c/o = care of. However, these should never be used in formal written communications, where the word should be shown in full.<br>Be careful not to confuse the slash and the backslash in computer commands – particularly if both are used. |
| Tilde (~) | This mark is placed over a letter in some Spanish words to indicate a particular nasal sound, eg mañana. |
| Umlaut (ü) | Sometimes called a diaeresis, this is a mark of two dots above a vowel to indicate that the vowel is sounded separately, eg Zoë or naïve. |
| Virgule | This is the American term for a slash or oblique. |

## Test your understanding

Select any *six* of the punctuation signs above and write a sentence clearly illustrating its correct usage.

# COMMUNICATION IN PRACTICE

## Test your skills

**1** The following are all modern words and phrases. In each case give the meaning and then say if the term could be used in formal business communications. Compare your answers with other members of your group.

- **a** photo opportunity
- **b** couch potato
- **c** on a roll
- **d** brownie points
- **e** computer virus
- **f** brainchild
- **g** lifestyle
- **h** infrastructure
- **i** backlash
- **j** whole new ball game
- **k** interface
- **l** ecosystem

**2** Newspapers had a field day when Silentnight, the bed manufacturer, bought the company Rest Assured, another bed company for £3 million.

**a** From the brief extract below, how many figures of speech can you identify?

**b** Now try your hand at writing two or three paragraphs yourself in the same style. Compare your efforts as a group. Do note that they should all be fit for publication!

**Two in a bed and the little one said £3 million!**

*The business world awoke to the news yesterday that two Northern firms had decided to bed down together from now on. The magnificent four-poster of a firm Silentnight announced its intentions to cement its relationship with Rest Assured – a mere bunk bed or even sleeping bag in comparison.*

**3** Joan Parkinson is a long-standing customer of Hightown Garden Centre. She retired several years ago and has always paid her bills regularly, although now she is getting older she sometimes becomes forgetful. Your boss, Alan Hammond, has pointed out that she still has not paid her last three bills – dating back over three months. He has telephoned her twice, but thinks she forgets afterwards. He doesn't want to be cruel, but obviously the firm cannot continue to supply her with plants unless she pays for them. Alan has asked you to write to her in the hope that a letter will have more effect – but has asked you to word it carefully. She is 'Miss Parkinson' and doesn't like modern terms such as 'Ms'. She lives at 112 Cedar Road, Hightown, HG3 2DN. Draft a letter for Alan to sign.

**4** Identify and correct the error(s) in each of the following sentences.

**a** His resume was sent to Senor Cuidad yesterday at his box number c\o Mahon Newspapers.
**b** It is appaling how little he has learned from the expereince.
**c** Targett marketting is the vision of the future acording to the sales manager.
**d** Your hair is a different colour than mine.
**e** I wish to see you only about this, and no-one else.
**f** I am annoyed at Bill for voluntering me for this job.
**g** To make sure you are sitting properly, check your own posture or ask a co-worker to.

## Apply your skills

Although you helped out only once or twice at Hightown Garden Centre Ltd, spring is approaching, which means increased business, and Alan Hammond has asked if you will work for a week or two for them. The Garden Centre has grown considerably over the past few years and several new staff have been employed to help. Two years ago Alan

Hammond introduced a mail-order side to the business, which has been extremely successful. He now has several staff permanently employed receiving and processing phone orders. To improve matters he has decided to introduce a computerised system of orders and stock control so that the staff can enter the details on computer immediately and check if items are available. He has also introduced a new e-mail system to reduce the number of memos.

Today Alan has called you into his office to discuss the tasks he wants you to carry out. The documents to which he refers are shown in Figures 15.9 and 15.10.

*I'm very concerned that we're not up to speed on health and safety issues as they relate to computers. Can you look into this for me and produce a report with a few recommendations about what we need to be doing? You'd better make it fairly formal – I'd like to present it to the Board of Directors when we meet next Thursday, and some of them are fairly fussy. If I want more money to be allocated I need their support.*

*You may wish to research this yourself, but if it's any help I've a paper which might help you. You'll also need to look around and talk to the staff who are using the computers. Have a word with Fred, too, will you. Don't make the report too long – a couple of pages at the most – and you'd better use the standard headings.*

*I'm also a bit worried about staff attitudes to e-mail. I spotted one sent by Fred Jenkins to one of his staff really ripping her off for a minor mistake, which just won't do. I've also got a feeling that new lad – Brian – has been chatting up Claire by e-mail, but obviously neither will own up to it. A friend of mine has given me an article on e-mail usage that could be useful. Not all of it is relevant. We don't have the Internet here – our system is small and internal – so you can ignore references to external users and things like encryption. However, I think you should mention the password bit – which is important whether the system is internal or external. Please summarise the main points in a notice we could put on the staff noticeboard.*

**COMPUTER SAFETY IN THE WORKPLACE**

The use of computers in the workplace is largely covered by the Health and Safety at Work Act and related regulations, particularly The Provision and Use of Work Equipment Regulations 1992 and The Display Screen Equipment (DSE) Regulations 1992.

The following issues are particularly important:

- All workstations must meet the minimum requirements specified for display screen equipment. All furniture and software must also meet certain standards. For instance, display screens must have a stable image, be capable of being tilted and swivelled,and have characters of a reasonable size. There must be no reflective glare.
- Keyboards must be tiltable and separate from the screen. There should be a rest space on the desk in front of the keyboard.
- Work surfaces must be sufficiently large and of a low reflective finish. The equipment must be moveable to suit the needs of the user.
- Work chairs must allow easy movement and a comfortable position. The seat height must be adjustable and seat back tiltable to give good back support. Foot rests must be provided on request.
- There should be satisfactory lighting but as little glare as possible. Windows should have blinds and workstations should be positioned to avoid reflection.
- Training must be given on the software and systems used to minimise stress.
- Activities should be planned so that users have regular breaks during the day. It is illegal for operators to work continuously at a computer all day.
- On request, an eye examination must be offered for those who use a VDU for more than one hour a day. Special spectacles must be provided if the test shows that these are required.
- All users should receive health and safety training relating to their equipment to minimise the risk of repetitive strain injury (upper limb disorders).

***Figure 15.9*** *A paper on health and safety relating to computers*

*On that issue, send a short memo to Brian Griffiths and to Fred Jenkins for me, telling them to stop abusing the system. You'll have to be careful what you say – just say we are concerned about recent attitudes to e-mail and that they may find the attached information helpful, and attach a copy of your notice to each memo.*

**THE DO'S AND DONT'S OF E-MAIL**

Recently, Norwich Union was sued for libel in respect of an ill-written internal e-mail. This cost the company £450,000 in damages. For this reason, if no other, it is important for organisations to have in place clear guidelines to govern the use of e-mail.

1 E-mail is virtually instantaneous and senders therefore expect a rapid response. **For that reason all users should check their e-mail regularly.** If there is no time to respond in full, a brief acknowledgement should be sent.

2 E-mail is much less formal than conventional letters and faxes. The odd spelling mistake, typographical or grammatical error may be forgiven more readily. However, this is no excuse for users not checking their e-mail before transmission.

3 Some users like to use abbreviations or other devices to keep the e-mail as brief as possible. This is useless if the meaning is then not understood by the recipient. It is also possible to offend people if the e-mail is too terse or 'sharp'. By and large, it is better to think of e-mail as just another communications medium, which must follow normal conventions.

4 Most e-mail systems automatically print the name of the sender at the top. **Never send an e-mail as someone else** (eg by using his or her mailbox facility).

5 There is no need for Dear . . . . . or for Yours sincerely (some people type Y/S), but if you are writing to a stranger it is recommended you include your full name, organisation, department and job title if appropriate.

6 E-mail is poor at conveying humour, which is often misinterpreted as sarcasm. Some users include smiley faces such as ☺, or marker words surrounded by asterisks such as * JOKE * to convey humorous intent. This technique is not to be recommended for business e-mails.

7 Whereas some disagreements may be expressed over e-mail, users must be careful they cannot be accused of harassment or intimidation. Abusive e-mails are known as 'flames' and should be avoided. Flames sent deliberately by senior and middle managers to junior staff should be subject to disciplinary action.

8 The law of copyright means that users must be careful what they include in an e-mail. Confidential information should not normally be transmitted by this means.

9 Security aspects are very important. Files from external sources should be checked for viruses. All users should be careful never to disclose their password to any e-mail correspondent, no matter who they claim to be. If someone asks for a password and is entitled to know it then that person should already have the means to find it out!

10 Most e-mail systems allow a reply to be sent that includes the original message. This can become a problem where messages and replies continue over a period of time. It is sensible to quote only the relevant part of the message when replying.

11 Junk e-mail is known as 'scamming'. It is much resented. Management should be informed if any external sites start to transmit junk e-mail to the site.

12 An important limitation of e-mail is lack of security unless messages are encrypted. Encryption utilities are readily available, and can be installed on most systems.

***Figure 15.10*** *An article on e-mail usage*

**Personal observations on computer systems**

1 Equipment and workstations all new. Documents show that systems conform to new regulations.

2 One workstation has not yet been delivered – computer is on a table and user sitting in ordinary chair. User complains regularly of backache. Supplier says problem with order is our fault – order was completed incorrectly. Documents support this claim.

3 No blinds at windows and walls painted white. This creates glare on screens.

4 No foot rests.

**Interviews with staff**

1 None has received any health and safety training and none knew about eye tests or foot rests.

2 Staff recommended to Fred reorganisation of furniture and asked for blinds at windows several weeks ago. Both would improve matters. Nothing has been decided, as yet.

3 Fred is said to get annoyed if they take a break – apart from normal coffee breaks.

**Interview with Fred**

1 Fred had no knowledge that there were legal requirements in relation to computer usage. He says he is concerned with the quantity of work at present and whilst the computers have helped, there has been a problem coping with the new system and all the orders at the same time.

2 He says the problem has been made worse by staff absences, but appreciates these may have been caused because they are more stressed.

3 He will build in suitable rest breaks from now on, but thinks this could result in orders not being processed as quickly.

***Figure 15.11*** *Your notes on the computer system*

*Finally, I noticed that new girl – Joanne Evans – was late again, for the third day on the trot. I've had a word with Mary Jenkins, her supervisor, but no-one knows of any personal problems affecting Joanne. Just write a short memo please, saying I've noticed the problem and obviously it won't do. If she wants to see me to talk about the situation then that's fine – but unless there's a very good reason I'll expect an immediate improvement. Thanks.*

After talking to Alan about some general issues you decide to walk around the office area to talk to staff working on the computers and to make some observations yourself. Your notes are shown in Figure 15.11. Prepare the five documents Alan requires.

*WORD WIZARD*

## New words for old

The technical name for new words is 'neologism'. This refers to an old word used in a new way or a completely new word.

### OLD WORDS – NEW WAYS

How many 'old words in phrases' can you identify in the following? Can you give both the old and new meanings, and say to what the writer is referring?

> Apparently I need a new chip before I can get on the Web or access the Net. At present I am short of memory. The last time I tried to install a program my system crashed before I had saved my files and I was locked out. I tried to quit using my mouse but a virus had wiped my back-up. Even the menu was down. None of my keys will work and I can't use Windows at all.

### NEW WORDS

Every year a number of completely new words enter our vocabulary. From all the words and dates given below, try to guess when each was 'officially' recognised in the major dictionaries. Answers are given on page 314.

| Word | Dates |
|---|---|
| VAT | 1988 |
| Information Superhighway | 1996 |
| Television | 1973 |
| Radar | 1971 |
| Lager lout | 1926 |
| Walkman | 1911 |
| World Wide Web | 1936 |
| Alcopop | 1959 |
| Air raid | 1953 |
| Hovercraft | 1960 |
| Rock 'n' roll | 1981 |
| Teddy bear | 1941 |
| Robot | 1902 |
| Mickey Mouse | 1994 |
| Bikini | 1995 |
| Silicon chip | 1986 |
| Workaholic | 1920 |
| Laser | 1993 |
| Mexican wave | 1958 |
| Road rage | 1946 |

# 16

UNIT

## IN THE SPOTLIGHT – APPLYING FOR A JOB

Whether you are applying for your first job or your tenth, applying to a new organisation or wishing for promotion with your existing employers, the process of preparing an application and attending an interview brings together virtually all of your communication skills:

- your ability to write an effective letter of application
- your ability to summarise your achievements in your CV
- your ability to complete an application form neatly, accurately and appropriately
- your ability to listen, respond and interact with an interviewer.

For most people this is a nerve-wracking experience. It can also be an elating or depressing one, depending upon the outcome. This unit has been designed to enhance your skills in all of these areas and to improve your prospects of being the successful candidate.

## FINDING AN APPROPRIATE JOB

Once you are employed, you will spend many hours of your life at work. It is therefore important that you think carefully about the job you want to do. After all, no-one wants to spend the greater part of their waking time feeling unhappy. If you have any worries about your future career or job prospects, seek expert careers guidance and counselling – either through your college or by visiting your Careers Office or Job Centre. Make an interview with a careers adviser, who will discuss your options with you.

Be realistic about your first job after completing a course of study. Although you may have achieved several qualifications, to an employer you still have to prove yourself. If you are too ambitious, you may find yourself having to cope with many rejections, and this can make you dispirited. An old maxim is that it is always easier to find a job once you already have one! Remember this and be prepared to take an appropriate (rather than ideal) job to gain experience and then move on.

There are several ways in which you can find out about suitable jobs.

- Read the papers – this means buying local and national papers that contain job advertisements. Often there is a specific day or night for advertising certain types of jobs, which means you don't have to buy a paper every day.
- Ask friends and relatives about vacancies in organisations where they are employed. Often, employees learn about vacancies first from the firm's noticeboard.
- Visit the Careers Office or Job Centre and read the noticeboards. Ask for further details if there are any jobs in which you are interested.
- Visit a local recruitment or employment agency. These usually have both permanent and temporary vacancies. Note that there is no charge to the client, but some are more ethical than others. Don't be persuaded by one of their recruitment consultants into applying for any job if you don't like the sound of it. Equally, don't be put off if you are asked to undertake a skills assessment of some kind – the more reputable agencies often ask for this. They can then match candidates more precisely to suitable vacancies.
- Surf the Net. More and more organisations and agencies are advertising vacancies. In addition, several people now put their CVs on the Net in the hope that an organisation will contact them.
- If you are particularly keen to work for one type of organisation or industry, you could write an unsolicited (look up this word!) letter telling them about yourself. If your letter is good enough, you may be contacted later if there is a suitable vacancy. However, be aware that some organisations – particularly in the media – receive thousands of unsolicited letters each year. Another technique is to write to these companies asking them about the qualifications you should obtain to be eligible for a particular type of job. Then set about achieving them before you write again!

## Job advertisements, job descriptions and person specifications

When you first open a newspaper full of advertisements, scan the job section to see if there is anything of interest. If you find an interesting advertisement you need to read it carefully to see how well you are likely to fit the job, and think about how well the job (and the organisation) are likely to fit you.

You will find that many advertisements distinguish between attributes that are **essential** and those that are **desirable** – although the advertisement may not use these words. Synonyms for 'essential' include expressions such as 'must have', 'must possess' or 'will be expected to have'. If you cannot match the essential criteria, it is unlikely you will be offered an interview. Desirable requirements are more flexible. Synonyms here include 'would be an advantage', 'would be useful' or 'special consideration will be given to candidates who have'.

To understand these terms it is useful to know a little about what happens in an organisation when a vacancy occurs. Many organisations first prepare two documents – **the job description** and **the person specification**. The job description is a brief description of the responsibilities and the duties of the position. It also often gives information such as working hours. It does not

**JOB DESCRIPTION**

| | |
|---|---|
| **TITLE** | Customer Assistant |
| **DEPARTMENT** | Housing |
| **HOURS OF WORK** | 37 per week – flexitime |
| **RESPONSIBLE TO** | Housing Care Manager |
| **RESPONSIBLE FOR** | N/A |
| **JOB SUMMARY** | To provide support for Housing Management Team in dealing with customer enquiries and liaising with support services. |

**DUTIES**

1 Attend to customers and callers both face-to-face and over the telephone.

2 Log requests for housing repairs on computer system and check/instigate follow-up procedures as required.

3 Provide and despatch information on current lettings to enquirers.

4 Provide and despatch information on rent enquiries and liaise with rent officers as required.

5 Provide and despatch information on grants and other forms of financial assistance to enquirers.

6 Deal with all other tenancy enquiries as required.

7 Maintain computer database of tenants.

8 Communicate verbally and in writing with other council departments as required.

9 Undertake any other duties commensurate with the position as required by the Housing Care Manager.

***Figure 16.1*** *An example of a job description*

**PERSON SPECIFICATION**

**POSITION: CUSTOMER ASSISTANT, HOUSING DEPARTMENT**

1 PHYSICAL ATTRIBUTES

| *Essential* | *Desirable* |
|---|---|
| Good communicator<br>Neat and tidy appearance | Good health record |

2 ATTAINMENTS

| *Essential* | *Desirable* |
|---|---|
| Communications qualification<br>Basic IT/WP qualification<br>Some experience of dealing with the public | Housing qualification (or willingness to study for same)<br>Knowledge of basic benefits<br>Keyboarding skills |

3 ABILITIES

| *Essential* | *Desirable* |
|---|---|
| Able to deal effectively with customers and clients<br>Well organised | Neat handwriting<br>Good numeracy skills |

4 PERSONALITY

| *Essential* | *Desirable* |
|---|---|
| Ability to work unsupervised<br>Ability to work as member of a team | Ability to cope with stress<br>Calm and patient |

***Figure 16.2*** *An example of a person specification*

usually give the salary or conditions of employment, as these may change more frequently than the job description. Many organisations will send a copy of the job description to all applicants as a matter of routine. An example of a job description is shown in Figure 16.1.

From this document a person specification is prepared. This identifies the essential and desirable attributes of someone who would be capable of undertaking the duties in the job description.

When the applications are received, it is normal to expect *all* those chosen for interview (known as short-listed candidates) to meet the essential requirements. If a large number of applicants qualify on these grounds, the applications will be scrutinised again to see which qualify most on the 'desirable' attributes. Therefore, the more exactly you match the specification, the more likely you are to be asked for interview. Some organisations send a copy of the person specification to candidates. A copy of the person specification linked to the job description in Figure 16.1 is shown in Figure 16.2, and the resulting advertisement is shown in Figure 16.3.

# MAKING AN APPLICATION

If you decide to make an application, you need to check

- whether you should telephone or to write for further details or for an application form and, if so, whether you need to enclose a stamped, addressed envelope
- whether you have to write a full letter of application
- whether you are expected to send your CV and a covering letter

HIGHTOWN BOROUGH COUNCIL

Housing Care and Neighbourhood Services Department

**CUSTOMER ASSISTANT**

**Scale 2/3 £9,350 to £10,870 pa (under review)**

You will work as part of the Housing Management Team providing counter service to callers and telephone cover. In addition your responsibilities will include dealing with repairs, lettings, responding to rent queries and other tenancy matters.

You must have experience of working directly with the public and be proficient at inputting information into computer systems. The successful applicant will hold a relevant communication and IT/WP qualification and be of neat and tidy appearance. Ability to work unsupervised, operate as a member of a team and be well organised is essential.

A knowledge of basic benefits, a qualification in housing (or the willingness to study for this) and basic typing skills would be an advantage. It is also desirable that candidates have good written and numeracy skills and can remain calm and patient even in stressful situations.

**Closing date for this post is 15 September 199-**

Application forms are available by telephone on (01928) 502893. Completed forms should be returned to the Personnel Department, Hightown County Council, Cheyne Walk, Hightown HG1 8EG, quoting **reference 894.99.**

*Hightown Council is an Equal Opportunities employer and welcomes applications from all sections of the community*

***Figure 16.3*** *The job advertisement for a Customer Assistant*

- to whom you must address your letter
- whether you must quote a specific reference number
- the closing date, if any.

Note that if you misread any of these instructions, you are likely to blot your copybook right at the start.

You also need to know what all the abbreviations used in the advertisement mean. The Wordbank section on page 298 should help you.

## Test your understanding

**1** What specific facts would you have to bear in mind if you were applying for the job illustrated in Figure 16.3?

**2** Read the advertisement in Figure 16.3 carefully and identify *all* the essential requirements and desirable requirements of the job. Check you are correct by referring back to Figure 16.2.

**3** When you ring for an application form, what questions do you think you would be asked, and how would you prepare for making this call?

**4** As a group, brainstorm what you would do if you obtained an application form and then lost it!

## Your application letter

Most advertisements ask you for a 'covering letter' and CV. This means that you need to write a brief letter to accompany your CV rather than a full letter of application. For your first job your covering letter should be fairly short. As you progress in your career you may be expected to give more details and provide more information on your achievements. In other cases, there may be space for these on an application form.

Bear in mind that even the simplest covering letter should mention at least one fact that distinguishes you from other candidates. Identifying this fact and writing about it, however, can be extremely difficult. Most people struggle when they have to promote themselves or write positively about their accomplishments. They feel as if they are boasting. To put this into context, think about the situation from the point of view of the person who is wading through dozens of applications. If *you* don't give him or her any incentive to choose you, who will?

## Your curriculum vitae

Your curriculum vitae is a brief account of your education, qualifications and experience to date. The term means 'list of life' in Latin. It *must* look professional. It should be an original document (not a photocopy) and it is sensible to prepare it on a word processor and keep it stored on disk.

You should continually update your CV. It is said that if you have nothing to add over 12 months or so, then you do not deserve to progress in your career! However, most people are continually gaining experience and qualifications, particularly when they are young, and it is a much harder task updating a CV prepared several years ago than doing this routinely every few months.

The points you should bear in mind when preparing your CV are as follows.

- It is usual today to put your name as the heading, rather than the words Curriculum Vitae.
- It is sensible to keep your CV relatively short – two pages at the most.
- Put personal details first, but keep these relatively brief.
- Put information in reverse chronological order – so that your most recent qualifications and experience are first in the list.
- Omit anything you did or achieved pre-GCSE.
- Use different sizes of type, emboldening and spacing to emphasise different sections and set out your CV attractively.

***Figure 16.4*** *Jaclyn's covering letter and CV*

23 Beveridge Road
HIGHTOWN
HG7 2SP

6 September 199-

The Personnel Department
Hightown Borough Council
Cheyne Walk
HIGHTOWN
HG1 8EG

Dear Sirs

**CUSTOMER ASSISTANT – REFERENCE 894.99**

I refer to your recent advertisement in the Hightown Gazette and would like to be considered for the position. I am particularly interested in the job you advertise as I have recently moved to the area and until June I worked as a customer assistant at Waverley District Council offices. During this time I successfully achieved my NVQ level 2 Customer Service award. Although I was not specifically involved with housing issues I do have a basic knowledge of this area and would be very interested to specialise in housing and to study for any relevant qualifications.

I have pleasure in enclosing my curriculum vitae for your information. This gives further details of my previous employment and current qualifications.
I would add that when I studied for my GNVQ Intermediate Business I also studied the Key Skills of Communications, Numeracy and Information Technology, in addition to obtaining additional IT qualifications as listed on my CV.

I enjoy meeting members of the public and dealing with their enquiries and would welcome the opportunity of developing my skills in this area. I can be available to attend an interview at any time and would appreciate the opportunity to discuss my application in more detail.

Yours faithfully

Jaclyn Griffiths (Miss)

Enc

**JACLYN GRIFFITHS**

| | |
|---|---|
| Address: | 23 Beveridge Road, Hightown, HG7 2SP |
| Telephone: | (01928) 662880 |
| Nationality: | British |
| Date of Birth: | 20 April 1979 |
| Marital Status: | Single |

**EDUCATION**

| | | |
|---|---|---|
| 1996–1997 | Waverley Tertiary College | Business with IT course |
| 1991–1996 | Waverley High School | Studying for GCSEs |

**QUALIFICATIONS OBTAINED**

| | | |
|---|---|---|
| June 1998 | Royal Society of Arts | NVQ Customer Service level 2 |
| June 1997 | BTEC | GNVQ Intermediate Business |
| June 1997 | Royal Society of Arts | Computer Literacy and Information Technology |
| June 1997 | Royal Society of Arts | Text processing Stage 1 |
| June 1996 | Southern Examining Board | GCSEs<br>English Language (B)<br>Business Studies (C)<br>Maths (D)<br>Computer Studies (D)<br>History (D) |

**WORK EXPERIENCE**

| | | |
|---|---|---|
| 1997–1998 | Waverley District Council | Customer assistant |
| 1996–1997 | Tesco Ltd, Waverley | Part-time cashier and customer service assistant |

**ADDITIONAL INFORMATION**

Holder of St John's Ambulance basic first aid award.
Clean driving licence

**REFEREES**

Mr D Stanton, Customer Care Officer, Waverley District Council, Bradshaw Road, Waverley WV2 8DL Tel: (01276) 440983
Mrs J Parkin, Lecturer, Waverley College, Clements Street, Waverley WV1 3SL Tel: (01276) 309820

23 Beveridge Road
HIGHTOWN
HG7 2SP

6 September 199-

The Personnel Department
Hightown Borough Council
Cheyne Walk
HIGHTOWN
HG1 8EG

Dear Sirs

**CUSTOMER ASSISTANT – REFERENCE 894.99**

I refer to your recent advertisement in the Hightown Gazette and would like to be considered for the position. I am particularly interested in the job you advertise as I have recently moved to the area and until June I worked as a customer assistant at Waverley District Council offices. During this time I successfully achieved my NVQ level 2 Customer Service award. Although I was not specifically involved with housing issues I do have a basic knowledge of this area and would be very interested to specialise in housing and to study for any relevant qualifications.

Prior to this I undertook a Business Studies and IT course at Waverley College where I successfully achieved my GNVQ Intermediate Business qualification which included the Key Skills of Communications, Numeracy and Information Technology. I also obtained the Royal Society of Arts Computer Literacy and Information Technology award and Text Processing Stage 1 qualification. I took this course to obtain relevant business and IT qualifications after completing my GCSEs at Waverley High School, where I obtained GCSEs in English Language (C), Business Studies (C),Maths (D), Computer Studies (D) and History (D).

During my time at College I worked part-time for Tesco Stores in Waverley where I gained check-out skills and worked on the customer service desk. I also obtained my St John's Ambulance basic first aid award. I have a clean driving licence.

I enjoy meeting members of the public and dealing with their enquiries and I would therefore welcome the opportunity of developing my skills in this area. I am available to attend an interview at any time and would appreciate the opportunity to discuss my application in more detail.

Yours faithfully

Jaclyn Griffiths (Miss)
Enc

***Figure 16.5** Full letter of application drafted by Jaclyn Griffiths*

- A photocopy of a CV should never be sent. You *must* send an original print-out. Otherwise you give the impression of sending out dozens each month!
- Check with your referees *before* you include their names whether they would be prepared to give you a reference. It is not wise (nor is it good manners!) to put anyone's name down without prior agreement.

## Test your understanding

A brief covering letter and the CV of an applicant for the job in Figure 16.3 are shown in Figure 16.4. Read these carefully and then answer the questions below.

**1** Why might Jaclyn Griffiths have spoiled her chances of getting an interview by simply sending these documents?

**2** Compare the covering letter Jaclyn sent with the *full* letter of application (see Figure 16.5) she originally drafted before she decided to send her CV. What differences can you identify?

**3** What do you think is the most persuasive point in Jaclyn's application – and why?

**4** As a group, critically assess Jaclyn's letters. Do you think she has done enough to 'sell herself'? If not, what improvements could you suggest?

## Completing a job application form

You have already read about form completion and form design in this book. However, job application forms deserve their own section because they are one of the most important forms you will ever complete. A silly mistake and your chances of an interview can rapidly vanish. Turn back to pages 88–89 to refresh your memory about form-filling before you continue reading.

The most difficult part on the form is the section, which may be as large as an A4 page, which asks you to detail your achievements or to state why you are suited to that particular job.

This is one occasion where the 'third person' is definitely not appropriate. You *must* use the word 'I' and talk about yourself positively. Forget everything you ever heard at school about 'bragging'. The employers to whom you are applying will, if you are successful, 'buy' your services or abilities and they need to spend their money wisely. You are drafting an advertisement about yourself to tempt them to find out more by inviting you for interview. You may find this easier to do if you have kept an up-to-date Record of Achievement and can use this for inspiration. Otherwise, start by listing all your strengths and positive points. Then add all your achievements, then things you like doing. Put all this information in a logical order (with the most impressive first) then join it together. To help you, a worked example is shown below.

## A WORKED EXAMPLE

Let us assume that Jaclyn Griffiths read the advertisement properly and sent for an application form. When it arrived, she noticed that there was a box as follows:

> *Please give below any information relating to your own abilities and achievements in support of your application. Include, for instance, your career plans and give details of any responsibilities you have had over the last few years.*

Jaclyn prepares her notes under various headings, as follows. Note that throughout this process she links her abilities to those detailed in the advertisement.

**Jaclyn Griffiths**

| | |
|---|---|
| Strengths: | Well-organised, patient. Experienced at dealing with members of the public. Used to working as a member of a team, and have always worked well with colleagues. Good at English and fluent communicator both verbally and in writing. Accurate typist. Good computer skills. Excellent attendance record at work and at college. |
| Responsibilities: | Worked alone on customer service desk at Tesco during busy periods (Friday evenings and Saturdays). Worked alone at customer information bureau of Waverley District Council when colleague(s) absent or on lunch break. Responsible for completing documentation neatly and accurately, finding out a variety of information relating to council services and greeting visitors. Kept database of information up-to-date using PC. |
| Achievements: | Gained NVQ level 2 Customer Service award and first aid award during first year at work. Was appointed First Aider for department in March 199-. |
| Career Plan: | To improve customer service skills and to specialise in one particular area. Would like to stay in local government if possible and progress. Willing to study for additional qualifications in own time. |

Jaclyn now uses these notes to prepare the text to go in the allocated space. This time, however, she writes in sentence and not note form. She retains her headings to make the information easier to read.

## Test your understanding

**1** Select the information under any *one* of Jaclyn's headings and write this out in continuous text. Check your finished work with your tutor.

**2** Prepare a strengths/achievement/responsibilities/career plan document for yourself – firstly in note form and then in sentence form. After your first draft in note form you may find it useful to talk this through with your tutor in a tutorial, when you can discuss in private your strengths and potential career plan.

**3** Many people include this type of information if they have to send a covering letter and CV. There are two ways of doing this.

**i** You can write a paragraph (or two) detailing this information in the letter.

**ii** You can include the information in your CV. In some cases, specialists advise writing a punchy sentence or two immediately underneath your name to describe yourself in glowing terms. In other cases, applicants prefer to detail the information about 'responsibilities' directly under the reference to the job(s) they have held, and to put other details under 'Additional Information'.

**a** As a group, discuss the merits of putting the information in the letter or the CV. Which do you think would be the most effective and why?

**b** If you put the information in the CV, where would you prefer to insert it? Again, discuss where it would be most appropriate and how it could be worded.

**4** Assume you are applying for the job advertised in Figure 16.3 and that a covering letter and CV are acceptable. Prepare your own application and submit it to your tutor for his or her opinion.

## *WORDBANK 13*

Abbreviations and jargon are frequently used in job advertisements. If you are thinking of applying for a job it helps to know what they mean. Below are the main ones you are likely to meet.

AAE – average annual earnings

bens – benefits (eg luncheon vouchers, discounts on company goods etc)

box number – a number allocated to an advertiser who does not wish to give the name of the organisation or firm. Be suspicious of these advertisements – reputable organisations are prepared to advertise their names.

casual work – work that is both temporary and variable in hours

circa – about – usually used in relation to salaries, eg circa £9,000

DTP – desktop publishing

FAO – for the attention of – sometimes used to indicate to whom you must address your application

| | | |
|---|---|---|
| flexitime | – | flexible starting and finishing hours, although each job holder must normally work a number of 'core hours' eg between 10 am and 4 pm each day |
| freelance | – | someone who works on a self-employed basis but is contracted to do a specific job for an organisation |
| GSOH | – | good state of health |
| K | – | thousands – again used in relation to salaries, eg £12K = £12,000 |
| neg | – | negotiable – means salary is not fixed, but will depend upon experience and qualifications |
| O/T | – | overtime |
| OTE | – | on target earnings – used where your salary would comprise a basic rate plus commission. Bear in mind that the OTE figure is often optimistic rather than realistic |
| pa | – | per annum (per year) – usually used in relation to salaries, eg £9,800 pa |
| PAYE | – | Pay As You Earn – the tax system in operation for employees |
| pro rata | – | proportional – used for part-time jobs where you need to work out the salary as a proportion of the full-time rate, depending upon the number of hours to be worked |
| SAE | – | Stamped Addressed Envelope – may be required if you are sending for details or information |
| scale post | – | an official salary scale is in operation with specific salary points, called increments – it is normal to rise one increment each year until the post holder is at the top of the scale |
| statutory days | – | official holidays, eg Christmas Day, May Day, etc |
| superannuation | – | the term used in the public sector for pensions (eg if you work for a local authority or the civil service) |
| temporary work | – | a job that lasts only a short time |
| under review | – | the salaries quoted are currently being reviewed and may be increased shortly. |

## Test your understanding

**1** Look back at the advertisement in Figure 16.3 and look for any terms used which are mentioned above. Check that you now understand what each means.

**2** In the advertisement, Hightown Council claims it is an 'Equal Opportunities employer.' As a group and with your tutor, discuss what this means and how effective you think these policies are likely to be.

**3** Collect at least four advertisements from your local or a national newspaper to illustrate *at least* six of the terms used above.

## TOOLS OF THE TRADE – interview skills

Few people enjoy being interviewed. There is always the worry that you will be asked a question you do not understand or cannot answer. Some people are very shy and have great difficulty speaking fluently and clearly. Others can be viewed as over-confident because they seem very sure of themselves, but display little enthusiasm for the job! When you are offered an interview for a job, there are two major considerations if you wish to make a good impression.

1 Your performance will be directly linked to how well you prepare for the interview.

2 You should remember that an interview is a two-way process. The interviewer is trying to assess if you will fit in with the organisation. You are trying to assess if you will like the job. However, unless you appear interested and enthusiastic, you are unlikely to be given the opportunity of turning it down!

If you dread interviews of any kind, and consider them a terrible ordeal, try to change your attitude. Instead of thinking of them as an inquisition, consider them an opportunity to demonstrate your accomplishments and talk about what you have achieved. Remember that the worst that can happen is that you may not be offered the job – which may be upsetting, but is hardly life-threatening!

# INTERVIEW PREPARATIONS

You are likely to be informed by letter that you have been given an interview – unless you are sent for interview by an employment agency. In either case, as soon as you receive the details, you should start your preparations.

1 Check the basics – day and date to start with. Then make sure you know where the organisation is situated and how to get there. This may mean have a practice to find the premises and check bus or train times. Remember, you *must* allow plenty of time for the journey.

2 Scrutinise your appearance. Remember that the interviewer is more likely to be of your parents' generation, so don't reject the type of clothes that they prefer! The type of organisation should also influence your decision about what to wear. A bank or a firm of solicitors is likely to be more conservative than an advertising agency or a record company. Seeing the clothes worn by existing employees will give you the best indication of what is acceptable and what is not. Choose an outfit you like and can wear comfortably (tight clothes are normally unsuitable). Preferably select something crease-resistant. Check that your shoes aren't down at heel or covered in scuff marks. Keep items you have to carry to a minimum (even an umbrella can be a nuisance at an interview).

3 Investigate the organisation. What does it do? Is it local or nationwide? Have you read any of its advertisements? Is it a large company where you could send for information? (Someone applying for a job at your college, for instance, could obtain a copy of the prospectus in advance to see the

number of departments and the types of courses on offer.) Prepare two or three questions to ask the interviewer which show you have done your homework and enable him or her to give you further useful information about the organisation. These could include questions such as:

**a** I've learned what I can about your organisation, but if I was fortunate enough to be offered the job I would like to learn more before I start. Could you tell me if you have any literature available?
**b** Are there any periods or seasons during the year when you are particularly busy and when I would be expected to work late?
**c** Could you tell me if your organisation would support me if I wanted to continue my studies?
**d** If I worked hard and did well, what would be my promotion prospects?

4 Consider the type of questions you are likely to be asked:

**a** where did you go to school/college?
**b** what did you like the best/least when you were studying?
**c** what is your favourite subject and why?
**d** where are you working now?
**e** why do you want to leave?
**f** what skills/abilities do you feel you could bring to this job?
**g** why do you want this particular job?
**h** what are your hobbies and interests?
**i** how would you describe yourself?

Prepare a suitable answer for each and, if possible, ask someone to give you a practice interview beforehand.

5 The night before, prepare your clothes, re-read the job description and check your timetable. Remember, punctuality is *vital*. Aim to arrive early, rather than at the last minute, so that you are cool, calm and collected rather than hot and flustered. If a last minute emergency occurs, telephone the organisation *immediately*.

## On the day

1 Arrive in plenty of time and give your name and reason for visiting to the receptionist or at the security gate. If the organisation is very large you may have to walk a considerable distance from the security gate to the appropriate building – you should allow time for this.

2 Expect to be shown into a waiting area. You may be offered a cup of coffee while you are waiting. Don't attempt to take this into the interview room with you, in case you spill it. In some cases, you may prefer to refuse the offer altogether!

3 When you are shown into the interview room remember to look the interviewer in the eye and *smile*. It makes all the difference if you look pleasant rather than sulky at first sight! Be prepared to shake hands (so don't hold anything in your right hand or have anything draped over your right arm). A good interviewer will help you to relax at the outset by following a fairly standard formula for the interview.

**a** The first part is likely to comprise simple opening courtesies.
**b** The interviewer will then check basic facts from your letter, CV or application form.

**c** There should be a definite section where you are given more information about the job itself and the tasks involved. This should also include such details as the salary and conditions of employment.

**d** The first questions you are asked should be fairly basic and concentrate on linking your application to the job.

**e** More in-depth questions may follow, to assess your motivation, interest in the job, personality and ability to cope with the demands of the job.

**f** The interviewer should ask if you wish to ask any questions. It is always better to have one or two questions up your sleeve rather than look blank! This is where your 'homework' questions can come in. You should also make queries if you are unsure about something you have been told. Try to avoid asking about holidays and time off, though!

**g** At the end of the interview you should be told what happens next – so that you have some idea of how long you will have to wait before a decision is made, and how you will be notified of the outcome.

Not all interviewers are experienced at coping with either interviews or candidates. This is more likely to be the case in a small firm than in a large organisation. In this situation, you cannot rely on the interviewer learning all about your strengths without any assistance from you. It is sensible to make sure you have the opportunity to mention anything you think is important.

**4** Throughout the interview you will be assessed on:

**a** your attitude to relevant matters
**b** how well you are likely to fit in with existing staff
**c** how long it takes you to understand and respond to a question
**d** whether you can speak clearly and fluently
**e** whether you can interact with your interviewer at the right level (relatively formal but not distant)
**f** how enthusiastic you appear to be
**g** what your priorities are (eg whether you are a hard working or feet-up type!)

If you are asked a particularly difficult question – or a question you do not understand – you can gain thinking time by asking for the question to be rephrased. Say quite simply, 'I'm sorry, I'm not sure what you mean. Could you repeat the question, please?' Remember that your body language, too, plays a key role in projecting a positive image. Lean forwards, not backwards. Don't cross your arms or legs, or clutch a bag or folder to your chest. Look animated, not bored! Take deep breaths if you are feeling nervous, and speak slightly more slowly than normal.

**5** At the end of the interview it is likely that the interviewer will stand when you do and show you to the door. Be prepared to shake hands again. Put any doubts behind you at this stage – if you haven't been successful tell yourself it wasn't meant to be – and regard the interview as good practice.

## Test your understanding

**1** As a group, decide on an additional *four* questions that could be asked by a candidate at an interview.

**2** Prepare your own answers to the interview questions on page 301. As a group, compare your ideas and decide which type of responses would create a good impression with an interviewer and which would not.

**3** Divide into groups of 3 or 4. Decide upon a suitable job vacancy and write an appropriate job description and person specification. From these documents, prepare an advertisement.

Circulate the advertisements among the class. Each person should apply for one of the jobs advertised. The group that placed the advertisement shoud acknowledge all applications and arrange interview times.

Within your group, decide upon suitable questions you will ask the job applicants. Then hold mock interviews, with your tutor as observer, to give feedback both to candidates *and* interviewers.

**DON'T YOU DARE!**

*...commit any of the following cardinal sins at an interview!*

- *be late*
- *be unprepared*
- *be unresponsive so that every answer has to be dragged out of you (this exhausts the interviewer!)*
- *whisper every response*
- *boast excessively about your achievements*
- *bite your nails or fiddle with your hair*
- *give long rambling explanations that no-one can follow*
- *be too informal or over-familiar with the interviewer*
- *use repetitive and annoying words and phrases (particularly slang)*
- *be vague or give the impression you rarely see things through to completion*
- *be tactless or undiplomatic*
- *be critical about authority*
- *blame others for your misfortunes.*

## MAKING HEADWAY – personal communications

Throughout this book you have learned to communicate in a variety of situations relating to your existing or future workplace. However, the benefits of being a good communicator don't apply only to your job – numerous advantages are to be gained in your personal life. You should, for instance, be able to:

- speak to strangers confidently
- express yourself (whether verbally or in writing) clearly and unambiguously
- listen carefully – and remember what has been said or agreed
- find out information you need
- complete a wide range of forms accurately and without hesitation
- contribute positively to a joint discussion or meeting
- write letters that look and sound professional – so that you are almost guaranteed a response.

This last skill is extremely important, even in an age when many communications are face to face, over the telephone, by e-mail or fax. There always seems to come a time when you need to write a letter – and having the skill to do this is invaluable.

Quite apart from job application letters, you may also need to write:

- letters of confirmation for a booking or to confirm an arrangement
- a reminder letter to a friend or an organisation about fulfilling a promise
- a letter of enquiry about something in which you are interested
- a letter of complaint if you are dissatisfied with something
- a letter of request if you want someone to do you a favour
- a thank you letter to someone who has helped you
- a letter of condolence or sympathy if someone you know has had a dreadful experience or suffered a bereavement
- a letter of resignation if you wish to leave an organisation.

Some of these letters will be fairly straightforward. Others require the skills of tact and diplomacy discussed in Unit 14. Most letters are better typed and printed, particularly to business organisations. Others may be better if they are personally written, such as a letter of condolence or sympathy. Obviously your style and wording will vary depending upon whether you wish to write formally, or informally to a close friend.

25 Galway Close
WESTBURY
W3 4WL

24 June 199-

Mrs Karen Walker
Department of Business and Technology
Hightown College
HIGHTOWN
HG3 2MP

Dear Mrs Walker

You may remember that I was a student in your Business Communications and IT group between 1996 and 1997. When I left the college I was fortunate enough to gain employment with DPTS Software Systems and have worked for them for two years now, progressing from Clerical Assistant to IT Coordinator.

Whilst I enjoy my work, DPTS is a small organisation and my promotion prospects are very limited. For a few months, therefore, I have been considering changing my job if a suitable opportunity arose.

Last week I read an advertisement by Johnson, Thames and Watson, a large firm of accountants in Westbury, who are looking to develop a service to assist clients with their IT needs. I have sent for an application form for the position of IT Marketing Services Coordinator and would like to put forward your name as referee. I am hoping that you remember me as a keen and conscientious student who did well in her final examinations!

I hope you are keeping well and that your current students are succeeding in their studies. Please remember me to the other staff who taught me, particularly John Turner and Margaret Smith.

Kind regards

Yours sincerely

Lucy Thomas

***Figure 16.6***
*A letter requesting a reference*

The first four types of letters mentioned above should cause you few problems as they require skills you have already learned. The others may cause you more difficulty, as they often involve personal relationships. The following guidelines may help.

## A letter of request

One request most of us need to make at some time is to ask someone for a reference. If you have not seen this person for some time or if he or she lives some distance away, you may wish to put your request in writing rather than telephone. Some tips include:

- keep your letter fairly short and to the point – but not so brief that it sounds curt
- ask pleasantly and give all the details the person will need to help you (this may involve reminding your recipient who you are!)
- use the opportunity to give an up-date on what has happened since you last saw the person concerned, if this would be appropriate.

An example of a short letter requesting a reference is given in Figure 16.6. Check that this includes all the information Mrs Walker would require. Note that the writer has adopted a slightly formal, rather than informal approach. This is normal if there has been a time gap in the relationship.

## Test your understanding

Assume you are Lucy Thomas. You are fortunate enough to get the job at Johnson, Thames and Watson and your interviewer refers to the excellent reference he received from your former tutor at Hightown College.

Write a letter thanking Mrs Walker. You may find it useful to compare your completed letter with those produced by other members of your group.

## A letter of sympathy

Sympathy letters are always difficult to write. In this section we are not looking at personal letters to close friends, which are outside the remit of this book, but shorter notes you may send to less intimate acquaintances. The first point to note is that it is always better to write *something*, rather than decide you don't know where to start and therefore do nothing. A useful tip is to buy a card – one without a message is often better – as this limits your space and therefore the number of words you have to think about.

- Start by expressing your sadness about the situation. Standard phrases include:

  *I was deeply distressed by the news that ...*
  *I was very sorry to hear ...*
  *It was with sadness that I learned about ...*

- Continue by giving some words of comfort or consolation. If you have problems with this part, focus on the person about whom you are writing, eg

  *I will always remember your uncle as a kind and helpful man ...*
  *I know that when I worked with your wife she was always a wonderful colleague ...*

- If the situation is such that assistance would be appreciated – and if you are prepared to follow up any promises you make – then you may wish to make an offer of some kind, eg

  *This will obviously be a difficult time for you. If I can help in any way, please do not hesitate to contact me.*

## A letter of resignation

A letter of resignation is easy to write if you work for a large faceless organisation or have been employed by them for only a short time. If you work for a firm where everyone has treated you wonderfully from day one, your letter may be difficult to compose – particularly if you think your boss will be upset to receive it. Do remember, however, that you can soften the blow by being generous in your remarks. Conversely no matter how much you are dying to leave you shouldn't say so in your final letter. You never know when you may need a reference in the future!

25 Galway Close
WESTBURY
W3 4WL

30 June 199-

Mr D Williams
Director
DPTS Software Systems Ltd
23 Park Road
WESTBURY
W2 6EF

Dear David

I wish to inform you that I have been offered a new job as IT Marketing Services Coordinator with a large firm of accountants in Westbury. I therefore wish to give one month's notice of my intention to leave DPTS on 31 July, 199-.

It is with considerable regret that I am resigning from my present job. I have thoroughly enjoyed my time with your organisation and appreciate all the assistance and training I have been given during the past two years. My new job will give me the opportunity to develop my skills still further and to take on new and challenging responsibilities. I therefore do not feel I can sensibly refuse the opportunity.

I would like to take this opportunity to thank you personally for all the help and advice you have given me since I started working for DPTS, and to wish you and the company every success in the future.

Yours sincerely

Lucy Thomas

***Figure 16.7** A letter of resignation*

- Start by giving the facts.
- Progress to writing a few kind words and phrases.
- End with a courteous sentence or two.

Lucy's letter of resignation to her boss at DPTS is shown in Figure 16.7. If you were David Williams, how would you feel when you received it, assuming you had helped Lucy considerably during her time with you?

## Test your understanding

1 David Williams has to write a formal reply to Lucy, accepting her resignation. Again he can take the opportunity to end the relationship on a pleasant note by writing a few appropriate words.

   As David Williams, draft an appropriate reply to Lucy.

2 Three months after leaving, Lucy bumps into a friend from DPTS who tells her that David's partner at the firm, Paul, has died following a serious car accident. Paul was very helpful to Lucy when she worked there and she knows that he and David had built the firm from scratch over a period of 10 years or more. She decides to write David a short, personal note. As a group, decide the wording Lucy should use in this situation.

## DOUBLE TROUBLE

Select the correct word for each sentence from the pairs shown below. In each case, write a sentence to show you clearly understand the meaning of the other word.

1 There is a distinct/distinctive difference between the weather in December and the weather in May.
2 I am fed up with bailing/baling him out when he is in trouble.
3 I knew that if you said her name it would strike a cord/chord.
4 He offered her a derisory/derisive salary to do the job – no wonder she refused!
5 He has a very equitable/equable temperament – nothing seems to upset him.
6 It is a facility/fallacy that all rich people are happy.
7 The little girl has an imaginary/imaginative friend with whom she pretends to play when she is lonely.

**8** You'll jam/jamb the machine if you try to put all that paper in the tray.
**9** It is very risky/risque to tell deliberate untruths at an interview, as you are likely to be found out.

## THE GOOD GRAMMAR GUIDE

### Conjunctions

You probably think of conjunctions as 'joining words' that enable you to write longer sentences. This is their main value. However, to express the meaning of the sentence correctly it is important to select the most appropriate conjunction. It is also useful to know how you can vary the position of the conjunction to add variety to your writing.

There are two main types of conjunctions.

**1** Those that join items of equal value or status, eg

*We ate fish* ***and*** *chips*
***Both*** *Mark* ***and*** *Stephen are going to the concert*
*She wanted to visit Paris* ***but*** *could not afford it*
*She finished the work,* ***then*** *left for the evening.*
*She didn't go on Friday* ***or*** *on Saturday.*

In all these cases, the meanings of both parts of the sentence could stand alone, eg

*We ate fish. We ate chips.*

*She wanted to visit Paris. She could not afford to visit Paris.*

When the conjunction relates to the same person or item, you do not need to repeat this noun or pronoun. Other conjunctions that operate in this way include *so, for, yet, whereas, either..or, neither...nor*.

**2** Conjuctions that join a main clause in a sentence to a dependent clause. In this case the second part of the sentence could not stand alone because it 'depends' upon the main clause for its meaning. Therefore you could say

*I am going shopping before I go to work.* You could not say.

*I am going shopping. Before I go to work.* The second sentence would not make sense.

We select a particular conjunction describing the relationship between the clauses, such as the following.

- **Time relationships** use *before, after, since, until, when, now,* eg

  *I can visit your office* ***after*** *I have spoken to that visitor.*

- **Place relationships** use *where, wherever,* eg

  *We are leaving for Spain tomorrow,* ***where*** *we intend to spend four weeks in the sun.*

- Some relationships indicate a possible **problem**, such as *except, if, unless,* eg

  *He has promised to attend* ***if*** *he is free on that date.*

- Some relationships give a **reason**, such as *because, in order to, rather than,* eg

  *I have to stay late on Monday* ***because*** *I must finish this report.*

You can vary your writing in two ways by using conjunctions.

- you can change the order of your clauses and write the dependent clause first, eg

  *I am going shopping before I go to work* or *Before I go to work I am going shopping.*

- You can write a longer sentence by using more than one conjunction, eg

  *I am going shopping before I go to work because I need to buy Kim's birthday present before lunch.*

## Test your understanding

**1** Link each pair of clauses below by selecting an appropriate conjunction from the list given in Figure 16.8.

**a** I wrote the report in a hurry (............) it is needed today.
**b** We will visit Tewkesbury tomorrow (............) I lived as a child.
**c** You will miss the post (............) you run to the Post Office.
**d** The fax has been faulty for several days (............) it worked for me this morning.
**e** They cannot confirm we will have an extra day's holiday next year (............) the directors have met next Tuesday.
**f** He said he would notify me (............) they have another vacancy.
**g** You can borrow my car (............) you return by 3 pm (............) I have a dental appointment.
**h** We will all go for a walk (............) the weather is dreadful.
**i** She has worked for the company (............) it was founded in 1972.
**j** She will always help out (............) there is a crisis.

**Commonly used subordinating conjunctions**

| | | | |
|---|---|---|---|
| after | although | as | as if |
| as soon as | because | before | even if |
| even though | except | how | however |
| if | in case | in order that | in order to |
| rather than | since | so that | that |
| though | unless | until | whatever |
| when | whenever | where | whereas |
| wherever | whether | which | while |
| who | why | with the result that | |

***Figure 16.8*** *Select appropriate conjunctions from this list*

**2** Select any four of the sentences above and reword it by putting the dependent clause at the start of the sentence.

## SPELLCHECKER 15

Below is your final set of words in this book. In each case check that you know both the spelling and meaning of the words.

| | |
|---|---|
| aggregate | ascend |
| automatic | contagious |
| deterrent | dossier |
| dubious | harassment |
| incessant | inertia |
| irrevocable | maintenance |
| manoeuvre | miniature |
| ominous | perseverance |
| proprietor | spontaneous |
| transparent | vehement |

# COMMUNICATION IN PRACTICE

## Test your skills

**1** Review your discussion skills. Read the extract below and then form two groups, one to support the first argument and one to support the second. Debate each objectively and decide, as a group, which argument to support.

*Some English teachers and scholars have long been appalled by the cavalier disregard shown by the advertising industry for English grammar and spelling. They argue that it is difficult to teach students to write correct English while their pupils are being bombarded by illiterate notices and advertising slogans. They point to 'howlers' such as 'almost unique', 'near perfection'; phrases such as 'feel like' (instead of 'feel as if'); Apple's ungrammatical 'Think different' slogan, Heinz's spelling of 'Beanz Meanz Heinz', Mercury's 'Who would you most like a One2One with?' and – possibly the worst one of all – 'Does you does or does you don't take Access?' According to the Plain English Campaign, such bad grammar and spelling are very confusing for those who struggle to write or speak the language correctly.*

*The advertising agencies stoutly defend their approach. They argue that there is a need to communicate quickly and in a style people understand and use every day. Moreover, many advertising messages are not only grammatical but quite clever in their creative use of words. And anyway, no-one confuses witty slogans or names with correct English usage – the shop Toys 'Я' Us even uses a jokey backwards 'R' in its name. English is an ever-changing language with fluid usage rather than rules set in tablets of stone. In their view, language should reflect current trends and the way it is used in society today – and not be dictated by rules devised years ago.*

**2** Revise your letter-writing skills.

**a** You have seen a music centre advertised in a magazine. It is available by mail order. You have tried to phone three times to check if there is a CD, tape deck, record deck and radio because the advertisement is unclear. You also want to check the size and to find out whether different sizes of speakers are available.

The firm's name is Supra Sounds, 15 Chesterton Way, Westbury WS4 3LT. Write a personal letter to the manager (whose name you do not know) asking for this information.

**b** Three weeks later you are still waiting for a reply. Write a brief reminder letter to Supra Sounds, asking for an immediate response.

**c** The manager of Supra Sounds, Ken Watkins, eventually writes to you enclosing a leaflet on the music centre. He also gives you details of the different speakers available with the system and the sizes. After two or three telephone conversations you agree to purchase the system for £699, payable on delivery. Ken Watkins has asked you to let them know, in writing, when you will be at home for the system to be delivered and set up by their engineer. He has asked that you give at least three days' notice. Decide on a suitable time and date and confirm the arrangement.

**d** The day before the system is due to be delivered Supra Sounds telephone to tell you there is a slight delay. The system, you are told, cannot be delivered when requested, because the engineer is ill. They promise you that the system will be delivered four days later. On that day you take the afternoon off work, but by 5 pm no-one has arrived. When you telephone Supra Sounds you are told Ken Watkins is out and no-one else knows anything about the order.

**i** Assuming you still want the system, write a letter of complaint to Ken Watkins, insisting that a definite arrangement is made immediately to deliver the music centre, or you will cancel your order.

**ii** Assuming you have decided that Supra Sounds is at best disorganised and at worst a very dubious organisation, write a letter stating your dissatisfaction and cancelling your order.

## Apply your skills

**1** Select an advertisement in a local or national paper for a job that appeals to you.

**a** Identify those requirements that are essential and desirable from the details given in the advertisement.

**b** Check that you understand all the abbreviations and jargon that may have been used.

**c** Write brief notes outlining your own strengths and other attributes, which would enable you to 'sell' yourself in a letter or on an application form.

(If you cannot find a suitable advertisement, choose the job advertised in Figure 11.1 on page 193.)

**2** Write a covering letter to apply for the job, assuming that you have to write a letter and send your CV. Include at least one point from your notes or by referring to the advertisement which would make your application stand out from the rest.

3 Prepare an up-to-date and well-designed CV to go with your letter.

4 You are invited for an interview, so prepare for this by deciding on questions you are likely to be asked and how you will answer. In addition, if you are using a real advertisement, find out something about the organisation. If possible, arrange to have a mock interview with your tutor and ask him or her to give you feedback on your performance.

5 You wish to ask Josie Sharples, the manager at Brightside Stores, Watery Way, Westham, WS3 4MP for a reference. You have worked at Brightside Stores every weekend for the past two years. You also worked there all last summer and know Mrs Sharples will be happy to let you name her as a referee but feel it would only be courteous to write asking her first. Prepare a suitable letter.

6 You are delighted to have been offered the job following your interview.

   **a** Write a letter to Mrs K Taylor, the Staffing Manager at the organisation, to confirm your acceptance and starting date.

   **b** Write a second letter to Mrs Sharples, thanking her for her reference. At the same time, inform her that as you will now be working full-time you will no longer be able to work at Brightside Stores every weekend. Express your regrets as Mrs Sharples has always been very kind to you and has done her best to give you extra work when you have needed the money.

## WORD WIZARD

By now, you should be able to spot words that have been used incorrectly, ungrammatical sentences and poor punctuation. The following passage was kindly provided by Dave Williams. It may test your skills a little but will give you some light relief. The test is firstly to understand it and then to rewrite it sensibly and grammatically, with no spelling or punctuation errors!

*Anyone desirable to write books or reports, be they short or long, should strive too maximise they're optimal use of one's english grammar and obliviously there is an need for correct spelling two one should not neglect punctuation neither.*

*Frequent lea, many people and individuals become confusing or just do not no it, when righting, when words that mean different, when sounding identically, or when pronounced very similar, are knot too bee spelled inn the same whey. The quay two suck seeding is dew care, a lack off witch Leeds too Miss Spellings that mite otherwise of bean a voided. Word Process sore spell chequers donut find awl missed takes.*

*Invariously, one will also knead to in sure that you didn't Mick's up the prone nouns or tens mid sent tens. Equally impotent that you don't also never double nor not even triple use of the negative. Of cause, when writing correct, the ordering, within a sentence, of constituent phrases, needs care full planing, which should always be done. Moor over, frequent repetition as well, if used over and over again, many times, can additionally often also render illegible text. This can be sighted as one of the many egg samples which is difficult or all most impassable for a reader to die jest. Another is split infinities, with which readers can find it incredulously difficult to really notice.*

*Despite all the pitfulls how ever, with practise, patients and the right altitude, any one can soon become a commandable writer and effluent speaker, as what I did.*

## Solution to crossword puzzle on page 147

| 1 C | O | 2 L | L | 3 E | A | G | 4 U | E | | 5 A | 6 Q | U | 7 A |
|---|---|---|---|---|---|---|---|---|---|---|---|---|---|
| A | | I | | S | | | N | | | | U | | U |
| 8 T | R | A | N | S | M | I | T | | 9 Y | I | E | L | D |
| A | | I | | E | | | I | | | | U | | I |
| 10 L | O | S | I | N | G | | 11 D | 12 I | 13 S | S | E | N | T |
| O | | E | | T | | | 14 Y | E | T | | | | O |
| G | | | | I | | | | | A | | 15 D | | R |
| 16 U | L | 17 T | R | A | | 18 C | A | U | T | I | O | U | S |
| E | | H | | L | | R | | | I | | G | | |
| | 19 F | E | W | | 20 M | I | C | R | O | | 21 M | R | 22 S |
| 23 O | | I | | 24 M | | M | | | N | | A | | H |
| 25 P | E | R | M | I | T | S | | 26 C | E | N | T | R | E |
| T | | | | N | | O | | | R | | I | | E |
| 27 S | T | A | T | I | O | N | A | R | Y | | 28 C | O | N |

## 'Opposite view' extracts to compare with those on page 186

*Extract 1*

*Critics of the European Working Time Directive argue that the benefits are very limited given all the qualifications and exemptions. None of the regulations apply to transport, fishing or junior doctors. In addition, apart from the holiday entitlement, workers in industries which must provide continuity of production or service are also exempt. This includes telecommunications, public services and the security industry – notorious for its long hours.*

*Extract 2*

*The difficulty for the Lord Chancellor has been that only 46 of this year's 511 applications to be a QC were received from females. Ten of these 46 were chosen, whilst the remaining 50 new QCs were male. Unless more women apply, they will continue to be very much in the minority.*

*Extract 3*

*The ONS was very critical of regulations introduced by the previous Government which tightened up the rules for claimants. The ONS estimated that at least 20,000 genuine job-hunters lost their entitlement to benefit as a result of one of the changes and a further 150,000 were probably prevented from claiming as a result of the introduction of the Jobseekers Allowance, which replaced Unemployment Benefit. Over the past ten years, successive rules and regulations have effectively prevented many people from claiming, and 'massaged' the figures downwards statistically if not in reality.*

## Key to Word Wizard on page 190

*None* of the statements can be proved to be accurate from the passage.

## Key to Word Wizard on page 290

| **Word** | **Dates** |
|---|---|
| Teddy bear | 1902 |
| Air raid | 1911 |
| Robot | 1920 |
| Television | 1926 |
| Mickey Mouse | 1936 |
| Radar | 1941 |
| Bikini | 1946 |
| Rock 'n' roll | 1953 |
| Silicon chip | 1958 |
| Hovercraft | 1959 |
| Laser | 1960 |
| Workaholic | 1971 |
| VAT | 1973 |
| Walkman | 1981 |
| Mexican wave | 1986 |
| Lager lout | 1988 |
| Information Superhighway | 1993 |
| World Wide Web | 1994 |
| Road rage | 1995 |
| Alcopop | 1996 |

YEOVIL COLLEGE
LIBRARY